W9-AQL-831

How to Build Your Own Web Site With Little or No Money:

The Complete Guide for Business and Personal Use

By Bruce C. Brown

EXTRA MATERIAL! Take a closer look at HTML examples & what they generate at
http://www.atlantic-pub.com/extras/buildwebsite/bonus.htm

HOW TO BUILD YOUR OWN WEB SITE WITH LITTLE OR NO MONEY: THE COMPLETE GUIDE FOR BUSINESS AND PERSONAL USE

Copyright © 2010 Atlantic Publishing Group, Inc.
1405 SW 6th Avenue • Ocala, Florida 34471 • Phone 800-814-1132 • Fax 352-622-1875
Web site: www.atlantic-pub.com • E-mail: sales@atlantic-pub.com
SAN Number: 268-1250

Library of Congress Cataloging-in-Publication Data

Brown, Bruce C. (Bruce Cameron), 1965-
   How to build your own web site with little or no money : the complete guide for business and personal use / by Bruce C. Brown.
      p. cm.
   Includes bibliographical references and index.
   ISBN-13: 978-1-60138-304-4 (alk. paper)
   ISBN-10: 1-60138-304-5 (alk. paper)
   1. Web site development--Amateurs' manuals. I. Title.
   TK5105.888.B768 2009
   006.7'6--dc22
                                    2009040371

Printed in the United States

PROJECT MANAGER: Melissa Peterson • mpeterson@atlantic-pub.com
ASSISTANT EDITOR: Angela Pham • apham@atlantic-pub.com
INTERIOR DESIGN: Holly Marie Gibbs • hgibbs@atlantic-pub.com
INTERIOR LAYOUT: Antoinette D'Amore • addesign@videotron.ca
COVER DESIGN: Meg Buchner • meg@megbuchner.com
JACKET DESIGN: Jackie Miller • sullmill@charter.net

Printed on Recycled Paper

Atlantic Publishing Group Inc. is honored to thank our nation's service men and women. The sacrifices and achievements of the brave men and women of our armed forces can never be understated. The staff at Atlantic Publishing Group asks each of you to take time to remember our service men and women who are currently serving overseas in harms way and those who are protecting and defending our homeland today. Atlantic Publishing Group has partnered with the VETERAN TICKETS FOUNDATION to support our United States veterans. A portion of the profits of this book will be donated to the Veteran Tickets Foundation.

- Douglas R. Brown & Sherri L. Brown

It's In the nature of Veterans to step up — so we did.

The kind of people who volunteer to serve their country, the ones who put their nation first and their own lives second, are the kind of people we need to honor every day — not just on Memorial Day, Veteran's Day, and the Fourth of July, but every day.

Through Veteran Tickets Foundation, now those who care about veterans have a way to give back. Every day, In every city, there are events with empty seats that could be filled by those who served. More than that, the average person cannot afford many of these event tickets. The Veteran Tickets Foundation believes the events that bring Americans together in the spirit of celebration, competition, and camaraderie, those all-American moments, are the times we should welcome and acknowledge our veterans.

The Veteran Tickets Foundation is a national nonprofit, nongovernmental 501(c) (3) tax-exempt organization (IRS application pending). All contributions made to the organization are deductible under Section 170 of the IRS Code. But most importantly, it is a dedicated group of business people who are also veterans. They served our country, and now it's their privilege to serve veterans and to provide an opportunity for the rest of America to express its thanks and gratitude.

When Veterans go to an event or their favorite sports team for free, we want them to feel a collective "**thank you**" from all of us to all of them. You can join the Veteran Tickets Foundation at **www.vettix.org/donate.php**.

Veteran Tickets Foundation
3401 East Turquoise Ave.
Phoenix, Arizona 85028

Dedication

This book is dedicated to my beautiful wife, Vonda.
In June, we celebrated our 25th wedding anniversary, and
I'm looking forwarding to sharing the next 25 years — and
many more — of my life with you. I can't put into words how
important you are to me, or how deeply I love you.
Thank you for making my life complete!

"It's going to be legendary."

— Barney

"A haiku is just like a normal American poem,
except it doesn't rhyme and it's totally stupid."

— Mr. Garrison

"There's a time and a place for everything, and it's called college."

— Chef

Table of Contents

Foreword

Launching or managing a business in today's economy can be an exceptional challenge. As the market becomes more competitive than ever, businesspeople are forced to reduce costs and come up with creative strategies to continue marketing and maintain sales.

Recently, the Web has evolved into the fastest growing marketplace, and businesses or individuals who do not have a Web presence are losing an enormous share of the market.

You have probably picked up this book because you are looking to build a Web site for your business on a budget, or perhaps you are interested in finding creative ways to improve the current Web site you may already have. No matter the size of your business or your field, *How to Build Your Own Web Site With Little or No Money: The Complete Guide for Business and Personal Use* is an essential tool for business owners who wish to launch a professional-looking and functional Web site without investing in expensive Web design companies.

My best advice for building a highly professional and great-looking Web site is to hire a professional Web site designer. Aside from their experience, vision, and skills with tools and aesthetics, an experienced Web site designer will pay for itself by saving you time and projecting your business ahead of your competition. However, if you elect to design your own Web site without assistance from a professional, below are some tips in addition to the invaluable information this book contains.

As the founder of **www.crea7ive.com**, a Web site design firm that has been named one of the best in the country, I have 10 years of experience with Web site design. I am familiar with the tools, procedures, and even short-cuts available for Web designers. I am very impressed with the complete-ness of this book, and I highly recommend it to business owners who want to design their own Web site because it compiles insightful information in a straightforward, well-organized, step-by-step approach that will allow average individuals with little to no Web design knowledge to create a professional-looking Web site.

Whether you are on a strict budget or you have no budget at all, the process of building a successful Web site begins with organization. Prior to getting your hands on image and HTML editors, dedicate the necessary amount of time to planning all the details of the site — from registering the domain name and planning the title and content of each page, to hosting and mar-keting. It is important to remember that time is money, and with every day that goes by, you may be losing potential business by not having an online presence. So, when it comes to decision-making, be practical, reasonable, and, most importantly, proactive.

With my years of experience with project management in the Web site de-sign industry, I have dealt with hundreds of businesses, and below are some clear-cut tips to get you started.

The first step to creating a Web site is choosing a domain name (the "www.yourname.com" every online site must have). When choosing a domain name for your brand new Web site, it is very important that it is easy to re-member and easy to spell and, if possible, it contains keywords about your services. This is highly important for search engine optimization (SEO), as you will read ahead in the following chapters. For example: If your Italian restaurant is called Mario's, you may want to purchase the domain name **www.MariosItalianFood.com**.

Once you have decided your domain name, purchase it immediately. It is extremely important you do this as soon as possible, as it may lose availability if you let time go by. I have seen this happen, so move fast and purchase it from any of the main domain registry providers before someone else does it. You can register a domain name for approximately $10 per year.

The next step is to determine the purpose of your Web site and what content it will include. Keep in mind that a well-designed site must be the founding structure for changes you may want to make in the future. You must design a site map that will be flexible enough to make those changes and that will not require you to restructure your Web site completely if you wish to add or remove pages.

After you have chosen a domain name and content for the Web site, you must decide on the design elements for your Web site, starting with a logo. If you do not have a professionally designed logo, find a professional to create one. Unless you are an experienced designer, do not attempt to design your own logo, because this will be the base for everything you do and the future image of your business. You can find an affordable logo designer online using logo contest Web sites or by hiring a freelancer. On the other hand, if you already have a professional logo, you can move forward with selecting colors and the style of your Web site. The colors and style should match your logo, of course. Check out other Web sites to find a Web site design you like. Check out your competitors and the leaders in your industry. What do their sites look like? This will give you an idea of what you like — and what you do not — so you can begin creating your own.

Do not forget to research online marketing techniques upfront; you will be surprised by how much you can do to expand your Web site even before it launches.

Hopefully, these tips will get you pumped to get started; you can access **www. Crea7ive.com** for more tips and examples of award-winning Web site design.

Enjoy the drive.

Maria Pia Celestino
Account Manager & Art Director
Crea7ive
www.crea7ive.com

Maria Pia Celestino is the founder and president of Crea7ive.com, an awarded design and advertising firm that has been named one of the best in the country. Crea7ive has worked with hundreds of entrepreneurs and executives from several countries around the globe and served many of the world's major companies and personalities. Maria Pia has an extensive background in design, Web development, e-commerce, and marketing that has been honed through years of experience and continuous training.

Born in Buenos Aires, Argentina, Maria Pia has resided in Florida for eight years, where she has watched her company, Crea7ive.com, evolve to being one of the most well-known brands for Web site design. Maria Pia has conducted seminars about the Web, e-commerce, and online advertisement throughout the state of Florida.

Maria Pia's mission is to continually improve services and products offered by Crea7ive to help its clients grow.

BEST in
SEARCH
JUN 2009
†OPSEOs
WEB DESIGN

2nd Best
Web Design Company
awarded by †OPSEOs

As featured in
Entrepreneur CNN SmartMoney

Introduction

What qualifies someone to be a "Web designer?" The answer depends on whom you are asking. I started designing Web sites in 1997, using basic HTML to code pages. Over the years, I increased my skills and started to use Web development applications to improve the quality of my Web sites, interact with databases, and automate processes. Web design applications such as Microsoft Office FrontPage®, NetObjects® Fusion™, and early versions of Adobe Dreamweaver® were amazing technological advances for Web designers.

This brings us back to my original question. If you are a beginner working with basic HTML code or using the latest products such as Microsoft Expression® Web, you are a Web designer, though your skill level will increase over time. If you have advanced training and are an established industry expert, you are a Web designer just as much as the beginner who is trying to develop his or her first Web site. This book is all about free or low-cost Web site design, and for that reason, we will concentrate on the best techniques and products to get you started. You can sink an enormous amount of money into Web design, and in some cases, you may need to if you have a truly complex site. However, it is possible to design a highly effective site with little or no money.

Web sites can be expensive, but they do not have to be incredibly difficult or challenging to build. I built my first Web site with no experience, and while by today's standards it was probably not the best-looking site I have ever developed, it served its purpose well. You may find there are times when you need the services of an experienced Web site designer and Web developer; however, this book will arm you with the knowledge, skills, and confidence necessary to build your first Web site for little or no money. You will also be introduced to some no-cost alternatives to building a Web site that will still help you establish a Web presence.

Anyone has the capability to build his or her own Web site. You do not need to be a trained Web designer to build your very first Web site and achieve your goals. In my book *How to Use the Internet to Advertise, Promote, and Market Your Business or Web Site With Little or No Money*, I revealed a variety of design techniques and marketing tools you could implement with little or no investment to achieve the best possible search engine rankings and increase Web site visibility within all of the major search engines. This book will help you to design, develop, and produce your very first Web site on your own. Also included is an index of professional Web designers who can help if you have advanced needs such as electronic commerce, shopping carts, database integration, and more. Anyone can design and develop a Web site, and this book will help you to achieve just that.

Whom This Book is For

This book is written for anyone who is considering designing and developing a Web site, whether they are a small business, large business, or sole proprietor. It is intended to act as a guide for anyone who is interested in making money, increasing Web site traffic, driving up revenue, improving the financial posture of his or her organization, and establishing a Web presence at little or no cost. While this book will give you the basics for Web design, it is not an intense Web development guide. It will help you understand Web site design, search engine optimization, and other essential components of a Web site and overall marketing campaign. This will ensure that your Web site is highly effective, is visible in search engines, and will ultimately achieve your goals.

How This Book is Organized

This book is organized to help you build a highly successful Web site. Below is a chapter summary of what you will find in this book:

- **How can I become a Web designer, and what do I need to be successful?:** While specialized training will certainly help you refine and hone your Web design skills, and may open the door to advanced Web design techniques, the reality is that Web design is not very difficult. There are many tools that can help you design a highly effective Web site, and this chapter will give you the confidence and inspiration to begin. It will also cover basic terminology, domain names, Web hosting, and equipment requirements.

- **Developing a successful business and marketing plan & finding your niche:** Businesses must develop a marketing plan, ascertain achievable goals, and establish overall objectives. This brief introduction to marketing, market research, and analysis will help ensure that your Web site design efforts support your overall objectives and goals and set you up for success in a highly competitive marketplace.

- **Web site design 101 & HTML fundamentals:** You must understand the basic concepts of Web design as well as Hypertext Markup Language, better known as HTML coding, and other basic principles of effective Web site design. In this chapter, you will learn the fundamentals of Web site design, receive a comprehensive introduction to HTML, and take a quick look at XHTML™, or

Extensible Hypertext Markup Language. With this chapter, you will be well on your way to building your first Web pages.

- **Web site design applications — tools to achieve your goals:** A convenient benefit of building your own Web site is that you do not have to hand-code them anymore. There is a plethora of tools available that let you build Web sites in a Graphical User Interface (GUI), and the application builds the HTML code for you. Though you do need to understand the basics of HTML coding, these applications, such as Adobe® Creative Suite 3 and Microsoft Expression Web, do the hard work for you, letting you concentrate on building great Web sites. This chapter will discuss and preview a variety of Web design applications.

- **Web site organization and navigation fundamentals:** One of the biggest challenges for Web designers is Web site organization and navigation. You need to do some thinking and design work before you start coding Web pages. Ideally, you should have already mapped out how your Web site will be organized and how you want to integrate site navigation. A simple-to-navigate Web site is absolutely critical to achieving success on the Web.

- **Web site content and design:** Content and design are two critical elements of an effective Web design. How your material is organized and what content the site contains will mean success or failure for your Web site. You must design a site that is appealing, functional, and meets your goals. Likewise, you must have effective site content to attract the attention of others, provide them with the information they seek, and keep them interested in your Web site. If your goal is to sell products, you must ensure that your design and content are well-defined and support your e-commerce goals. Often, a Web site is so disorganized that the content is out-of-date, it contains broken links, or it is simply not possible to find what you are looking for.

- **Web site graphics:** This chapter will clear up the mystery of which format of images and graphics you can use on the Web, and which are the best and why. This chapter also explains how you can use images to create an appealing and effective Web site that is optimized for download speed.

- **Web page formats, JavaScript®, and cascading style sheets:** There is a wide variety of Web page formats. This chapter explores each and defines why you may choose — or need — a certain Web page type versus another. It also includes an in-depth look at cascading style sheets (CSS) and why you should use them, as well as a thorough introduction on how to create your own CSS. An introduction to JavaScript and XHTML is also provided.

- **Electronic commerce and shopping carts:** One of the most common goals of both individuals and businesses is to sell products online. You can find nearly anything for sale online, and the competition is fierce. To sell products online takes special applications known as shopping carts. E-commerce opens the door to selling products, accepting credit card payments, using the PayPal® payment system, and other methods of monetary exchange. However, this requires more advanced Web design skills and requirements. This chapter will cover the basics of e-commerce and introduce you to PayPal, shopping carts, and Secure Socket Layer Certificates.

- **Optimize your Web site for search engines:** To get the most out of your Web site, you need to ensure it is optimized for search engines. This chapter will guide you through the principles of how to design your site for maximum search engine optimization (SEO). This is one of the most critical phases of Web design, and often the most overlooked. If people cannot quickly find you in search engines, this chapter will help you overcome this major obstacle.

- **Generating Web site traffic:** This chapter will provide you with tips and tricks on how to generate Web site traffic, as well as increase your overall rankings in search engines. Creating a Web site is the first step, but to achieve success, you need to ensure that people can easily find and navigate your Web site.

- **Introduction to pay-per-click advertising:** This chapter will provide you with a general overview of pay-per-click (PPC) advertising, how it works, how it compares to other marketing techniques, and how to effectively design a PPC campaign for maximum success. It will also discuss what happens when a site visitor clicks on an advertisement, how it is tracked, and how this can generate Web site traffic and increased revenue. You will be provided with a comprehensive introduction to all components of Google PPC applications, including detailed setup, campaign design, and management of Google campaigns. This chapter will delve deep into Google advertising campaigns and reveal a multitude of tips, tricks, and secrets detailing how to maximize the effectiveness of PPC campaigns utilizing Google.

- **Increase profits with Google AdSense™:** This chapter is an introduction to the Google AdSense program, which is another opportunity for you to generate income by allowing other advertisers' PPC advertisements to be placed on your Web site. This no-cost program is an excellent tool to generate revenue at no cost. When you complete this chapter, you can start earning Google AdSense revenue in fewer than five minutes.

- **Generating income with affiliate marketing:** This chapter explains how you can incorporate affiliate marketing into your Web site, how it works, and the multitude of variables involved. You will learn the finite differences among affiliate programs, affiliate networks, and affiliate marketing techniques so you can choose the method that will work best for your company or Web site and maximize your revenue potential. You will also discover how you can start an affiliate program that will directly improve the overall marketing strategy for your business or Web site and increase your revenue bottom line. This chapter covers the basic options for affiliate programs and is a critical step in helping you to determine whether you want to become an affiliate or host affiliates. Both options have varying degrees of complexity, responsibility, and revenue streams, and this chapter will discuss them all so you can make the most educated decision.

- **Harnessing the power of blogs:** This chapter is all about blogs. Blogging is simple and can be a powerful partner to your Web site. To fully understand how blogging can benefit your business or cause, you need to understand blogging itself. This chapter will provide you with all the information you need to know about blogging, including the history of blogging, how it works, and how you can start blogs that will directly improve your overall marketing strategy for your business, Web site, or other worthy cause. Blogging is powerful and very simple. This chapter will give you a crash course on the basics and more. You may even find that a blog is really the ideal solution to your needs. You can create free blogs that may, in fact, serve the same needs as a Web site — moving you onto the Web in minutes, for no cost at all.

- **Social networking:** Social networking is growing in popularity with sites such as MySpace™ and Facebook™. These sites truly show the power of social networking. Social networking sites can also directly impact your Web design and search engine visibility efforts. This chapter is dedicated to introducing you to social networking, as well as showing how you can incorporate social networking into your overall online marketing plan to generate traffic for your Web site. Social marketing is one of the most powerful — and free — marketing tools you have at your disposal. It is not just for teenagers.

- **Interviews with Web design experts:** This chapter contains interviews with many Web design experts and professionals — and a few novices — that will help you with your own Web site design efforts. These experts give practical advice as you learn how to develop your Web site. Learn from those who build Web sites for a living or have gone through the trials and tribulations of creating their own Web site. This is one of the most important chapters in this book because of this valuable advice from experts.

- **Web site design success stories:** This chapter is a compilation of success stories from businesses or individuals who designed and built their own Web site and achieved success. You can read their stories, which will inspire you even more as you design and develop your own Web site. In this chapter, you will see how creating a Web site has impacted the lives of the people featured.

- **Summary:** This chapter contains some final words of encouragement and advice. Building a great Web site is something everyone can do. Although some advanced Web sites may require the assistance of Web site professionals, the majority of Web sites can be built on your own, for little or no money.

- **Recommended reference library:** Atlantic Publishing Company has a wealth of great reading resources. This chapter contains references that every Web designer and online business owner should possess.

- **Glossary:** The glossary will help you understand the terminology you need to know before you build your own Web site.

The Internet is the ultimate marketing tool, giving you immediate access to billions of people worldwide, and by building your own Web site, you can make your presence known for little investment. After reading this book and applying the principles and techniques contained within, you can empower your Web site to achieve success.

This book was designed for the small business or individual who does not have an information technology or Web design staff and is limited on their technology budget and technical knowledge. If you are the owner, proprietor, or manager of a traditional brick-and-mortar or online business, or simply an individual who wishes to build your own Web site, you can save thousands of dollars in costs for Web site design services.

With the help of this book, both the novice and the expert can discover the easiest and least expensive ways to build a Web site for personal or business use. You will assemble a plan that describes in detail your goals for the site, as well as who you are trying to reach and what you plan to offer to make the site unique. Other areas will include some of the pitfalls to avoid, and the design schemes that best fit your personal or professional needs. This book will touch on the terminology you need to know, such as HTML, XHMTL, and Secure Socket Layer Certificates. You will learn basic HTML and evaluate the wide array of software available to build and maintain your Web site without having to hire a professional company to update it.

Many of the discussions within will center on the use of commercial Web design programs such as Adobe Dreamweaver, Microsoft Office FrontPage, Microsoft Expression Web, Serif® WebPlus™ X2, and other programs that are similar but available as open-source software. You will learn where to find these free software platforms and determine which are better with some help from the experts. As you begin implementing the Web site plan and designs, you will check into the different types of open-source software that are available, such as WordPress™ and Joomla!™. These software programs will help you create the platform that will allow you to build virtually anything you want. This book will also evaluate free HTML editors, such as Nvu and Microsoft Live™, a free Internet-based service. You will navigate a variety of avenues to use for building a Web site that is user-friendly and eye-catching.

This book will help you create a Web site that draws your target audience, regardless of whether the site is designed to be informative on news and events in a local region, sell products or services, or just created for family and friends to catch up on what is happening in your life. You will learn some of the dos and don'ts of borrowing text from other sources, sizes and types of fonts to use, how to create your own text, and resources to contact for help with this portion of the design plan.

This book will provide you with all the tools you need to bring your design to life and harness the power of the Internet. If you follow the guiding principles contained in this book, you will discover how satisfying it is to build your own Web site and prove that you can be a successful Web designer. Every chapter of this book could be a standalone book on its own, as the topic is so broad. Though it is impossible to fit everything into this one book, the bare essentials you need to get started are laid out in these pages. However, you may need to expand your knowledge with other resources, such as books on PPC marketing, HTML, JavaScript, XML, XHTML, and other advanced topics.

Chapter 1

HOW CAN I BECOME A WEB DESIGNER & WHAT DO I NEED TO BE SUCCESSFUL?

Being a Web designer is not as difficult as you might imagine. You do not need years of training and experience. In fact, by the time you finish this chapter, you will have started down the path of becoming a Web designer and developer. To be fair, though, you need to set realistic expectations. Some Web sites and Web site technologies are complex and may require advanced skills to effectively reach your end goal. However, this book is designed to help you build your own basic Web site for little or no money and ensure that you can establish a viable, functional Web presence that is SEO-friendly.

To fully understand the concept of building a Web site, you must first understand the terminology. This chapter will discuss some of the terminology used by Web builders, such as domain names, disk space, e-mail accounts, forums, Web hosting, virtual servers, dedicated servers, and FrontPage extensions. For some, these may be common terms, but it is still necessary to discuss each of these in order to build a solid base of understanding before delving deeper into Web site design fundamentals.

Web Designer versus Web Developer

A Web designer is the individual who creates the overall design, look, and feel of a Web site and all of the pages contained on the Web site. A Web site must be designed to achieve the site owner's goals, support the business brand name, and incorporate a variety of fonts, colors, navigation, layout, images, and page content to present to the Web site visitor. A Web designer will typically take his or her design plan and turn it into an HTML (or other format) template, incorporate cascading style sheets (CSS) to control the overall look and feel of the Web site, and incorporate all images, content, and files to produce a Web site.

CSS is a formatting language. The template you may use is either static HTML templates or created through the use of CSS, images, and other page elements to create a Web page that can be reused over and over again throughout your site. You can add new content, but the overall format, style, and layout is controlled by CSS. Using CSS allows you to have a single CSS document that will determine the formatting for all the page elements, which gives you the ability to change the font color, borders, padding, margins, and other formatting options for an entire Web site; however, CSS is not your actual Web page template. Typically, once the Web site is built, it is published to the Web and is visible to search engines, and site visitors can then navigate your Web site.

A Web developer, on the other hand, is tasked with all programming needs for a Web site. Typically, this includes implementing e-commerce capabilities or adding advanced functionality, database connectivity, or search tools. In the case of most small businesses and individuals, you will perform duties as both the Web designer and the Web developer. Often these terms are used interchangeably, but there is a distinctive difference in function. In most cases, when designing and building your own Web site, you serve in both capacities.

The General Structure of the Internet

To understand Web design, it is important to understand the general structure of the Internet. Knowing how the Internet works allows a Web designer to properly serve his or her clients. Background information about the emergence of the Internet helps in developing effective strategies for Web site function. In particular, designers need to look at the general structure of the Internet, including some of the most widely recognized features of the World Wide Web, like Internet Protocol (IP) routing and hypertext links.

The World Wide Web, a different entity from the Internet, is a large database of interlinked forms of information, documents, images, and just about any other form of data you can think of. All of this information is linked together by hyperlinks and URLs, which connect servers — the computers that store the originals of the data — to other computers.

When an Internet user types in an HTTP address, they call up a specific block of data using its assigned code. Let us take Amazon.com®, for example. Somewhere out there, the documents, images, and sound files that make up Amazon.com are stored on a server computer. When you, the Internet user, type in the HTTP address **www.amazon.com**, your computer communicates with the Amazon.com server computer. Data transfer begins: Your computer requests information from the Amazon.com server, which then transmits copies of the original files over to your computer.

Web Site Fundamentals

There are really only two basic components to a Web site. They are your Web pages, the compilation of HTML pages you have designed, and the images, content, and other information that will be displayed on your pages. Your individual Web pages collectively create your Web site. Your Web site can be as small as one page, or it can be thousands of pages. All Web sites have a home page. The home page is the page that site visitors are taken to when they type in your Web site domain name into a browser. From your home site, visitors can navigate your site and visit other Web pages on your site. All Web sites consistently change as new content and other Web pages are added; thus, although you may complete your initial design and publish your Web page, typically, your site will require further maintenance, updates, and revisions. The most challenging part of creating a Web site is developing a blueprint for how you want your site organized, what pages it will contain, how content will be organized, and how your pages will be laid out in relation to others as you design your navigation and page relationships. Design your pages individually, formulate what each page should include, and flesh out the actual content and site design later. You can do this work on a piece of paper or even with sticky notes on the wall, as this will help you visualize the layout.

One of the first aspects to recognize when building a Web site is that you will need some type of software program — or you will have to learn HTML coding and build your site from the ground-up. For those determined to learn all of the coding necessary to build and maintain a Web site, we will explore these options later in the book, starting in Chapter 3, as well as look at a variety of software options to help you with your design goals. Most of the Webmasters interviewed for this book say that starting out with the ability of adding interactive content and items to your Web site is the best route to take because even if you do not plan to use them in the beginning, you will most likely use them down the road. In later chapters, we will look at Web development applications such as Microsoft Expression Web, Adobe Dreamweaver, Serif WebPlus X2, and Microsoft Office FrontPage. When approaching your Web site design, it is usually best to keep colors and fonts at a basic level.

There are four main components of a Web site:

1. **Domain name:** This name is registered and corresponds with where your Web site is physically located on a Web server, and it is also used for your e-mail accounts.

2. **Web hosting:** This is the physical "storage" of your Web pages on a server that is connected to the Internet. This machine "serves" your Web pages as they are requested by a Web browser, and this machine has an IP address. The Domain Name System (DNS) trans-

lates your domain name into your Web account IP address and serves up the appropriate Web pages as requested. Your domain registry will store the IP address of your DNS. The concept may sound difficult to understand; however, it is actually quite simple.

Your Web site consists of a series of Web pages. These Web pages are files, which are stored on a Web server along with images and other content on a Web server. This Web server has an IP address, which is a unique machine name for that Web server. DNS servers translate your domain name (e.g. www.myWebsite.com) into the IP address where your site is actually hosted, and your Web server then serves your page to the Web browser of your site visitor. Therefore, it is critical that your DNR account (the company where you bought your domain name) is updated with the physical IP address of your DNS (provided by your hosting company). This ensures that anyone who searches or types in your domain name into a browser window will be directed to the DNS, which then translates this to the IP address of your site, ensuring that your Web pages are properly displayed at all times.

3. **Web pages:** These are the Web pages you created and published to your Web server. You can create Web pages with programs such as Microsoft Office FrontPage, Microsoft Expression Web, Adobe Dreamweaver CS4, and many other applications, including free design applications.

4. **Optional items:** These might include shopping carts, forms, or databases. While none of these are required for Web sites, you may find that your needs may change over time, so keep that in mind during the planning process.

Web Design Hardware Requirements

You do not need to invest significant funds to be able to create your own Web sites; you only need to have a reliable computer. Web sites can be designed and tested on your personal or business computer, and you do not need to have your own Web server — in fact, you should avoid this cost. Many Web designers work exclusively from their laptop computers, which is a great way of having mobility so you can keep working on your Web pages no matter where you are. My minimum recommendation for a laptop is an Intel® Core™2 Duo Processor, although you do not need the fastest model on the market. In fact, any mid-range processor will more than meet your needs for a long time. On the desktop, the Intel Core 2 Quad models are highly suggested because of the ability to effortlessly multitask.

You also need to have a fast, reliable Internet connection. It really does not matter what you choose — as long as it is high-speed broadband, which is reliable and cost-effective. Do not cut corners on your Internet speed, and do not use dial-up because it is far too slow and you will become frustrated with its limitations very quickly. You may want to use an external 1GB hard drive for regular backups, while programs like Carbonite™ are extremely useful for full backups of Web sites. You can get a free trial of Carbonite at **www.carbonite.com**.

For graphics editing, popular options include Corel® Paint Shop Pro® X2 and Adobe Photoshop® CS4. Some well-known examples of Web design software include Microsoft Office FrontPage, Microsoft Expression Web, and Adobe Dreamweaver CS4. Other design applications such as Serif WebPlus X2 offer great tools for the novice designer. That said, you do not need to invest significant funds into advanced Web design applications. There are also many freeware, or free software, offerings for both your Web design and graphics editing needs, which will be discussed later on in Chapter 4. Also, it is important to recognize that most Web hosting companies also provide easy-to-use Web site templates as part of your hosting package, enabling you to create a great-looking site quickly and very easily. My recommendation, however, is that you invest in Microsoft Expression Web and Corel Paint Shop Pro X2, as they are both very good applications offered at a reasonable price, and will meet the needs of nearly all Web development efforts. However, other design applications, such as Web-PlusX2, offer great tools for the novice designer — and there are plenty of free Web site design and graphics editing applications available.

In the Web design and development communities, you will see two distinct groups: the Microsoft group and the Adobe group. The Adobe group uses Adobe Dreamweaver CS4. Most Web developers consider Dreamweaver to be the professional Web designer's product of choice. In comparison, many used to consider Microsoft Office FrontPage to be the beginner's tool. Microsoft changed that with the release of Microsoft Expression Web, which matches up favorably with Dreamweaver. FrontPage is no longer officially supported by Microsoft, but it is still readily available for purchase. It is a good beginner tool that provides you with the what-you-see-is-what-you-get (WYSIWYG) environment where you create in design mode and the software writes the HTML code for you. WebPlus X2 is also a great design application for those without any HTML experience.

Web Site Hosting

Web hosting is a bit more complex than simply buying storage space, though that is essentially what you are doing. You are paying a provider to "host" your Web site on their Web server. The Web server has special software that lets the server operate as a Web server, and as pages are requested from your Web site, it "serves" them to the Web site visitor. A Web server can host hundreds of Web sites simultaneously, which is how you can buy Web hosting services relatively inexpensively. Web servers have a unique IP address to identify the machine your site is hosted on. DNS servers translate your domain name into that IP address, and this is how your Web pages are served to your site visitors. If you type in **www.atlantic-pub.com**

(Atlantic Publishing Company) into your browser, the DNS server that is specified in your domain name registry translates this URL into the corresponding IP address for the Web site and serves up the Web site to the site visitor.

In most cases, you will buy hosting from a commercial service provider, though you can host your own Web site on your own servers. But hosting is cheap and reliable, and buying hosting services puts the burden of supporting the equipment, leased high-speed Internet connections, and back-up services and applying patches and upgrades on the service provider. Let your hosting provider deal with all the costs and challenges associated with keeping your Web site available; it is not worth investing in your own Web server equipment.

A Web host is the foundation you will need to build your Web site; without it, you cannot begin to implement your design plans. The Web host provides you with the disk space, e-mail accounts, and secured shopping carts. Although this book is all about finding the least expensive or free way of building Web sites, there are times when choosing the free route might end up costing you more money and headaches in the long run. One of the key factors in using a free Web host might include limiting your ability to create interactive pages or having enough space to build the site you have designed in your planning stage, and in most cases, none will support e-commerce or other advanced Web development needs.

While there are "free" Web hosting services available, most of them push advertising onto your Web site and limit your creativity by forcing you to select from a limited number of Web site templates. If you want to build a site that contains 25 pages, many of the free Web hosts will not support that many pages or offer the ability to increase to that number as your Web site needs grow. The last thing you want is to build a site and then have to move it because the host you chose does not offer the support or tools you need to maintain it. Moving a site is not only costly, but time-consuming as well.

You can use Google or any other search engine to find reputable hosting service providers, both free and cost providers: **www.doteasy.com**, **www.mister.net**, and **www.Webs.com** are just a few of the dozens of free hosting providers. Each of these sites have specific limitations, so you should carefully review them before you decide on free versus pay options. As you will find, feature-rich Web hosting packages can be readily obtained for under $100 a year. An index of Web hosting companies is provided in the back of this book. Applied Innovations (**www.appliedi.net**) is one such company. Their ValuePlus™ hosting solution features multiple domain support so you can actually host two individual domains on the same account. While you will most likely never use many of the features included in this plan, the ValuePlus plan does include the most important features you should look for: 2,000 MB of disk space, 50,000 MB of monthly data transfer, advanced statistics reporting, and unlimited e-mail accounts. When you own and host your own domain name, such as **www.brucecbrown.com**, your hosting account comes with e-mail accounts as well.

Another factor to consider is what you plan to use your site for, as there is a major difference between the needs and support for a personal site and a business site. It is not recommended to use a free Web host for a business site. Personal Web sites used to be very popular to share photographs and information with family and friends, but now social networking sites, such as MySpace and Facebook, or personal blogs may actually be a better alternative than designing and hosting your own Web page. They are completely free, which makes this an attractive route.

If you choose to build a personal site versus a business site, Lisa Irby, founder and Webmaster of **www.2createaWebsite.com**, recommends using WebSite Tonight® from Go Daddy® because it is reasonably priced and browser-based, meaning there is no software to download. It allows you to create message boards, video, Adobe® Flash® introductions, text, pictures, chat rooms, shopping carts, and games.

At **www.GoDaddy.com**, hosting plans are relatively cheap, and you can upgrade to a virtual dedicated server with full administrative access or sign up for a dedicated server with administrative access. A virtual dedicated server has several businesses using it, but all are separated from each other by allotments of space and security, whereas a dedicated server is all yours — no one else uses any portion of it. People often ask whether you need a virtual dedicated server or a dedicated server. A virtual dedicated server is suitable 99 percent of the time. There is a steep increase in price between the two, and unless you have a need for a massive, e-commerce-enabled Web site with thousands of site visitors simultaneously, there is no need for a dedicated server — so save your money. Whichever server suits your fancy, all plans offer full customer support and include routers, servers, firewalls, and Google Webmaster tools. As with most hosting sites, the costs can rise exponentially if you pile on the extras. No matter what site you use, research and read the fine print to understand exactly what you will get with the different packages. One thing to look for is whether any site-building tools and templates are included in the package you choose, if you want to create quick and easy Web sites on the fly.

When using a free Web hosting server, it appears that the Internet spiders find the advertising on the pages, but often not your site content, which is one reason why many people say free hosting does not work as well as commercial hosting. Free hosting and software sound like great concepts, but using them is one of the first pitfalls Web builders recommend against because, as the old adage goes, you get what you pay for. Free services might not be worth the headaches you will face as you begin building your site.

According to Lisa Irby, the disadvantages of using a free hosting service far outweigh the advantages. On her Web site, Irby emphatically writes, "After my nightmare experiences with using free Web hosts, I vowed to never go the free route again because it is definitely better to invest a small amount of money." The following list from Irby's Web site at **www.2createaWebsite.**

com/prebuild/create-free-Website.html illustrates the disadvantages of using a free Web hosting site to build your new Web site.

Disadvantages of Free Web Hosts

- You have limited Web page space.

- You cannot add interactive features, such as chat rooms, message boards, games, and online ordering.

- Search engines often ignore them because they do not actively help you with keywords the search engines look for, and overall, this is a huge disadvantage.

- Your visitors may doubt your credibility.

- You may have banners and/or pop-up ads on your home page — or all of your pages — which will cost your customers or visitors because most users block pop-ups and will stay away from your pages if they have to deal with them.

- You are usually assigned a long and hard-to-remember Web address, which means that you do not choose your own short domain name. For instance, it could be something like **www.freeWebhost. com/yourdomainname**.

- No guarantees of site availability and longevity.

- No branded e-mail addresses, such as **you@yourdomain.com**.

- Poor help and support options, if any are offered to begin with.

- These services may not be free forever; unless you read the fine print, the free Web hosting may be only temporary and could end up costing you much more than if you had started out with a company that is up-front about its costs.

Using free hosting and software might sound like a simple route to take, but when doing so, remember that it usually means you are getting exactly what you paid for — which is nothing. Another detail to remember is that despite the claims that these free Web hosting sites offer, they are not cheap to run because someone has to pay for the space they are offering you for free. This could ultimately end up with the hosting site losing so much money that they fold, or your Web site becoming overrun with advertising to pay for these "free" services. Typically, banners and pop-up ads are how these free Web hosts provide you with a free site. Most, if not all, free Web hosting sites do not offer any guarantees that protect you against your pages being shut down without notice or suddenly changing their terms and converting to a paid hosting system.

Another downfall to free Web hosting is that search engines have a more difficult time finding your site and, in many cases, simply don't index it and include it in their databases. When you are building a Web site to make money, those search engine results are critical. You will never gain any momentum without the major search engines like Google and Yahoo!® finding your Web site.

Here are the main reasons why "free" hosted Web sites are normally not found in search engines:

- **Too small and "unimportant"**: Most free sites are generally small and are not of significant value because they do not contain a solid theme or concept, and they usually have more links to external sites than to their own internal pages. Content is one of the specific types of information search engines look for, and this means content that has a particular focus and a large number of pages.

- **Minimal updating of site content:** Many people build a Web site, publish it, and never update it. Search engines are getting smarter, and the formulas they use to determine page rankings might not recognize free Web hosting sites. When a site is shown as being hosted on a free Web host server, the search engines appear to have greater difficulty indexing them — or they just exclude them entirely.

- **No links pointing to the Web site:** Many Webmasters or Web directories will not link to a site built on a free host. One reason is these sites might not look professional, and few people want to link to a poorly developed site with pop-ups and banners all over the place because it creates a negative image for their site. Another issue is that most Webmasters know that free sites generally have short life spans. These days, the kinds of Web sites linking to you are important for achieving a good search engine rank, as you will discover later in this book. The truth is that free Web sites get little respect on the Internet.

When choosing a hosting plan, remember to research the company and find out what types of customer service they offer; whether you can update your site when you want to; and what types of e-mail accounts and support the host provides. On the Web site **www.top-10-Web-hosting.com**, the ten best Web hosting sites according to their survey of 58,000 Webmasters are ranked and updated daily.

Domain Names

You must own your own domain name if you want to have a serious Web presence. Your domain name is your brand name on the Web. It is the address every site visitor will type in to visit your Web site, and it is critical that you choose a good domain name and host it with a reputable provider. There are dozens of companies you can purchase your domain names from. Most offer convenient control panels that let you update settings, including DNS server IP addresses. If you have your own company exchange server, you will also be able to change IP addresses for your mail servers if you do not wish to use the provided POP — post office protocol — e-mail accounts with your hosting account. This will also allow you to update your contact information, name, address, and e-mail addresses.

Your domain name should uniquely identify your business. The general rule of thumb is that the shorter the domain name, the better, and it should be relevant to your company name, service, or products. If you already have an established corporate name or identity, you should try to base your domain name on that corporate identity. This will allow customers to identify your company name with your domain name. For example, Atlantic Publishing Company's domain name is **www.atlantic-pub.com**. We also highly recommend that you secure any similar domain names, with the main reason being to protect your identity from others who may use a very similar sounding or identical domain name, with a different extension. Using the example above, you would also want to tab **www.atlanticpub.com**, **www.atlanticpub.net**, and **www.atlanticpublishing.com**. Your primary domain name should be the domain name that is "hosted," while others may be parked at no additional cost and pointed to the main domain name URL. This way, you only pay for one hosted domain name but utilize many domain names on the Internet, all directing site visitors to your main hosted site.

It is important that you name your Web site after your domain name. The primary reason for this is so that people know your Web site and business by name. CNN® stands for Cable News Network, but no one calls it that; CNN is simply known as CNN, and the domain name is CNN.com. While this may be a simplistic explanation, your domain name should easily relate to your company name so your brand or company name can be easily recognized and memorized.

Many professional Web designers recommend using keywords in your domain name rather than your company name. For example, the **www.strugglingteens.com** domain name specifically targets the industry of private schools and programs by using the keywords "struggling teens." Therefore, when you type the keywords "struggling teens" into the Google, Yahoo! and Bing search engines, this Web site pops up in the No. 1 spot under the paid ads. Your domain name may have relevance in how some search engines rank your Web site, so embedding keywords into your domain name may help you achieve better search engine success.

Another option you may consider is to purchase both: domain names identifying your business, and those using keywords. Put your Web site files on the domain name with the keywords, and redirect the domain names with the company name to the keywords domain name. This will allow you to market the domain name with your company name, which helps with branding and has the benefits of having the actual Web site located under a domain name with keywords.

Keywords built into Web site content and meta tags are essential to obtaining and maintaining visibility with these major search engines. This will be discussed in detail in later chapters of this book. Keywords are not something you implement once and forget; the keywords must be constantly updated to ensure immediate success in gaining visibility and to keep your site listed on the first page of the search engine results. Few people look beyond the first page of search engine results, so if you are located on page ten — or even page two — you may never be found.

Domain names should not be extremely long; this is going to be your URL address for your Web site, and the last thing you need is a long address that no one can remember. Although some people may bookmark your page in their Internet browser, just as many, if not more, will not. You could lose valuable traffic if your Web site address is too long. If you are determined to have a long URL address, hyphenating the words will make it easier to read.

There was a time when domain names were readily available, but today you will find that many domain names are already registered by someone else. Typically, there are variations of your desired domain name available, or perhaps other domain name extensions such as .org, .net, or .us. You can check the availability of a domain name by going to **http://who.GoDaddy.com/WhoIsCheck.aspx**.

Advantages of Owning Your Own Domain Name

- You have full creative control over your domain name.

- It is easy to get it listed with the major search engines, which in turn makes your site easier to find.

- You can have multiple branded e-mail addresses, e.g. **you@your domain.com**.

- There is plenty of Web page space for site expansion when hosted.

- There are no worries of your site being removed unexpectedly when hosted on a free hosting provider with a virtual domain name.

- It looks more professional than virtual domain names.

- You have more flexibility for design and functionality.

Web Site Design Fundamentals

As a Web site designer, the focus of your creativity should follow a similar path. Focus not simply on developing a Web site that sells a product or service. Using the right side of your brain, you should be able to take the specifics for your client's Web site and brainstorm a creative branding solution for them. One Web site designer was approached by a small business owner who needed to generate a brand for five Web sites. The designer was awarded the project not because they were offering the best rate for the sites — although they were — but because they immediately had the idea that the sites would work best as part of a brand if they were all designed according to a template. For the Web designer, this meant that only one template needed to be created, and it could be applied to all five of the Web sites the client needed.

Set a series of goals for each of your Web site design projects. Even if you are designing a relatively small site, establish some sort of schedule for your work. Determine your goals for the project with clear priorities and an understanding of what needs to be done when. When making a Web site, have more than one goal. For example, your immediate goal might be to develop a good home page for the Web site so that you can at least post this key page and have it running live relatively quickly. On one level, a Web site design is an art form. It is a presentation of a concept and idea through the use of HTML coding, just as a painting is the presentation of an idea rendered using paints of various colors and other such media. To determine what type of pages you need for a Web design project, begin by determining what you expect your site to look like. Below are some considerations to take into account:

- **Consider the amount of information you have and how to organize it.** Under no circumstances should the site visitor be overwhelmed by the content. On one hand, your client might not want to develop a site that only has a few pages, a couple of pictures, and some spattering of text. On the other hand, you want to make sure that visitors are going to be sufficiently engaged to stay on the site. If there is too much information, you will probably have to think about creating a database to manage it all. Ordinarily, however, you should just think about developing a reasonable amount of information per page.

- **Consider how visitors are likely to use the information.** Most Web sites allow the user to simply sit back and read information. Most people spend their time online reading e-mails, catching up on the latest news, or occasionally tracking the financial markets.

Online banking is big, too. Most of these activities fall somewhere between being entirely passive and being moderately passive, but that does not mean that people do not enjoy interactive Web sites and online activities. One of the ways you may be able to help your client keep their visitors on the site for the maximum amount of time is by finding some way to establish interactive activities on the site, whether that involves taking part in quizzes and survey polls, or posting opinions on message boards for all to see. Also consider whether there is going to be any need for visitors to download content, such as video or audio files. Does your client want to stream video, for example?

- **Consider users' expectations.** As you develop a concept in your design process for a site, it is important to have a fairly clear idea of what people are going to want from the site when they visit. Most designers develop a practice of visiting Web sites that are, in one way or another, similar to what they have been asked to design to get an idea of the features and functions people are going to be expecting. Because most users have a pretty clear idea of what they expect when they go looking for a particular Web site, it pays to look closely at what features are common among sites that are relevant to your project.

For the layout and multimedia content of the site you design, think about the best way to organize the information you need, and the best way to meet the expectations of site visitors. Most sites have a unique home page layout and two or three subordinate page designs. Uniformity is important as an aesthetic element, too; people do not want to be overwhelmed by too many different page layouts any more than they want to be overwhelmed by too much information or too many multimedia features. Select the best elements — the top three or four page layouts, the best three or four colors, a single font style — and stick with them, applying a single resolution to all the pages. Web sites are always a work in progress. There will constantly be products or information to add; these updates will liven up your page and garner more page views. Aim for a site that is content-rich with images that catch the eye, but is still easy to load and navigate. Many buttons, icons, and frames are good if they serve a purpose and make the site more organized, but if they serve as a distraction or a nuisance, people will look for a site that is less complex. However, just as there are some sites with too much, there are sites that are full of "under construction" pages and black holes. A messy, incomplete site will also steer the average browser to a better place, even if you do offer a better product or service. You never want to put a site up that is not ready for potential clients to see. They may think your work on their site will be incomplete and messy. A small, comprehensive Web site is a good foundation for better, more complex features as you learn more and grow. You can add new features after you have established your basic Web site with all the necessities.

Plotting out how your Web site will be seen is another vital part to creating a winning Web site. No amount of advertising or quality content can make up for an unattractive, sloppy design and layout. Many Web sites have amazing content, but rarely are seen because they are not appealing to a user at first glance. Take some time and plot out what you want to do on paper. List all of the links you want to have on your home page. Color is crucial and should be given plenty of thought. A dark or heavily patterned background with a light text is hard to read and can divert people's attention from your products. Everyone has had this problem at least once and had to resort to highlighting the text in order to read it. Someone who has searched and found other Web sites with similar content or products will pass your site up for one that is easier to read.

Backgrounds should be white or a light color that dark text can stand out on. A dull Web site with no personality is not going to win you regular visitors, either, so go with a combination that is universally liked by most people. Brightly colored text should only be used for highlighting words. If you choose to use a color other than black for your main text, make sure it is dark. If black is too plain, opt for a chocolate brown or navy on a light background. Color is an area where you, as a Web site designer, must choose good combinations. If a potential client sees your Web site and it has a color scheme they hate, they will probably find a better option that fits their tastes. It is crucial to find combinations that appeal to the eye and are easy to read. Black text with a white background is not the only option. Some combinations that also work well, for instance, are a light blue with a dark, chocolate-colored text, or a light green background with a navy blue text.

The layout of a page and its components will make or break your Web site. You have limitless options in the layout of your Web site, but there are some general rules to follow that will make your page standard enough for even the extreme novice to use and understand easily. Avoid making your page so busy that no one can focus on a single piece of your Web site. Including plenty of space where there are no graphics, text, or links is key to making a Web site clear and easy to maneuver. If you make it easy for your visitors to completely explore your site without any problems, they will come back for more.

The top of a page should be reserved as a marker for the name of the Web site or business. Think of it as a small billboard or a calling card. You can include a logo or another identifying image of your client's brand. Keep it simple and concise. The best positioning is in the middle third of a page. It will be front and center and impossible not to notice when a home page loads.

The first portion a visitor will look at is the top middle-third of a Web site. Make sure this area is neat, but still has personality and flair to give your client or their company an identity. Make sure it is not a template or plain text that is boring and seen all around the Web. Links to other pages on a Web site, called navigation buttons, are typically positioned in one of three ways. You can place them across the top, down the left side, or down the right side of each page. If you choose, you can place two sets of links at the top and bottom, allowing the visitor to click on links whether they have scrolled all the way down or up the page.

Give your visitors options to increase the likelihood that they will move on to other pages on your site. If you have many different links on your home page, you may choose to place them vertically on the left or right side just because of how many there are. A list down either side of the page is much neater than having several that stretch across the screen and out of the main view. If you can limit yourself to one or two lines at the top without having this problem, that is all right. If you have several links and the top of the page looks like a large block of links clustered together, go with a listing on the side.

Labels for links should also be short. They should convey the message of what it connects them to without being too wordy. For instance, instead of "All about us and our history as a company," go with "Company Bio" or just "About Us." Whenever you add a link that is extremely long, the entire page is skewed off its streamlined look. Keep it short and sweet. People constantly play a game of "word association," especially when scanning through a site. If they are looking for something in particular, there may be a few words in their head that they are searching for. If someone is looking for information about your company's history, they will probably be scanning the page for "Bio," "About Us," or "History." Look at other Web sites and see what phrases pop up. It is a good idea to go with the grain. If you want to be unique, you can come up with your own link words, but make sure that people can make the connection you intend.

Every computer will view a page differently as well. Your site should be designed to look good no matter what the resolution or page view settings are configured on any computer. Using a percentage setting on your Web site can make it look good on a wide range of screens, not just yours. With 80 to 90 percent, your page will fill 80 to 90 percent of the screen width of every computer. Keep in mind that most monitors sold today are high-resolution, wide-screen LCDs. Some images you add can pose a problem if they are too big to fit within the percentage view. You should still check your page in all possible resolutions whenever you are going live for the first time, or after you have added new pages.

One of the great benefits from using programs such as Dreamweaver or Expression Web is that they come with an arsenal of powerful tools for creating very impressive Web sites fairly easily. With these programs, it is also easy to create advanced effects such as rollover buttons, forms, navigation menus, and database integration. With the click of your mouse in Expression Web, you can create HTML pages, ASPX, PHP, CSS, Master Pages, Web Templates, JavaScript, XML, and .ASP Web pages.

CSS will be discussed more in Chapter 8, but Expression Web does most of the work for you by letting you choose pre-defined CSS layouts to help you lay out the sections of your Web pages.

Expression Web (and other applications) can create style sheets for you, and you can customize your style sheets as you work through them. By using CSS to lay out your Web site, you eliminate the need to use HTML tables. Expression Web even lets you create dynamic rollover buttons quickly and easily. You can also create amazing rollover navigation menus in a matter of minutes.

Make sure you are consistent throughout your Web site. Text that is "clickable" should be a different color from standard text. Fonts should be standardized throughout your site and, generally, your Web pages should be based on the same template, so they appear seamless as they are served up one after the other by the Web server. CSS gives you enormous control over the look and organization of your Web pages, but you can still achieve this without the use of CSS. Make sure you test out your pages in a variety of browsers on a variety of monitor sizes and resolutions. Design for a 1024x768 resolution, which is the standard today.

This chapter has provided you with a great deal of information for Web site designers, Web site hosting service providers, and recommended products, vendors, and software. But in addition, you may find that you need to use the services of a freelance designer, graphic artist, or SEO expert. One good source is **www.guru.com**. Individuals can post a no-obligation project to Guru.com™ and begin receiving competitive quotes from freelance experts in hours. Alternatively, one can also search Guru.com by skill category to locate the highest-ranked freelancer and invite him or her to work on a project. This strategy is especially helpful if you are unsure of how to define your project needs on your own, or if you just need the best expert you can find with a specific set of skills.

This chapter has provided you with the basic knowledge of Web site design fundamentals and explained the requirements for hosting and publishing a Web site to the Internet; Chapter 2 will show you how to develop a marketing plan before digging deeper into Web site design fundamentals.

Web Design Advice, Hints, and Tips — by Vickie Acklin

You can design your own Web site for very little money. An online Web site editor is the most cost-effective way to build your own site. You can usually purchase your domain name, set up Web site hosting, and build your Web site using an online editor, all in one place. One thing to make sure of is that you use a known company for your Web site. Find out how long they have been in business. See if they offer support if you need help.

Using an online editor such as GoDaddy's WebSite Tonight will save you time and money. Online editors are not developed to let you design a very complicated Web site, but you will be able to design a good Web site if you take time with it. Even though it is termed "WebSite Tonight," do not try to get your Web site online in one night. Spend some time designing a quality site.

Most online editors are pretty easy to use, but you still need to take the time to look at all of the options the program offers and get familiar with them. With online editors, you will usually choose a color and design theme. Once you have made your decision, you simply add your text and images. Online editors have a basic gallery of images you will choose from if you want to place an image on your site.

If you want to spend a little more money and also have the time to learn a software program, you can purchase a Web site editor at many stores. Dreamweaver is good, but can be complicated to learn. CoffeeCup® software is much easier to use but also creates much simpler Web sites. And there is still a learning curve with CoffeeCup. You will need to use the help files that come with any editor you purchase and become familiar with the program. Most offer tutorials.

When you design your own Web site, always remember that you are designing it for the public and not for yourself. You want to design your site as though it is your store. Make it easy for visitors to find their way around your Web site. Set up your links logically.

Start simple with your first new site. Get the basics online and preview it often. As you start to gain confidence with the Web site program you are using, you can add more color and design. The best advice here is to not get in a hurry. It takes a professional designer some real time to develop those excellent Web sites you see on the Internet; it should take you some time, too.

Keep your Web site colors toned down. Some color is all right, but you do not want to "scream" color. Use Web-safe fonts on your Web site only. Web safe fonts are the fonts that most everyone has preinstalled on their computers, such as Arial®, Tahoma®, Verdana®, and Times New Roman®. If you use a special, fancy font and your visitor does not have that font installed on his or her computer, the browser will substitute a font, and it may look bad on your particular Web site. If you stick to Web-safe fonts, your visitor will view the Web site the same as you do. Note: If you use a special font in an image, everyone can see it — even without the font installed in their computer.

Vickie Acklin is an independent Web site designer and developer who has owned her own business since 1999. She designs for small to medium businesses and has a niche in which she offers design packages. You can visit Vickie's Web site online at **www.Websitedesigntexas.com** *and contact her at vickie@Websitedesigntexas.com.*

Web Hosting Advice for Beginners — by Vickie Acklin

When choosing a Web site hosting company, do not look for free Web site hosting. That is a mistake many new Web site owners make. Free Web site hosting is very basic and will have very limited features. Free Web site hosting companies are free because they place advertising banners on your site. These advertisement banners are the way in which the free hosting company makes enough money to offer free hosting. If you are putting a business Web site online, an advertising banner at the top of every one of your Web pages is not going to look good. In addition, the free Web site hosting company usually also places an advertisement for their free hosting on your Web site, too.

You should set up low-cost Web site hosting. The features offered with basic, inexpensive plans are usually enough for a basic Web site. If you decide to add interactive features to your Web site, basic hosting will usually be adequate. If you need more hosting space or features, it is usually simple to upgrade without having to move your Web site or start over.

Whichever company you choose, make sure to choose one that has been in business for a while. The hosting company you choose should have good support and designers on hand. This way, if you need help, you can pay their support to help you.

Vickie Acklin is an independent Web site designer and developer who has owned her own business since 1999. She designs for small to medium businesses and has a niche where she offers design packages. You can visit Vickie's Web site online at **www.Websitedesigntexas.com** *and contact her at vickie@Websitedesigntexas.com.*

Nine Tips to Change a Web Site from "Created" to "Completed" — by Paul Pennel

1. Test browser compatibility

Does your Web site work in every Web browser, such as Internet Explorer™ or Safari™? Unfortunately, just because your Web site looks great in one browser does not mean it looks great in every browser. If this is not addressed, your Web site may not look as professional to everyone who views it as you originally desired. Does your Web site work on a Mac® as well as a PC, or personal computer? If you do not have both a Mac and a PC, make sure to find a friend who can look at your Web site on whatever machine you do not own.

2. Contact information

Do you have easy-to-find contact information on your Web site? You need a phone number, an e-mail address, and preferably an e-mail form. You want your customers to reach you in a manner they are comfortable with. If you have a physical location, be sure to include your store address as well. This information should be an in easy-to-find location such as your header, which is the top of the Web site home page.

3. Marketing

To market your Web site, it should be submitted to all of the large search engines, such as Google and Yahoo! If you are not listed in search engines, nobody will be able to find your Web site.

Are you advertising your Web site in other ways? If you are a "solopreneur," you may not have much of a budget for marketing. However, that does not mean you should ignore marketing altogether. If your budget is tight, the best way to do this involves a large amount of time on your part, but the good news is this method is free of cost. Essentially, you should be promoting yourself on other Web sites. As part of owning your own business, you are probably already reading articles and forums related to your field. As you do this, you should comment on the articles and post on the forums. In some forums, the guidelines may even allow you to post a link to your Web site. Be careful not to blatantly advertise yourself; instead, provide useful feedback on these forums. The more links to your Web site, the more ways people can find your site. This will also affect the visibility of your Web site in search engines. While there are other factors involved, this is one that you can help to control.

You may be tempted to place advertisements on your Web site. If you have a large amount of traffic and the ads do not take away from your message, this can be a good way to make some money. However, if you do not have a lot of traffic, it is probably more cost-effective for you in the long run to avoid the advertisements and just concentrate on your message.

4. Repeat visitors

You have committed much of your time and/or expenses to attract people to your Web site; now, how do you make sure they keep coming back? The more often they visit your Web site, the more your name is in their minds and the more likely they are to purchase from you. Something like an online forum or a blog that has useful information will keep people coming back for more current information. Consider having a signup that entices people to receive a newsletter you publish in your area of expertise. Your newsletter should be regular enough so you stay in people's minds, but not so frequent that they get annoyed and ask to be removed from your mailing list.

5. Building trust

As a "solopreneur," you will not have the same built-in trust as a well-known online company, like Amazon.com, has with customers. Therefore, you will have to design your Web site in a way that will have people visiting the Web site trusting it — and trusting you. Testimonials from previous satisfied customers are a great way to do this. Also, a picture of you will give the Web site more personality and will create the feel that you are not a faceless Web site that may disappear at any moment. If you have a building, include a picture of it along with an address.

The more information you provide upfront on your Web site, the more people will trust you. Creating a detailed "Frequently Asked Questions" page is valuable. An "About Us" page is good as well. If you allow sales directly from your Web site, have them done on a secure connection and make that very obvious to your customers. Give your customer some form of guarantee. An example of this could be providing a money-back guarantee if they are not absolutely satisfied with your product.

6. Have your Web site reviewed

A professional opinion about your Web site would be ideal, but these can be hard to acquire. Instead, have people you personally know review it for you. If you are targeting a certain market, ask friends in that market to take a look. If your reviewers are afraid to offend you, then their feedback will not be of any value. Therefore, make sure to tell them to be brutally honest with their opinions. You, too, should review your Web site multiple times to make sure the content and design are consistent and easy to read from page to page. Also remember to check your spelling and grammar.

7. Favorites icon

When customers visit your Web site, the Web address is located in the Web browser's location bar. A favorites icon is a small image shown next to the address. It is also seen if the customer has your Web site bookmarked in their browser. The favorites icon is a good way to brand your Web site and increase its prominence in a bookmark menu. It is simple to set up, and for such little icon, it definitely helps make your Web site stand out. If you already have a logo or some image you want associated with your Web site, go to **http://tools.dynamicdrive.com/favicon** and follow the instructions. It automatically converts your image to the correct size and file name; all you have to do is copy the file to your host.

8. Statistics

Viewing real-time statistics for your Web site is desirable. Google Analytics™ is a way to easily see how customers find your Web site, how many customers visit on a given day, and what pages those customers are most interested in It also gives you a graphical overall view of your customer traffic. It is a free tool and easy to implement. Go to **www.google.com/analytics** and follow the directions. You should be able to set this up within 15 to 30 minutes. There are other similar statistic tools available on the Internet; just be sure to use one that works for your Web site.

9. I'm done, right?

"OK, I've done all of this for my Web site. I'm done, right?" Nope — you are never done with your Web site. If you put out a great Web site in January but never update it, then by July, it is going to look out-of-date. Make sure you keep some kind of current information about your industry or your company on your Web site so visitors can see you are an active and thriving organization. Just because your Web site is great today does not mean that it should not be completely redesigned every couple of years to keep it fresh. If your Web site looks professional and current, people will view your business the same way.

Minnow Web Design offers solutions for small businesses or organizations with big ideas. Owner and designer Paul Pennel combines 12 years of information technology experience with a desire to make great Web sites affordable. Paul can be contacted at paul@minnowWebdesign.com or on the Web at www.minnowWebdesign.com.

You Must Do This Before You Begin — by Erin Pheil

Because the process of planning, designing, and creating one's own Web site is exciting and fun, people often begin their projects filled with energy, brimming with enthusiasm, and bubbling with ideas.

What many people fail to realize, though, is that all the enthusiasm and energy in the world cannot create a successful Web site if the site has no clear goal or purpose.

Time and time again, businesses build their own company Web sites without understanding why they were building them:

- "Well, all of our competitors have Web sites, so we need one, too."

- "We've been told we need to have a Web site to be successful."

- "Our summer intern knows how to build Web sites, so we figured we'd have her build a company site for us."

Without fail, these "Web sites without purpose" end up providing the least return on investment, doing the least amount of good — and sometimes even causing harm for the people and businesses that built them.

Fortunately, it is easy to set yourself (and your Web site) up for success; simply follow this one tip before you begin even the first steps in your Web site creation process: Clearly define at least one goal or purpose for your Web site. People build Web sites for different reasons. Why, exactly, are you building your site?

- Do you wish to educate potential customers and decrease confusion about your various services and offerings?

- Are you looking to increase your monthly income through online sales?

- Would you like potential clients to be able to browse through photos of past projects?

Make sure you write down the main reason(s) you are building your Web site on a piece of paper; a written goal is much more powerful than one that remains trapped in your head. Writing down the goal(s) for your site will streamline your project, focus your energy and enthusiasm, and help you make smart choices as you move forward.

Then, each time you need to make a decision about your site, simply stop and ask yourself, "Will this help me reach my goal for the Web site?"

For example, say you have decided that your Web site's primary purpose is to collect feedback and reviews from existing clients. Halfway through your project, you happen upon a Web site offering an animated slideshow that would easily integrate into the site you are building. The slideshow is slick, professional, and impressive; better yet, it only costs $9.

Should you integrate the slideshow into your Web site? It would look impressive — but what specific purpose would it serve? If you think back to your main goal of collecting customer feedback, you can quickly determine that an animated slideshow would not move you forward toward your goal; instead, it would likely do little more than add clutter and detract from your site's effectiveness and ability to collect customer feedback.

Without a goal to work toward, the process of building your own site will likely feel akin to a dreadful, confusing chore instead of an exciting, fun experience. Without a goal, enthusiasm is drained, energy is wasted on pointless tasks, and time is almost always spent moving down dead-end paths. This is why sites without clearly defined goals often end up looking and feeling like patchwork quilts. Photos, text, and components are thrown together for no specific reason. The content in these sites often appears disjointed or incomplete. Site visitors often have frustrating experiences and feel unsure as to what they are supposed to do.

Without a clearly defined goal, your Web site will just sit there. There will be no way to determine if it is successful or effective, if it was worth all of your time and effort, or what — if anything — could be improved. Conversely, a clearly defined goal helps you to determine whether your Web site is successful. Is your Web site actually doing what you wanted it to do? Is it collecting customer feedback, bringing in extra money each month, or encouraging new customers to reserve consultations with you? If not, you know more work needs to be done.

Make sure you set yourself up for success before you begin your Web site project. Determine why you are building your site and allow this purpose to be your guide as you plan, design, and develop your Web site.

Erin Pheil is the founder of Timeforcake Creative Media, Inc., a boutique Web and graphic design company that specializes in creative, effective Web site and graphic design projects. You can learn more about Erin and Timeforcake at ***www.timeforcake.com****.*

Chapter 2

DEVELOPING A SUCCESSFUL BUSINESS AND MARKETING PLAN & FINDING YOUR NICHE

If you are building a business Web site, an essential step before you begin to design and develop your site is to craft a thoroughly thought-out marketing plan for your business. A good marketing plan is critical for you to map out your future goals and achieve success. Writing one is a fairly straightforward process that requires you to set clear objectives and determine how you will achieve them. This chapter is entirely optional in relation to Web design efforts, but often many Web sites are built and published without a marketing plan, which is a critical mistake. Despite the best of intentions, there are times that a well-conceived Web site will ultimately fail because of little or no marketing.

A marketing plan must be achievable, realistic, cost-effective, measurable, and flexible. One of the main objectives in developing a marketing plan is to establish your budget. Your marketing plan may consist of:

- Market analysis
- Business objectives
- Marketing strategies
- Steps to achieving business objectives
- A realistic budget
- A realistic timeline

Performing a Market Analysis

You need to be flexible based on your budget, marketplace competition, business objectives, and both internal and external influences. Market analysis helps you determine if there is a need for your supplies or services. Understanding the marketplace, the desire for your products, and your competition will help you better understand how to establish a successful business in a competitive environment. If there is no need for your products, you will likely fail — unless you establish your presence in the marketplace. Likewise, if there is a high level of competition, you must develop a marketing plan that allows you to compete in product, quality, availability, or price. Knowing the marketplace needs and how they are currently serviced are essential in developing your marketing plan; you cannot realistically build your Web site and just expect customers to find you. Chapter 11 concentrates on search engine optimization, which is absolutely critical for all Web sites to achieve search engine rankings and indexing with Google and all other major engines. But even if you achieve great search engine ranking results, if there is no demand or desire for your products or services, you will fail. Marketplace analysis must be done in advance to ensure there is a viable market for your products or services in the first place.

The following questions will help you perform a basic market analysis:

- What market am I trying to enter?
- What or who is my current competition?
- How successful is my competition?
- What is the market share of my competition?
- Is the market saturated or open?
- What is the market size? Is there room to grow?
- Is there stability in the market, or is it volatile?
- How are my competitors marketing their goods or services?
- What do customers seek in regard to my products?

- What is most valuable to my customers?
- What are customers willing to pay for my products or services?
- What do I offer that my competition does not?
- What effect will the current economy have on my business goals?

You should analyze current or previous marketing strategies, as well as those of your competition, both successful and unsuccessful. Understanding failure is as important as understanding success factors. These questions may help you analyze your potential for success in a competitive marketplace:

- Am I offering a new product line, new service, or unique product?
- What marketing strategies have I used successfully? What was unsuccessful? Have I used online marketing in the past? What was the success rate or return on investment?
- Have I evaluated the results of previous marketing plans? What was the impact on sales?
- Are we currently using any strategies?
- What strategies are my competitors using?
- How much money is allotted in my current budget? How much am I currently spending? How much was my marketing budget in the past?
- Why would someone choose our product over our competition?
- What do we do to distinguish ourselves from our competition?
- Why would someone trust us, more than our competition?
- Who are our customers?
- Where do our customers come from?

You must perform what is known as primary and secondary research. Primary research includes phone interviews, surveys, Web-based surveys, and focus groups. Primary research is the most current information available. Secondary research is data that has already been collected for other purposes but may assist you with your market research. Examples of secondary research may be libraries, blogs, or other online resources.

Establishing Business Objectives

Nearly 50 percent of new businesses will fail within four years. This is also true for online businesses; however, they do have some distinct advantages over traditional brick-and-mortar businesses, as well as some overarching challenges. With an online business, you may have fewer employees, less building space, and less overhead. However, without the traditional storefront, you also do not have a physical presence. Instead, you have a virtual presence online. You need to develop a long-term business plan that will map out your path toward success, usually called a strategic plan or strategic goals. To develop your strategic plan, simply organize your goals, objectives, and timelines in a written format. This document is intended to be "living," and can be easily adjusted based on the current operating environment. You will need to complete your market analysis in order to better prepare your long-term business objectives.

You may be asking, "How can I know what my objectives and timelines are when I don't know how successful I will be in the future or what will happen to my company in the next few years?" The point of determining business objectives is not to predict the future, but to establish the desired course of action while setting strategic goals along the way. Your objectives should be attainable and must be measurable so you can evaluate your success in meeting, or failing to meet, these objectives. Ensure that you update your business objectives at least annually — perhaps even semi-annually — during your initial operating years.

If you are an existing business, you should first perform a comprehensive evaluation of your current business state. What have you accomplished, and what have you not? Are you profitable, or operating at a loss? What and who is your competition? What are the industry trends in relation to your products or services? Use resources to help you research and establish your business objectives, such as the Small Business Administration, which can be found online at **www.sba.gov/library/pubs.html**, or your local chamber of commerce, industry associations, and libraries. Similar research and market analysis must be completed for new online businesses as well.

Document your initial findings and business objectives. Review goals with your employees, as they may provide input or ideas that you have not considered. Ensure that your plan addresses all aspects of your organization such as sales, marketing, human resources, advertising, customer service, and information technology.

Develop a mission statement for your company as well. A mission statement captures your organization's purpose, customer orientation, and business philosophy. Share your mission statement with both employees and customers, and post it prominently.

Establishing Marketing Strategies

You must establish a clearly defined, written strategy and marketing plan for your online business. Consider all marketing strategies, and implement those that are most relevant to your business operations and offer the most potential for increased customer base and return on investment. At a minimum, your marketing strategy should include:

- A profile of the target consumer
- Competitive market analysis
- Distribution plans for your products
- Product price strategy
- An advertising budget
- An advertising and marketing strategy analysis to evaluate potential methods
- Your corporation vision and business objectives
- Brand uniqueness or image for your products
- Evaluation of your products and services
- Distinction of your company and/or products from competitors

Implement and evaluate your marketing strategy as it relates to achieving your corporate business objectives. Some marketing plans may take significant time and investment; think long-term and do not be too quick to change your objectives because you are not meeting the goals in your specified timelines. Be flexible, but allow your marketing strategies the time to grow and mature.

Your online marketing plan does not need to be overly complex and should be not a time-consuming process, but it is important to map out your objectives, budget, and critical success factors so you can measure and evaluate your success in achieving them. An average marketing plan may be fewer than a couple of pages in length and is a map for your company to achieve success on the Internet.

Media exposure is a key component in developing a successful marketing profile and strategy. Your customers will form their opinions, either positive or negative, based on what they hear and see in print, on television, on the radio, or on the Web. Recognizing the importance of media exposure and dedicating resources to promote your online business can boost the sales of your products or services. That positive media exposure is also a major step toward maintaining credibility in your online marketplace and channeling more traffic to your Web site.

Developing a tactical approach to media exposure should be part of your overall business objectives and marketing plan. There are several actions you can take to promote your offline media exposure. These may include:

- Approaching your local chamber of commerce and requesting that they write a short article about you and your business. Even if you are an online-only business, local exposure is important. You can then take that article and publish it on your Web site as another promotional tool, or use it in an online e-zine campaign.

- Offering to be a speaker at a seminar, or being a leader at a workshop in your area of expertise. This is a great way to gain media exposure that is incredibly positive and community-oriented, thus earning you credibility and trust among potential clients. Circulate your URL and business information at the seminar. Put your Web site URL on everything you distribute: fliers, promotional items, business cards, and letterheads.

- Following up any correspondence or phone calls from the media with a letter or phone call. Make sure to leave your Web site URL on their voice mail. This strategy will earn you a reputation as a conscientious, courteous entrepreneur with the media.

Share your knowledge by writing articles and professional opinions for online publications, and upload them to automated, e-zine syndication sites. These syndication sites are perfect for having immediate hotlinks back to your Web site and other specific landing pages. Remember to include your e-mail or picture in the byline, as well as brief biographical information on yourself and your business. The more exposure you generate, the more successful your business will become. Give permission to authors to use your articles in their books, magazines, or other publications, and be sure to require them to include a corporate biography and contact information in exchange for the permission.

Develop tactics to make media exposure and coverage work for you. Make media friends wherever and whenever the opportunities present themselves, all in an effort to increase media awareness and promote public relations. You will have to earn media exposure, but the time and effort you expend will be your investment in having a positive public profile both on- and offline.

Most columnists will give their e-mail address in their byline at the conclusion of their article. Send them a note with your comments and views while offering your expertise as a source for future quotes. Optimize your media exposure whenever possible; the returns for your business will be substantial.

Gaining the trust of your customers is extremely critical in developing a continuing relationship that rewards your online business with repeat customer sales. The one-time sale may boost your immediate sales numbers, but returning customers are what take your business from mediocre to fantastic profits. Your goal is to build quality customer relationships — and then maintain them.

Media exposure, both online and offline, opens the door to a potentially long-term relationship with customers by using implied third-party credibility, thus legitimizing you as the expert in your field. Once you attract the prospects, you still have to deliver your goods and/or services and ensure that the customer is completely satisfied. One of the major advantages of using Google marketing tools, for instance, is that the Google name is already equated with trust. Google's reputation is superior, and you can leverage that reputation and trust in your marketing campaigns.

Increasing Your Public Profile

The more positive your public profile, the more success you will have both on- and offline. This ties into gaining credibility with the public and with your customers. Your public profile is your trademark for success and profits, and your online profile and business rating is critically important to how customers perceive you. Local and state Better Business Bureaus are great organizations to join and obtain positive ratings. Other online business profile ratings services worth considering are **www.resellerratings.com**, **www.epinions.com**, and **www.consumerreports.org**. Do not underestimate the impact of a review of your business and/or products and services. You must ensure 100-percent customer satisfaction in both service and product quality to ensure you gain only positive reviews for you and your company.

Positioning yourself and becoming known as an expert in your market takes time, patience, and personal confidence. Just knowing the advantages of effective marketing is half the battle. The combination of media and marketing communicates the benefits and unique aspects of your business, which in turn drives customers to your Web site. When you establish yourself as an expert in your market, others will be drawn to you for advice, sponsorship, professional opinion, and branding — all of which will have a dramatic, positive effect on your online business.

When it comes to sharing your expertise, you goal should be to publish for free, thereby allowing many other organizations, news services, and other publications to distribute your article in return for links back to your Web site and direct product promotions to thousands of potential new customers. There are ways that you can publish a full-page ad promoting yourself and your business without spending a dime. Contact editors of publications and offer them your press release to add content to their next publication. Many editors are looking for useful and relevant content so they can meet deadlines. Take advantage of this opportunity and create the perfect article for publication. Always ensure that you require a corporate biography and full contact information to be published with your articles. Target newspapers, magazines, newsletters, Web sites, and e-zines; magazines that have both an offline and an online image are excellent for increased exposure.

Creativity and Planning

The first step in undertaking a Web site design project is the planning stage. With every Web design project you encounter, clarify what exactly is needed to complete the project satisfactorily, defining the precise scope of the project and establishing a program for completing the project over a given period of time.

Defining the audience of a Web site is the second and most crucial step. One of the audiences for your Web site is always going to be the group of people your client targets as their primary market. These external visitors might well be targeted through advertising programs, such as PPC or Google ads. The demographics of that target market group provide you with the basis for your primary audience of external visitors and serve as your first audience reference point.

As Web site developer, you should create a profile for your target audience based on general research. Who are the average members of your target audience? Determine what they look like, how old they are, where they live, what they do for a living, how much money they have, and what their hobbies are. This information will help you incorporate an understanding of their specific needs and preferences in the development of your Web site.

The Two Sides of the Web Designer

There are two traits you need to succeed as a Web designer. The first relates to the programming and general computing aspect of Web design. There is a certain amount of the "computer geek" personality required to undertake the work successfully. You need to understand computers in general, if not in considerable detail. You have to be able to troubleshoot should something go wrong. You should also have a knack for creating cool, new, and innovative Web site designs to keep your clients happy. Make sure that every aspect of the Web site you design works perfectly online, and that all potential clients can visit the site without issue.

You also need to have an artistic streak in your personality. Web site designers are generally artistic, creative people. Many graphic designers and regular artists have determined Web site design to be a lucrative side business, or even a lucrative primary business. You need to have something of an eye for artistic design and Web layout design so that you can appeal to your customers.

Establishing Your Business

Creating an effective business plan is a two-stage process. First, you need to get a strong handle on the type of business you are becoming involved in. Fact-finding, as you might call it, is going to take some time, so be prepared. You will need to analyze the market you are planning on entering, what is involved in the type of work you are looking to secure, and what potential customers are looking for.

Your business plan should include a summary of the approach you want your business to take — your company mission and objectives. Include a review of the market and an analysis of your place within that market. Describe the products and services you are going to offer to customers and how you are going to reach out to customers. Your business plan will describe your marketing strategy and your sales strategy. It will also describe and analyze the effectiveness of the staff you decide to put together. Not everyone wants a staff to support their business, but it is one more aspect to think about.

Once you have a first draft for your business plan, you should have plenty of time to consider which scenarios — good or bad — you are most likely to face with your business as you implement your plans. If you need further assistance in analyzing the general climate for your business, here are some resources to consider:

- The Small Business Administration: **www.sbaonline.sba.gov/ starting_business**
- Nolo®: **www.nolo.com**
- Palo Alto Software, Inc.: **www.paloalto.com/ps/bp**
- Inc.: **www.inc.com**
- The Small Business Development Center: **www.sbdcnet.utsa.edu**
- Bplans: **www.bplans.com**

Most of these online resources provide good reference points for creating a business plan, particularly with a view toward secure financing for the business venture. Nolo is particularly useful for addressing legal issues related to business startups.

A good business plan is one that is regularly updated and altered to reflect changing patterns and objectives of a company and the market in which it operates. Your business plan should help you plan your income and expenses, manage your marketing campaigns, and monitor your sales if you use it properly.

Generally speaking, a business plan should contain the following sections:

- Executive summary
- Mission statement
- Company objectives
- Personal evaluation of the business owner
- Description of services and products
- Company overview (a review of location, personnel, and resources)
- Market analysis (a review of the business niche and competitors)
- Advertising and marketing summaries
- Financial projections

If you are establishing a business, you must complete the required steps, such as obtaining a license, permits, and registrations. Consider the precise nature of the business you decide to establish. There are several different business structures to consider: sole proprietorship, partnership, corporation, and limited liability company (LLC). You should consider the pros and cons of these various business structures with input from your attorney and your accountant. In most cases, a sole proprietorship or an LLC is more than adequate for most small business purposes. Here are each of your options:

- The **sole proprietorship** is one of the easiest entities to understand. The status is exactly what it sounds like; it means that you, the business owner, are the only one responsible for your business. The status is simple to set up, and compliance is easy, too. The accounting system you use for a sole proprietorship is straightforward. All of your income and expenses are considered business income and business expenses. There is no reference to a business structure. The major disadvantage of this particular status is the lack of protection offered for either you or your business. You accept full responsibility and the full risk of your business because there is no separate legal structure to protect you. Anyone can sue you, and they can sue you for anything pertaining to your business.

- A **partnership** is fairly similar to the sole proprietorship status, except more than one person is involved. You may remain primarily responsible for the business, depending on how you determine dividing up responsibilities with your partner. When you decide to form a partnership, it is crucial that you address the nature of the partnership in all of its intricacies. Think about how profits will be divided and how expenses, including startup costs, will be managed. Partnerships in business are much like marriages in life; without strong foundations and open communication, you will be in trouble. You should plan in advance for the eventual breakdown of your partnership to determine how everything will be divided.

- An **LLC** is usually the best choice for a Web site design business. An LLC protects your assets like a corporation, without the burden of corporate maintenance. This status has become the most popular way to start a business because it offers limited liability to its owners. An LLC is a business entity that has the characteristics of both a corporation and a partnership. With an LLC, you can elect to be taxed as a corporation, or avoid double taxation by choosing to be a "pass-through," or nontaxable, entity. For any legal assistance in developing your business, consider using the cost-effective solutions offered at **www.legalzoom.com**.

- **Corporations** take you one step further, providing you with protection against potential business problems. If you set up a corporation, you are demonstrating that you do not own the business; that is, your assets are not linked to the business, and you are not responsible for the debts of the business. When you incorporate, you do not actually own your business in the legal sense. You may own all the shares, but technically speaking, you are actually hired by the shareholders of the corporation to manage the business interests, even if the only shareholder is you. It may sound odd, but the major advantage of this structure is that you have considerable protection in the event of legal problems, and you can sell shares to others to generate some working capital for the expansion of your business.

• A **subchapter S Corporation** is a dramatically simplified version of a standard corporation. The paperwork is comparable, but the structure offers the same protections as the corporation structure, along with simplified filing systems.

Employer Identification Numbers & Business Licenses

The first step you should complete is to obtain an Employer Identification Number (EIN), also known as a Federal Tax Identification Number, which is used to identify a business entity. This is typically required for you to obtain a business license in your state and county. The EIN is your permanent number and can be used immediately for most of your business needs, including opening a bank account, applying for business licenses, and filing a tax return by mail. However, no matter how you apply — either by phone, fax, mail, or online — it will take up to two weeks before your EIN becomes part of IRS permanent records. You must wait until this occurs before you can file an electronic return, make an electronic payment, or pass an IRS Taxpayer Identification Number matching program. The IRS Web site will guide you through the process of obtaining an EIN at **www.irs.gov/businesses/small/article/0,,id=97860,00.html**. The IRS offers a wealth of information regarding tax benefits and the form of your business. More information and comparison charts are available at **www.irs.gov/businesses/small/article/0,,id=154770,00.html**.

Research and determine the requirements in your state, county, and city for obtaining business licenses, permits, and tax receipts. This information can usually be found on the Internet. If you are the sole proprietor of your business, you will also most likely need to register a fictitious business name, assumed name, or "doing business as" (DBA) name in your state. The Web site **www.business.gov/guides/business-law/business-name/dba.html** lists all the requirements and provides links for each state. You must also check with your county and city. Most will require a county or city business license or tax receipt, and they may also have additional requirements for personal property tax and other important local legalities with which you must comply. The site **www.business.gov** is a great overall resource for starting your own business.

Finding Your Niche

After determining whether your Web site will be used for personal or business use, it is time to decide what content, navigation, and features you want to include on your Web site. Here are some basic questions to get you started:

1. What specific niche or arena are you seeking with your Web site?
2. What are some tips in finding that niche?
3. Who is your target audience?
4. What steps should be taken to reach that specific audience?
5. What are the primary differences between building a Web site for business or pleasure?
6. What are some of the key areas to keep in mind when deciding on a name for your Web site?

Most new Web builders know one thing: Either they are out to make money with their Web site, or they are creating some type of personal site to reach friends, family, or their local community. Topics and services are as limitless as the people who build Web sites.

With business Web sites, the ultimate goal is to draw visitors in, retain their repeat visits to your site, and grow your customer base. Many experts recommend avoiding any topic involving "how to make money." With how rampant junk e-mails and spam have become, most people will initially react with suspicion; the last thing they want is to have their personal information shared with the millions of other sites that send out additional junk and spam e-mails. There is no such thing as a "get rich quick" idea; in most instances, these are schemes to get your money. Therefore, you do not want to fall into this type of niche.

This is not to say that you cannot make money on your Web site — it just means that starting out with something simple is often better than trying to recreate the success of MySpace or Facebook, for instance. These sites allow you to create your own personal, simple Web page, and though it appears easy when you do it on these sites, what you do not see are the professional Webmasters and programmers they have hired to create, maintain, and constantly update these pages. This is exactly the reason that MySpace or Facebook personal pages may be more appropriate, cheaper, and easier than trying to create your own individual Web site. Sites like YouTube®, Facebook, and MySpace are complex, interactive sites that require someone with an extensive background in programming to be developed. If you are determined to build a highly interactive site, you will either have to learn all the programming codes needed, or hire someone to do it for you. It is suggested to start with a simple design and a small Web site that can evolve over time into something more complex and interactive.

Regardless of what type of site or topic you decide on, it is important to monitor your site. If it is a business site, you also want to provide additional security measures to protect your visitors from someone who might try to hijack your site for client information or scam your customers without your knowledge. Security is imperative when you are dealing with customers and clients. You own the Web site, and your clients or customers are putting their trust in your ability to protect them while they are on your site. If someone's information is hijacked and used illegally due to visiting your Web site, you might find yourself with serious legal problems.

Whatever your topic or idea, it must be something that you enjoy or have a passion for, because a Web site requires constant updating and maintenance to keep it moving forward.

How do you reach a specific audience? Figure out exactly who would benefit from your site and add that to your initial design plan. For example, say you want to publish a magazine of some kind and have determined that your target audience is the 15 to 25 age bracket. The next step is to decide what type of content will reach your target audience; it is critical, especially with the teen market, to ensure that your Web pages are age-appropriate. Maybe you want to produce a site that offers tips for teens ages 13 to 16; if so, you need to determine what types of tips would be appropriate to share with teens within that target age range. Also keep in mind that though parental controls are available, some parents may not consider the possibility that their child might inadvertently be visiting Web sites that are not appropriate for his or her age group.

11 Small Business Web Site Don'ts — by Paul Pennel

1. **Have your cousin create your Web site.** Your cousin might be a great person, but unless he or she is a professional Web designer, he or she is likely to create a Web site that is almost unusable for first-time visitors.

2. **Leave "Under Construction" pages.** In 1996, it was common to have Under Construction pages on Web sites, but today they make a Web site look unprofessional. Do not link unfinished pages to the Web site until they are done being constructed.

3. **Force visitors to view a splash screen before entering your real Web site.** Customers are looking for information, not impressive graphics. If they have to wait 30 seconds to get through your introductory screen before actually viewing your content, they will leave.

4. **Create confusing navigation.** Content is very important, but the best content in the world is useless if customers cannot find it. Put your navigation, or list of links, on the top or left-hand side, where people are used to finding it on most Web sites.

5. **Make visitors guess what your business can do for them.** If a customer comes to your Web site and cannot figure out what you can offer them within 20 seconds, they will leave. On your home page, prominently display the purpose of your business in a few sentences.

6. **Hide your contact information.** You want customers to be able to communicate easily with you. If they get frustrated trying to find a way to contact you, they will likely leave your Web site and visit a competitor.

7. **Fill your Web site with every piece of information you can think of.** Overloading customers with information is a very common mistake. But more is not always better. A clean, easy-to-read Web site is more desirable than one cluttered with unnecessary content.

8. **Use free Web hosting.** Free hosting comes with a different kind of cost. Free hosts add banners and pop-up ads, which make your Web site look cluttered and unprofessional.

9. **Have out-of-date content.** Nothing makes a Web site look more irrelevant than outdated information. Revisit your Web site often to keep it updated.

10. **Ignore submitting your Web site to search engines.** Even the best-designed Web site is useless to your business unless people can find it. Submit your Web site to all of the major search engines, such as Google, Yahoo!, and Bing.

11. **Test your Web site in only one browser.** Unfortunately, every browser interprets a Web site differently. Yours could look great in Safari on a Mac, but look awful in Internet Explorer on a PC.

*Minnow Web Design offers solutions for small businesses or organizations with big ideas. Owner and designer Paul Pennel combines 12 years of information technology experience with a desire to make great Web sites affordable. Paul can be contacted at paul@minnowWebdesign.com or on the Web at **www.minnowWebdesign.com**.*

Chapter 3

WEB SITE DESIGN 101 & HTML FUNDAMENTALS

When building Web sites, you need to cater to a large global audience with a variety of connection speeds, monitor sizes, and resolutions. Consider accessibility issues and design to World Wide Web Consortium — or WC3® — Web standards. This chapter will discuss Web site design fundamentals in depth and give you a crash course in HTML.

Start your Web design projects with a piece of paper and pencil. Map out the pages you know you want, review other sites for ideas, and build a skeleton model of your site's layout. This is the fundamental building block of your Web site's navigation structure. Design the layout, then fill in the keyword-rich content. Depending on the content and context of your Web site, your site design will take you in a variety of different directions and involve various colors, fonts, and images.

As you build your site, you will add Web forms, navigation, interaction with databases, searches, and other interactive features to bring your pages alive. Your Web site content is the most critical component of your Web site. It must quickly convey the intended message, capture the interest of the readers, and keep their attention. Site navigation is crucial in allowing site visitors to quickly move from page to page on your Web site; poor navigation will lose visitors quickly. Audio and video content are very popular to embed in Web pages. However, it is recommended to never use audio content because it may drive users away. If you must insist on including audio, include the option to turn it off on the Web page and make it easy for your site visitors to find. Video is acceptable, but let the visitor have the ability to start and stop the video. Looping video may drive away site visitors as well. Be cautious in your font selections and use Web-friendly fonts. Keep the colors organized and standardized — CSS is great for this — and do not use dozens of fonts in a variety of sizes and colors. The look and flow of your site is just as important as the content.

Web pages are electronic documents written in HTML, and each page has its own unique address, or URL, that identifies where it is located on the Internet. Web sites have at least one, but normally many more, linked or related Web pages. These pages are linked together by the use of hyperlinks. This allows visitors to your Web site to click and navigate from page to page without leaving your site. If you have links on your site to other sites, you can set these links up so that they open a new browser window, which again ensures that your visitors never really leave your site. The IP address is used to reach a Web site. The visitors type the common domain name into the address bar of the Web browser, and a DNS server translates this into the actual IP address that corresponds to the Web site. Here is an example to better illustrate this point: Type **http://69.147.114.224** into your browser address bar and load it. You will see the Yahoo! home page. Typically, we simply type in **www.yahoo.com**. Remembering those numbers is not necessary because these servers automatically translate the domain name into the IP address for any Web site.

The Web page we see in the Web browser is in HTML format. HTML has a specific number of elements that control the text or other objects we see on a Web page, and visitors use different applications known as browsers to see the content of the site. The World Wide Web is the collection of all publicly accessible Web sites.

Another important term is the URL, which can be compared to an address, but is, in fact, more than that. URL has three parts: protocol, do-name, and path. Here is an example. Take a look at the following URL: **http://www.washingtonpost.com/wpdyn/content/article/2009/07/10/ AR2009071003506.html.**

- The first part of a URL (http://) — is the protocol. This tells the browser about the type of the server it is taking. The protocol HTTP means Hypertext Transfer Protocol.

- The second part is the domain name of the Web site that is displayed in the Web browser. Here, the domain name is **www.washington post.com**. If you type this address in the address bar, you will see the home page of this news site.

- The third part is the path. In the above URL, this is the longest part: /wp-dyn/content/article/2009/07/10/AR2009071003506.html. This path directs you to a specific news article on the news site.

While researching and looking at other Web sites, you have probably noticed that many designs are similar to a magazine layout, with a logo or name of the site at the top. Off to either side or under the header is usually a list of the articles or topics available on the site. Some sites may offer descriptions of the articles, while others might just have headlines that are text links to the full article or other pages on the site. Text links are created in HTML and usually appear in a different color than the rest of the text. These links may take you to other sites or pages on the site you started on, and when you move your mouse over them, the hand appears on your mouse cursor, telling you this is an active link to another page or site. All you have to do is click the link, and a new page will open up in a separate window or the same window, depending on how the Webmaster created the link.

Placing too many links on your Web pages may confuse your visitors. Make a bold statement with your headline so your visitors want to continue reading. Boring headlines will not catch their attention. Content should subtly direct them to the next place to go, whether it is for more information or to purchase something. Keep it simple by using a headline, content, and call to action; do not overcrowd your site, and use graphics only where appropriate. Each Web page should have its own theme and focus. Find a keyword that is in line with your niche to build each new page around, and design the page for that topic. Research other sites that are similar to the one you are building to see how they have been laid out for more ideas.

A "sitemap" allows Web site visitors to find specific information and different sections of your Web site from one central page, and is critically important for search engine optimization. Sitemaps are essential to have on large sites that have many pages of information, products, or links. There are Web sites that can automatically generate sitemaps for you to add to your Web site, but before delving any deeper into how to build Web pages, it is important to dispel some myths about Web site building.

1. **Web design is only for "geeks."**

   This statement could not be further from the truth. Basic Web design is easy, especially when you use a good HTML editor such as CoffeeCup, Adobe Dreamweaver CS4, or Microsoft Expression Web 3. These programs also come with pre-built templates that allow you to insert and upload text to your site, or save it directly to the Web, if your hosting site supports the software you have chosen.

2. **Flash will enhance your Web site.**

   Flash is an animation feature many beginning Web builders want to use immediately, but Lisa Irby, founder and Webmaster of **www.2createaWebsite.com**, recommends using it sparingly. Flash is a fun tool to use, but if you have too much of it on your site, it can be very distracting. And Flash makes your pages load slower, even with a high-speed Internet connection, as it allows the builder to include things like audio and video content, but the pages often load with a delay as a result. If you are intent on including Flash on your Web site, test it out on a sample audience with a wide range of connection speeds and get feedback before making it a permanent feature. Make sure to include a "skip intro" button on your page as it loads to give your visitors the opportunity to move into your Web site — without having to wait for the Flash animation.

3. **The more colors, the better.**

Although color may look great in a hardcopy print of a newspaper or magazine, Web pages are different; colors are not always a good idea. Irby points out that if your visitors' eyes hurt from reading your pages, they will not return. If you want to use colors, limit the number and mix, which means that you should not use more than two or three colors. Choose lighter colors, not dark.

4. **You can never have too many images.**

Ideally, Web pages should not be any larger than 30 KB, including images and HTML, and it is important to include the height and width HTML attributes on all of your images so that your text loads before the images.

5. **Your site is always viewed equally.**

Just because your site looks good on your computer does not mean it will look the same on someone else's monitor. Monitor and screen sizes, shapes, and resolution can make a Web page look very different than what you might be seeing. This can be an irritating experience for the visitors because if they cannot see part of the page, they will get frustrated and not return to your site. There are few things more annoying than trying to read text that trails off the page and does not allow you to scroll far enough to the side to see the remaining words. Different Web browsers view your pages differently, so you should check your Web pages on a variety of monitors, with a variety of Web browsers at varying resolution settings. If you are using tables, set the widths in percentages rather than pixel values, because if you have your width set for 80 percent, it will take up 80 percent of your screen — no matter what resolution your visitors have their screens set at.

This is where the usage of fixed or flexible layouts comes into play. A fixed layout will allow you to build a page that is designed specifically for any screen resolution your visitors may use. Your content will not get lost in the sides of the screen and require your visitors to scroll back and forth. One downside of this is that on large screens, there may be some unused portions of the page, which can create a layout that looks unprofessional.

According to the Lynch and Horton Web style guide at **www.Webstyleguide.com/wsg3/index.html**, when using a fixed-width table, you must define cell widths with absolute values to keep the tables from expanding to fill the window. The site says the next step is to ensure the tables will not collapse by including an invisible image that is equal to the width of the cell in each table cell. These two steps will force the table cells to maintain their dimensions, regardless of the browser window size.

Creating your own flexible layout requires a deeper knowledge of HTML, such as how it is used in different platforms and browsers, and how it requires users to give up some control of their page design. However, many Web developers believe it is the best option because it offers a flexibility that the fixed layout does not. For example, the fixed layout does not allow you to change your pages to a flexible one down the road. But the downside is that you will need to learn the HTML coding required to build tables and create layout templates. Decide whether you want to spend the time and money it will take to learn how to do these types of layouts yourself, or buy the pre-built templates or software packages that include the templates. Keep in mind that both flexible and fixed Web sites can be created utilizing Cascading Style Sheets by properly formatting CSS positioning and DIV areas as the main page structuring element.

The next step in your design plan should be site navigation. Many Web sites use button links somewhere on the home page to lead you to different sections of the site, but there are many ways to do this, and it all depends on the method you want to use. There is no one way to build your site navigation; it is dependent on your needs and the size of your site. The larger the site, the harder it often is to find information.

One mistake many first-time Web builders make is trying to label their navigation bars with unusual titles. It is recommended to use clear and concise title names when listing your different pages on the navigation bar or buttons. People will not return to your site if they get lost or confused because you did not create labels that were easy to understand. The design of your site navigation bars should be fluid and easy to update, and change with the growth of your pages.

There are three basic types of Web site navigation. The first is hierarchical, which is best-suited for sites where there is a large amount of information available on a variety of topics that allows the user to dig deeper and deeper as they proceed through the pages. This type of setup is commonly used by large sites like the Google and Yahoo! search engines. One of the downfalls to this type of navigation system is that you have to hit the "back" button to return to earlier pages if you want to check out some other link you saw previously, or if you simply want to get back to the home page. For example, imagine doing a Google search and following the links from one Web site to another to find additional information. This is great for a one-way trip, but it can be a hassle when you have to retrace your steps to find a particular page that offers a different perspective relative to the topic you are researching.

The next type of navigation is global, which is best for easily jumping from page to page, where the information may be in broader categories within the entire Web site. Conversely, local navigation — the final type of navigation — is used for sites with in-depth information located in more specific or localized areas of the site. As was discussed in Chapter 2, many designers will include a trail of embedded links within their articles. These links are a different color from the rest of the text, and if you click on them, they open a new window or take you to the new site via the same window. Do not use these as a replacement for a good navigation bar.

Some of the most common navigation bars are located on the left side of the page or at the top of the home page. While you might be tempted to place it somewhere else, most people will look in these areas first. In the end, though, it is a matter of choice, and there are no real rules governing where you place your navigation. First, decide whether you want to use a bar, tabs, or buttons. Once you have determined this, the next step is to return to your design plan and make a list of the different sections or pages you want linked to your navigation bar.

Use the tools you have in your Web design applications. They will do most of the work for you: creating tables, links, image maps, bookmarks, and navigation buttons, as well as connecting to databases and shopping carts. While it is usually important to know how things work, you do not need to know how to create the HTML to make them work properly.

How to Approach Web Design

You must approach Web design depending on your overall objective. Your site has to be functionally sound to attract your target audience. Another important feature is usability. Usability refers to the ease in which your site visitors can navigate and use your site. The first duty of a Web site is to convey your target message to site visitors. Your site has to be organized in such a way that all relevant information can found easily and quickly. If visitors have to work hard to get the necessary data from your site, they will be distracted and will typically leave quickly. In many cases, Web designers make sites attractive but lose sight of functionality and usability. When designing a Web site, a designer also has to think like a site visitor. Organize all the pages so you can easily find information, navigate the site, and convey your target message or purpose.

Web Site Functionality

Functionality refers to the speed of page load in the browser, as well as the management of broken links and Web site errors. Before your site is live, you need to test it often to ensure everything is working properly. As the administrator, you control how your Web page will look, but you never have control over client-side issues, such as whether a visitor is using broadband or a slow, dial-up connection. Make your Web site friendly to all users, and ensure cross-platform compatibility. You can also offer high-speed and low-speed versions of your Web site to cater to both audiences.

Another important fact is browser compatibility. Older browsers may not show information on a site as you expect or desire. Design considerations should be made to ensure backward-compatibility with older browser versions and various browsers, such as Internet Explorer and Mozilla® Firefox®. In all cases, consider the user audience, and try to account for as many technical variations as possible.

Web Site Branding

Whether you offer a product or service, branding is always important. A brand name is not just a word; it is also a trademark of the product. When you are creating your Web site, be careful choosing the logo and the tagline. Both will bear your product name and may be difficult to change in the future. A logo should be clearly visible on the home page and all other pages. Logos represents the market value of a product. You can use creativity and have fun with your logo. For example, some companies slightly change the theme of their logo for targeting different occasions, such as Christmas, Halloween, or Valentine's Day.

Types of Web Sites

Web sites can differ in format, based on the kind of information you provide to your visitors. Web sites can be categorized as such:

Informational Web site

An informational Web site provides information on different topics. It could be a report on a global news event, or national news related to pop culture. Examples of such are **www.CNN.com**, **www.Greenpeace.org**, and **www.FOXNews.com**™.

Advocacy Web site

An advocacy Web site is one sponsored by an organization, or a group of organizations attempting to manipulate public opinion to agree with their ideas. The Sierra Club, the Democratic Party, and the Republican Party are examples of those with advocacy Web sites.

Business/marketing Web site

A business or marketing Web site is one sponsored by a commercial enterprise. These sites usually have pages containing information as text, photos, and videos, all of which are trying to promote or sell products made for a specific purpose. You can easily identify them by their domain name extension, which is .com. **www.Sony.com** and **www.Amazon.com** are some of the most well-known among the millions of business or commercial Web sites.

Personal Web site

Individuals usually keep this kind of site to share personal information, or to showcase expertise in a particular hobby or profession.

Blogging is one example of this approach, in which an individual shares his or her thoughts with millions for free. It can be a useful source for gaining insight from people's personal opinions. If you are considering a personal Web site, you may want to establish a free blog, or use social networking and save the costs of building your own Web site.

Social networking sites

Social networking sites have become very popular. People across the world become connected through these sites by sharing messages, photos, songs, and ideas. Facebook, MySpace, and hi5™ are a few of the most popular social networking sites. YouTube is also considered a social networking site, albeit primarily through video, and it was used effectively, for instance, during Barack Obama's presidential campaign.

Static Web Sites

A static Web site has Web pages stored on the server, and when the user types the URL into their Web browser, the pages appear in the browser. These types of sites are primarily coded in HTML, and CSS is used for the presentation of the information. JavaScript may be used for client-side scripting when required. This type of Web site displays the same information to all visitors. The main objective of a static Web site is to present and provide consistent, standard information for an extended period of time. To update the new information, the owner has to edit the information manually, which includes modifying text and adding or removing photos. With the use of software like Dreamweaver, FrontPage, or Expression Web, as well as some basic Web design knowledge, a Web site owner can easily create and modify a static Web site.

Dynamic Web Sites

A dynamic Web site changes and customizes the content of the Web page automatically and frequently based on certain criteria. Suppose a person from New York and a person from Sydney, Australia each have a Yahoo! account. Their personal information, such as their contacts or e-mails, are different, but they are sharing the same Yahoo! platform. When they sign into their accounts, depending on the login information, data is shown tailored to their specific account and region. This is an example of a dynamic Web site.

The main purpose of a dynamic Web site is to make it easier to maintain the site by controlling a few template pages and a database. Otherwise, the site owner or the developer would have to build and update hundreds or thousands of different Web pages and links for different purposes.

A dynamic Web site takes information from users, and matching with that data, it imports all the necessary information from databases, then shows it to the user. Dynamic Web sites interact with users in a variety of ways, including by reading cookies; recognizing users' previous history, session variables, and server side variables; or by using direct interaction.

Web Site Commonalities

Almost all Web sites follow a common skeleton of Web pages, but they usually differ in their provided services and appearance. Almost all Web sites share information by providing text and photos. Another common feature is similar pages, such as contact pages; the format of Web pages should remain consistent in all pages. If your site has a lot of text as information, then you can include a search option in which a visitor can search the desired term and get results quickly. Yet another good option is having a Frequently Asked Questions (FAQ) section.

What makes a site most universally appealing? While appearance may be the obvious answer, content is still overall king. You might run a wonderful advertising campaign for your site and include some flashy imagery, but unless your Web site is rich in content, you will not be satisfied with your results. Content that is useful, valuable, informative, and educational will attract the right audience like nothing else. Content is the most vital part of a Web site, but often site owners become distracted by the design and features of a Web site, and the central message is neglected. When developing your content, you need to keep in mind the purpose of your site. To create a content-rich Web site, there are some key guidelines to follow:

- Construct the content in a way so that it meets your desired goal or purpose.
- Make the content attractive in form, tone, and length.
- Organize the content with relevant sources.
- Provide more than one way to reach the content.
- Quality review of your site.

When you define your goals, you have to keep in mind that the content you are presenting should:

- Be informative, useful, and flawless.
- Accurately convey your message.
- Avoid creating confusion.

Break apart large portions of text into smaller sections so they can be easily read and understood, and make sure content is written with the same goal in mind. Try to minimize the number of links on the page, as having too many distracts the reader from the main content. Mention your key point without any descriptive introduction — get to the point quickly. Avoid narrative or descriptive writing. Too much advertising and promotion can affect the main goal.

Try to organize content so it does not take up too many pages. It should seem to readers as though they are just one or two clicks away from their target. Also try to use smaller text. If a user has to scroll, there is again a chance for distraction. Make an effort to keep readers on your Web site. If a person spends five minutes on your site, make sure it is meaningful and leaves a lasting impression.

If you provide more than one way to reach Web pages or content, visitors will feel comfortable and never feel lost. You should form a team that will go through every single detail of your site and make a log describing all potential bugs and errors. When this is done, update or modify the problems according to the report.

Hypertext Markup Language (HTML)

Everything you see when browsing a Web page is presented through HTML. It is easy to learn, and this chapter includes a beginner's guide to get you started. HTML includes many defined tags, such as heading, italic, and bold. The forms you see in the Web pages can be made with HTML, though to make those interactive, you typically need JavaScript.

HTML can be integrated with CSS and JavaScript for more efficiency. HTML consists of a series of short codes typed into a text file by the site author; this is known as a tag. The text is then saved as an HTML file and viewed through a browser. This browser reads the file and translates the text into a visible form, rendering the page as the author intended. To see a complete list of tags and elements, visit **www.w3.org**.

There are different versions of HTML, from HTML 2.0 to the latest XHTML 2.0. XHTML is a separate language that began as a reformulation of HTML 4.01 using XML 1.0. You will find that most modern Web pages today are created in XHTML, which is a cross between XML and HTML.

HTML Web Page Design Fundamentals

This section of the book will provide you with an overview of HTML and how to create basic Web pages using HTML code.

What is HTML?

HTML is a language used to describe Web pages. HTML is not a programming language; as the name implies, it is a markup language consisting of various markup tags. By using these markup tags, Web pages can be made.

Markup Tags

Markup tags are also known as HTML tags. By using angle brackets "<" and ">" around a keyword, we can make a tag, such as <html>. These tags always come in pairs, which are made by using forward slash "/", as in <html>, paired with </html>. The first tag in the pair tag is the starting tag, and the other is called the ending tag.

HTML Web Pages

HTML Web pages are HTML documents that contain HTML tags with plain text. Web browsers such as Internet Explorer or Firefox read the HTML document and display it as a Web page in the browser window.

Requirement for Making HTML Web Pages

The simple and efficient feature in HTML is that you do not need expensive tools or software to make Web pages. All you need is a text editor, such as Microsoft Notepad®.

Write your HTML tags in Notepad, save the file with any name of your choosing with file extension **.html** or **.htm**, and you have created your own HTML Web page. Make sure to use either **.html** or **.htm** as your file extension so the browser can read it and display it as a Web page.

Sample HTML Document

These instructions will help you create an HTML document in three simple steps; this is the basic layout of all Web pages created in HTML. This section will also show you how to put more content on the page, and where to put all the text so it displays properly.

The following figures will show you, step-by-step, how to create an HTML document, save it, and view it in Internet Explorer.

Step 1: Open Notepad and type the HTML tags as shown below:

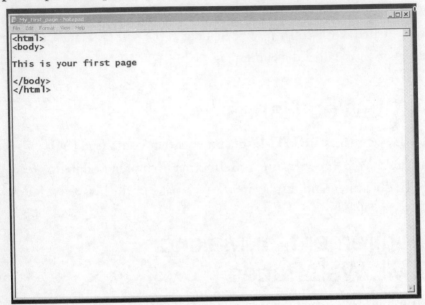

Step 2: Save the file with extension .html as shown in the figure below:

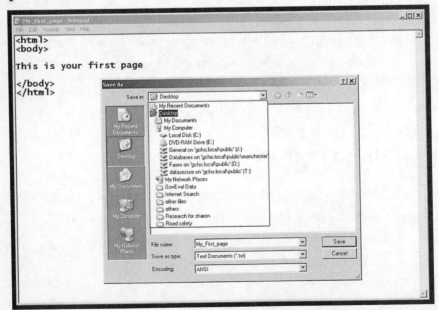

As shown in the above figure, the file has been named as "My_First_page" with file extension ".html." You can save the file wherever you want. In this example, it is being saved on the desktop.

Step 3: After saving the file, double-click the newly created HTML file icon to open and view your Web page. As shown below, you just created a basic Web page, which says, "This is your first page."

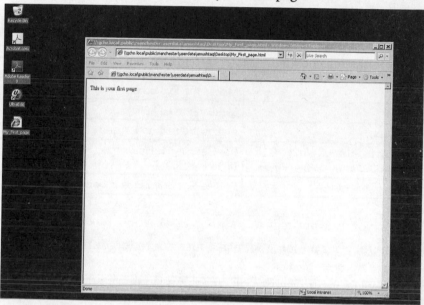

Sample document
(My_First_page.html) explanation

As you can see from the sample, there are two main pair tags: **<html>...**
</html> and **<body>...</body>**. There is also the plain text, "This is your first page."

The first paired tag tells the browser that it is an HTML document and is starting from **<html>** and will end on **</html>**. The second paired tag, e.g. **<body>**, is the main area where you put what you want on your site. The ending body tag, e.g. **</body>**, tells the browser that this is where the body is ending. There are many other things that can be done with the text in the body area. You can format the Web document as you choose using similar tags.

List of Formatting Tags

The following list includes the basic tags you can use to format your Web document, what they are used for, and their written code and output:

Tags	Description
**\ **	Used to insert a line break
\<p>...\</p>	Used to form a paragraph
\...	Makes the text bold
\<i>...\</i>	Makes the text italic
\</u>...\</u>	Makes the text underlined
\<h1>...\</h1>, \<h2>...\</h2>, \<h3>...\</h3>, until \<h6>...\</h6>	For Heading 1, Heading 2, Heading 3, up to Heading 6
\<center>...\</center>	Places text or images in center of the page

Note that you can put tags in between tags, as in **\\<i>\<u> your text \</u>\</i>**, but in doing so, make sure not to forgot to close the tags.

The following figure shows all the above tags used in the written HTML document:

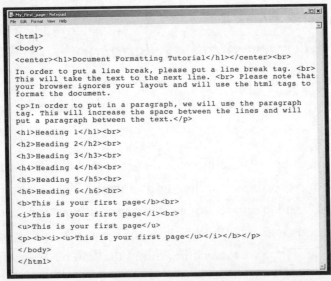

The following figure shows the Web page output of the written HTML tags:

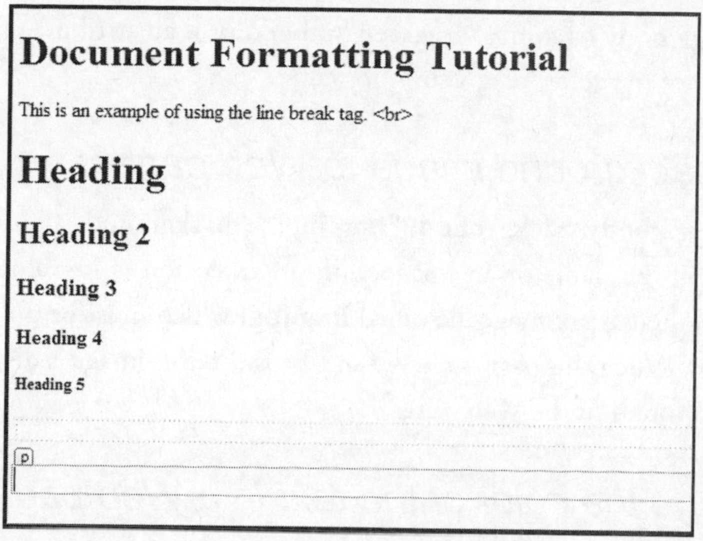

Document Formatting Tutorial

This is an example of using the line break tag.

Heading

Heading 2

Heading 3

Heading 4

Heading 5

[p]

By using these formatting tags, you can format your documents any way you want: Your browser ignores your layout and will use the HTML tags to format the document. You must use the formatting tags to format your document unless you are using other methods to control layout, such as CSS, which will be discussed in Chapter 9.

HTML Attributes

HTML tags are also called elements, and in HTML, you can add attributes to HTML elements/tags. Each of these attributes have names and values specified with them. These attributes are specified in the opening tag, and normally look like this: **name="value"**.

HTML tags with attributes allow you make your Web page more attractive by adding background color or background images. You can use the following attributes:

Add background color to a Web page

In the tag **<body bgcolor="seagreen">**, **bgcolor** is an attribute name, and the name of the color, **seagreen**, is its value.

Add background image to Web page

In the tag **<body background="img.jpg">**, background is an attribute name, and the name of an image with an extension is its value. In this example, there is an image file called **img.jpg**, which must be uploaded to the server. When this page is viewed in a browser, this image is displayed in the background of the Web page.

Change the color of the text in a Web page

In the tag **<body text="white">**, **text** is an attribute name, and the name of the color, **white**, is its value.

Note that either background color or a background image can be used, but not both at the same time. Here are the screenshots of the HTML tags and the attributes created above:

This image shows a background color by using the **bgcolor attribute**.

Document Formatting Tutorial

This is an example of using the line break tag.

h1
Heading

Heading 2

Heading 3

Heading 4

Heading 5

This Web page shows a background image using the **background** attribute.

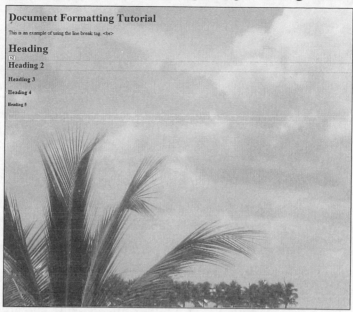

This Web page shows text color by using the **text attribute.**

Basic HTML Tags

There are more features you can add to your Web page, such as showing images on the page, adding links to different pages, creating tables, making forms, and making lists.

HTML Image

In order to put images on your Web page, you need to use the following HTML tag: **<img src="image name.extension">**. For example, in the tag **<img src="Sunset.jpg">**, here **<img>** is an HTML tag with the attribute name **src** and value **Sunset.jpg**, which is an image file that must be loaded on the Web server. You can also define the size of the image by using the **width** and **height** attributes. To apply a border to an image, use the **border** attribute.

A complete HTML tag for image with width, height, and border will look like this: **<img src="Sunset.jpg" width="100" height="100" border="10">**. You can change the values for width, height, and border as you wish. You would also normally use an **<alt>** tag to give the image a description; this will be discussed later in Chapter 11.

The following screenshot shows how to embed an image in an HTML document:

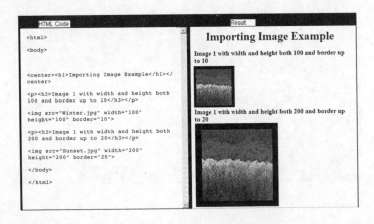

HTML Hyperlink

As established earlier, a Web site is a combination of different Web pages hosted on a Web server under a common domain name. Web pages can only be "linked" with each other by using a hyperlink HTML tag, as shown here:

<a href="page name.extension">Name of page to be displayed on the Web page</a>

Here is an example: **<a href="page2.html">Link 1</a>**. This tag includes an anchor tag **<a>,** with attribute **href**, then the name of the Web page to link to, **page2.html**, and the title of the link to be displayed on the Web page, **Link 1**.

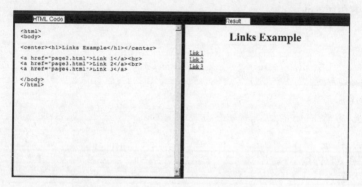

HTML Tables

Tables are very useful in Web page design. They help you to keep your Web pages clean and aligned properly. The table tag looks like this:

<table width="100%" border="1">

<tr>

<td>…. </td>

</tr>

</table>

The starting tag is **\<table>**, which tells the browser to display a table. **\<tr>** is used to show the number of rows, and **\<td>** is used to show data within those rows, as shown in the example below:

```
<table width="100%" border="1">
<tr>
<td>Name</td>
<td>Age</td>
</tr>
</table>
```

In order to show more rows, you simply add more **\<tr>** tags, as in this example:

```
<table width="100%" border="1">
<tr>
<td>Name</td>
<td>Age</td>
</tr>
<tr>
<td>Simon</td>
<td>25</td>
</tr>
<tr>
<td>Andrew</td>
<td>23</td>
</tr>
</table>
```

When displayed in the browser, a table may look like this:

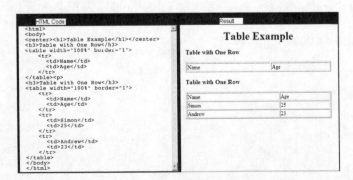

You can put as many tables with as many rows as you want in one Web page. In order to make tables without borders, you simply change the attribute to **border="0"**. Then the browser will display the data without any table borders.

HTML Forms

Forms are used to take information from the Web site visitor and store it in a database on the server, or e-mail it to a designated e-mail account. Storing data in a database and e-mailing data from forms is advanced, but this next example will demonstrate how to create basic forms and capture data from them.

Form HTML Tag Format

<form>
First Name <input type="text" name="firstname">
</form>

The above example shows how to create a form on Web page by starting with the **<form>** tag, an opening tag that tells the browser that there is a form in the Web page. The **<input>** tag shows what type of input is required from the user. In the above case, it is a simple text field taking the first name from a user.

Other Form Input Tags

Name	Description
<input type="radio" name="sex"> Male	Used to insert a line break.
<input type="radio" name="sex"> Female	Radio input tag is used for "yes" or "no" type responses, such as male or female.
<input type="checkbox" name="vehicle">	Checkbox tag is used to show checkboxes in order to select multiple options. An example of this can be hobbies such as fishing or biking.

Name	Description
<input type="submit" value="submit">	This tag is use to put a submit button at the end of the form so all the input information is either stored or sent via e-mail, depending on the action specified in the form.

<select>
   <option>Option 1</option>
   <option> Option 2</option>
   <option> Option 3</option>
   <option> Option 4</option>
</select>
	The **<option>** tag defines an option in a select list.

<textarea rows="2" cols="20"> **</textarea>**	The **<textarea>** tag defines a multi-line text input control. You have to specify the rows and columns to be displayed in the browser.

Whenever you use **<input type="submit" value="submit">**, you have to specify what action should take place after clicking the submit button. To do this, you must use an action attribute with a method in the starting **<form>** tag. After inserting the action and method, the form tag will look something like this:

<form action="form_submit.asp" method="get">

The image below uses all the form tags discussed above:

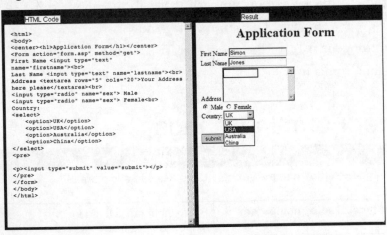

If a Web site visitor fills out the form and clicks the "Submit" button, the browser will send your input to a page called **form_submit.asp**. The page will show the received input.

HTML Lists

HTML lists are similar to bullets used in Microsoft Word®. There are two types of HTML lists: an ordered list and an unordered list.

Ordered list: An ordered list is used to show a list in order with numbers. Below is an example of an HTML ordered list tag:

```
<ol>
<li>Item 1</li>
<li>Item 2</li>
</ol>
```

The above tag will show the list in an order. The **<ol>** tag tells the browser it is an ordered list, and the **<li>** tag is used to show the list. You can include as many items in a list as you would like by repeating **<li>** tags.

Unordered list: In order to show an unordered list, simply change the **<ol>** tag to a **<ul>** tag:

```
<ul>
<li>Item 1</li>
<li>Item 2</li>
</ul>
```

The following screenshot shows both ordered and unordered lists:

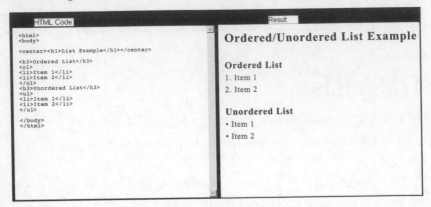

More HTML Tags

All the HTML tags discussed above are standard tags. But there are many more HTML tags used to format Web pages in more detail, such as providing information about what type of data is being used in the document by using **metadata**, how to include **comments** while writing HTML tags, and how to use **block quotes**. A few other tags, like **<pre>**, **<head>**, and **<font>**, will also be discussed.

Head tag

The **<head>** tag is specified between the starting **<html>** tag and starting **<body>** tag. The **<head>** tag is used to specify the heading part of a Web page. The format of the **<head>** tag looks like this:

<html>
<head>
<title>Your First Page</title>
</head>
<body>
</body>
</html>

Metadata Tag

Metadata is the information about the data to be used in the HTML document. Metadata is typically used to specify page description, keywords, and the author of the document. Metadata is not displayed in the browser window. Meta tags will be discussed in significant detail in Chapter 11 of this book. The format of the metadata tag looks like this:

<head>
<meta name="description" content="Your First Page"/>
<meta name="author" content="Your Name"/>
</head>

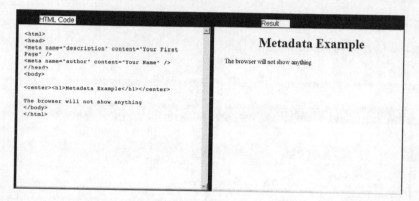

Comments Tag

This tag is very useful in writing HTML or any other programming language. A remark made within a comments tag will be ignored by the browser and is used to explain your code, which can help you when you edit the source code at a later date. The comment tag looks like this:

<!--This is a comment. Comments are not displayed in the browser-->

Comment tags can be specified anywhere in the HTML source document and are not displayed in the browser window.

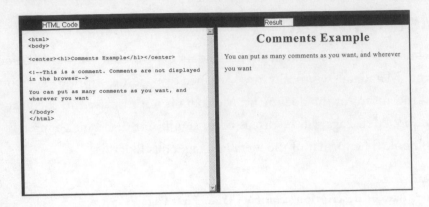

Font Tag

The font tag is very useful to specify the font face, font size, and font color of text. The font tag looks like this:

<font size="3" color="red" face="verdana">this is your first page</font>

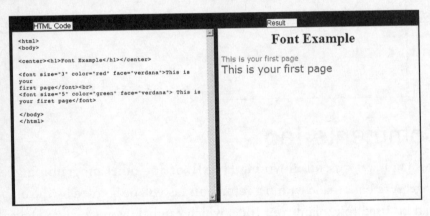

One suggestion is to create a new folder in your My Documents folder to save all of your content, images, and other Web site files in one place. This keeps the Web site organized and efficient. It is difficult to manage a Web site when all of the files are stored in the root folder. As you have already seen, there is simply too much HTML code to memorize. Some of the codes are simple to use, such as the opening tag ****, which is the HTML code for bolding text on your Web pages, and the closing tag ****, which indicates the end of the bolding. The same is true if you want to use italics or even a combination of the two, as in this example: **my text<i>additional text</i>**. In this instance, the second portion of the text would be both bolded and italicized, and the first part would just be bolded. Remember to keep the text attached to the tags, meaning there is no spacing between the tag and the first or last word of the text. For normal content, you would use the opening tag **<p>** and the closing tag **</p>**. Again, you could mix it up by using **<p>textadditional textmore text</p>** and have a combination of both normal text and bolded text in the same sentence or paragraph.

There are four different types of tags that should be included in every HTML document. These tags define the type of document you are building and the primary sections within that document. These tags are **<html>**, **<head>**, **<title>**, and **<body>**. In a basic HTML document, you might see something like the following example:

```
<html>
<head>
<title>Eat more Vegetables</title>
</head>
<body>
Eating more vegetables is good for you.
</body>
</html>
```

Though these tags should be used in all HTML documents, there are some exceptions. Some Webmasters believe that using the **<html>** and **<head>** tags are important, while others believe they have little or no use in an HTML document because they do not appear to have any visible effect on a Web page or how it is displayed in the browser. However, the general consensus is that these tags divide your Web pages into sections that make them easier to understand and edit. These tags help you to create nice-looking and easy-to-use pages that include individual sections to help your visitors find what they are looking for.

Nested HTML tags have an opening tag and a closing tag, as discussed previously. For example, if you want to set your font color and size with bolding, you would use the following code:

<font color="blue" size="3"><b>Physical fitness is a great way to stay healthy!</b></font>

It is important to remember that if you begin your tag with **<font>** and include bolding, it must also be closed at the end with **</b></font>,** not **</font></b>.** Follow the order in reverse to close the tags out.

Anchor Tag

The anchor tag helps you use HTML to insert a link into the text of your document that takes you to another page or a new Web site. To use anchor tags, decide which site or page you want to link to, then use the following HTML code to set it up:

<a href ="www.ruralnorthwest.com">RuralNorthwest</a>

The **<a>** tag is the anchor tag, while **href** is the HTML code that specifies that this is a hyperlink or URL to another page or Web site.

Bookmarks

This same anchor tag will provide easy linking to other pages on your Web site, but do not use this as a replacement to your navigation bar. In most instances, these types of internal links are used to help the reader explore additional information about the topic you provided, but this is not a replacement for site navigation. When providing links to other parts of the same Web page, you can use what are known as bookmarks. You must use the HTML **<a>** tag to create your page bookmarks. The HTML bookmark tag links to a corresponding anchor tag, so when someone clicks on the bookmark, they are navigated to your anchor point. For example, if you wanted to provide a link to your bio, which is located at the bottom of the Web page, you can create an anchor tag with **name="bio"** just before your bio text as follows:

<a name="bio">Biography of Bruce C. Brown</a>

The above HTML link works as a bookmark link. You can navigate to this bookmark by using **href="#bio"** in another HTML **<a>** tag link: **<a href="#bio">Read Bruce's Bio</a>**. This HTML bookmark works within the same page you are currently on, and it can also be modified to jump to a bookmark on another page within your Web site.

<a href="sales.htm#bio">Read Bruce's Bio</a>

HTML bookmark link tags are most beneficial for long pages, such as FAQs. You can use anchor tags to create links to other pages or sites, or you can create a link that opens a new window, which prevents your visitors from being diverted away from your site. This is called target control. A target code includes four predefined values: **blank** loads the page into a new browser window; **self** loads the page into the current window; **parent** loads the page into the frame that is superior to the frame the hyperlink is in; and **top** cancels all frames and loads in a full browser window. It is important to use an underscore and lowercase text when using a predefined target. Here is an example of how an anchor and target code would look:

<a href="http://www.ruralnorthwest.com" target="_ blank">

The next topic involves how to use "name" anchors so that your visitors can click on subheaders at the top or side of your Web page when reading extremely long documents. This allows the reader to skip over the information that is of no interest to them and click the subheader for the section of the document that contains the information they want. This type of anchor differs from a hyperlink in that it does not take you to another page or Web site, and it is not a different color from the rest of the text in the document, unless you specify certain colors and font size differences in the anchor.

For example, say your content is about accounting, and your reader is looking for information on billing schemes. You can create a name anchor to lead him or her directly to the information on billing schemes. You would use the following type of coding:

<h2><a name="billing schemes">Billing Schemes</a></h2>

Though these anchors do not link to anything outside of the current page, you can include the href or hyperlink coding to create links to the name anchor by using the following additional code within the HTML:

<h2><a href="forexample.html#billing schemes">Billing Schemes </a></h2>

If you wanted to create a hyperlink to the named anchor on the same page, you would use the following code:

<a href="#billing schemes">Billing Schemes</a>

It is important to remember to use the hash (#) mark because without it, these links will not work.

DocType

Although it is not technically a tag, one of the codes used by most Webmasters to ensure that their pages are visible on all Web browsers is the Document Type Declaration, using the tag **<!Doctype...>**, which tells the browsers what edition of HTML code you are using to write your pages. For example, if you are using the 3.2 version of HTML, the code would look like this:

<!DOCTYPE HTML Public "-//w3c//DTD HTML 3.2 Final//EN">

For HTML version 4.0, it becomes a little more complicated:

<!DOCTYPE HTML Public "-//w3c//DTD HTML 4.0//EN" "http://www.strugglingteens.com/TR/REC-html40/strict.dtd">

According to **www.w3.org**, DTD stands for "document type definition," which allows the browsers to determine which version of HTML you are using. The usage of "strict" tells the browsers you are conforming to the strict rules that apply to this type of coding.

For XHTML, DOCTYPE may look like this:

```
<?xml version="1.0" encoding="utf-8"?>
<!DOCTYPE html PUBLIC "-//W3C//DTD XHTML 1.0 Transitional//EN"
"http://www.w3.org/TR/xhtml1/DTD/xhtml1-transitional.dtd">
<html>
```

An example of what a basic Web page would look like with HTML and XHTML coding is as follows:

```
<!DOCTYPE html PUBLIC "-//w3c//DTD XHTML 1.0 Strict//EN"
"http://www.strugglingteens.com/TR/xhtml1/DTD/xhtml1-strict.dtd">
<html xmlns="http://www.crystalriverhouse/server/xhtml">
<head>
<title>Crystal River Vacation Rental</title>
<meta http-equiv="Content-Type"
        content="text/html; charset=utf-8" />
</head>
<body>
<h1>Headline For This Section</h1>
<p>Where you write your content.</p>
</body>
</html>
```

The previous example shows the opening and closing tags, and the attribute element is **<html xmlns="http://www.crystalriverhouse.com/server/xhtml">**. The next element in this coding example is **<title>Crystal River Vacation Rental</title>**, which tells the Web browser what to display at the top of the page in the title bar and is critical for indexing by major search engines. Another element used in the example is the meta element, **<meta http-equiv="Content-type" content="text/html; charset=utf-8" />**, which is not visible on the screen but can provide additional information to Web browsers and search engines. Meta elements are also described as "self-closing," as shown with the **/>**. In the example, the meta element is simply telling the browser which character set to use, specifically UTF-8.

According to Ian Lloyd, author of *Build Your Own Web Site the Right Way Using HTML & CSS*, published by SitePoint Pty. Ltd., 2006, the UTF-8 character set is a critical component to use because it ensures that all of your visitors will see your pages as you see them. He explains that if you do not use UTF-8, people from other countries who view your site might not be able to see what you have on your site because they are reading it in a different language, which is why the UTF-8 element is so important. It allows visitors from all over the world to see your Web pages as they appear to you, no matter what language they are using to view them.

Headings

Headline tags can also be used like this:

<h1>First Level Heading</h1>
<h2>Second Level Heading or Sub-heading</h2>

and so on for **<h3>**, **<h4>**, **<h5>**, and **<h6>** subheadings, which are defined by different font sizes that are mostly larger than the text portion of your page. There is an exception when using **<h6>**, because it normally appears to be about two or three sizes smaller than your content. You should use all of the headline tags sequentially so as not to confuse the reader. If you use an **<h1>** header throughout the page, it will be difficult to determine whether this is an ongoing theme, or if there are completely different topics. In other words, begin with your main heading, then use the tags listed previously to implement one or more subheadings so that your content is clear to the reader.

The final element of the example is the **<body>**. This is where all of your hard work on content comes together to create the main portion of your Web site. When writing the text to put into the **<body> ... </body>** portion of the code, one suggestion is to do it in an easy-to-use text editor such as Notepad. If you make mistakes or want to rewrite something, it is much easier to make all of the necessary changes in Notepad than to try to rewrite your content within the **<body>** coding areas. Again, most Web design applications will let you enter content into the design interface and will simply create the HTML code for you.

Paragraph Tag

Another tag to remember in HTML is the paragraph tag, which looks like this:

<p>text inserted</p>

This tag allows you to separate your body of text into paragraphs.

Ordered and Unordered Lists

If you wanted to create content that contained bulleted lists with both ordered and unordered points within the body of your page, you would use the following code:

```
<!DOCTYPE html PUBLIC "-//w3cs//DTD XHTML 1.0 Strict//EN"
"http://www.strugglingteens.com/TR/xhtml1/DTD/xhtml1-strict.dtd">
<html xmlns="http://www.strugglingteens.com/2006/xhtml">
<head>
<title>Check Out The Points Below</title>
<meta http-equiv="Content-Type"
        content="text/html; charset=utf-8" />
</head>
<h1>Introduction To Key Physical Fitness Points</h1>
```

```
<body>
<h2>Headline For This Section</h2>
<p>Where you write your content.</p>
<ul>
<li>This is the code for a bulleted list</li>
<li>Additional bulleted item</li>
</ul>
<p>The following is another list, but this time it is ordered:</p>
<ol>
<li>An ordered list is numerical, not bulleted</li>
<li>One more for good measure</li>
</ol>
</body>
</html>
```

In this example, the unordered list has the opening tag **<ul>** with the **<li>** tag to indicate an unordered bulleted list, with **</ul>** as the closing tag. The ordered list — which can be numerical, in Roman numerals, or alphabetical — uses the opening tag of **<ol>** with the **<li>** tag and **</ol>** for closing the list.

Tables

Tables are a major part of any Web page design. In HTML Web sites, they allow the site builder to create a much more attractive page design. In CSS-based Web pages, CSS uses tables for informational display purposes and not as a page element to define the page layout. There are three important tags for tables, which include the opening table tag, **<table>**, and the table row and table data tags, **<tr>** and **<td>**, respectively. The following examples illustrate how to use the tags and create tables on your Web pages. The **<tr>** tag represents a row for the table, while the **<td>** tag represents a cell, or column, inside the row.

```
<table>
<tr>
<td>A</td>
<td>B</td>
```

```
<td>C</td>
</tr>
<tr>
<td>X</td>
<td>Y</td>
<td>Z</td>
</tr>
</table>
```

Notice that by looking at the code, you can tell how many rows and columns are included. For example, the two opening **<tr>** tags indicate two rows, and the three opening **<td>** tags on each line represent three data cells or columns. If you wanted to add another row, you would just add another **<tr>** tag at the beginning of the code.

In the next example, a table with borders is created by inserting the border attribute to the opening table tag. As you can see, in the beginning of the table border tag there is a **"2,"** which indicates how thick you want the border to be. If you set the border to **"0,"** there would not be a border, whereas if you put it at **"8,"** your border would be much thicker than at **"2."**

```
<table border="2">
<tr>
<td>A</td>
<td>B</td>
<td>C</td>
</tr>
<tr>
<td>X</td>
<td>Y</td>
<td>Z</td>
</tr>
</table>
```

The next example illustrates how to change the color of your table border by adding the **bordercolor** attribute:

```
<table border="2" bordercolor="red">
```

```
<tr>
<td>A</td>
<td>B</td>
<td>C</td>
</tr>
<tr>
<td>X</td>
<td>Y</td>
<td>Z</td>
</tr>
</table>
```

Another aspect to creating tables is the ability to increase or decrease the amount of space between the table cells, called **cellspacing**, or changing the amount of space within the cells by using **cellpadding** attributes.

```
<table border="2" cellspacing="10" cellpadding="3">
<tr><td>A</td> <td>B</td> <td>C</td> </tr>
<tr><td>X</td> <td>Y</td> <td>Z</td> </tr>
</table>
```

If you were to set the cellspacing attribute to **"10,"** it drastically increases the spacing between the cells, and if the cellpadding attribute is set to **"3,"** it adds a little space within each individual cell. However, if you want to have a table border but no border around the letter, set the cellspacing to **"0."** In many instances, Webmasters will use pixels to set table widths, but using a percentage makes it easier to determine the amount of space your tables will fill on a page. The following example shows how to set your table widths using percentages:

```
<table width="100%" border="2">
<tr>
<td>A</td>
<td>B</td>
<td>C</td>
</tr>
<tr>
<td>X</td>
```

```
<td>Y</td>
<td>Z</td>
</tr>
</table>
```

If you prefer to use pixels, use the following table settings to achieve the same result of 100-percent usage of your space. In this instance, you would set it at 300 pixels rather than 100 percent, as follows:

```
<table width="300" border="2">
<tr><td>A</td> <td>B</td> <td>C</td> </tr>
<tr><td>X</td> <td>Y</td> <td>Z</td> </tr>
</table>
```

The next example shows how to adjust your column widths by setting the values on your table data **<td>** cells by using percentages or pixel widths. The column width in the following code shows that the first column in both rows is set to 70 percent, while there is no value set for the other two columns. The table width is set to 300 pixels, with the first column taking up 70 percent of those 300 pixels, roughly 210 pixels. The remaining two columns will divide the existing 30 percent of the table equally into roughly 45 pixels apiece:

```
<table width="300" border="2">
<tr>
<td width="70%">A</td>
<td>B</td>
<td>C</td>
</tr>
<tr>
<td width="70%">X</td>
<td>Y</td>
<td>Z</td>
</tr>
</table>
```

If you decide to use pixels instead of percentages, your table coding will look like this:

```
<table width="300" border="2">
<tr>
<td width="210">A</td>
<td width="45">B</td>
<td width="45">C</td>
</tr>
<tr>
<td width="210">A</td>
<td width="45">B</td>
<td width="45">C</td>
</tr>
</table>
```

Using percentages ensures that the table uses the same amount of screen, no matter how large or small the user's screen resolution is set. For example, if you are using a 21-inch monitor to view your site and you have a table width set to 300 pixels, the table will show up very small on their screen. If you set the table width to 70 percent, it will take up 70 percent of the screen, no matter the size of the monitor. If you create a table that is 760 pixels wide that is viewed on a 15-inch monitor set to a 640 x 480 resolution, the user will have to scroll left and right just to see the entire table. If your table is set to 100 percent, it will fit any screen, regardless of the resolution settings.

These examples illustrate setting table height, horizontally aligning content within the tables, vertically aligning content, and creating a left navigation bar layout with tables.

The first example is adding the height code:

```
<table height="250" width="300" border="2">
<tr>
<td width="210">A</td>
<td width="45">B</td>
<td width="45">C</td>
</tr>
<tr>
```

```
<td width="210">A</td>
<td width="45">B</td>
<td width="45">C</td>
</tr>
</table>
```

The next example shows how to use horizontal alignment, such as a left alignment inside a cell for your content. All you have to do is change the **"left,"** **"right,"** or **"center"** tags with the **align** attribute to change the alignment:

```
<table width="300" border="2">
<tr>
<td width="210" align="center">A</td>
<td width="45">B</td>
<td width="45">C</td>
</tr>
<tr>
<td width="210" align="center">A</td>
<td width="45">B</td>
<td width="45">C</td>
</tr>
</table>
```

In this example, we illustrate how to vertically align the content within the table's cells by changing the alignment to top, bottom, or middle by using the **valign** — or vertical align — tag and changing the **"top," "bottom,"** or **"middle"** tags to indicate where the content will appear within the table cell:

```
<table height="250" width="300" border="2">
<tr>
<td valign="top" width="210">A</td>
<td width="45">B</td>
<td width="45">C</td>
</tr>
<tr>
<td valign="top" width="210">A</td>
<td width="45">B</td>
<td width="45">C</td>
</tr>
</table>
```

Any Web application will create tables for you automatically, and there are table generators available on the Web for free. Tables and lists are the two most confusing HTML topics, and the ones that get you in trouble the fastest. It is usually not worth trying to hand-code tables in HTML. Let the Web design applications do the work for you and provide you with error-free HTML code.

HTML Practice

Open Notepad on your computer and perform the following tasks to ensure that you have grasped basic HTML concepts:

- Create a Web page in which you discuss a topic, with details and images.
- Create a Web page that includes links to other Web pages.
- Create a table to show the name, place of birth, and date of birth of your friends.
- Create a Web form to capture name, place of birth, and date of birth.
- Create a Web page with both an ordered and an unordered list showing the items in your house.

The below screen shot is a picture of a Web page for a luxurious rental property located in Crystal River, Florida. This is a very straightforward Web site that uses static HTML design based on a layout with tables:

Before taking a look at the coding for this page, you should examine some of the key coding elements contained within. This Web page uses a background image called **beach_bg.gif**, which is coded as such:

<body background="images/beach_bg.gif">

This Web page uses tables to properly align the page elements. The **<table>** tag specifies the cellspacing and cellpadding, and it also specifies a total table width of 770 pixels. The page is centered in the Web browser by using the **align="center"** attribute. This page also uses an image called **crystal river.jpg** with a width of 277 pixels and a height of 65 pixels that is used as the heading of the page. This image uses an **alt** attribute to display text when the mouse moves over the image, which is also critical for search engine optimization purposes. This Web page uses various fonts, colors, and an embedded hyperlink to the e-mail address info@crystalriverhouse.com, which has a predefined subject when clicked and opened in an e-mail application such as Microsoft Outlook®.

```
<table cellSpacing="0" cellPadding="0" width="770" align="center" background
="images/beach_bg.gif" border="0" id="table1">
    <tr>
        <td width="345" bordercolor="#FFFFFF">
        <p align="center">
        <img    border="0"    src="images/crystalriver.jpg"    width="277"
height="65" alt="Welcome to Crystal River Florida - An ideal Rental Paradise
on the Gulf of Mexico"></td>
        <td width="345">
        <div align="center">
            <font face="Arial, Helvetica, sans-serif" color="#ffffff" size="4">
            <b>&quot;</b></font><font face="Lucida Handwriting" size="4"
color="#FFFFFF">Casa
            Dos&quot;</font><font face="Arial, Helvetica, sans-serif" color=
"#ffffff" size="2"><b> Crystal River Vacation
            Home</b><br>
            <aclass="sitecredits" href="mailto:info@crystalriverhouse.com?subject
=Crystal River Rental Information">info@crystalriverhouse.com</a><br>
             </font></div>
        </td>
    </tr>
</table>
```

The site utilizes unordered lists to properly align the bulleted text:

```
<ul>
<li><b><font face="Arial, Helvetica, sans-serif" size="2">
Incredible Waterfront</font></b><font face="Arial, helvetica, sans-serif" size="2">
spacious property set along the beautiful Florida Gulf Coast.  Warm trop-
ical breezes, casual relaxation and comfortable living create the ideal Florida
vacation paradise....
```

This next piece of HTML shows a line item in an unordered list with an
embedded hyperlink to the Citrus County Chamber of Commerce:

```
<li>
<font face="Arial,Helvetica,Geneva,Swiss,SunSans-Regular">
<b><font size="2">Watered by seven spring-driven rivers</font></b><font
size="2"> and wrapped in verdant forest.
```

<a target="_blank" href="http://www.citruscountychamber.com">Citrus County </a> may be Florida's most natural attraction! If variety is the essence of the Florida experience, then from its unspoiled shore on the Gulf of Mexico to its rolling hills and sparkling lakes, Citrus County has it all. </font>
 </li>

Web Forms

This example Web site utilizes a Web form to allow customers to make reservations online. In this case, the site uses Microsoft FrontPage extensions to manage the form automation process. FrontPage extensions make the handling of form data very simple, as you can use the extensions to have your form submitted to a database, e-mail address, static file on your Web site, or a combination of the three. You must have a Microsoft Web server for FrontPage extensions to work. Although they are called "FrontPage" extensions, they work equally effectively with Expression Web:

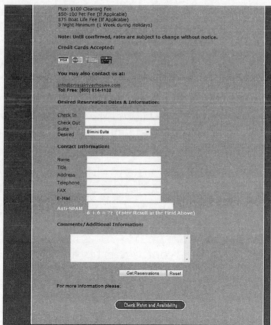

Here is a look at this form's HTML code so we can understand how it works and how it was created. Because the amount of HTML code to create a form is extensive, this example will only involve a few pieces of the entire form. This form uses FrontPage extensions to handle the data, so it uses the **"POST"** method and the action calls the FrontPage **WebBOT**. When the form is submitted by the site visitor, it sends an e-mail with the form field data completed by the site visitor. Most of this code is generated by FrontPage:

```
<form method="POST" action="--WebBOT-SELF--" onSubmit="return
FrontPage_Form1_Validator(this)" language="JavaScript" name="FrontPage_
Form1">
    <!--Webbot bot="SaveResults" s-email-format="HTML/UL" s-email-
address="sales@crystalriverhouse.com" b-email-label-fields="TRUE" b-email-
replyto-from-field="TRUE" s-email-replyto="info@crystalriverhouse.com"
b-email-subject-from-field="FALSE" s-email-subject="Crystal River Reservation/
Info Request" s-date-format="%A,%B %d, %Y" s-time-format="%I:%M:%S %p"
s-builtin-fields="Date Time" u-confirmation-url="confirmation.htm" startspan
--><input TYPE="hidden"zNAME="VTI-GROUP" VALUE="0"><!--Webbot
bot="SaveResults" endspan i-checksum="43374" -->
```

The actual form fields for **"Check In"** and **"Check Out"** are displayed below. The width of the form field is specified:

```
<input name="Checkin" value size="35" tabindex="3"></font></td>
    </tr>
    <tr>
        <td align="left" width="119"><font size="2">Check Out</font></td>
        <td width="531"><font color="#000080" size="2" face="Verdana">
<input name="Checkout" value size="35" tabindex="4"></font></td>
```

The form also includes a submit button labeled **"Get Reservations."** The HTML code below shows how this button is created. There is a reset button to clear the form data in addition to the submit button. When the submit button is clicked, the FrontPage extensions form handler submits the data to the recipient e-mail address. You will also notice the closing **</form>** tag, which completes the form code:

```
<inputtype="submit" value="GetReservations" name="Reservations"></font><font
face="Verdana"><input type="reset" value="Reset" name="B2"></font></p>
        </form>
```

HTML 5 was released on June 10, 2008 by the W3C (The World Wide Web Consortium, **www.w3.org**), and the latest version was released on April 23, 2009. In this version, new features are introduced to help Web application authors, new elements are introduced based on research on prevailing authoring practices, and special attention has been given to defining clear conformance criteria for user agents in an effort to improve interoperability. For more information on the status of the technical report and other superseding documents that may be published later, visit the W3C Web site at **www.w3.org/TR**.

Although this was just a brief overview of HTML, you now know the basic fundamentals to recognize and work with HTML. There are many Web sites that offer further help and advice on HTML coding, such as **www.htmlcode tutorial.com** and **www.w3schools.com/html**.

Introduction to XHTML

This section is a brief introduction to XHTML. There are many great books on the Web that are devoted to XHTML. You should be aware that both Expression Web 3 and Dreamweaver CS4 fully support XHTML and, in fact, XHMTL is the standard for most modern Web sites.

XHTML is a language used to reformulate the contemporary technology provided by HTML. It is used to make Web sites easier to get find, build, and use. XHTML was created to remedy the fragmentation issues that are caused by HTML elements that are not standardized. XHTML forces designers to program to specific strict code standards and ensures maximum browser compatibility so that your Web pages appear exactly as you want them to.

- As its name indicates, XHTML is a language formed as an extension of HTML.

- XHTML is a language formed by combining HTML and XML.

- XHTML is agreed on by the W3C. This ensures the uniformity of the structured data.

- You can use XHTML in your Web pages because it is backward-compatible.

- There are many languages that are used for creating Web pages. XHTML works with all those languages.

- All XHTML codes have to have a closing tag, which differentiates it from HTML.

Why should you use XHTML?

- **Extensibility:** XHTML, which is essentially the "latest" version of HTML, ensures compatibility with future standards. Browsers and design applications will be built upon the XHTML standard.

- **Portability:** With the growth in popularity of the Apple® iPhone™ and similar devices designed to access the Internet, XHTML ensures compatibility for cross-platform deployment, meaning your Web data will appear properly in a portable device.

- XHTML is used to increase compatibility and conformity.

- XHTML is approved by the W3C, so it will be more durable.

- XHTML can be used in a number of devices.

HTML versus XHTML

XHTML is an enhanced version of HTML, but there are some distinct differences between the two.

Even though they are similar, they differ in syntax.

Syntax for HTML:
<img alt="Portrait a"

```
src="/images/a.jpg">
```

Syntax for XHTML
```
<img alt="portrait a"
src="/images/a.jpg" />
```

The chance that errors will occur is more likely in HTML than in XHTML simply because there are stricter rules for XHTML than HTML, and thus errors are spotted easily. Note the closing tag. Also, XHTML is written only in lower case. **Doctype** is required in HTML, whereas in XHTML it is not necessary.

Benefits of XHTML

There are many benefits of using XHTML. It is able to adapt to all browser types, including mobile browsers. The use of XHTML ensures future compatibility.

The most stunning feature of XHMTL is its adaptability to support technologies with iPhones, pocket computers, and Personal Digital Assistants (PDAs). This enables them to display the text in their respective windows in a compact manner.

The good news is that programs such as Dreamweaver and Expression Web do the work for you by default creating the XHTML-compliant code.

Extensible Markup Language (XML)

XML is a markup language for documents containing structured information. Structured information can be words or pictures. The XML language defines a standard way to add markup to documents so they can be cross-platform. This works when all browsers have the same structure.

Here is an example of XML:

```xml
<?xml version="1.0"?>
<note>
    <to>Obama</to>
    <from>Sarkozi</from>
    <heading>Congratulations</heading>
    <body>In the war against terrorism, you'll find us on your side.
</body>
</note>
```

A unique feature of XML is that you can create your own definitions. Unlike with HTML and XHTML, the tags are not fixed. XML was created so that richly structured documents could be easily used in different platforms on the Web. A great article on using XML can be found at **http://geekswithblogs.net/maisblog/articles/80683.aspx**.

JavaScript

JavaScript is a lightweight programming language that works with both HTML and CSS to make a Web site interactive. It is a client-side programming language that runs in the browser, not on the Web server. When a page is loaded, any JavaScript on the page is then run by the browser. JavaScript is simple to learn, easy to use, and can be used to change information automatically on a Web page, enable pop-up windows, cause text to change upon mouse rollover, and many other uses that increase interactivity and functionality on Web pages. There are hundreds of sites with JavaScript tutorials and thousands of scripts available for free download and use on your Web site, covering a wide range of uses and functionality. One of my favorites is **www.javascript.com**, which has thousands of free JavaScripts you can embed into your Web pages. JavaScript syntax is easy to learn for anyone who has ever programmed in an object-oriented language. JavaScript, CSS, and XHTML form a new format called dynamic HTML, or DHTML.

Cascading Style Sheet (CSS)

CSS is a style sheet language used to describe the presentation of data . CSS is most commonly used to format and style Web pages written in HTML and XHTML. It can also be integrated with XML. To make sites more interactive, use CSS.

CSS code is inserted in the head of the HTML tag. CSS helps Web pages stick to a specific design. Your site can be seen differently in different browsers, but CSS controls this by forcing a standardized appearance.

Active Server Pages (ASP)

Active Server Pages (ASP) programming is code that enables the delivery of dynamic, database-driven content to Web site visitors. ASP code is placed within HTML pages and enclosed in special tags, and the files have a file extension of .asp. ASP allows Web sites to interact with databases by running the code in the client-side browser but giving Web sites the functionality of database interactivity. This is useful for data validation or presenting data to a user from a database, such as product information, pricing, or inventory levels.

PHP®: Preprocessor Hypertext

PHP is a scripting language used to create dynamic Web pages. It is used extensively in Web site development and is embedded into HTML. PHP page code is stored on the Web server and configured to be dynamically generated when the page is called by the Web browser. Because PHP is free and cross-platform, it can be run on most Web servers and is widely used today for dynamic page generation.

Structured Query Language (SQL)

SQL is a database computer language that is used to manage data in relational database management systems (RDBMS). You should use SQL for data query and update, schema creation, and data access control. Most Web hosting companies support SQL, which will allow you to manipulate data in databases. Some shopping carts also require you to run SQL to manage data in the shopping cart application.

Chapter 4

WEB SITE DESIGN APPLICATIONS — TOOLS TO ACHIEVE YOUR GOALS

There are dozens of software applications on the market to help you create Web sites quickly and easily. Some of these help automate the creation of HTML if you want to work in an HTML environment, while others let you create Web pages in a design environment where the HTML is written for you. This chapter will provide you with an extensive review of several of the most popular Web design applications on the market, such as Dreamweaver CS4 or Expression Web 3. Often, it simply comes down to personal preference and what you are most comfortable with.

Another available avenue is to use a content management system (CMS), such as Joomla! or Mambo. These programs offer tools to create, modify, and organize information on your Web site. However, they do require some technical savvy to install and set up, so unless you truly need a CMS, this option is not typically recommended for beginners.

Other suggestions for simple Web site development may be through your Web hosting provider. Many offer custom templates and simple applications to expedite Web development and let you have a site created and hosted within hours. Hosting providers like PowWeb (**www.powWeb.com**) and Applied Innovations offer free page-building tools, a large amount of space for your Web site, and all of the interactive capabilities you may want to incorporate either now or later. The only drawback of free applications such as these is you are limited in creativity because you have a limited set of options to manage and design your Web site, and often it can be very difficult to "move" your site to another hosting platform if required at a future date.

This chapter will also give you an overview of some free HTML editors, such as Nvu and WYSIWYG Web Builder ("what you see is what you get"), and whether you need these editors once you have built your site. Other topics will include learning what open-source software like WordPress and Joomla! offer, how they work, and how you can use them to create a platform for your Web site. It will also touch on the hosting systems that some of these open-source software programs need to be fully functional.

Joomla!

Joomla! is a CMS that helps users build Web sites. Not only is this software free to use, but the Joomla! site at **www.joomla.org** also provides a forum where users can find additional support and answers to their questions. Joomla! allows users to download an easy-to-install package that provides Web site builders with the ability to add, edit, and update images. It utilizes a simple browser interface that allows users to upload new items, job postings, images, and staff pages. It also allows users to create a subscriptions feature, which is helpful in learning who visits your Web site.

This software offers multiple applications to allow Web site builders to create add-ons and extensions. Some of the examples listed on the Web site include form builders, business or organizational directories, document management, image and multimedia galleries, e-commerce and shopping cart engines, calendars, forums and chat software, blogging software, directory services, e-mail newsletters, data collection and reporting tools, and banner advertising systems. To find additional options, go to **www.extensions. joomla.org**. Joomla! is a great free, open-source application you may wish to consider if you want a robust, flexible CMS.

WordPress

WordPress, at **http://wordpress.com**, is another free, open-source option for building a blog. Blogs can be — and often are — used as Web sites. This is an attractive option to some people because blogs are free and easy to use. Many businesses have abandoned the idea of maintaining both a blog and a Web site in favor of just a blog. This is also a good option for creating personal Web sites. Blogs will be discussed in greater depth in Chapter 15.

Homestead®

Homestead, found at **www.homestead.com**, offers many options for making your site extremely simple, interactive, and user-friendly. Homestead is designed to work with small businesses and help them reach out to find new customers, while also getting their sites noticed by some of the major search engines like Yahoo! and Google. This site provides more than 2,000 Web site templates, which you can either use individually or use to create your own customized template. You can also start from scratch and build your own template if you so choose.

A unique aspect of Homestead is that it offers you the capability to edit text right on the Web page, or completely replace it with your own content by pasting it on the page. You can upload images from your computer's hard drive or use some of the more than 250,000 images available to you for free. Homestead will also provide support in transferring your current domain name, and even help you to create a link to redirect your traffic to your new site. You can add forms to collect information from your visitors so that you can send them e-mail promotions and newsletters, or you can get a guestbook and allow your visitors to post comments. The site includes a PayPal shopping cart you can set up to make it easy for your customers to purchase items or services without having to use a credit card, and it has an e-commerce option if you want to set up a larger business site. Homestead is a great option if you do not want to learn a Web design application and want to create an attractive site quickly.

Nvu

Nvu, pronounced "en-view," is an open-source software program that was designed exclusively for the Linux computer operating system. If you are a Linux user and need an easy-to-use Web authoring system, Nvu may be your solution. Nvu is free and originated from the Mozilla Composer code base. According to the Nvu Web site at **www.nvudev.com**, it takes the basic functionality offered by Composer and adds new levels that allow "integrated Web site management, better form and table support, and better browser compatibility." One of the advantages of using Nvu is that it allows an easy-to-use system for Web file management and WYSIWYG Web page editing ("what you see is what you get"), which makes this software a good choice for someone with little or no HTML code experience.

Although Nvu was primarily designed for the beginning Web builder, the site explains that it is also a great tool for advanced Webmasters because it reduces the amount of time required to build a professional-looking site. Nvu is not an exact clone of FrontPage and Dreamweaver, which use the Windows operating system, but it is similar because it incorporates many of the same easy-to-use features of these products.

Microsoft Office Live

Another Web site hosting service that offers free site building software is Microsoft Office Live Small Business. This host offers free hosting, domain registration, e-mail, and tips for getting traffic to come to your site. When you sign into the site at **http://smallbusiness.officelive.com** and click on the "design a Web site" tab, a design window pops up that allows you to use a predesigned table format to build your site. You just type in the information you want included on your site. It comes with a navigation bar set up on the left with pre-labeled tabs for "Home," "About Us," "Contact Us," and "Site Map." At the top of the design page, there are options such as fonts, colors, font sizes, site theme, styles, navigation options, inserting your logo, headers, and footers. There are also image, document, and template galleries that you can browse and select from to build your page.

This option for hosting and building your Web site is self-explanatory, and everything you need to build a personal and small business site is available. You will need to log in using your Windows Live™ ID, or register for a free Windows Live ID to access the site and begin building your own Web pages. There are definite limits to this option: You cannot use your own domain name because Live assigns one to you, and you have limited control over the content of your site.

There are many other free Web design applications and solutions you can use. You can do a search on your favorite search engine with the keywords "open-source HTML editors" or "open-source Web building software." This will pull up thousands of sites to choose from. However, use caution and read all the fine print to ensure you are not downloading and building your site on a software program that is just a free trial version with a 30-day usage. Many of the trial or demo software programs do not provide the full software capabilities, and they will shut down your entire usage capabilities at the end of the free trial, leaving you with a completely constructed site that you no longer have access to — unless you pay for the full version of the software.

Now that you have an overview of the free options, this next section will give you an in-depth review of some of the most popular commercially available Web design applications on the market and will compare features among these applications. You must choose which path you are willing to take to build your own Web site. If you want a quick, easy site and do not want to spend money, there are plenty of options for basic Web sites or blogs. If you want to create highly customized or advanced Web sites and avoid using templates, you need to use a more advanced Web design application such as Dreamweaver, Expression Web, or WebPlus X2.

The SeaMonkey® Project

The SeaMonkey Project is an open-source project by Mozilla, the company that manages and distributes the popular browser Firefox. The SeaMonkey Project (**www.seamonkey-project.org**) includes a Web browser, an e-mail and newsgroup client, an HTML editor, an Internet relay chat (IRC), and Web development tools. The SeaMonkey Internet Suite is completely free and is a great way to learn HTML. The SeaMonkey Internet Suite is available for Windows, Mac, and Linux-based systems. It also supports CSS and other advanced languages. The HTML editor produces HTML 4.01-compliant code, but it does not produce XHTML or XML. The HTML editor does not support all elements, but does allow for elements from other HTML documents to be pasted in.

The SeaMonkey Composer, its WYSIWYG Web design program and HTML editor, features four different views in its user interface: Normal (WYSIWYG) ("what you see is what you get"), HTML tags, HTML code, and browser preview. Because the program is open-source, there is a large community of support and plenty of documentation to help people who are working with SeaMonkey.

Microsoft Expression Web 3

Microsoft Expression Web, part of the Expression Studio suite, works with the SharePoint® Designer to replace the Microsoft Office FrontPage product previously included in the Microsoft Office suite. The Microsoft Expression Web program is a WYSIWYG and Web authoring program meant to help people design Web sites and Web applications that use ASP.NET or PHP. The second version of Microsoft Expression Web also includes full support for Microsoft Silverlight™.

Microsoft Expression Web is currently in its third version. The Microsoft Expression Studio suite includes: Expression Web, Expression Blend™, Expression Design, Expression Encoder, and SketchFlow. All of these programs work together, similar to the programs in the Adobe CS4 Design Suite.

When compared to its major competitor, Adobe Dreamweaver, many believe that Expression Web is the better program for designers, and that Dreamweaver is the better program for coders.

Benefits of Microsoft Expression Web 3

Microsoft Expression Web is a cost-effective solution for many Web designers because it is generally $100 cheaper than Dreamweaver. For those on a budget who still need a top-of-the-line development program, this makes Microsoft Expression Web a viable solution.

For those who are used to FrontPage or the Microsoft Office suite, the program is easy to learn. The fact that it shares a common user interface makes it easier to pick up than other programs. Microsoft Expression Web has support for several different development languages, including XML, CSS, PHP, and ASP.NET. It is important to note, however, that PHP was not supported in the first version of the program. The support for several coding languages makes this a good program option for those who work with several different languages.

When coding with these various languages, Web developers can rest assured they are using the most standard compliant WYSIWYG program available. This means that people who are using the program to design their Web sites will be able to learn correct coding practices by studying the code that Expression Web generates for them. When a designer uses "bad" coding practices, Microsoft Expression Web alerts the user that the code is not considered standard and tells the user it should be changed.

Microsoft Expression Web also offers support for CSS, something not generally seen in many other Web design and development programs. It is easier to use than several other CSS editors on the market today. The program facilitates "add-ons," or third-party applications, to enhance the program to the specific needs of the Web designer. Just as FrontPage had several different "add-on" options, Microsoft Expression Web does, too.

Drawbacks of Microsoft Expression Web 3

Microsoft Expression Web comes with fewer features than Adobe Dreamweaver. This may be a good thing for some designers, such as those who are just getting started and do not want too much to overwhelm them. For more seasoned designers, however, this could be a major pitfall of the program as compared to Dreamweaver.

There is no CSS validator. Just as HTML needs to be validated to make sure it is code-compliant with all the W3C standards, the CSS code should also be validated. For the program to have such a heavy base in CSS and so many CSS features, the fact that it lacks its own CSS validator is a drawback. However, with the number of CSS validators available online, this is not a major issue — apart from the inconvenience of having to use another service to validate the CSS code.

Several wizards and features from FrontPage are no longer available, which means Web designers need to take time to find third-party add-ons, or manually develop the items once easily done with the wizards. Additionally, there may be a steep learning curve for any non-basic tasks. The fact that you can use Expression Web to do more complicated tasks such as developing AJAX applications is a plus, but the fact that beginners do not have much help in learning how to do such tasks in Expression Web detracts from this.

Features of Microsoft Expression Web 3

Professional design environment: The professional design environment allows designers to accomplish more in a shorter period of time because the placement of the menus and tools you need are conveniently found. This means you can spend more time focusing on the actual design rather than worrying about how to find the tools and features you need. You can also import Photoshop files to use as your graphic designs.

Standards-based site design: This tool will make sure all your coding is compliant with the standards set forth by the W3C. Good coding practices help with the server's ability to correctly display your Web site. This also helps with search engine indexing, which means you have a better shot at getting a steady flow of traffic to your Web site.

CSS layout: This feature makes it easy to separate your Web site design from Web site content. With features like drag-and-drop margin control, visual hierarchy of coding, and color-coded code, you will be able to design and develop CSS layouts with ease.

CSS site templates: Quickly set up a design for your site using CSS site templates. Make adjustments to colors, fonts, and styles to make it your own.

CSS style application: You can choose between automatically generated CSS styles, or create them yourself for ultimate control over your Web site design.

CSS management: This makes it easy to manage complex CSS-based sites because the rules are provided for you.

Property task panes: The panes allow you to see everything you have at your disposal in terms of coding attributes and styles.

ASP.NET 3.5: Render all sorts of ASP.NET modules without any coding knowledge.

Edit PHP pages: The second and third versions of Microsoft Expression Web offer support for PHP editing.

Microsoft Office FrontPage

Microsoft Office FrontPage is a WYSIWYG Web design and Web site administration program produced by Microsoft. The most recent version of this program is FrontPage 2003. This program is meant for those who are not familiar with HTML and Web design technology. FrontPage is integrated with a Microsoft Office interface so as to make the program work seamlessly with the others many people are already familiar with from the Microsoft Office suite.

It was designed for Windows-based systems, though a Mac version was released in 1998. The Mac version of the program came with fewer features than the Windows version, and because of this, the program never received any updates.

Benefits of Microsoft Office FrontPage

Microsoft FrontPage has several benefits, including a shared office interface, a WYSIWYG editor, help for novice designers to learn HTML code, and a low-cost availability.

The shared Office user interface: Because FrontPage looks like the other programs in the Microsoft Office suite, it is quite easy to learn how to use. It does not take much to pick up the structure of the program for those who are already familiar with programs such as Microsoft Word and Microsoft PowerPoint®.

The WYSIWYG editor: This is the greatest benefit to the program for those who are not familiar with HTML. It allows user to drag and drop their design elements onto the page, and the program generates the necessary HTML coding. It allows users to see their design, rather than simply stare at the code.

Helps novice designers learn HTML code: As designers become more comfortable with HTML and Web design, they have the option to view the HTML code for specific areas of their design, thereby allowing them to learn more HTML and have the program grow with them. It is a valuable teaching tool for classrooms and for anyone who wants to turn a hobby into a profession.

Low cost: Microsoft Office FrontPage is available at a lower cost as compared to its Dreamweaver competitor from Adobe.

Drawbacks of Microsoft Office FrontPage

As with every program, there are drawbacks to using FrontPage, including a decreased usage in the program, non-compliant HTML, and difficult optimization for any browsers other than Internet Explorer.

The program is no longer widely used because it has been succeeded by Microsoft Expression Web and Sharepoint Designer. Though it is no longer supported by Microsoft, there is no shortage of support for the program from other users, so those who are looking to save some money and still want a Microsoft-based product may be satisfied with FrontPage. You can upgrade to Expression Web in the future, if you so desire. The automatically generated HTML is non-compliant with HTML standards set forth by the W3C. The code is hard to edit for compliance and is proprietary to Microsoft.

Features of Microsoft Office FrontPage

Split view: In FrontPage 2003, the user has the ability to see the code and the design view at the same time, saving the time and hassle associated with having to alternate between the two view options.

Dynamic Web templates: Also in FrontPage 2003, the use of Dynamic Web Templates was introduced to allow users to designate a template to use for a Web page or an entire Web site. These templates greatly reduce design time and look very professional.

Interactive buttons: Save time and cut costs by creating graphics and interactive buttons without a program such as Adobe Photoshop.

IntelliSense®: Save time by using this form of auto-complete in code view. While in the code view mode, IntelliSense will suggest tags and other codes to stop the user from having to type the complete command.

Accessibility checker: Make sure your Web site is completely accessible to all users with the accessibility checker. It will make sure the pages are optimized for Web users with disabilities and will also help with HTML code compliance. It even includes an HTML optimizer to ensure your Web site is completely accessible to everyone.

Code snippets: Avoid writing code yourself and save time with the code snippet library, full of various code snippets to help you with your design.

ASP.NET support: FrontPage 2003 includes support for the coding language ASP.NET. Previous versions of the program did not support the language.

Automatic Web content: Create content for your Web site with ease, as you can insert MSNBC® headlines and weather forecasts, search, and other tools directly into your Web site. These will automatically update so you will have fresh content without having to continually update your Web site.

Photo gallery: Quickly create a photo gallery for personal or business use. The templates can be edited so you can change the layout to suit your needs, and you can quickly add captions to each photo. This is a great timesaver as compared to manually creating the gallery.

PowerPoint-like drawing tools: Draw graphics with ease using tools found in PowerPoint.

Usage analysis reports: Take a look and see what is being used on your Web site by whom. You can get these reports daily, weekly, or monthly. These can be exported into Microsoft Excel® so you can take a closer look at them later to make sure you are getting the most of your Web site design.

Central commerce manager add-in: Make e-commerce easier on your Web site with this add-in. Easily track your product catalog and purchases.

Discussions and subscriptions: Discussions and subscriptions can be used with SharePoint Team Services to post and reply to comments on any Web site on the Internet and keep up with them with e-mail. This feature is useful for Internet marketing.

Document libraries: You will be able to store documents for the entire team of people working on the Web design in one place, making it easier for the entire team to know what is where and how to get to it. It will streamline the production process for everyone involved.

Adobe Dreamweaver CS4

Adobe Dreamweaver is a combination WYSIWYG Web design program ("what you see is what you get") and text editor to allow for both visual design and line-by-line hand coding. Originally owned by Macromedia®, the program debuted in December 1997. Macromedia was acquired by Adobe in 2005, and since the acquisition, Dreamweaver has been updated to version 10.0, more commonly known as CS4. Dreamweaver is considered an industry standard for Web design because it is widely used in many institutions. Adobe chose to discontinue its GoLive® competitor product when it acquired Dreamweaver from Macromedia.

Benefits of Adobe Dreamweaver CS4

There are many different benefits of using Adobe Dreamweaver if you are a Web design novice. Simply being able to point and click, rather than having to remember and type extraneous amounts of code, saves time. In studying the resulting code, users can teach themselves HTML and CSS with the designs they are already working on.

The use of this WYSIWYG program allows designers to place more emphasis on what the design itself looks like, instead of placing emphasis on what the code looks like. Dreamweaver formats and color-codes the actual scripting of the pages to make learning and editing the code easier for the designer.

People without any HTML or coding knowledge at all can use this product with ease, and there is plenty of support to be found. Dreamweaver is also suitable for Web designers who use other programs in the Adobe suite, including Flash, Fireworks®, Photoshop, and Illustrator®. There are several integration tools, meaning you can use a file from one program in another.

Drawbacks of Adobe Dreamweaver CS4

Dreamweaver comes with a steep learning curve and is also pricier than its competitors. While this is a drop in the bucket for Web design firms and larger corporations, this cost is not very feasible for many small businesses, let alone individuals who want to learn how to code and design their own Web sites.

Features of Adobe Dreamweaver CS4

New user interface: The new user interface in the latest version of Dreamweaver has been designed to match all the other programs in CS4 to help users work faster and smarter, adding cohesiveness to all the programs. Users now have the ability to stack panels and menus where they need to, in order to create the most productive working environment.

Cross-product integration: This allows people who use more than one Adobe product to easily move files back and forth and work between the programs at the same time.

Related files and CSS navigator: As the use of CSS continues to grow, more and more programs like Dreamweaver are making support for this programming language available in their programs. The updated properties panel in version CS4 allows for quick and easy edits to CSS styles to adjust the appearance of a Web site.

Integrated coding: Designers can use the integrated coding feature for coding hints to make sure their code is clean, compliant, and quick.

Advanced language support: Dreamweaver has support for many different programming languages, which makes it a great tool for those who do more than HTML and CSS. In addition to those two common languages, Dreamweaver will also help designers code XHTML, XML, JavaScript, AJAX, PHP, Adobe ColdFusion® software, and ASP. Using the same editor for these various program languages keeps things simple for Web designers so they can focus more on their projects and clients.

Cross-platform support: Many Web designers work on both PC and Mac systems. Though two different versions of the program will be needed — one for each system — the flexibility to use the same program across platforms gives designers an edge, ensuring the Web sites they design will look the same regardless of the system they are viewed on.

Flash video support: Many Web sites use Flash video because the Flash player is something found on the majority of computer systems today, and Flash video cannot be saved to the viewer's hard drive as with other video file formats. The ability to support Flash video means Web designers will be able to save time when choosing to integrate video into their designs.

Live view: With the newest version of Dreamweaver, designers can preview their designs in a number of browsers without having to let go of direct access to the code. This is not much different from previous versions' preview functions, though it will save time in the long run.

HTML data sets: This feature allows for using dynamic Web design features without having to learn additional coding languages and information in order to create these features. It is useful for tables that require sorting; adding these to your Web site is as simple as a few clicks.

Photoshop smart objects: All you need to do is drag a Photoshop document (PSD) into Dreamweaver and any updates you make to the PSD file will reflect in the Dreamweaver file. It will provide a tight link to the photo and the source, along with aiding in time efficiency.

Advanced JavaScript functionality: Dreamweaver has support for the jQuery, Prototype, and Spry frameworks. All designers need to do is attach the correct JavaScript files externally, and Dreamweaver will help by displaying the correct coding hints.

Code hinting for AJAX and JavaScript frameworks: As JavaScript usage becomes an increasing trend in Web design and development, more designers are making it a point to learn about it. With this feature, there are tool tips and other hints to help designers make sure their code is clean and debugged.

Related files and code navigator: These tools will provide more efficiency by giving easier access to all the files associated with the project in one window. Designers can navigate through whatever files they need as they need them, regardless of file type.

CSS best practices: Now designers can make sure their CSS code is proper and compliant without actually having to type any code. With tool tips, designers can get a simple explanation of all the properties and how to make sure they are correct to ensure the CSS is ready to go.

Adobe InContext editing: This simple, easy-to-use feature allows content authors to make changes to Web site content without actually having access to the Dreamweaver program, which means designers can focus more on design and worry less about content.

CoffeeCup

CoffeeCup Software is an American software development company based in Atlanta, Georgia. They have been creating programs to help with Web design and development since 1996.

The CoffeeCup Software lineup includes:

- **The HTML Editor 2008:** This program is an HTML and CSS editor to help you design Web sites.
- **Visual Site Designer 6.0:** This is a WYSIWYG Web design program.
- **Shopping Cart Creator 3.1:** Create a shopping cart for your Web site.
- **Web Form Builder 8.0:** Build interactive Web forms with ease.
- **Direct FTP 6.6:** Upload files to your domain and server to get them live on the Web.
- **Photo Gallery 5.9:** Create a photo gallery with ease.
- **Website Access Manager 2.0:** Password-protect portions of your Web site.
- **Google SiteMapper 4.7.1:** Create a Google Sitemap and allow users to search your Web site.
- **Web JukeBox 4.5:** Add a music player to your Web site.
- **Web Video Player 5.2:** Convert your videos to Flash and put them on the Web.
- **Flash Firestarter 7.2:** Make Flash effects.
- **LockBox 3.1:** Store your usernames and passwords.
- **Website Font 4.1:** Use any font for your Web site.
- **Flash Menu Builder 3.4:** Build Flash menus.
- **Flash Website Search 5.0:** Build a customized Flash search function.
- **Live Chat 6.0:** Create a live chat room for your Web site.
- **Ad Producer 3.0:** Create ads to advertise your Web site.
- **RSS News Flash 4.5:** Use this program to add content from other sites via Really Simple Syndication (RSS).
- **Web Video Recorder 3.0:** Record video with your Web cam, edit, and create text to add videos to YouTube or MySpace.

- **Web Calendar 4.2:** Add a Flash calendar to your Web site.
- **Flash Blogger 4.5:** Create and maintain a blog.
- **PixConverter 4.0:** Convert photos to different formats for Flickr® and other photo Web sites.
- **Website Color Schemer 4.0:** Create color schemes for Web sites.
- **Image Mapper 4.2:** Create image maps.
- **StyleSheet Maker 5.0:** Create CSS with ease.
- **WebCam 4.1:** Upload live Web cam shots to your Web site.
- **GIF Animator 7.6:** Quickly and easily create animated graphics interface format (GIF) files to use on your Web sites.

There are many different programs that can be used together to create professional-looking Web sites. These programs are much cheaper than larger programs such as Microsoft Expression Web or Adobe Dreamweaver. These programs are well-suited for novice Web designers and work seamlessly together. Once you purchase and download the program, you will receive free updates and support for life.

WebSite X5 Evolution

WebSite X5 is a Web design product developed by Incomedia, Inc., a privately owned company with operations based in Europe. The program boasts that you can create your Web site in just five easy steps. It is a WYSIWYG program that allows you to publish a personal or business Web site with ease, and it includes e-commerce support. Website X5 Evolution version 8 is available in English, German, Spanish, Italian, and French.

There are several benefits to using Website X5 Evolution. All you have to do is drag and drop the design elements into the template, and your Web site is done. There is no need to learn code.

The program uploads the site to the Web at the end of your creation process, so there is no need for an external FTP program. The program adheres to all programming language standards set forth by the W3C, which means the site will be easier to index in search engines and will be properly displayed in a variety of Web browsers. This program offers many of the same features as the larger software giants such as Microsoft Expression Web and Adobe Dreamweaver.

Namo WebEditor

Namo WebEditor is a WYSIWYG HTML-based editor meant for designing Web sites and other Web applications. The current version is available in English and German.

The Namo WebEditor is available for a much cheaper cost than Adobe Dreamweaver or Microsoft Expression Web. This program is good for beginners to learn how to use HTML and other Web design skills, but will work well for skilled Web designers, too. The program can edit several other languages for Web designers who want to learn more advanced coding languages.

AceHTML Pro

AceHTML Pro is a Web development program created and distributed by Visicom Media, Inc. This is not a WYSIWYG editor.

This program offers many of the same features as the software giants, such as Adobe Dreamweaver and Microsoft Expression Web, without the high cost associated with those two programs. AceHTML Pro is an excellent option for novice Web developers who need to learn more about the various coding languages used in Web development because it supports programming languages such as HTML, JavaScript, CSS, ASP, and PHP. This program allows Web designers and developers to customize the interface to their needs.

HomeSite®

HomeSite was originally owned by Macromedia, Inc., but was acquired by Adobe. Development of this program was officially ended by Adobe on May 26, 2009. This is not a WYSIWYG editor.

It is a lightweight, code-only editor to help Web designers and developers create their Web sites. It is only available for Windows. HomeSite+ is a feature included in all versions of Dreamweaver past MX 2004.

Serif WebPlus X2

Manufactured by Serif, a leading developer of professional and consumer-oriented desktop publishing, design and graphics software, WebPlus X2 was released in 2008.

The most recent version of Serif's Web site design powerhouse, WebPlus X2, enables Web designers of all abilities to build high-end, full-featured Web sites without having to learn to use HTML code. Highlights of the program include:

- Desktop publishing-style approach to Web design, making it as easy to create a Web site as it is to create a printed document.
- Built-in multimedia and Web 2.0 support for adding Flash animations, videos, blogs, podcasts, and polls.
- Integrated e-commerce, enabling any business to create a fully transactional Web site.
- Optimization and analytics to aid in search engine optimization and tracking visitor trends.

It is simple to use and creates attractive Web sites quickly, and includes 12 months of Web hosting for free. There is also a chart included that compares features between WebPlus X2 and several other major Web applications.

Chapter 5

WEB SITE ORGANIZATION AND NAVIGATION FUNDAMENTALS

How you organize your Web site is critical to its success. Organization increases the functionality and viability of your Web site. It will bring in return visitors and inspire your current site visitors to stay longer as they explore your site. Site structure is a critical element to designing your Web site.

Home Page

Every Web site has a home page. Typically, this is the first page a site visitor will see, and it is therefore the anchor of your Web site. The focus of your design efforts should concentrate on your home page, and it should serve as the launch pad to other parts of your Web site. Some Web sites may use a splash or entry page before you hit the home page; usually these are done in Flash as an "intro" page, and they can normally be quickly bypassed to get the visitor to the main site content. If you type in **www.crystalriverhouse.com**, you are navigated to the home page of the Web site, **www.crystalriverhouse.com/index.htm**. You specify your home page in your Web server software: Index.htm, home.htm, or index.asp are very common home pages.

This is the most important page on your Web site. This is the page that every visitor will see first, so you must quickly convey your message, offer simple site navigation, and grab the interest of the site visitor. This page must have defined navigation that is quick to find and use. You should have navigation links or navigation buttons, as well as excellent Web content that is keyword-rich and is easily read and understood by the site visitor. Other common pages in a navigation structure include pages such as "Contact," "About Us," "Photographs," "Product Information," "Company Information," "Terms and Conditions," and "Feedback." Ideally, you should be able to link to all pages of the site from any page on the site with not more than two mouse clicks. Burying pages in layers of obscurity will ensure that they are never visited.

It is highly recommended that you design a site template to be used throughout the site for uniformity and consistency. A Web site is easier to navigate and manage when it is standardized. You can do this in Expression Web or use CSS or table layouts. Because your home page is the first page a site visitor sees, this is your one chance to make the best impression possible. A home page that is organized, is easy to read, and that contains the perfect balance of text and visual content is critical to the success of your Web site. You need to make sure site visitors know who you are, so you should display your logo prominently. Ensure that you have displayed contact information and e-mail addresses, and make sure your message is delivered in a consistent, easily read format.

Chapter 7 is an entire section dedicated to images on a Web site. Images truly paint the picture you cannot convey with words alone and can make your Web site a work of art and inspiration. Use high-quality images saved in a Web-friendly format to speed the loading of pages in a browser. Choose image size and placement carefully to enhance your Web site, and not just cover it up with images.

Web Site Navigation

The importance of Web site navigation cannot be understated. One of the great features of FrontPage is the ability to create navigational views of Web sites, as shown in the following:

Navigation through a Web site can be complex. When you integrate e-commerce into your Web site, make it easy to navigate, simple to find products, and effortless to check out and pay for products. Too many sites make it difficult to find and pay for products, and they lose potential customers who do not have the patience. You must also provide superior customer service and timely responses to inquiries and support issues. Providing static Web pages to address some of the most commonly asked questions will help you to avoid many issues, but you have to be ready to respond to customer inquiries in a timely manner.

Every Web site must use some form of advanced applications, such as form handlers, database interactivity, or JavaScript integration. Some of these are fairly simple if you use FrontPage extensions but, in many cases, you must have some working knowledge of scripts, ASP, or Common Gateway Interface (CGI) to configure these services. JavaScript is simply script that is interpreted by the browser and run as it is loaded on a Web site. These scripts can provide a wide array of advanced features and functionality, and are an essential part of any Web site. Typically, you do not need to know how to write JavaScript to use existing scripts and embed them into your Web pages, but you do need to understand how it works.

Flash is a programming language that can add advanced animation and graphics to your Web sites. Many Web sites are built entirely on Flash technology. As mentioned in the last chapter, Web site organization will pay dividends as your Web site grows. Keep your images in an images folder, keep your documents in a documents folder, and if you have shopping cart applications software, do not install it in the root of your Web site so that it is intermingled with your actual Web pages.

Consider multiple navigation systems to ensure that there is more than one option to navigate throughout a Web site. Common navigation features are left-hand menus that list various pages or sections of your Web site, as well as tabs across the top to improve quick navigation to particular content-specific section of your site and emphasize the most important areas of your Web site. A JavaScript drop-down menu on each page offers redundancy to ensure that each page can link to any other page on the Web site, as customized content and color can help a site visitor realize what section or content-specific area of a Web site they are in.

The Web page below from the Atlantic Publishing Company Web site illustrates some of these navigational features:

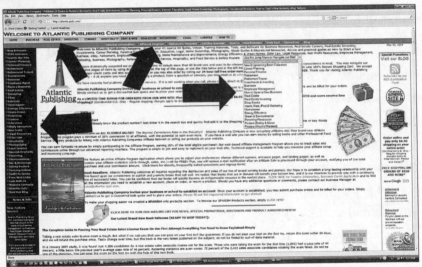

Site navigation is a fairly simple concept: Provide site visitors an easy way to find their way around your Web site. You can do this in a variety of ways, but keep in mind that search engines handle navigation differently, depending on if the navigation is based on actual button images, HTML text, or through other methods. Search engine optimization will be discussed later in Chapter 8 of this book, and you should consider SEO when designing all portions of your Web site — your navigation system in particular. If you are going to use buttons or other images for navigation, make sure each image has an **<alt>** tag with a text description because this text will be indexed by search engines. Many navigation systems now use or are designed using JavaScript, Java™ applets, or Flash technology. JavaScript typically is not as problematic because it often uses images with **<alt>** tags or text-based navigation, such as drop-down menus, so the text can be indexed.

Common Web Site Navigation Styles

The most common navigation styles are:

- **HTML links:** Simple, efficient, and great for search engines, but not as appealing as fancy buttons or other methods.

- **Bread-crumb trail:** This system uses a single line of text to show a page's location in the site hierarchy. This should only be used as a secondary navigation system, but it is very useful in showing the site visitor where they are in a Web site's hierarchy. This navigation technique is increasingly beneficial to users.

- **Navigation bars or buttons:** By far the most common type of navigation. Typically found on the left-hand side of a Web page or across the top of a Web page.

- **Tab navigation:** First made popular by Amazon.com, this can be considered a secondary navigation system as well, but it provides a direct link to specific sections of a Web site.

- **Sitemap:** A single Web page that shows the complete navigation structure for your Web site. This is critical for SEO as well.

- **Drop-down menu:** A menu, typically across the top or left-hand side of a Web page, that drops down or expands into sub-menus as the mouse is moved over them. This allows you to put many links into the navigation, but these menus stay collapsed except when used. These are typically made from JavaScript, DHTML, or CSS.

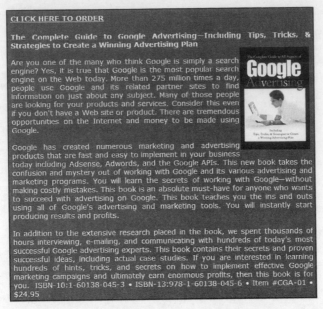

Sample Web Page with HTML Link

Sample Bread Crumb Trail Navigation

Sample Tab Navigation System

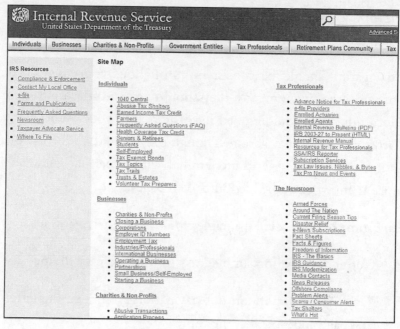

*Sample Sitemap at **www.irs.gov***

Sample Drop-Down Menu

The bottom line is that simple, effective, user-friendly navigation is one of the most important elements of Web design. It is recommended that you spend some time visiting other sites to see how different navigation methods are employed. This will not only give you great ideas for what to do for your own site, but it will also help you determine what you should not do. Keep with what works — we read left to right and are trained to look at the left side, or top, of a Web page for navigation. Do not bury your navigation at the bottom of the page or stick it on the right side of the page.

Your navigation should be consistent throughout your site. If you use buttons and drop-down menus, they should appear on every page, in the same location. You should embed hyperlinks into your Web pages as an alternative method to navigation. Though they should not be the primary navigation system, site visitors are familiar with hyperlinks and can easily recognize them when embedded into Web pages.

Here are some basic guiding principles for Web site navigation:

- Keep site navigation simple, easy to use, and easy to find.

- Placement is important; put navigation systems in the left side of each page and/or across the top.

- Ensure that you have multiple navigation systems in place on your Web site.

- Keep your navigation manageable; do not overwhelm site visitors with complex menus that offer too many choices.

- Use simple, easy-to-understand verbiage in you navigation menus, e.g. "Home," "About Us," and "Contact Us." Links should be clear, concise, and precise.

- Ensure that your navigation system is "above the fold." This is a term taken from the newspaper industry that means that the important stories are placed above the "fold" in a newspaper, and less important stories are placed below the fold, where they are not seen when initially viewing the front page. The concept translates well to Web pages. You only have so much real estate in a monitor, and you cannot always fit your entire page into the browser window, forcing users to scroll to read more content. Make sure your navigation systems are "above the fold" on a Web page — users should never have to scroll to find your navigation system. The same applies to Web page content; put the important information above the fold if you want site visitors to see it.

- Make sure you have a "Home" navigation link on every page. Provide your site visitors with an easy way to get back to the home page.

- Ensure that your site layout and navigation menus are consistent throughout your site. Every page should have the same navigational layout and placement.

- Large sites are challenging because of the number of pages. Organize your site by category, section, and products to simplify navigation. Users should be able to get to any page with no more than two mouse clicks. Do not bury pages on your site by requiring multiple mouse clicks to find them — they will likely never be visited.

- Make your navigation systems attractive through the use of graphics, images, and advanced features, such as rollover buttons that change color when a mouse is moved over them. Microsoft Expression Web has a great feature that lets you create interactive buttons on the fly.

There are many free options for Web site navigation, and Dreamweaver and Expression Web both offer fairly robust integrated solutions to create accessible and functional site navigation options.

Search Options

You must integrate some form of search capability into your Web site. This can be done with a site map as well as through additional applets from Google and other companies that will index your Web pages and give you free search capabilities.

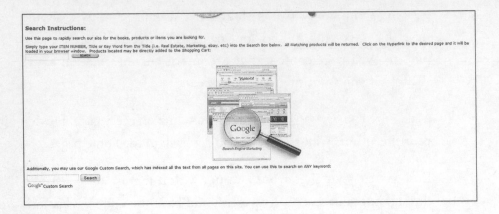

One option is to use the Google Custom Search, which can be obtained at **www.google.com/searchcode.html**. There are many other examples you can find with a quick Web search.

Frames

Frames were very popular in the 1990s and were a way to take multiple Web pages and display each of them in one browser window. The heading would often be in one frame, the navigation on the left side of a page in another frame, and the main page content in a third frame. Each frame typically scrolled independent of other frames. This method was popular because you could maintain one Web page for navigation, for instance, and have it display on all your Web pages. There are now other, much better ways to do this, by using tables, CSS, Include Pages, and Server Side Includes (SSI). Do not use frames; they bring no value that you cannot gain from another method, and they have more issues than they are worth.

Web Site Templates

There are thousands of Web site templates available for you to use when developing your Web site. Many of these are very high in quality and designed specifically for Dreamweaver, FrontPage, or Expression Web. These applications even come with built-in templates, as does WebPlus

X2. "Template" is not a bad word, and you should consider commercial templates as a starting point for your Web design efforts. Although the templates included with FrontPage were not very good, Dreamweaver and Expression Web include more professional templates that utilize CSS and typically meet accessibility standards. Also, WebPlus X2 offers attractive, professionally designed templates that are included with the software at no additional charge. There are dozens of Web sites that also sell customized templates, such as PixelMill™, available at **www.pixelmill.com**.

Most templates take advantage of Include Pages, which were touched on earlier. These allow you to have portions of Web page "call" data from other pages through an "include," and display the data on that page. To the site visitor, it is seamless, and for you, it simplifies maintenance and changes. If your entire site navigation is an include and you have 300 Web pages, you can edit the one navigation page, and it is updated instantly on 300 pages. The alternative would be to update 300 pages individually.

You should utilize CSS in your Web design efforts as well. With CSS, you control the overall appearance, font sizes, and colors of your Web site from a master CSS file. Your page reads the CSS file and applies the appropriate standards to your Web page so it is displayed properly. This standardizes every page on your site from one single file. Both Expression Web and Dreamweaver have extensive CSS support built into their applications.

Chapter 6

WEB PAGE CONTENT

This chapter will discuss the importance of content, including why it is so imperative to have solid content, no matter what type of business or service you are providing. Even if your Web site or blog is for personal use, content drives search engine visibility and is vitally important to achieving success on the Web. Content is critical not only in drawing visitors into your site, but also getting them to return time and time again. Writing solid, comprehensible content means two things: You need to know your topic, and you need to have a good grasp of how to build your content into something of value.

Search engines look for well-written, interesting, and unique content that is updated and relevant. Content should be written so that it can be easily scanned, because site visitors may not have time to read lengthy text. Include bold-faced headlines with text to make it easier for visitors to find what they are looking for — without having to read everything. Four basic tips for writing good Web content are: include keywords; use clear titles; keep it short and sweet; and forgo the sales pitch so your visitors can get to the real meat of the site.

Your first sentence and paragraph is going to determine whether your visitors will read the entire Web page. One of the first lessons that students learn in journalism is how to write a lede, which is that first sentence you read in most newspaper stories. It must be a selective introduction that grabs the reader's attention; it is best-served with a solid verb to describe what the article is about. Make sure your content is not only timely, but relevant to your readers as well.

Remember to spell-check everything. Do it as you write, and again when you are finished. Also make sure to check your grammar closely. Using fancy fonts will not help you to retain visitors because they are just too difficult to read and are often not Web-friendly, nor are they universally visible.

It is essential to write about something you know and have researched extensively. Just throwing words on a page is not the way to write your content. You must have a clear focus on what you are trying to sell or offer to your clients. If you do not understand the topic you are attempting to write about, neither will your audience. Do not be too wordy; use clear, concise descriptions. That does not mean that you cannot write longer copy when necessary — it just means you do not want to write more than is required to explain your product or service. When using the Web, potential clients want the information to be quickly and easily digested, so your goal is to describe your product or service in such a way as to get them to pick up the phone or use the shopping cart method to purchase what you are selling.

Only hyperlinks to other pages or Web sites should be underlined. There are many other ways to emphasis a specific area of your content, such as bolding or italicizing sub-headlines to divide your content into predetermined areas. You can also implement bullets or numerical lists. Within the text and in sub-headers, you may create links to different areas of your Web site; single pages on your site; different sections of a document on the same page; or other Web sites. In doing so, however, remember to use the keywords you have chosen to promote your site with search engines.

Another factor to remember is to leave enough space between your content and graphics or images. Do not allow your content to flow under or over these items. If you have content that is buried or unreadable, you will irritate your readers, and may even lose current and future customers because the site looks unprofessional.

There is one final detail regarding any type of Web writing, and that is to choose your words and way of writing them carefully. For example, most people today know and understand basic Web communication, which means that if you choose to use all-capitalized words in your e-mails and chats, your customers or clients might feel as if you are yelling at them. On the Web, you can easily offend people by using all-capital letters to make a point. So unless this is your intent, use capitalization carefully and sparingly in all communications with your visitors. There are numerous methods you can employ to draw visitors to specific areas of your content without resorting to excessive capitalization.

Content Keywords

Web site traffic is the number of visitors and visits a Web site receives. It is important that you implement SEO techniques and embed keywords in your Web page content to raise the visibility and ranking of your Web site within search engines. One major step is to determine what keywords or key phrases your potential customers may use when seeking out your company, products, or services. A keyword is a word or phrase that people would employ to locate information on the products, services, or topic they seek.

How to Develop Keywords

One of the biggest challenges when establishing your Web site is developing your initial list of keywords and key phrases. Key phrases are simply keywords that are joined together. They refine the search and narrow down generalized searches into very specific result sets. Such phrases are often overlooked as people create keyword lists, but they are just as vital to SEO for your Web site. You must develop a list of potential keywords or key phrases before producing your content. Here are some tips to guide you:

- Screen your employees, friends, and customer base for a list of all the possible keywords or key phrases you believe they might use to try to find your Web site.

- Screen your competitors' sites for a list of all the possible keywords or key phrases on their Web site.

- Brainstorm a list of any relevant keyword or key phrase you can think of. Take some time away from the list; then, over the course of a week or so, keep adding more potential keywords and key phrases to the list.

- Be sure to incorporate your company name, catch-phrases, slogans, or other recognizable marketing material into keywords.

- Add both the singular and plural spellings for your keywords.

- Take a peek at the meta-tags on competitors' Web sites, in particular the "keywords" tag. Review this list and add them to your own keywords list.

- Avoid trademark issues and disputes. Although there is some degree of latitude in regard to trademarks, it is recommended to avoid using other companies' trademarks unless you are an authorized distributor or reseller of their products.

Design your Web site so that it provides the information people are looking for, with simple navigation and usability to navigate your Web site. Embed your keywords or key phrases into your Web site content. Utilize your Web server logs to research what keywords or key phrases people are using to find your Web site; this will likely help you refine your keyword and key phrase lists. Keyword density is also important in Web site design.

You need to feature keywords in your Web site content, but you must also ensure that the page content still reads properly. The number of keywords embedded into page content in comparison to your other text determines the "density" of a keyword. The proper keyword density for a Web page is typically considered to be from 5 to 10 percent.

Ensuring that you have a proper balance of keywords or key phrases will ultimately help you to reach thousands of potential site visitors. Google PageRank™ is a useful tool when developing your Web page content. Make sure that you constantly analyze your keyword or key phrase performance through Web logs. Optimize your Web site content by increasing the frequency of productive keywords to increase visibility and traffic. More than half of all Web site traffic and searches land on your home page; therefore, devote significant time to analyzing your Web content, embedding your keywords and phrases, and optimizing your site for search engine visibility.

How Users Read Web Pages

People seldom read Web pages word-for-word; instead, they sweep the page, selecting various words and sentences. In researching the way in which people read Web sites, it was discovered that only 16 percent read word-for-word. Consequently, Web pages must use analyzable text and employ accentuated keywords. Additionally, Web pages must contain significant sub-headings, bulleted lists, and ideas organized by paragraph.

Rules of Web Writing

Your Web site is your professional calling-card, your main entrance, and is your first impression upon site visitors. A well-written Web page explains what your Web site is all about, who you are, and what products or services you offer. It must be captivating and easy to read. People often make instantaneous decisions based on what they see, and the content of Web sites is no exception. Here are some general guidelines for creating Web page content:

Create content for the site visitor

Perhaps the most challenging part about the developing strategies of content for Web sites is to determine what is important for your readers, which may be in opposition to what is important for the business. Your goals are typically aligned, but from time to time, they can be in conflict. Ensuring that you create content for the Web site visitor is critical in order to meet their needs, capture their attention, and convert visitors into clients.

Convey the advantages

Content must clearly convey the advantages and benefits of visiting your site or using your products or services. Give visitors the information up-front. People are constantly seeking information that will help them work more effectively, improve the quality of their life at work and home, and help them complete their objectives. Convince the site visitor that you can achieve these goals.

Write to reach your visitors

Write your content in a conversational tone. This ensures a much clearer model of writing.

Web page formatting for ease of scanning

Web pages are often filled with long, uninterrupted paragraphs that are nearly impossible to read. Your site visitor typically only sweeps over these pages. Capture the main ideas, concepts, and key points in your documents so the reader can skim the content without losing the main purpose and meaning.

Optimizing Content for SEO Keywords

A keyword is a simple expression that reflects the topic or the principal idea of an entry of blog, article, or the other contents of Web site. Search engines such as Google employ keywords as a basis for their system of indexing a Web site. When each new entry, article, Web page, or blog is indexed by a search engine, the algorithm of the search engine detects expressions of keywords to determine the purpose of the content of the Web site and ranks the pages accordingly into its database of Web pages. When an individual types a series of words in the search box of a browser, the search engine extracts corresponding results based on the keywords used in the search and returns the results to the browser in ranked order.

A good keyword or key phrase is one that reflects with precision what a person would enter into a search engine, returning the result most closely matching their desired content. Keywords must be specific and relevant. Keywords are useless if too broad. Optimal density of keywords is between 5 and 10 percent. Web sites with a density of keywords above 10 percent are likely to be penalized by search engines.

Using Images with Web Page Content

The use of images and visual impact is necessary in order to seize the attention of site visitors. You must gain their attention immediately, and the creative use of images is one of the best ways to do that. Once you do so, your content should provide them with the information they are seeking. Keep in mind that the content is what is most important. Unlike window shopping, visual appeal of a Web site will not garner attention; someone must be searching on keywords to find your Web site. But the images you use will complement your content and provide a balanced presentation of your Web site. Images should be used strictly to enhance your content.

Chapter 7

WEB SITE GRAPHICS

The saying "A picture is worth a thousand words" still holds true in this digital age. When used properly, pictures and images are able to convey ideas and concepts in ways that words cannot. But they can just as easily become a distraction — and an eyesore. The use of images in the right places on a Web site can enhance the user experience and drive more traffic to your Web site through word-of-mouth advertising, as well as search engines. But you must ensure that your images do not detract from your keyword-rich Web page content.

Images are one of the main details that set a Web site apart from other sites dealing with the same topic. They can make the Web experience more desirable beyond text-only material. Images can define the character of a Web site at first look. Excessive use of images characterizes a page as a hobbyist or entertainment page, whereas reserved use of images is usually correlated with information and news-related sites. Images can be used for representations of data in forms such as graphs and charts, without having to script the necessary code to parse and display such information dynamically. They can be used to set the tone of an article through pictures and photographs, and can also be used to enhance the style of a Web site through advanced graphics techniques that mimic a three-dimensional look or create effects of reflection. The importance of graphics and images on the Web is undeniable.

In order to learn how to incorporate images into your Web site, it is essential to have a firm understanding of several fundamental aspects of graphics and images. This chapter will cover the basics of using free graphics and editing programs to create images, will provide an in-depth look at two commercial photo-editing applications, and will also explore the similarities and differences among different image formats.

Images and graphics are key components to Web site design. You must balance text with graphics and white space; you do not want to drown out your written content with too many pictures, graphics, or clipart. Most Webmasters believe the rule of thumb is to use no more than three pictures or graphics on any given page, and resize them to no more than 72 DPI, or dots per inch, to ensure they load quickly. Balance and space images so the written content is clearly visible on the page, which allows your visitors the opportunity to begin reading your content as the pictures load. Be cautious with the sizing of your fonts — too large a font is not professional and is distracting; too small, and it cannot be easily read.

Images, graphics, and pictures provide an added value to your site, but if there are too many, they can also detract from your site and make it look less professional. Clipart should be used with extreme caution because it tends to make your site look amateurish in nature. Most of the clipart and graphics available for free download are low-quality. One of the best Web site investments you can make is to obtain royalty-free stock photos. These can add a touch of class to your Web pages and are absolutely free. They provide a visual center of interest on an otherwise plain Web page and can add spice and color.

Use CSS when possible to control font size, color, and layout. External style sheets are typically used for this purpose because they control the entire site. The style sheet is actually a file on your Web server that stores all your CSS preferences. You embed HTML code into each Web page, and your style sheet is applied when the page is loaded in the browser. You can also use internal style sheets, which control only the page they are on; this is useful if you need one page to function or appear differently than the others.

Image File Formats

The three main formats of images seen on the Web are JPEG, PNG, and GIF. TIFF and BMP are other familiar formats. Although they might all look the same at first glance, each has its own advantages and disadvantages.

JPEG stands for Joint Photographic Experts Group, the committee that created the standard. Its most common file extensions are .JPG or .JPEG. This is one of the most popular graphic formats on the Web because it is usually the default output format for most cameras and other imaging devices. However, default and most popular does not always mean the best. Certain versions of JPEG use an interlaced, progressive loading style. The rough outline of the image is displayed first before the details slowly start filling in. The difference is almost unnoticeable for smaller images, but on larger JPEG images viewed through slow connections, you can see the image slowly being formed as it loads. The advantage of this is that the user can view a low-quality, but full, version of the image before the high-quality version of the image loads. This is contrary to the linear loading style used by PNGs and other formats, where the image is loaded line by line, pixel by pixel, in its full quality.

One disadvantage of JPEGs are that they do not support an alpha component, so this format can only be used for full-size images without any transparency. This is one of the main reasons why JPEGs are not often used in features like menus and navigation bars that use irregular shapes like round edges or circles with transparent backgrounds. JPEGs can be compressed to your bandwidth needs, though this is at the cost of quality. Quality also varies based upon the system because some browsers take shortcuts to decompress the file faster. The lossy compression is one of the main problems with JPEG. It is infamous for leaving behind artifacts. You can notice the JPEG artifacts by comparing the original and the compressed version of the file and looking for blocks of color and loss of minor details.

Portable Network Graphics, or PNGs, are a newer file type with support for many features. They stand apart from JPGs in the fact that they have an alpha channel, allowing transparency in PNG images. They also support indexing options that allow you to reduce the file size of an image by narrowing down the number of colors used in the image pallet. PNGs also differ from JPEGs in that they have support for loss-less compression, which preserves the original quality of the image. The advanced preprocessing techniques this format utilizes for compressing files come at the minor cost of speed. It also comes with a gamma channel to adjust the brightness of the image. The main highlight of this format is its extremely efficient compression. So if you are looking for a small file size that is light on the bandwidth without any loss of quality, then PNG is your format.

The Tagged Image File Format (TIFF) is a universally accepted file format for images compatible with most Window, Mac, and UNIX™ operating systems. TIFF images incorporate a loss-less compression, giving you small file sizes without loss of any quality. This is an important factor to consider when storing any quality-sensitive images. Compression always comes at the cost of speed in opening and saving files. Although the difference is minute with modern processors, the speed might be a factor to consider for images and files that need to be repeatedly opened or saved. TIFF files are used mainly for the purpose of printing and archiving.

Bitmap, or BMP, is another common file format. Bitmaps are usually uncompressed, leaving their file sizes much larger than equivalent PNG or JPEG files. There are multiple versions of BMP available, including a 32-bit version supporting an alpha channel for transparency. BMP files can be manually compressed into a fraction of their original size using free compression programs such as 7-Zip.

GIF images are one of the original image formats of the Web, and they are usually used for animations. Their use is limited because GIF images limit your pallet to 256 colors. Because of this, gradients and other shades are often hard to achieve within the limits of GIF, unless it is used for small images, such as logos. Programs such as GIMP, the GNU Image Manipulation Program, can allow you to draw your graphics in full color and then reduce the pallet down to the essential 256 colors. This often results in grainy pictures. The main advantage of GIFs is that they offer a simple alternative to bandwidth-intensive video. GIF files also support JPEG-like interlacing options that allow a rough image to be downloaded before the full detail image. This is especially useful for users with a slow Internet connection. The format also uses a lossless compression technique to compress the images into a smaller file size.

SVGs are Scalable Vector Graphics files. Unlike JPEG or PNG files, SVG files store information as vectors. This allows you scale the image indefinitely without losing any of the quality of the image. This makes it an optimal file type for logos and other images that are repeatedly resized, as resizing often causes blocky pixelization with most other file types. The features of SVGs are limited when it comes to more advanced enhancements, so consider saving a basic outline of your images as an SVG, then doing the final touch-up on it and saving it as a high-resolution JPG or PNG.

Images and HTML

The way an image is incorporated into a page is important when it comes to SEO, usability, and accessibility. The following is an example of how to embed an image into an HTML document. Open Notepad or another HTML editor and create the following Web page:

```
<head>
<body>
<img src="Images\SampleImage.png"></img>
</body>
</head>
```

Save it to your desktop or local folder. In the same location, create an "Images" folder and place a sample image in the folder from your system. You can edit the **src** attribute of the image to point to your particular image. It is also possible to add in an image without the end tag **</img>** by using this format:

```
<head>
<body>
<img src="Images\SampleImage.png"/>
</body>
</head>
```

Run the sample Web page file in a Web browser to see the output. The code displays the image **SampleImage.png** from the Images folder in the local directory. The default position of the image is at the top left corner. You can move the image around the screen by doing this:

```
<head>
<body>
<div style="position:absolute;left:40px;top:20px;">
<img src="Images\3.png"></img></div>
</body>
</head>
```

The line **<div style="position:absolute;left:40px;top:20px;">...</div>** moves the image 40 pixels right and 20 pixels down. You can also align text as top, bottom, middle, left, or right by doing this:

<div style="align:center;position:absolute;left:20px;top:350px;">

It is possible to add borders to images by using the border attribute with the number of pixels as the parameter:

```
<img src="Images\3.png" border="10">
```

If you want to set an image as the background of a page, just add the background attribute linking to the background image to the **<body>** tag:

```
<html>
<body background="Images\background.jpg">
</body>
</html>
```

Although it is recommended that you do the formatting for images beforehand, it is sometimes necessary to do basic adjustments to the image while it is being displayed. You can adjust various properties of an image such as its source, width, height, and border though these lines:

```
<img src= "Images/sampleImage.png" width="1024" height="768"
hspace="0" vspace="0"></img>
```

The **width="1024" and height="768"** attributes resize the image to 1024 x 768 pixels. Keep in mind that it can sometimes reduce the quality of the image if the original ratio is different from the new one. The **hspace** and **vspace** options adjust the vertical and horizontal spaces around the image. Setting these to 0 will align it to top corner of the page. Adjusting this value is also a way to move the image around the page without relying on the **<div>...</div>** tag.

Search Engine Optimization & Images

Naming your image properly will help optimize it for search engines, allowing users to easily find the image. The mouseover-text description, or tooltip, of an image is another factor to consider for SEO. Properly tagging images drives search engine traffic to your Web site. Proper tagging will also aid users with images disabled to navigate the site without trouble. Try the following code without having **"SampleImage.png"** in the local directory:

```
<img src="SampleImage.png" alt="Sample Image" />
```

The Web page will display a blank square with the image not found symbol and the text from the **<alt>** tag. The **<alt>** tag still shows up whether or not the image is there. This adds an extra layer of protection to your Web page because it is still usable even without the images. The **<alt>** tag will also make your Web site more accessible to users with disabilities because it is compatible with most assistive software such as Microsoft Narrator. You can further improve accessibility while optimizing for search engines like Google and Yahoo! by using "D" links and **longdesc.**

```
<img src="SampleImage.png" alt="A sample image showing the use
of HTML attributes" longdesc="sampleImageDescription.htm"><a
href="sampleImageDescription.htm" title="Sample Image">D</a>
```

The page that the **longdesc** points to can contain a further description of the image, allowing you to describe the image in higher detail while squeezing in a few more keywords related to the image. A sample description could look something like this:

"The image shows a sample image used commonly to demonstrate sample features. The sample image is ambiguous in nature. The blank background blends in nicely with the blank foreground. It also uses the PNG format, referring to another part of the article. The image shows how simple tags can be decorated to make it more accessible while also optimizing it for search engines."

The **<alt>** tag can contain a basic description of the image with a few keywords, while the longdesc should either be a longer sentence or should link to a better description of the image. One of the main differences between **<alt>** and longdesc is that the description in the **<alt>** tag is visible when you mouse over the image, while the description in longdesc is not. Do not, however, stuff either of the descriptions with keywords. Modern search engines use spam filters that look for the excessive use of catch phrases without any real content. The **\<alt\>** and the longdesc should be a textual replacement for the image without being simply a list of tags. Also note that decorative eye candy is usually not tagged. This is to help keep the HTML page simple and clean without any unnecessary information. Ask yourself if the speed and bandwidth costs are worth the extra tag.

Another factor that search engines consider is the file type. JPEGs are often associated with photographs, while GIFs are assumed to be site graphics. Make sure to choose the right file type so that your images are categorized correctly. Using just one copy of an image and then referencing it consistently throughout your Web site could help its page ranking in search engines like Google. PageRank is Google's technique for determining the relative value of a page or a file based upon the number of inbound and outbound links. It is often referred to as the probability of a user randomly clicking links reaching a particular Web page. PageRank, like most modern search algorithms, is based on the quality as well as the quantity of links. This is one reason why you should always license your images correctly so as to protect them from being leeched to other sites. External sites can, however, link to them. This improves your page rank while protecting your Web property.

Copyrights and Licenses

When using content from other sites, always give proper citation. A simple link with credit to the photographer and a short note about the license is usually enough, but check with the original author to see if they have any special preferences. Proper citation in accepted formats such as that of the Modern Language Association (MLA) is another one of the factors that search engines consider. This is one reason why Wikipedia® pages often get a high page rank.

You should always host all important image files on your own server. Files hosted on free image hosting servers are convenient for larger, more bandwidth-intensive elements of the site, but should not be used for main parts of the site such as navigation and logos, as many of these sites are prone to downtime and file loss. Image leeching is considered bad manners in the world of Web development. Never use an image from another Web site without the expressed written permission of the Web site owner to make sure you are not violating any copyright laws. There have been instances in which the original image owner replaced the images with "Don't Leech" signs. The signs can appear on the leechers' Web sites without their knowledge because the file link is still the same. This could cause a tarnished reputation of the Web site in question because hundreds of users might notice the signs before the site developer does.

Hosting images on your own server will take the element of risk and surprise away from all important content crucial to your Web site. You can find many free images online that are released under free and open licenses. Look for images marked "copyleft" or those released under the Creative Commons License. Be sure to read the license carefully to make sure you comply with the requirements listed before using the image for your Web site. If you cannot find what you are looking for, consider using one of the following programs to create new and original graphics for your Web site.

Free Graphics Editing Software

GIMP (GNU Image Manipulation Program) is a widely used graphics editing program. It is a free, open-source graphics program released under the GNU General Public License (GPL). Its functionality is similar to Photoshop in the sense that its main focus is to edit and enhance photos and other pictures. It supports all of the basic features such as cropping, color filtering, brightness and contrast, hue and saturation, and color modes. It also comes with many filters and plug-ins for the more advanced editing requirements. These include blur, sharpen, oilify, edge detect, lens flare, fractal rendering, solid noise, plasma, ripples, and waves. Additional plug-ins can be created or downloaded from the official GIMP Web site. GIMP allows you to open and save your files in a variety of file formats.

Note that you can work with Photoshop files in GIMP because it supports .PSD, the Photoshop file format. One disadvantage is that, like Photoshop, GIMP can sometimes be very resource heavy. If you plan to add more plug-ins and external features to do more advanced editing, make sure you have a system that can support the RAM and processing needs of GIMP. The support for brushes, patterns, and add-ons combined with a myriad of built-in features make GIMP a serious alternative for Adobe Photoshop. You can download the latest version of GIMP for free from **www.gimp. org**. It is also possible to download past versions of GIMP if the current version is not working for you. If you are a programmer, the source code is also available at the site.

Microsoft Paint, also known as MS® Paint, is the built-in graphics program for Windows®. Although it comes with the bare minimum in features, it is an easy-to-use, always-at-hand option for simple tasks. The main focus of Paint is pixel-based drawing. It will take a lot more work to get the same effects from Photoshop or GIMP in Paint, as almost all of the work done by filters in GIMP must be done manually in Paint. Paint does allow you to switch between three modes of painting: pencil, brush, and airbrush. You can zoom in and work on individual regions of the picture in detail, then zoom out for a higher-quality finished product. There are tools to create ovals, rectangles, polygons, straight lines, and curvy lines. If you are running a Windows system, MS Paint should already be on your system. Go to **Start > Run >** and type in "MS Paint." It should launch the Paint program.

Inkscape® is a vector graphics editor. It is used to create SVG files. It is the perfect tool for creating buttons, logos, and other simple graphics in a snap. You can also create a custom character set to use as a font for your site in Inkscape. The Calligraphy Tool is perfect for such tasks. If your mouse handling is not so great, draw rough outlines in Inkscape, then use the Node Tool to edit it to your liking. Because SVG files are actually just XML files, it is actually possible to edit SVG files with any text editor. That, however, can be very tedious. Inkscape is an easy-to-use program that allows you create amazing artwork using simple shapes and tools. Inkscape can be downloaded for free from **www.inkscape.org**. You can take a look at the screen shots and the documentation available on the Web site to learn more about all of the smaller details of the programs.

Paint.NET is another graphics program offering features similar to GIMP and Inkscape. It comes with the simplicity of MS Paint, the usability of Inkscape, and some of the advanced features of GIMP. Its main use, like GIMP, is photo manipulation, and it supports all of the popular file formats. The two programs are almost exactly same in many aspects, but the interface of Paint.NET is different than GIMP in the sense that it only displays the basic tools and features. It offers features similar to, but better than, regular MS Paint, but without the high-tech features of GIMP. You can download Paint.NET at **www.getpaint.net**.

The decision of picking which of these four free programs to download and use is a simple matter of time, place, occasion, and personal taste. Each offers unique features and capabilities that, when combined, can allow you to create eye-catching graphics without the cost of expensive and bloated software like Photoshop. All of these programs are being actively developed at their corresponding sites, so expect bigger and better features to be added to the bundles in the future.

Commercial Graphics Editing Software

Adobe Photoshop is the most popular graphics editing software on the market. It is geared toward professionals and is incredibly complex and very expensive. However, it stands out among the competition for its incredible depth of features, functionality, and power. It is the best graphics editing software on the market. A great review of Adobe Photoshop CS4 is available here: **www.pcworld.com/reviews/product/35706/review/photoshop_cs4.html**.

Corel Paint Shop Pro Photo X2 is a much cheaper, yet still feature-rich, alternative to Adobe Photoshop. The bottom line is that it is an excellent program that will meet the needs of most graphics challenges and is not overly complicated to learn. Corel Paint Shop Pro Photo X2 balances user-friendly design with powerful features at a reasonable cost. A great review of Corel Paint Shop Pro Photo X2 is available here: **www.pcworld.com/ reviews/product/30516/review/paint_shop_pro_photo_x2.html**.

Logos and Banners

Logos and banners are another aspect of Web design that is intertwined with graphics and animation. Creating a logo requires a great amount of patience and care. Logos tend to become the "face" of a company. They set the mood of a Web site. Your logo should stand out and be easily recognizable. It is often a good practice to integrate the name of the company into the logo itself, like with the logos of Google and Coca-Cola®. The color scheme of the logo usually tends to become the color scheme of the entire Web site. This consistency is necessary in order to preserve the flow of the site. You should also consider other places the logo might appear — e-mails, business cards, and page-headers — when you are designing it. Start brainstorming by thinking about how you would explain your Web site to a stranger. Write a few sentences or a paragraph about it. Then try to express that same idea on paper by sketching out a few pictures. Although there is no real right way to do this, ask others for their opinion when designing the logo. The logo is often what represents the site all over the Web in advertisements and other banners.

There are plenty of options for creating an outstanding logo. You can create it yourself or contract it out to a graphics design professional. There are also many software packages designed to help you create them yourself, such as AAA Logo. AAA Logo, found at **www.aaa-logo.com**, is one company that allows you to download the latest trial version of the software. Although this is not free software, AAA Logo is reasonably priced and provides the user with more than 8,000 unique logo objects and logo templates that can help you build your own logos, business cards, banners, headers, and icons for your site. This software allows you to create nearly any graphic you might need for your business or personal use. AAA Logo offers industry-specific logos in its pre-built templates, including technology, finance, health care, general business and retail, education and training, travel and tourism, organizations, sports and fitness, and food and beverage.

Another revenue stream you may consider is building logos for others and charging them a reasonable fee. If you purchase AAA Logos 2008, you can build and design logos to sell to other clients, and there is no limit on how many you can sell or create. There are also links on the home page of this site that explain how to print and export high-resolution 300- to 600-DPI logos for high-quality printing. There are many other such programs available on the Web — just Google the keywords "free Web logos" or "logo design companies," and dozens of other Web sites will appear in the search engine results. Take your time to research at least three or four of them before choosing which one you want to use.

Web site banners and advertisements are often the first impression a Web site has on a potential visitor. The two most common sizes for banners are 728 x 90 pixels and 468 x 60 pixels. Banners and advertisements must be interesting enough to capture the audience's attention. It is often a good strategy to ask a question or offer a sneak preview of the full content available at the Web site though headlines or catchy topic titles. This is enough to intrigue the audience, but not enough to satisfy its curiosity. Flashy, distracting advertisements are associated with scams and spyware more often than not, so their effectiveness has decreased dramatically. It is better to attract new users through content than through manipulation because it ensures that they will keep coming back.

Colors and Themes

When picking a color scheme, keep the feeling you want to create for the Web site in mind. Warm colors such as red, orange, and yellow can represent passion and energy, while cool colors like blue, green, and violet are used to create a sense of peace and serenity. Neutral colors like gray and brown are likewise neutral. Colors have meaning and emotions tied to them just like words and images. Look for colors that complement each other to give your Web site a nice flow.

The choice of colors is usually a personal one, as everyone has his or her own individual preferences regarding color. However, there are some basic rules that seem to be universal. Primary colors like red, yellow, and blue tend to emphasize simplicity as well as speed. Secondary colors are created by mixing two primary colors together. These include green, orange, and purple. Tertiary colors can be created by mixing secondary and primary colors together. When choosing the colors, first decide what parts of your Web site you want to stand out and what parts should flow. Use colors that are adjacent to each other to create a sense of consistency to your Web site. Use colors that are opposite of each other in the color wheel to highlight content by making it stand out. Over-contrasting everything could become an eyesore, so be picky in choosing what to emphasize.

Shades of gray are created when the red, green, and blue values are all the same (Ex: 127, 127, 127). Bright neon colors are created when one value is a lot higher than the two others (Ex: Neon Green: 0, 255, 0). Excessive use of neon colors is often considered an eye sore. Softer colors are created when the colors are closer together (Ex: 255, 200, 150). These should be used mainly for backgrounds and other large, solid-colored spaces. The colors on the foreground of the page should be at the opposite end of the color wheel so they are easily visible against the background. Red text on a red colored background is unreadable, while green or blue text can be easily read on the same page. Look around at other Web sites to find complementary images and colors.

Accessibility for vision-impaired users is another aspect to keep in mind when choosing a color scheme. While red text on a green background (or vice versa) stands out easily, it can sometimes be hard to read due to excessive contrast. To fix this problem, simply adjust the lightness of the colors so that the foreground is darker and the background is lighter. Easy readability is especially a concern if your Web site is for an elderly audience.

Typography

Typography is another factor to consider when designing a Web page. There are many free fonts available online. You can design a character set for personal use in Inkscape or GIMP. Choosing the right fonts and using them in the right places can really add to the style of a page. Be creative with titles, but be sure to choose a simple and easily readable font for the main text of the page. Text is as much a part of a Web site as images and should be cared for with just as much attention.

The use of typography can help to easily accent a site. It can add to the style of a site and make it stand out from other sites, just like images and colors. Choose fonts based upon the content you are focusing on. Some common fonts follow the themes of handwritten, calligraphy, graffiti, and mechanical writing. The choice of font can help set the mood and tone for the content.

The choice of font size is another important aspect of typography. Size 24 is commonly accepted as a good size for headlines, and size 12 is common for regular text. Keep your audience in mind when choosing the font size. Font sizes should be relative. If your main text is going to be in a bigger text, then the headline must be much larger also. The standard ratio between the body text and the title text is two to three times larger. Titles that are too large will attract attention, but it will seem unprofessional in nature. This is similar to the difference between tabloid headlines and newspaper headlines. If you want your content to be taken seriously, it must be presented seriously. Finally, always follow the basic rules of grammar and sentence and page structure. Never write in all caps, as it makes your writing seem as if it is aggressively screaming out the message.

Images Tips and Tricks

When deciding the size and ratio of images, use the "golden ratio," also known as phi. Phi is an irrational number often rounded off to 1.618. It is found in many places in nature and is considered the secret formula for beauty. Two successive numbers in the Fibonacci sequence create approximately this ratio. The Fibonacci sequence is a sequence of numbers where the next number is the sum of the two previous numbers. The first few lines of the sequence are 1, 1, 2, 3, 5, 8, 13, 21, 34, 55 ...

The eyes of visitors often tend to travel to four critical points that are all one-third of the way from the edges of the page. Place advertisements or other important content in these regions to gain maximum visibility. This rule also applies to the composition of an image. Place the important subjects of the image at these points to make them more noticeable at first glance.

Titles and images are easily noticeable to the user when the site first loads. A quick look at a picture should be able to explain the basic content of a page while leaving the visitor pondering a few questions. Images and graphics on a Web site should complement the text, not overpower it. You can say much more with an image than with a paragraph of text. Clear images give the reader a preview of the topic. They should persuade the reader to take the time to read the whole page. A page full of text can seem like an impenetrable wall of information. Adding a few images through an article or a blog post will soften the display. One good practice is to have a large title image related to the topic, and then add smaller images corresponding to each sub-topic in the post.

Simple-but-usable is always better than stylish but complex when it comes to Web sites. Take a look at the Google home page. The clean user interface allows even first-time users to navigate the site and access its features without any trouble. Simplicity also helps with loading time and bandwidth because there is less data to be sent and received. It reduces the strain on the user as well as the Web developer or Web host. Users will always prefer sites that are easy to use over the more complex alternatives. Simplicity sells.

Always have a backup copy of your Web site that you can revert to in case of an emergency. Make copies every month, week, or even every day based upon the frequency of change to your site. You can buy external hard drives or store files online for added security. Images tend to take up much room, so always compress images into Zip files for storage purposes. Name the files by content or by date of backup. You can choose to configure your server to automatically back up based on a schedule, if manual backup is too much of a hassle. Consider collaborating with other similar sites in order to gain more traffic. Referencing each other would help your users find more information. If the users are happy, they will keep coming back.

Think from the perspective of the Web site user. What would they want from your site? What information are they looking for? The content of the Web site should be focused around this topic. All of the images, graphics, and design elements of the site should be focused around the content.

As a general rule of thumb, images should be as small as possible to allow for faster load time of Web pages. Images should be saved at a resolution of 72 DPI, and image file sizes should be no larger than 20KB. Pixels are used to measure the height and width of an image file, and they are sized in kilobytes (KB) or megabytes (MB). If you have large image files on your site, you are driving away Web site visitors. Use <alt> tags for accessibility purposes and SEO.

How Palettes Help —
by Erin Pheil

Every so often, you might come across a Web site that just does not "feel" right. Something is off. The site does not feel polished, professional, or thought-out, but it is not immediately clear why.

Often these sites simply suffer from what we might affectionately call "palette malfunctions." Without a doubt, poor use of color is one of the main giveaways that an amateur designed a Web site. A professional Web designer will almost always have a color palette in mind before designing a site, and will therefore be less likely to use clashing or inappropriate colors.

Just as people should first determine a clear purpose for their Web site before getting to work, they should also determine their site's color palettes prior to starting in on their Web site's design. Fortunately, a wide assortment of online tools makes choosing color palettes a breeze. Adobe's Kuler™ is one such palette tool.

Prior to using an online tool such as Kuler, first think about a general color direction that would be appropriate for your site. If you own a spa, the use of soft, muted colors can help you achieve a calming effect on your site. If you own a forestry or tree services company, the use of green and/or earthy hues will let visitors quickly know they have arrived at the right site, whereas the use of, say, lime green and neon pink would likely confuse your site visitors and cause them to question your seriousness and professionalism.

Once you have brainstormed a few ideas about potential colors for your site, head on over to **http://kuler.adobe.com**. Type keywords from your ideas into the search box and begin browsing through potential color combinations. Try synonyms and alternative variations of your words, such as "earth," "earthy," "browns," or "natural."

Explore the site, check out other palette tools online, and keep looking until you find a palette that feels right for your site. Once you have chosen your palette, you will find that the color decisions you run into when designing your site — such as choosing link colors or determining which shade to use as your site's background — no longer seem intimidating or frustrating.

If you stick to your palette and ignore the temptations to introduce unrelated colors into your designs, your final Web site design will look more polished, more together, and more professional than those sites where colors were simply added haphazardly as the design evolved.

Erin Pheil is the founder of Timeforcake Creative Media, Inc., a boutique Web and graphic design company that specializes in creative, effective Web site and graphic design projects. You can learn more about Erin and Timeforcake at ***www.timeforcake.com***.

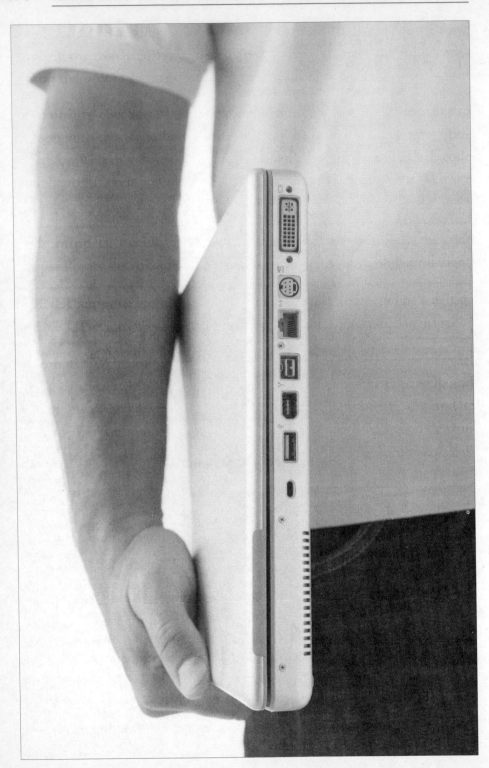

Chapter 8

WEB PAGE FORMATS, JAVASCRIPT, AND CASCADING STYLE SHEETS

The Web has evolved, and Web design has evolved with it. While .HTM or .HTML are the most common Web page types, there are a variety of others. All .HTML pages are static in nature, meaning the content displayed on the page will only change when it is updated by the Web site owner and it does not interact with a database or perform any other functions. This is not to say that .HTML pages cannot do many things; standard .HTML pages can be used for e-commerce and most Web online functions. A .SHTML page is a type of page that utilizes SSI; therefore, these pages are not static. SSI is a language used to create pages with dynamically generated content. ASP is similar, based on a Microsoft technology that contains Visual Basic (VB) code that the Web server executes when the page is loaded. This means the Web page interacts with databases and then lets you view and manipulate data from the Web browser. Java Server Pages, or .JSP, work in a similar fashion, but Java code is used instead of VB.

Another Web page format used to create dynamically generated Web pages is .PHP. This format is useful if you need to embed dynamic text into static HTML text and is primarily for integrating your Web site with a database. PHP is a scripting language similar to JavaScript, Java, and Perl™, but it is a server-side scripting language. The main difference is that the "work" or computing is done on the server and dynamically generated in Web pages in the browser. JavaScript and Java run on the client, meaning your computer does the work when the Web page is loaded. Server-side processing is typically faster and more powerful than client-side processing. PHP is commonly run on Linux Web servers. Perl, or .PL, is another scripting language that has all the same abilities as most other scripting languages, but is much easier to learn and use. Perl can run on Windows servers as well as Linux. However, it runs on the client side, so when a Perl script is loaded in a browser, it must be run on the fly, potentially slowing down the Web site experience slightly. The .CGI extension is a standard for interfacing external applications with Web servers and is yet another way to generate Web pages dynamically and interact with databases. There are many other formats, but for the purposes of this book, the chapter will concentrate on HTML code with JavaScript and CSS.

JavaScript

JavaScript is the most common scripting language in use on the Web. JavaScript is fairly easy to learn, and it adds functionality to Web page form. The best thing about JavaScript is there are many pre-written JavaScript codes for any conceivable need readily available on the Web. Some great JavaScript resources are **http://javascript.Internet.com, www.javascript-kit.com,** and **www.codelifter.com/main/javascript/index.html**.

- JavaScript is an object-oriented scripting language. It will enable the Web pages created to interact with your users. A response is always given by the Web pages to the action of the users.

- JavaScript is a programming language that can give your Web page dynamic abilities.

- JavaScript is a client-side programming language, which means it is browser-based and runs when the Web page is loaded by the browser.

- JavaScript is an interpreted programming language. Once the user's Web browser has downloaded the contents of a Web page, it can create a dynamic, interactive Web page for your users.

There may be confusion that Java and JavaScript are one and the same, but they are totally different languages; the only resemblance is in name. Both are client-side languages, and both follow object-oriented concepts, but Java is a complied language, whereas JavaScript is an interpreted language. A license is not needed in order to use JavaScript.

What is JavaScript?

- JavaScript is a programming language. It will make your Web site more interactive and dynamic.

- JavaScript is also a scripting language.

- JavaScript is a language that is added to HTML code of a Web page; it is not a stand-alone language.

- No groundwork compilation is needed in order to execute JavaScript.

- In JavaScript, a **<script>** tag is supplemented to each and every HTML command.

- JavaScript is platform-independent. It also supports cross-browser usage. It is for this reason that JavaScript became so popular.

- If JavaScript is the language attribute, then the commands that come within the **<script>** tag will try to execute.

- JavaScript has an extensive number of uses.

- You do not have to install any additional software to create and write JavaScript. The various text editors that come along with Windows, such as Notepad, are more than enough.

Why should you use JavaScript?

If you want to add effects or advanced form controls, JavaScript is the best way to do this. JavaScript is free, easy to use, and loads quickly in a browser. HTML is quite easy to learn, but HTML is not like JavaScript. HTML is static by nature, while JavaScript can make your pages come to life. There are a number of other programming languages that can make your Web pages interactive, such as Java, but JavaScript is the favorite of the Web design community. Your Web site should be able to process information and should be dynamic. If you combine JavaScript and CSS, you have successfully created DHTML. This is similar to HTML, but with DHTML, you can enable the movement of some parts of your Web page around the page. JavaScript is also a powerful tool for validating and checking contents of Web forms.

Many Web masters use JavaScript because it interacts well with all major Internet browsers. In most instances, those who build Web sites today are not programmers. They are normal people just like you, who might try to use JavaScript as a method of adding dynamic and interactive features to their pages. You can do a multitude of things with JavaScript, such as improving page design, validating forms before they are loaded on the server, detecting a wide array of browsers, and creating cookies. Cookies in the Internet sense allow you to store and retrieve information from your client's computer, which in turn allows a faster loading speed the next time that client visits your site. There are several different types of cookies. One example is a name cookie that requires your clients to sign in with their name, which is then visible when they return to your site. Another example is a password cookie, which is retrieved when your client returns and types in his or her password to enter your site or specific portion of the site, like a secured shopping area. Most people use their security software to scan and delete potentially hazardous cookies from their computers, but if the threat is low or nonexistent, the software normally recommends ignoring it during a scan.

One of the key elements to using JavaScript is to insert the **<script>** tag within the HTML coding on your page. For example, if you want to create a page with JavaScript embedded inside the HTML code, it would look something like this:

```
<html>
<body>
<script type="text/javascript">
document.write("How to Build a Web Site!");
</script>
</body>
</html>
```

In this example, the JavaScript begins after the **<html>** and **<body>** tags; the script tag **<script type="text/javascript">** tells the HTML page that the next portion is in JavaScript. The next portion of the script is **document.write("How To Build A Web Site!");** this is a command that tells the script what will show on the actual Web page. The closing tag **</script>** shows that this is the end of the JavaScript for this portion of the page. On your Web page, all you would see is the text "How to Build a Web Site!" This does not exactly show you the power of JavaScript, but you can at least understand how it functions. Often, JavaScript must be put in the **<head>** of a Web page so it loads before the **<body>** page content.

If you happen to have a browser that does support JavaScript, or if you want to be prepared for the visitors to your site who may not have the JavaScript capability, it is advisable to use the HTML tag **<!--** prior to the JavaScript statement to hide it, then use **-->** after the last JavaScript statement to indicate the ending. If you do not use these codes, the JavaScript will appear on the page as content. Most major browsers fully support JavaScript, but it can be disabled. You can also place JavaScript in the **<head>** and **<body>** sections of your page by using the following:

```
<html>
<head>
<script type="text/javascript">
document.write("How to Build a Web Site!");
</script>
</head>
<body>
<script type="text/javascript">
```

```
document.write("A guide for both personal and business use.");
</script>
</body>
</html>
```

Another example of using JavaScript might include running the same script on multiple pages of your site, which can be accomplished by writing the script in an external file and saving it with a .JS file extension. For a detailed explanation and tutorial on how to use external files and additional in-depth instructions on using JavaScript, visit the W3C Web site and walk through each step to get a feel for how it works. This Web site offers you the opportunity to try each code as you proceed through the steps.

In JavaScript, the navigator object contains information about a visitor's browser, such as the version of the browser, so your script will be executed correctly. You can go to the W3C Web site for a tutorial on how to use the navigator object, or go to **www.javascript.com**, where you can find additional options. Webweaver, at **www.Webweaver.nu/scripts.shtml**, provides free and fee-based scripts and applets you can use on your site, as well as design tools, hosting, Web site promotion, and clipart.

Here are a few more samples of JavaScript. While the following codes may look like HTML, they are not.

Mouseover effects are a type of code used to display a message in the status area of the Web browser when a mouse moves over a hypertext link:

```
<a href="mypage.html"
onMouseOver="window.status='The message'; return true"
onMouseOut="window.status=''; return true">
the text of the link</a>
```

This code is used to detect the visitor's browser and its version:

```
<script type="text/javascript">
var browser=navigator.appName;
var b_version=navigator.appVersion;
```

```
var version=parseFloat(b_version);
document.write("Browser name: "+ browser);
document.write("<br />");
document.write("Browser version: "+ version);
</script>
```

Output for this piece of code will look like this:

Browser name: Internet Explorer

Browser version: 8

This code is used for navigation with a popup menu within a form on a Web page:

```
<html>
  <head>
    <title>Pop-up Menu</title>
  </head>
  <body bcolor=white>
    <p>Where do you want to go?</p>
    <form>
    <select
      onChange="if (this.selectedIndex> 0)
window.location.href=this.options[this.selectedIndex].value">
      <option>Pick an area
      <option value="products.html">Products
      <option value="pricing.html">Pricing
      <option value="press.html">Press
    </select>
    </form>
  </body>
</html>
```

Cascading Style Sheets

Maintaining the format and appearance of Web pages has been a challenge for years. With CSS, you can now control an entire Web site's appearance and organization. Style sheets define how HTML elements are to be displayed in the browser, and CSS is now widely used by Web site developers.

There are three parts to CSS: the style, the placement, and the cascading effect. Styles are normally saved in external .CSS files that are stored on the Web server. However, you can also embed .CSS directly into individual Web pages. External style sheets enable you to change the appearance and layout of all the pages of a Web site by simply editing your style sheet. HTML coding and CSS can be used to create professional-looking borders, fonts, text alignment, and spacing.

CSS allows you to make changes to either one page or your entire Web site with a master list of fonts, colors, spacing, margins, and font sizes. These styles can be embedded inside your Web page or from an external page. With more advanced CSS techniques, you can control the layout of your pages without using tables or other HTML code. CSS allows faster and easier updates to your Web site because the coding is reduced, thus creating more efficient pages that require less bandwidth. This translates into cost savings for business owners. A CSS rule includes three primary elements, including the selector, the declaration (which consists of two parts), and the property, and it is critical to make sure the syntax of the command lines is correct to prevent errors.

The selector determines which HTML tag you are using, such as **<body>**, **<h1>**, or **<p>**. The declaration tells the browser what to do with the selected element, which is the property element that identifies font type, size, and color. The value causes the action that changes the font type, size, or color to the request made by the property. The declaration always contains brackets; the property must have a colon and ends with a semicolon. The correct way to write a CSS rule is as follows: **selector {property:value}**. An example for setting the font type and color would be: **h1 {color:blue; font-family:Arial,sans-serif;}**. This is done similarly with HTML, but the main difference between CSS and HTML is that in HTML you would have to code each page. In CSS, one simple code change, as shown previously, would change your entire Web site, or allow you to change it back if you do not like the look. CSS allows you to make changes quickly and efficiently while also offering you the freedom to experiment without the extreme hassle and loss of your time to change each page.

As with our earlier discussion surrounding HTML coding, be sure to use **Doctype** to tell the browser that your layout complies with the W3C standards and that you are using a transitional or looser page layout, which looks like this:

```
<!DOCTYPE html PUBLIC "-//w3c//DTD HTML 4.01 Transitional//EN">
<html>
<head>
```

As mentioned before, CSS can also be used in embedded style sheets, which means the style sheet is located between the **<head>...</head>** tags and the declarations are set between the **<style>...</style>** tags. Embedded style sheets connect only to the page you are working on; they cannot be used by another file like external style sheets. When using embedded style sheets in the second level of the CSS list of commands, site builders should keep in mind that these commands will supersede any commands used in the external style sheets. The next style of CSS is called inline style, which allows you to control the design of your site from one location or a set area of the Web page. It also gives you the freedom to control the font, font size, and color of an **<h1>** tag by using the following code:

```
<font-style="font-family:Arial,Helvetica,sans-serif;     font-size:22px;
color:red; text-decoration:underline;">
```

The next example illustrates how to use class styles, which allow you to create an independent style that is applicable to any HTML tag, written as such:

```
.headerfont {font-size:15px; font-family:Arial; color:red;}
```

This style requires a period before the selector, which in this case is **header-font**. Next, in the body of the HTML, you would add the following code:

```
<p class"headerfont">This is the Header</p>
```

There are no spaces or underscores in class names, and they must always begin with a letter.

The next examples will illustrate the ID styles used in CSS styles, which are similar to the class styles in that they create unique styles that are independent of the HTML tags. ID styles are used with JavaScript to identify unique objects on the screen. It is important to understand that you can only use an ID style once per page; they are best used to give an element or property a unique name or identity. The following example shows how ID styles look in coding:

```
#subheaderfont
{font-size:15px; font-family:Arial; color:red;}
```

When using an ID style, you would also put the following code into the HTML body:

```
<p class"headerfont">This is the Header</p>
```

It is a good idea to put the major structural elements of your site at the top of the style sheet. For example, the **<body>** element would be first, followed by the **<p>** styles, with the remaining styles in a logical order, such as alphabetically or by style type; you would also place the ID selectors ahead of class selectors. It is suggested that you add comments on external style sheets because this is a great way to search and quickly reference long lists of the style you are using. A comment line is identified by this code:

```
<!--add comment and close it like this -->
```

Web Site Templates

Web site templates are often debated and dismissed by professional designers. However, if you are a beginner and do not have the time, talent, and experience to create custom Web sites, templates are a viable option to use. They come with most every Web design application out there, including free design applications. These days, templates are created by professional designers and can eliminate much of the work creating your Web site. They can be bought or even found on the Web for free. With just a few mouse clicks, you can create a Web site from a template in Expression Web:

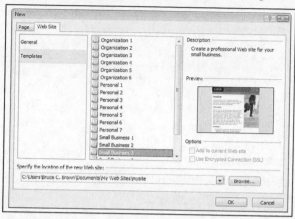

The Web site below was created in about 10 seconds with Expression Web and is ready to be customized. Expression Web creates a master template that protects the common areas of each page from being edited. This lets you create the navigation, heading, and logos in one master template and replicate them throughout all your pages with one click of the mouse. All you have to do is create the actual page content and images.

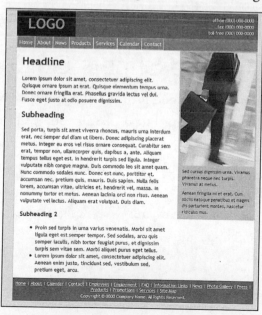

The example below illustrates the HTML code from this Web page. The highlighted areas are protected by your master template, and the rest are the regions you can edit and modify:

```
<!DOCTYPE html Public "-//W3C//DTD XHTML 1.0 Traditional//EN" "http://www.w3.org/TR/xhtml1-transitional.
dtd">
<html dir="ltr" xmlns="http://w3.org/1999/xhtml">

<!-- #BeginTemplate "master.dwt" -->

<head>
<meta content="text/html; charset=utf-8" http-equiv="Content-Type" />
<!-- #BeginEditable "doctitle" -->
<title>Home</title>
<!-- #EndEditable -->
<link href="styles/style3.css" media="screen" rel="stylesheet" title="CSS" type="text/css" />
</head>

<body>

<!-- Begin Container -->
<div id="container">
    <!-- Begin Masthead -->
    <div id="masthead">
        <img alt="logo" height="66" src="images/logo.gif" width="150" /><p>office (000)
        000-0000<br />
        fax (000) 000-0000<br />
        toll-free (000) 000-0000</p>
    </div>
    <!-- End Masthead -->
    <!-- Begin Navigation -->
    <div id="navigation">
        <ul>
            <li><a href="default.html">Home</a></li>
            <li><a href="about/about.htm">About</a></li>
            <li><a href="news/news.htm">News</a></li>
            <li><a href="products/products.htm">Products</a></li>
            <li><a href="services/services.htm">Services</a></li>
            <li><a href="calendar/calendar.htm">Calendar</a></li>
            <li><a href="contact/contact.htm">Contact</a></li>
        </ul>
    </div>
    <!-- End Navigation -->
    <!-- Begin Page Content -->
    <div id="page content">
        <!-- Begin Left Column -->
        <div id="column 1">
            <!-- #BeginEditable "content" -->
            <h1>Headline</h1>
            <p>Lorem ipsum dolor sit amet, consectetuer adipiscing elit. Quisque
            ornare ipsum at erat. Quisque elementum tempus urna. Donec ornare fringilla
            erat. Phasellus gravida lectus vel dui. Fusce eget justo at odio posuere
            dignissim.</p>
            <h2>Subheading</h2>
            <p>Sed porta, turpis sit amet viverra rhoncus, mauris urna interdum
            erat, nec semper dui diam ut libero. Donec adipiscing placerat metus.
            Integer eu eros vel risus ornare consequat. Curabitur sem erat, tempor
            non, ullamorper quis, dapibus a, ante. Aliquam tempus tellus eget est.
            In hendrerit turpis sed ligula. Integer vulputate nibh congue magna.
            Duis commodo leo sit amet quam. Nunc commodo sodales nunc. Donec est
            nunc, porttitor et, accumsan nec, pretium quis, mauris. Duis sapien.
            Nulla felis lorem, accumsan vitae, ultricies et, hendrerit vel, massa.
            In nonummy tortor et metus. Aenean lacinia orci non risus. Aenean vulputate
            vel lectus. Aliquam erat volutpat. Duis diam.</p>
            <h3>Subheading 2</h3>
            <ul>
                <li>Proin sed turpis in urna varius venenatis. Morbi sit amet ligula
                eget est semper tempor. Sed sodales, arcu quis semper iaculis, nibh
                tortor feugiat purus, et dignissim turpis sem vitae sem. Morbi aliquet
```

Cascading Style Sheets Guide

This comprehensive guide should give you the knowledge, tools, and understanding to successfully implement CSS in your Web site. This section is provided as a handy reference, but CSS can be a difficult concept to understand. CSS uses styles such as font, background, and color to manipulate the format or presentation of Web pages. You are much better off learning how to manage CSS in your Web design application than trying to create custom CSS by hand.

The most conventional among the types of style sheets is the external style sheet, which gives you the power to save a lot of work and can make your styling more flexible. What is the difference between CSS and HTML?

- HTML is designed as a common language and as a basis of the Web. By using hyperlinks, you can connect several or multiple pages together to make a Web site. HTML is used to structure text and multimedia documents, and to set up hypertext links between documents.

- CSS contains several additional codes to specify or format style elements such as fonts, images, positions, and colors.

Use of Cascading Style Sheets in a Web Page

CSS is merely a simple coding procedure used to control the format of a page using styles; you can use CSS to give yourself many options for creating, formatting, and designing your Web site.

CSS can be used for the following:

- **Coloring:** Examples are font coloring and background coloring. A quality CSS editor will provide you with many color choices.

- **Positioning:** Examples are image, text, and HTML tags positioned according to your liking. CSS positioning elements are powerful tools for Web page formatting because you can position anything anywhere on the Web page.

- **Sizing:** Examples are font and image sizing, with properties like dimensions, width, and height.

Benefits and Drawbacks to Cascading Style Sheets

Tremendous changes are rapidly occurring in terms of Web design, and many expectations and demands are being placed on Web developers. CSS popularity made a great impact on the Web developing and designing industry. Below is a list of advantages to CSS.

Benefits:

- **Accessibility:** CSS has the ability to tailor a Web page or Web site to different target devices, such as mobile phones. If the device will not be able to understand the styling, it still displays the contents.

- **Bandwidth/speed:** Style sheets are usually stored in a browser cache, so when you are loading Web site with multiple pages, for example, it will not be reloaded. This reduces data transfer over a network and increases download speeds.

- **Consistency:** Because styles can be "cascading" from another and it can be acceded or inherited by another, this allows consistency and equality upon styles, depending on the designer and user declaration. If, for example, you created a well-structured, CSS-based Web site but need to make changes to the structure and format, then instead of editing each page, you simply edit the global style sheet you created, which will update every page of your Web site.

- **Equality:** When you are working on multiple Web pages and want them to have equal styling and formatting, you can create one sheet for those pages.

- **Flexibility:** CSS gives you tremendous control over the overall look and feel of your Web site. You can easily make changes to your CSS template and change your Web site quickly.

Even though there are tremendous advantages to using CSS, there are some drawbacks as well.

Drawbacks:

- **Browser incompatibility:** Numerous browser bugs are possible because of the vide variety of browser types. Because of incompatibility issues, site owners are forced to use CSS "hacks" to implement the right layout for their Web pages. Commonly used browsers also have different recognition for pixels.

- **Column declaration short offs:** Layouts with multiple columns can be complex to use with current CSS. Floating elements are often rendered differently by diverse browsers and different screen shapes or resolutions.

- **Controlling shape elements:** CSS currently only supports rectangular shapes. But what about rounded shapes or rounded corners? Those shapes require a non-semantic markup to meet the shape requirement.

- **Elements with multiple backgrounds:** Developers currently have to choose between placing redundant wrappers around document elements or simply dropping the visual effects because graphical designs require several background images for every element. CSS can only support one.

- **Inflexible layout:** CSS is a styling tool, not a layout tool language.

- **Limitation of vertical controls:** It is normally easy to control horizontal element placements in CSS, but this is not the case with vertical element placements. It is not a simple task to center an element vertically or to place a footer no higher than the bottom of viewpoint, for example. This requires either intricate and unintuitive style rules, or undemanding but extensively uncorroborated rules.

- **Variable absence:** The absence of variable in CSS makes it essential to "replace all" when one desires to change a constant, such as dimensions and color schemes.

Code Syntax for Cascading Style Sheets

Syntax is a structure rule that is followed in creating CSS tags or any other programming languages. The CSS syntax consists of three elements:

```
selector{ property: value }
```

Selector: Selects the tag or element within the HTML tag that you want to style.

Property: The element you want to change in a selector.

Value: Defines the change to a property.

Note: The property and value is separated with a semicolon, indicating that property has a value. The property and value are closed with curly brackets, or braces.

Multiple declarations: Declaring more than one value within a property can be written as follows:

```
body {background-color:#FFD3D7; width:600px; height:500px;}
```

Note: Each value declared is separated with a semicolon, which indicates that there are multiple values you are declaring in one property.

There is also an option to make your code more understandable, especially in creating multiple declarations. Here is the code:

```
paragraph1{
    text-align:center;
    color:black;
    font-family:Arial, Helvetica, sans-serif;
    font-size:14px;
    width:500px;
    margin-left:200px;
    background-color:pink;
    padding-top:10px;
}
```

Group selectors: You can style a group of selectors in one declaration using a group selector. Here is the code:

```
h1,h2,h3,h4,h5,h6{
    color:gray;
    font-style:italic;
    font-family:Verdana, Geneva, sans-serif;
}
```

Once you have applied group selector, it will affect all the selectors declared within the group. In the example above, the **h1, h2, h3, h4, h5,** and **h6** selectors will affect all the properties. Text color will be gray, the font style will be italic, and the font family will be Verdana, Geneva™, and sans-serif. The comma is used to declare a group of selectors in one declaration.

Calling Cascading Style Sheets in a Web Page

You might be wondering how you can implement your CSS within your Web pages. There are different ways of calling CSS in HTML pages, including **inline**, **internal**, or **external**.

INLINE CSS: Inline CSS is used within the line of a selector within an HTML tag; you can use inline if you want to style a color from a sentence, for instance. Here is the code structure:

```
<selector style="property:value;">
```

Here is a sample code:

```
<h1 style="color:brown; font-style:italic"><strong>Sample paragraph 1</strong></h1>
```

Note: Inline CSS will only affect the line you have applied with the selector.

Embedded style type: The style sheet is place within the header. Here is the code structure:

```
<html>
<head>
<meta http-equiv="Content-Type" content="text/html" />
<title> Embedded Style Sample </title>
<style type="text/css" media="screen">
<!-- selector{ property-value:lightgreen; } -->
</style>
</head>
<body>
    Put your contents here
</body>
</html>
```

Here is an actual sample code:

```
<html>
<head>
<meta http-equiv="Content-Type" content="text/html" />
<title> Embedded Style Sample </title>
<style type="text/css" media="screen">
<!-- body{ background-color:lightgreen; font-style:italic; }
-->


</style>
</head>
<body>
    This is a sample embedded CSS
</body>
</html>
```

Here is the output:

```
This is a sample embedded CSS
```

External Type: This type of CSS calling is done by creating a CSS file that will call within the HTML code to take effect. Here is a sample code:

```
<head>
<link rel="stylesheet" type="text/css" href="mystyle.css" />
<title> Embedded Style Sample </title>
</head>
<body>
    <h1> This is a sample embedded CSS</h1>
</body>
</html>
```

Do not forget that you need to create the CSS file first before you can call it inside an HTML document.

How to Create Cascading Style Sheets

This section will illustrate the step-by-step process of creating CSS with the use of a text editor. A text editor is a type of program used for editing plain text files.

Note: It is highly recommended that when you start creating your HTML or CSS mark-up coding, you do it in a system default text editor. This will allow you to familiarize yourself with each tag.

Using a software editor: Install the software editor you want to use. The following sample uses Dreamweaver CS3. Try the following steps:

1. Click the "Start" button on the bottom-left part of the computer.

2. Click "Programs" and choose the Adobe Dreamweaver CS3. See the illustration below:

Note: You could also create a shortcut button on your desktop for a more convenient way to start the application.

3. Open Dreamweaver CS3. It will be shown as follows:

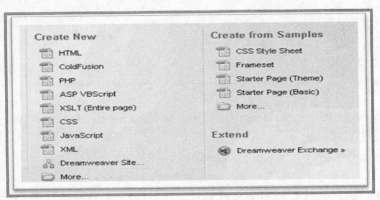

4. Select "CSS" to create a new CSS file, or you can start to create new CSS by going to "File" and clicking on "New." See the illustration below:

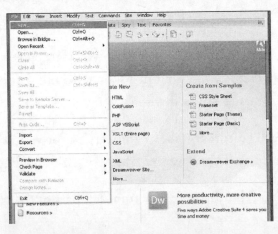

When you open a file, it will look like the following illustration. You can now start to do your mark-up coding.

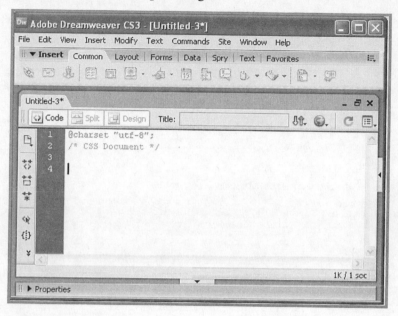

One main feature of Dreamweaver is that it can detect mistaken styling properties, tags, elements, or values; it marks a different color to emphasize wrong markup or color properties and values. In the following example, a red-colored text is displayed, indicating that there is a mistaken property within the selector.

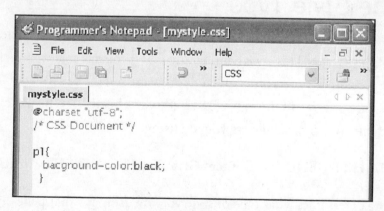

The correct code is illustrated below. You will notice in the program that the red marking has now turned to blue. This indicates that the property spelling of **"background-color"** is correct.

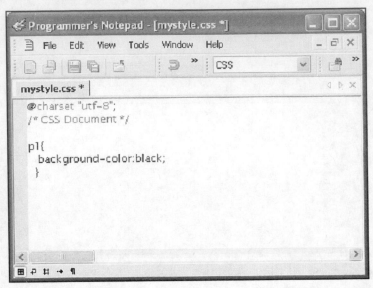

Browsers determine what styles to use when formatting a Web page design through the CSS indicated on the HTML file. There are three ways to call your CSS to work with your Web page.

Inline Style Type

Inline styles are added on a particular HTML tag. This comes in the form **<tag style="...">**. This style handles any CSS property relevant to the tag that is used. It is added on every tag you want styled. When using inline styles, you need to add the tag below inside the **<head>...</head>** tags for the default style sheet language you are using:

<META HTTP-EQUIV="Content-Style-Type" CONTENT="text/css">

This tag determines what type of style you are using for that page.

SYNTAX: <tag style="property:value; ">

Advantages of inline CSS

- Inline CSS is easy to add to HTML elements as needed. It minimizes adding another style on other declared CSS. You can quickly add it to the HTML tag.
- Inline style sheets are useful when an element has only few properties, such as if you want a word on your paragraph to be a different color from the rest.

Disadvantages of inline CSS

- Inline style overrides other CSS once declared on the tag.
- Because inline styles are added on every tag, when you want to make changes on your styles, you need to go over the document and change the desired properties yourself.
- If you want more styles for an element, your style code will become so long that you might get confused.
- If a page uses many styles, it might load slowly due to excess reading of styles. It is also time-consuming for a coder to maintain or modify styles.
- You need to set styles on every link you have.

Take a look at the following example to get a better idea of what inline CSS looks like:

```
<html>

    <head>

    <meta http-equiv="Content-Type"content="text/html" />

    <title>Inline Style Sample</title>

    </head>
```

Embedded Style Type

Embedded style is also called internal tag style. This type of CSS is set in the HTML **<head>...</head>** tag. This style is present on every page it is used. Embedded style sheets override declared styles in linked CSS for that document only.

SYNTAX:

```
<style                    type="text/css"
media="screen">
<!--
        Your styles here....
-->
```

TYPE: Determines the content style language.
MEDIA: Determines what media will use this CSS.

Here is an example:

```
<style type="text/css" media="screen">
        <!--
                p{   text-align:   left;   font-family:
Arial;}
                h1{ font-size: 3em; color: red;}
        -->
```

You can see that inside the tags **<!-- ... -->** we declare the properties and values of the styles. Here is a breakdown of the first example line:

p { text-align: left; font-family: Arial;}

- **p** is the selector.
- **text-align** is the property of the style.
- **left** is the value that determines what style to use.

Notice that opening and closing braces **{...}** hold the properties and values of the style. These braces group the styles that are declared in a particular selector or tag.

Note: Embedded styles are written inside an HTML comment **<!-- ... -->** tag. This is necessary to prevent displaying contents when styles are not supported by some browsers.

Advantages of embedded CSS

- Embedded style lets you modify only one portion of the document, since styles are piled up to the **<head>...</head>** tag.
- You can declare what media will use the particular CSS.

Disadvantages of embedded CSS

- Like inline CSS, embedded style makes your HTML load slowly if styles are used excessively, and the file size of the page is big.
- Your code source might become a long document using embedded style.
- It minimizes SEO. Search engines such as Google or Yahoo! can easily access Web sites that have lighter file sizes.
- Coders who want a clean HTML source code will have a hard time maintaining such a Web page because it takes time to determine which style an element is using.

Here are examples using embedded CSS:

```
<html>

  <head>

  <meta http-equiv="Content-Type"
content="text/html"/>

  <title>Inline Style Sample</title>

  <style type="text/css" media="screen">

  <!--

    body{background-color:lightblue;}

    p{text-align:left; font-family:Arial; font-weight:bold;
color:blue;}
```

Here is the output:

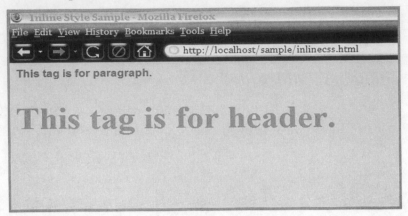

Note: When you do not specify a **font-family** property in your CSS, the browser will use its default font setting.

External Style Type

External or linked type CSS is done on a separate document that has the file extension .CSS. This type of CSS is linked in the HTML file to determine which CSS file a page will use. To call this external CSS on your HTML code, you need to use the **<link>** tag instead of the **<style>** tag inside the **<head>...</head>** tags. This references your CSS that is located in the separate file.

This type of CSS is the most used and recommended type for developing Web sites. Here are some advantages of using this type of CSS:

- Using external CSS allows a Web developer to determine the HTML code from the CSS styles. This is for easy file management.
- Styles within external CSS can be used by different Web pages by linking to the file. You can control styles on pages that have similar designs by customizing one file.
- Separating CSS from HTML code helps browsers show Web pages faster. Browsers download a few small files instead of one large file.

- It is easier for search engines to locate your Web site because there is less content in the HTML file.
- External CSS uses more organized and clean CSS declarations.

SYNTAX: Here is how you call an external CSS:

```
<head>
<title>…</title>
        <link rel="stylesheet" type="text/css" href="inline.css"
/>
```

- **<link>** is used to embed or call your CSS file.
- **rel** tells the browser that CSS is linked.
- **type** tells the browser what kind of file is to be used.
- **href** locates where your CSS file is stored.

Take a look at this example HTML code for a preview of how to use external CSS:

```
<html>
<head>
<title> Cascading Style Sheet </title>
    <link rel="stylesheet" type="text/css" href="inline.css" />
</head>

<body>
    <h1> Using External CSS </h1>
        <textarea>This is a sample code for using external CSS.
This is the recommended type used by most Web sites.
</textarea>
</body>
</html>
```

As you see in this image, HTML calls **inline.css** as the style sheet it will use. The image below will show how the external CSS file is coded.

```
inline.css  ×
/* CSS Document */
body{
        background-color:lightgreen;
}

h1{
        font-family: Georgia; }
```

It is not hard to use external CSS, as the coding is similar to embedded CSS; it is just saved in a different file. There are no tags used on this type of CSS. Only selectors, properties, and values are coded.

Here is an example of how CSS are referenced by the <link> tag. You can organize your HTML and CSS files in folders.

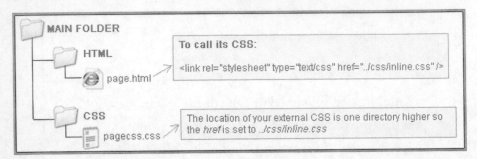

Note: Whenever you make changes in external CSS, all pages that link to the file will be affected. You can add more external CSS coding if you want other pages to have different design styles.

Import Style Type

Import CSS is somewhat similar to external and embedded CSS, but in this case, you include your external CSS in your HTML file and add some rules.

If you import two or more CSS files, the order of styles the browser will follow will go according to the order declared on the **@import** rule. Here is an example of import CSS:

```
<style type="text/css" media="screen">
       <!--
       @import url("mypage/css/style.css");
       @import
url(www.thepage.com/mix.css);
       body { background-color: lightblue;}
       -->
```

Note: The **@import** rule must come first before you declare any other CSS properties.

You can also import style sheets for specific media types you want to include. Just add the valid browser-supported media after **url("...")**, as in this example:

```
<style type="text/css" media="screen">
        <!--
        @import  url("mypage/css/style.css")  screen,  print,
tty;
        -->
```

Now that you have learned about CSS, its uses, and its types, you are now ready to delve deeper into designing your Web pages. You should now understand:

- How to set properties and values for each element you want to be styled.
- How to reuse style sheets and lessen your heavy coding. This helps your Web pages to download faster at browser views.
- What CSS properties an HTML element has.

Cascading Style Sheet Selectors

One of the primary components of this syntax is the selector. This is used to determine which part of the Web page is to be styled. Normally, HTML tags are the selectors used. The following sections will provide an overview of the types of selectors used in CSS.

Class Selector

Assume that you are working on different Web pages and you want your head titles to be of similar format. For example, you may want the heading to be a bigger size than the normal text and in a bold format. You would not want to repeat the property and value in every heading tag for every Web page.

The class selector can help you define styles for similar elements included on different pages. All you have to do is call a particular class name whenever you have to use it for an element, regardless of what part of the document it may be.

Declaring a class is done through the use of a dot (.) proceeded by the class name. You can give the class whatever name you want for the certain element.

> Declaring class selectors should be lowercase as in "class," and class names must not begin with numbers or contain spaces as some browsers like Mozilla Firefox may not acknowledge or be able to read these. Do not put a space between the dot (.) and the class name.

SYNTAX:

```
.classname{     property:}
```

Here is a simple illustration of using a class:

```
.mstyle{
     font-family:
Helvetica;
     color: red;}
```

When you want to call this class on your HTML element, here is what you do:

<h1 class="mystyle"> This heading uses a class selector. </h1>

This calls the class name you have declared in your CSS.

If you want to add another class name in one element, do so like this:

```
h1.mystyle{
    font-family: Helvetica;
    color: red;
}
h1.style2{
    text-align: center;
}
.common{
    background-color:
lightgreen; }
```

Here is an example of calling multiple classes in your HTML:

```
<h1 class="mystyle style2 common">
            This    heading    uses    a    class
selector.
```

NOTE: If you will have multiple classes, the class names to be defined within your **class="..."** attribute must be concatenated with a space between each name to tell that the element uses more than one style.

Descendant Selectors

There are instances where the use of class is overused, such as when working on **<div>** elements. Here is an example to illustrate this unnecessary code:

```
<body>
    <div class="maincontainer">
        <h1 class="title">Heading</h1>
            <p class="content">Paragraph</p>
        <h2 class="subtitle">Sub heading</h2>
            <span class="subcontent">Here's your sub content</span>
    </div>

</body>
```

Looking at this structure, you can immediately see that each element has its own class name. But if you added more elements to the same structure as written above, it would be confusing to go around the code and repeat these lines.

Web pages follow a hierarchy. This begins with HTML, then moves down to a structure containing other elements within the body. The image below illustrates an example of a hierarchy:

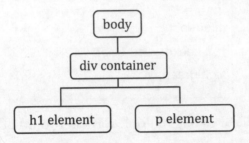

The **div container** in this illustration contains or handles two elements, **h1** and **p**. In this example, **body** contains a **div container**, which has **h1** and **p** as descendants.

Descendant selectors define the descendants of a certain main element where other sub-elements are factored in. This selector is useful to minimize the use of classes in elements. It is supported by most modern browsers. To give you an idea of how this selector works, here is an example to illustrate the difference from the previous sample:

```
<body>

    <div class="maincontainer">
      <h1>Heading</h1>
          <p>Paragraph</p>
      <h2>Sub heading</h2>
            <span>Here's your sub content</span>
    </div>

</body>
```

Here is an example code for a style sheet:

```
/* CSS Document */
div.maincontainer{
    main styles...
}
div.maincontainer h1{
    h1 unique styles...
}
div.maincontainer p{
    p unique styles...
}
div.maincontainer h2{
    h2 unique styles...
}
div.maincontainer span{
    span unique styles...
}
```

The code is much simpler. Now it is unnecessary to assign class names to each element. You can make the properties common for all the content under the **<div class="maincontainer">** tag and define a unique style for other content not specified within the tag.

ID Selectors

The ID selector is also called in HTML elements. This selector is a unique identifier on a page. Unlike classes, the ID selector is only applied to one element in your code. This is used to individually format the few elements that should not be repeated for any other content. With this tag, there will be no two attributes on your code that have the same style name.

To indicate this selector on an element, you would use **id="id_name"** as the property. On your style sheet, this is indicated with a slash (#). This selector is used in particular elements such as text boxes on forms. Like with the class selector, you will assign the ID name to the selector.

SYNTAX:

```
#idname{    property:}
```

Here is the previous example using an ID selector:

```
<body>

    <div id="maincontainer">
        <h1>Heading</h1>
            <p class="content">Paragraph</p>
        <div class="content">Another container added</div>




</body>
```

Here is the CSS code:

```
/* CSS Document */
div#maincontainer{
    width: 500px;
    font-family: Georgia;
}
div#maincontainer  h1{
    font-size:14px;
    text-decoration:underline;
}
.content{
    text-align: justify;
}
```

As you can see in the code, the **maincontainer** attribute has an ID selector identified in CSS by #. This ID is unique in the document; it cannot be called again by the other **div** element.

Take a look at this example:

```
<body>

    <div id="maincontainer">
        <h1 id="Head">This is My Title</h1>
            <p class="content">
            "The quick brown fox jumps over the lazy dog.
            The quick brown fox jumps over the lazy dog.
            The quick brown fox jumps over the lazy dog.
            The quick brown fox jumps over the lazy dog."
            </p>
        <div class="content">Another container is added on this part</div>
            <h1>This takes another style</h1>
            <h1>This takes the same style</h1>
        </div>

</body>
```

Here is the CSS property for this code:

```
/* CSS Document */

div#maincontainer{
    width: 500px;
    font-family: Georgia;
    background-color:yellow;
}
div#maincontainer  h1{
    font-size:16px;
    font-weight:bold;
    color: red;
}
div#maincontainer  h1#Head{
    font-size:40px;
    font-style:italic;
    color: orange;
}
div#maincontainer  p.content{
    text-align: justify;
}

div.content{
    width: 350px;
    background-color: lightgreen;
}
```

Differences between Class and ID Selectors

Before proceeding to the next selector, you should be aware of the differences between class and ID selectors, as these two are commonly used in elements. If you know these differences, you will not be confused with which to use on your styles:

- The syntax is different. For classes, you use a dot (.), while IDs use the slash (#) sign.
- Classes are used when you want your styles to be repeated many times within a page. IDs are used to call a unique style that is not repeated on any element on a page. IDs are only applied once on a page.
- It is possible to use multiple classes within an element, such as using **.style1 .style2 .style3** on your **h1** element. But IDs cannot have multiple IDs declared; only one ID name is to be declared in an **id="..."** attribute.

- IDs can be called by special browser functions such as JavaScript. A class does not have this capability.
- When dealing with links, you can assign an ID a **href** value. In the example **href="#maincontainer"** a browser locates where the **#maincontainer** is; when the link is hit, it will direct you to that location. This is another reason IDs are declared once in a document.

Similarities between Class and ID Selectors

Despite the differences mentioned above, IDs and classes also share some similarities:

- Both classes and IDs are case-sensitive. When you name one of these selectors **myStyle**, it is not the same as **mystyle**.
- HTML elements can have both ID and class as attributes. For example: **<div id="mystyle" class="styling">**.
- Using classes and IDs can expand content, and browsers can load HTML pages easier. Both also help cut down on time spent modifying styles.
- IDs can have the same properties and values that classes have.
- Both classes and IDs are essential in designing your Web page the way you want it to look. You can control your pages by using these selectors.
- There are no browser defaults for class and ID selectors. What you put in your style sheets are the values that a browser will carry for the page styles.

Universal Selectors

Universal selectors can be used anywhere that your page, and any element, can call them. This is represented by an asterisk (*). Here is an example of how this selector is used:

```
* {
        font-family: Arial;
        color: #333333;

}
```

This defines the font family and color for the all the pages on your Web site.

Group Selectors

There are instances when you may want to style a group of selectors with similar properties. You can do this by adding a comma (,) between each selector you will define. Here is an example:

```
body, h1, h2, h3, h4, h5, p, dl, dt, dd, ul, ol, li, img, caption, fieldset, form,
input, select, label {
        margin: 0;
        padding: 0;
}
```

This defines that the selectors or elements declared will have default margins set to 0 and padding set to 0.

Cascading Style Sheets Comments

CSS comments can help in finding where the style for a particular element is located. By using CSS comments, you can explain your code so other Web developers can easily find your styles when there is a need to modify the page design in the future. This will help them understand what that CSS is doing within your design.

Note: Comments are ignored by most browsers, but with some old browsers, these comments may cause errors.

Syntax for a CSS comment starts with /* and ends with */. Comments can be single lines or multiple lines, as long as words are within the /* */. When you include comments, be as brief as possible so the browser can load and detect your CSS quickly. Also avoid over-using comments; you do not have to include comments for every code in your document.

Here are few examples of using comments:

```
1. /*This is a simple single line comment. */


2. /*This is a multiple-line comment.
This can be a simple paragraph form.
Comment should be brief and concise.
*/


3. /*
CSS date created: 25-May-2009
CSS date last modified: 29-May-2009
Modified by Developer */
```

Here is a sample of CSS comment for our previous example:

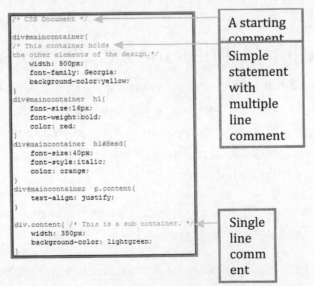

```
/* CSS Document */
div#maincontainer{
/* This container holds
the other elements of the design.*/
     width: 500px;
     font-family: Georgia;
     background-color:yellow;
}
div#maincontainer  h1{
     font-size:16px;
     font-weight:bold;
     color: red;
}
div#maincontainer  h1#Head{
     font-size:40px;
     font-style:italic;
     color: orange;
}
div#maincontainer  p.content{
     text-align: justify;
}

div.content{ /* This is a sub container. */
     width: 350px;
     background-color: lightgreen;
}
```

A starting comment

Simple statement with multiple line comment

Single line comment

CSS Properties and Values

Applying background color and image

Styling backgrounds for your Web site is essential. A common rule for this is to use a light background with dark texts to balance the design. You can choose your own scheme for colors and designs, but be sure that your styles are manageable and not annoying for visitors.

PROPERTIES

BACKGROUND COLORS: [background-color: value;]

Description: This property lets you set your desired background color. There are different ways to state your colors. They can be in hexadecimal, RGB, or word values. There are also good color mixers on the Internet.

- **Hexadecimal colors:** These are colors defined by their mixture in the RGB color model. These are colors from 0 to F.
  Examples: #ffffff; #000000; #fafad2

- **RGB:** Red, Green, Blue. This is the computer's native color space for taking images and displaying them on computer's monitor. The values are from 0 to 255.
  Example: 234, 192, 255

- **Word values:** These are colors that are stated in words. There are some browsers that take this value as an error. However, for beginners, it is helpful to use this to play around with styles and discover what word values are accepted by browsers.

Review these examples:

```
<h1 style="background-color: #fafad2; ">Applying back-
ground colors</h1>
```

```
<h1 style="background-color:  rgb(255,255,255); ">Applying
background colors</h1>
<h1 style="background-color:  green; ">Applying background
colors</h1>
```

BACKGROUND IMAGE: [background-image: url('location of image');]

Description: This allows you to use images as backgrounds for your layouts. If you have a gradient image that you want to become your background, you are free to style it on your design. It is also possible to add background images that are static and fixed, or backgrounds that follow when you scroll down the page.

Here is the code:

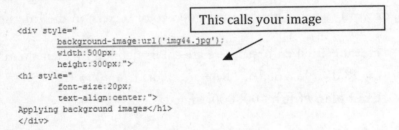

Here is the output:

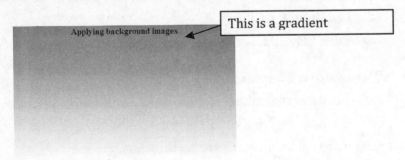

BACKGROUND REPEAT: [background-repeat: value;]

Description: This will make your backgrounds repeat on the screen. The following are values you can assign to do this:

repeat-x: Repeats your background horizontally.

repeat-y: Repeats your background vertically.

repeat: Repeats your background both horizontally and vertically.

no-repeat: Does not repeat your background.

```
<div style="
        background-image:url('img47.jpg');
        background-repeat: repeat-y;
        width:500px;
        height:300px;">
<h1 style="
        font-size:20px;
        text-align:left;">
Applying background images</h1>
</div>
```

Repeat your background

Here is the output:

Applying background images

Note: Your background will repeat vertically until your height reaches its span.

BACKGROUND POSITION: [background-position: value;]

Description: This sets the positions of your background where you want it to appear. By default, backgrounds are positioned at the top-left corner of the screen. You can use percentage (**%**), units (**cm** and **px**, for instance), and the words **top**, **bottom**, **right**, and **left**.

Here is the code:

```html
<body style="
    background-image:url('img47.jpg');
    background-repeat: repeat-y;
    background-position: 10%;
">
<div style="
        width:500px;
        border: 1px solid #333333;
">
<h1 style="
        font-size:20px;
        text-align:left;">
Applying background properties</h1>
</div>
```

Position your body background 10% from the left of your screen.

Here is the output:

You can see within the circle that the body gradient background starts 10% away from the left side from the border of the div element.

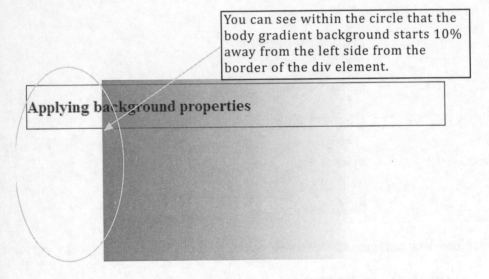

Applying background properties

BACKGROUND: [background: url('location') other property values;]

Description: Like other elements, you can also use a shorthand property for declaring backgrounds. This shortens your CSS code while compiling several properties in a single line. For example:

div#container{
        width: 500px;

background: url('image1.jpg') no-repeat fixed left top; }

CUSTOMIZING FONTS: <font>

Description: The **<font>** property is an element used to change the appearance of your text. This also enables you to choose what corresponding fonts you want to take place.

These are potential values under **<list-style>**, which will be discussed later in this chapter:

- **font-family:** This property is used to change the face of a font.
- **font-style:** This property is used to make a font italic or oblique.
- **font-variant:** This property is used to create a small-caps effect.
- **font-weight:** This property is used to increase or decrease how bold or light a font appears.
- **font-size:** This property is used to increase or decrease the size of a font.
- **font:** This property is used as shorthand to specify a number of other font properties.

To better understand the **<font>** property, look at the following examples:

PROPERTIES

FONT FAMILY: [font-family: value;]

Description: This will set the font family of an element. Possible values are any font family name.

Here is the code:

```
<p style="font-family:Tahoma, Geneva, sans-serif">
    This text will show you either Tahoma, Geneva, or sans-serif
    This will depend on which font you have on your system.
</p>
```

Here is the output:

> This text will show you either Tahoma, Geneva, or sans-serif.
> This will depend on which font you have on your system.

FONT STYLE: [font-style: value;]

Description: This sets the font style of an element. Possible values are
<normal>, **< italic>**, and **<oblique>**.

Here is the code:

```
<p style="font-style:normal;">
    This will show you the normal style
</p>

<p style="font-style:italic;">
    This will show you the italic style
</p>

<p style="font-style:oblique;">
    This will show you the oblique style
</p>
```

Here is the output:

> This will show you the normal style
>
> *This will show you the italic style*
>
> *This will show you the oblique style*

FONT VARIANT: [font-variant: value;]

Description: This will set the font variant of an element. Possible values
are **<normal>** and **<small-caps>**.

Here is the code:

```
<p style="font-variant:normal;">
    This will show you the normal variant style
</p>
<p style="font-variant:small-caps;">
    This will show you the small-caps variant style
</p>
```

Here is the output:

This will show you the normal variant style

THIS WILL SHOW YOU THE SMALL-CAPS VARIANT STYLE

FONT WEIGHT: [font-weight: value;]

Description: This property sets the font weight of an element. The **<font-weight>** property provides the functionality to indicate how bold a font is. Possible values could be **<normal>**, **<bold>**, **< bolder>**, **<lighter>**, **<100>**, **<200>**, and so on up to **<900>**.

FONT SIZE: [font-size: value;]

Description: This property sets the font size of an element. It enables you to adjust the x-height to make fonts more comprehensible. Possible values are size in pixels, size in percentage (%), any number, **<xx-small>**, **<x-small>**, **<small>**, **<medium>**, **<large>**, **<x-large>**, **<xx-large>**, **<smaller>,** and **<larger>**.

Here is the code:

```
<p style="font-size-adjust:0.53;">
    This text is using a font-size-adjust value to 0.53.
</p>
<p style="font-size-adjust:0.75;">
    This text is using a font-size-adjust value to 0.75.
</p>
<p style-"font-size-adjust:0.31;">
    This text is using a font-size-adjust value to 0.31.
</p>
```

Here is the output:

> This text is using a font-size-adjust value to 0.53.
>
> This text is using a font-size-adjust value to 0.75.
>
> This text is using a font-size-adjust value to 0.31.

Formatting and Styling Text

There are many ways to style your text. If you want to stylize text, make sure it is readable and clear enough for your viewers to see.

PROPERTIES

TEXT INDENT: [**text-indent: value;**]

Description: This allows you to indent paragraphs, sentences, or words. You can also assign negative values. When you do this, the first line of your text will be indented to the left.

Here is an example using this property:

```
a. p{
      text-indent: 15px;
   }

b. h1{
      text-indent: 20px;
   }
```

TEXT ALIGN: [**text-align: value;**]

Description: This sets the alignment of your text element.

Here are potential values under **<text-align>**:

- **left:** This is the default value on browser. It will align your text to the left.
- **right:** This sets your text on right alignment.
- **center:** This centers your text.
- **justify:** This value stretches your text lines so your left and right margins will be straight.

Here is the code:

```
p#a {
     text-align: left;
     }
p#b {
     text-align: center;
     }
p#c {
     text-align: right;
     }
```

Here is an illustration of how **\<text-align\>** works:

This text is left aligned.

This text is center aligned.

This text is right aligned.

TEXT DECORATION: [text-decoration: value;]

Description: This property enables you to add decorations or effects to your text.

Here are potential values under **\<text-decoration\>**:

- **none:** The text will stay as the normal declared text. It will not follow the decoration assigned if it is included on an element with declared decoration.
- **underline:** Puts a solid line under the text.
- **overline:** Puts a solid line over the text.
- **line-through:** Puts a solid line through the text. It is similar to strikethrough in a Word document.

- **blink:** Makes the text blink. This value does not work in IE.

Here is an example code:

```
a. <h1 style="text-decoration: underline;">Text underlined.</h1>
The text will look like this: Text underlined.

b. <h1 style="text-decoration: line-through;">Text strikethrough.
</h1>
The text will look like this: Text strikethrough.
```

Here is an illustration to show the styles for text decorations:

```
This text is underlined.

This text is overlined.

This text has strikethrough.
```

TEXT SPACING: [letter-spacing: value;]

Description: This value defines the spaces between letters or text characters.

Here is the code:

```
<span style="letter-spacing:5px;">
```

Here is the output on browser:

```
This is an example of a sentence using
letter spacing.
```

Borders and Outlines

Borders

Border properties define the thickness, color, and style of your element's border. Borders are commonly used for tables and containers. You can set border properties for the **top**, **right**, **bottom**, and **left**.

PROPERTIES

BORDER COLOR: [border-color: value;]

Description: This allows you to set the color(s) you want for your borders.

Here are potential values under **<border-color>**:

- Words such as red, yellow, and green
- RGB
- Hexadecimal; this color code is the most advisable form, as most browsers can interpret hexadecimal

Here is the code:

```
a. div{
    border-top-center: lightblue;
    border-right-color:
    yellowgreen;
    border-bottom-color: blue;
    border-left-color: green;
        }
```

```
a. div{

    border-top-color: # add8e6;    ←  light-blue

    border-right-color: # 9acd32;    ←  yellow-green

    border-bottom-color: #0000ff;    ←  blue

    border-left-color: # 008000;    ←  green

    }
```

. Here is the output for these two examples:

> different colors set in each side with border thick
>
> Individual borders set. This is an example.

Border width

Description: This sets the width of your border. You can define how thick or thin you want your border to be. You can assign values using px, pt, cm, thin, medium, and thick.

Here is the code:

```
div{
    border-top-width:10px;
    border-right-width:15px;
    border-bottom-width:4px;
    border-left-width:2px;
        }
```

Here is the output:

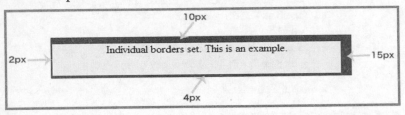

Border style

Description: There are eight different border styles you can choose from to add simple designs around your containers.

Possible values

SOLID BORDER: [border-style: solid;]

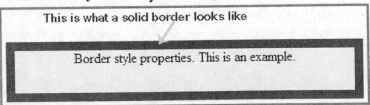

DOTTED BORDER: [border-style: dotted;]

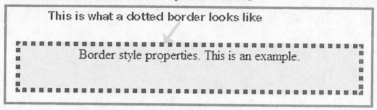

This is what a dotted border looks like

Border style properties. This is an example.

DASHED BORDER: [border-style: dashed;]

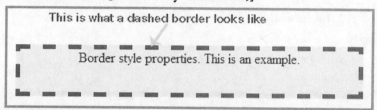

This is what a dashed border looks like

Border style properties. This is an example.

DOUBLE BORDER: [border-style: double;]

This is what a double border looks like

Border style properties. This is an example.

GROOVE BORDER: [border-style: groove;]

This is what a groove border looks like

Border style properties. This is an example.

RIDGE BORDER: [border-style: ridge;]

This is what a ridge border looks like

Border style properties. This is an example.

INSET BORDER: [border-style: inset;]

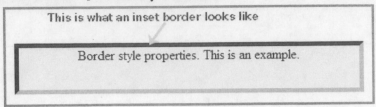

OUTSET BORDER: [border-style: outset;]

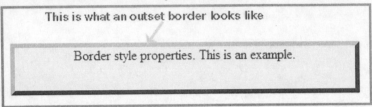

Border property

Description: This is a shorthand property that will help you define values for borders in a more concise manner. This property compiles the three properties discussed above in a single line.

Here is the code:

```
div#main{
    border: 3px dashed #009900;
}
```

Outlines

The outline property is a different property from the border property. This is used to draw lines around elements to make them stand out. These lines are drawn outside the border edge. Outline also has a shorthand property. Outlines are commonly used for visual objects such as buttons, active form fields, and image maps. They are also often used to highlight search terms. Here are the differences between outlines and borders:

- Outlines do not take space. Outlines do not affect the size and position of the element.
- Outlines do not have to be rectangular. While borders leave edges open when an element splits in several lines, outline closes the end of the line, then opens again on the next line.
- Outline properties are set the same on all sides, meaning the values of the width, style, and color should be the same on all sides.

PROPERTIES

OUTLINE COLOR: [outline-color: value;]

Description: This defines what color your outline will be. An outline color is set to one value for an element.

OUTLINE WIDTH: [outline-width: value;]

Description: This defines the width of your outline. Outline width is the same on all sides; even if you declare different widths on different sides, the browser will still interpret that your outline width is the same on all sides.

OUTLINE STYLE: [outline-style: value;]

Description: The outlines styles are the same as those for the border property.

- **none:** This sets the outline to 0, or no outline at all.
- **hidden:** This hides the outline. This is similar to the none value.
- **solid:** This sets a single solid line.
- **dotted:** This sets an outline in dots.
- **dashed:** This sets an outline in dashed lines.
- **double:** This sets an outline with two solid lines.
- **groove:** This sets an outline that looks carved on the page.
- **ridge:** This outline looks like an inverted carve on the page.
- **inset:** This outline looks like it is embedded on the page.
- **outset:** This outline looks like it is coming out of the element.

Here is an example using the outline property:

```
div#main{
    outline-style:dashed;
    outline-width: 2px;
    outline-color: #0000ff;
        }
```

This code produces the output below:

Outline style properties. This is an example.

Controlling Margins and Paddings

Margins and paddings are used define white spaces for elements, whether they be spaces on the top, bottom, left, or right of another element. Margins and paddings are different properties of CSS with different functions in creating spaces.

As you proceed with the next lessons, you will learn how margins and paddings work and what the differences are between the two.

Margins

Margins set white spaces around an element border. These are spaces outside the border or between the element that has the margin property and the other element near it. You can also set negative values for this property to overlap contents.

PROPERTIES

selector{ margin: value; }

Description: This sets the margin value for the top, bottom, left, and right sides. The margin size will be equal on all four sides of the element.

Here is an example code:

```
/* CSS Document */
h1.Title{
    width:500px;
    margin: 10px;
    border: 1px solid #666666;
    background-color: yellow;
}
```

selector{ margin: t r b l; }

Description: This sets the margin values of each side as a group. It is also called the shorthand margin property. The order of the sides goes clockwise from the top.

Here is an example code:

```
/* CSS Document */
h1.Title{
    width:500px;
    margin: 10px 15px 5px 20px;
    border: 1px solid #666666;
}
```

selector{ margin-top: value; }

Description: This sets the margin value at the top of the element.

Here is an example code:

```
/* CSS Document */
h1.Title{
    width:500px;
    margin-top: 10px;
    border: 1px solid #666666;
}
```

selector{ margin-bottom: value; }

Description: This sets the margin value at the bottom of the element.

Here is an example code:

```
/* CSS Document */
h1.Title{
    width:500px;
    margin-bottom: 5px;
    border: 1px solid #666666;
}
```

selector{ margin-left: value; }

Description: This sets the margin value at the left side of the element.

Here is an example code:

```
/* CSS Document */
h1.Title{
    width:500px;
    margin-left: 20px;
    border: 1px solid #666666;
}
```

selector{ margin-right: value; }

Description: This sets the margin value at the right side of the element.

Here is an example code:

```
/* CSS Document */
h1.Title{
    width:500px;
    margin-right: 15px;
    border: 1px solid #666666;
}
```

You can use the first example when the value of the margin you wanted to set is equal on all sides. However, the shorthand margin property is best used when you want to set margins in a more concise, easier way. Margins can be used on almost every element.

Important notes:

- Browsers set default margins for certain elements such as the body, form, and headings.
- To overwrite these defaults on browsers, you can declare a default value for these elements in your CSS by defining **margin: 0**. For example: **body{ margin: 0; }.**
- Firefox and IE each deal with margins differently. In Firefox, what you declare as a value is what the browser executes, whereas in IE, margins are executed double the value you have declared. For example, if your margin is **10px**, on IE it will look like you have input a **20px** margin.

Paddings

Paddings, like margins, are for white spaces between elements. Paddings differ from margins in that they insert white spaces between the element border and the content inside the element. This is also called "filling." Padding can be put on the top, right, bottom, and right sides of the element. While a margin affects the distance between elements, padding affects the distance between the border of the element container and its internal content. Unlike margins, you cannot put a negative value on paddings.

PROPERTIES

selector{ padding: value; }

Description: This sets the padding for the inner top, bottom, left, and right sides. All sides will have equal padding.

Here is an example code:

```
/* CSS Document */
h1.Title{
        width:500px;
        margin: 10px;
        border: 1px solid #666666;
        background-color: yellow;
}
```

selector{ padding: t r b l; }

Description: This sets the padding of each side in a simpler code. It is also called the shorthand padding property. The order of the sides goes clockwise from the top.

Here is an example code:

```
/* CSS Document */
h1.Title{
        width:500px;
        padding: 10px 15px 5px 20px;
        border: 1px solid #666666;
}
```

selector{ padding-top: value; }

Description: This sets the padding at the inner top side of the element.

Here is an example code:

```
/* CSS Document */
h1.Title{
        width:500px;
        padding-top: 10px;
        border: 1px solid #666666;
}
```

selector{ padding-bottom: value; }

Description: This sets the padding at the inner bottom of the element.

Here is an example code:

```
/* CSS Document */
h1.Title{
        width:500px;
        padding-bottom: 5px;
        border: 1px solid #666666;
}
```

selector{ padding-left: value; }

Description: This sets the padding at the inner left side of the element.

Here is an example code:

```
/* CSS Document */
h1.Title{
        width:500px;
        padding-left: 20px;
        border: 1px solid #666666;
}
```

selector{ padding-right: value; }

Description: This sets the padding value at the inner right side of the element.

Here is an example code:

```
/* CSS Document */
h1.Title{
        width:500px;
        padding-right: 15px;
        border: 1px solid #666666;
}
```

List Styling

Description: The **<list-style>** property is a shorthand property used to set the position and type of markers in a list; it can also be used to assign an image as the marker.

Here are potential values under **<list-style>**:

- **<list-style-type>**
- **<list-style-position>**
- **<list-style-image>**

To give you a better understanding of the **<list-style>** property, here are a few examples:

Here is the code:

```
<ul style="list-style-type:circle;">
    <li>HOME</li>
    <li>ENTERTAINMENT</li>
    <li>GALLERY</li>
    <li>DOWNLOADS</li>
    <li>CONTACT US</li>
    <li>ABOUT US</li>
</ul>
```

Here is the output:

- HOME
- ENTERTAINMENT
- GALLERY
- DOWNLOADS
- CONTACT US
- ABOUT US

Here is the code:

```
<ol style="list-style-type:decimal;">
    <li>ONE</li>
    <li>TWO</li>
    <li>THREE</li>
    <li>FOUR</li>
    <li>FIVE</li>
    <li>SIX</li>
</ol>
```

Here is the output:

1. ONE
2. TWO
3. THREE
4. FOUR
5. FIVE
6. SIX

Here is the code:

```
<ol style="list-style-type:lower-alpha;">
    <li>LETTER A</li>
    <li>LETTER B</li>
    <li>LETTER C</li>
    <li>LETTER D</li>
    <li>LETTER E</li>
    <li>LETTER F</li>
</ol>
```

Here is the output:

a. LETTER A
b. LETTER B
c. LETTER C
d. LETTER D
e. LETTER E
f. LETTER F

Here is the code:

```
<ul style="list-style-type:square;">
    <li>HOME</li>
    <li>ENTERTAINMENT</li>
    <li>GALLERY</li>
    <li>DOWNLOADS</li>
    <li>CONTACT US</li>
    <li>ABOUT US</li>
</ul>
```

Here is the output:

- HOME
- ENTERTAINMENT
- GALLERY
- DOWNLOADS
- CONTACT US
- ABOUT US

List Image

Description: The **\<list-style-image\>** property defines a pointer to an image resource which is to be used as the marker for list items.

Here are potential values under **\<list-style-image\>**:

- **URI:** The Uniform Resource Identifier works as a pointer to an image resource. If the URL cannot be resolved, then the property is treated as if the value were none.

- **none:** No image should be used as a marker for the element.

Here are some examples:

Here is the code:

```
<ul>
    <li style="list-style-image: url(images/arrow.gif);">HOME</li>
    <li>ENTERTAINMENT</li>
    <li>GALLERY</li>
    <li>DOWNLOADS</li>
    <li>CONTACT US</li>
    <li>ABOUT US</li>
</ul>
```

Here is the output:

Notice that in this example, an unordered list **\<ul\>** has been used, and it displays the image **arrow.gif** as the list indicator. Below you can see the effect of this in an ordered list **\<ol\>**.

Here is the code:

```
<ol>
    <li style="list-style-image: url(images/arrow.gif);">HOME</li>
    <li>ENTERTAINMENT</li>
    <li>GALLERY</li>
    <li>DOWNLOADS</li>
    <li>CONTACT US</li>
    <li>ABOUT US</li>
</ol>
```

Here is the output:

```
1. HOME
2. ENTERTAINMENT
3. GALLERY
4. DOWNLOADS
5. CONTACT US
6. ABOUT US
```

List Position

Description: The **<list-style-position>** property affects the placement of a marker in relation to the content of the list item.

Here are potential values under **<list-style-position>**:

- **inside:** The marker is made an inline element at the beginning of the first line of the list item's content.
- **outside:** The marker is placed outside the box containing the list item's content.

The following example is an unordered list using circle and square types as well as **<list-style-position: outside>** and **<list-style-position: inside>**.

Here is the code:

```
<ul style="list-style-type:circle; list-stlye-position:outside;">
    <li>HOME</li>
    <li>ENTERTAINMENT</li>
    <li>GALLERY</li>
    <li>DOWNLOADS</li>
</ul>

    <ul style="list-style-type:sqaure;list-style-position:inside;">
        <li>Music</li>
        <li>Photos</li>
        <li>Videos</li>
    </ul>

<ul style="list-style-type:circle; list-stlye-position:outside;">
    <li>CONTACT US</li>
    <li>ABOUT US</li>
</ul>
```

Here is the output:

- HOME
- ENTERTAINMENT
- GALLERY
- DOWNLOADS
    - Music
    - Photos
    - Videos
- CONTACT US
- ABOUT US

Table Styling

Border collapse

Description: The **<border-collapse>** property determines the border model used in the rendering of a table.

Here are potential values under **<border-collapse>**:

- **collapse:** Borders are collapsed to make a single border. Two adjacent cells will share a border.
- **separate:** Borders are separated. Every cell has its own border, and none of these borders are shared with other cells in the table.

Take a look at the following example of the **<border-collapse>** property.

Here is the code:

```
<style type="text/css">
    table.collapse {
            border-collapse:collapse;
    }

    table.separate {
            border-collapse:separate;
    }

    /* we gave a style for a <td> for you to better see the difference */
    td.1 {
            border-style:dotted;
            border-width:2px;
            border-color:#000000;
            padding: 10px;
    }

    td.2 {border-style:solid;
            border-width:2px;
            border-color:#333333;
            padding:10px;
    }

</style>
<table class="collapse">
    <caption>Example of a collapse border</caption>
    <tr><td class="1"> Cell A Collapse Example</td></tr>
    <tr><td class="2"> Cell B Collapse Example</td></tr>
</table>

<br />
<table class="separate">
    <caption>Exmaple of a separate border</caption>
    <tr><td class="1"> Cell A Separate Example</td></tr>
    <tr><td class="2"> Cell B Separate Example</td></tr>
</table>
```

Here is the output:

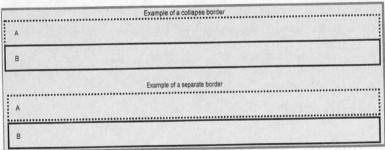

Table layout

Description: The **<table-layout>** property determines the layout method used in rendering a table.

Here are potential values under **<table-layout>**:

- **auto:** The table should be laid out according to some automatic layout algorithm. The browser does this automatically.

- **fixed:** The table should be laid out according to the provided fixed-table layout method.

Here is an example code:

```
<style type="text/css">
    table.auto
    {
    table-layout: auto;
    }
    table.fixed
    {
    table-layout: fixed;
    }
</style>

<table class="auto" border="1" width="100%" style="background-color:#9CC;">
    <tr>
    <td>The quick brown fox jumps over the lazy dog</td>
    <td>The quick brown fox jumps</td>
    <td>The quick brown fox</td>
</tr>
</table>
<br />
<table class="fixed" border="1" width="100%" style="background-color:#9CC;">
    <tr>
    <td width="50%">The quick brown fox jumps over the lazy dog</td>
    <td width="30%">The quick brown fox jumps</td>
    <td width="20%">The quick brown fox</td>
    </tr>
</table>
```

Here is the output:

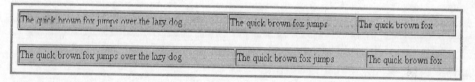

Cascading Style Sheets

Validation

Validation can be thought of as the markup version of a spell checker for errors in coding. Your markup codes should conform to a certain Web standard. Validation is one defense mechanism against errors. If you validate your Web site coding, you can always be sure that any problems or errors that may surface on your site are not due to your forgetting a closing tag, for instance. This makes it simpler to locate errors and perform testing, which in turn gives you more time to work on the actual design. The most important reason for validation is to ensure that your Web pages display properly and are optimized for search engines.

You can validate in three easy steps:

- Go to **http://jigsaw.w3.org/css-validator**.
- Put your Web address or URI in the white blank box.
- Click the "Check" button; you will then see if you have certain errors in your markup code.

Here is an illustration of the Web site:

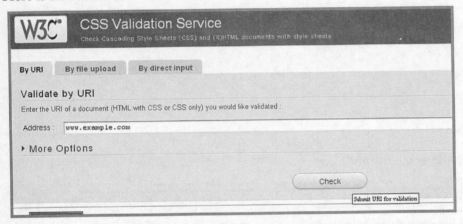

Here is an example of the output:

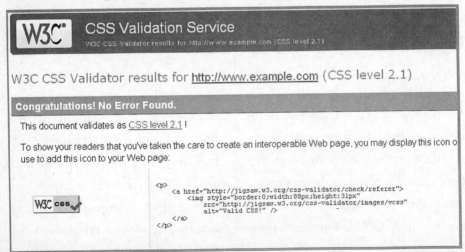

Chapter 9

ELECTRONIC COMMERCE AND SHOPPING CARTS

As your Web site or company grows, you may find yourself looking for ways to streamline your business activities. At some point, the expansion of your business will depend on how well you automate your various processes. One of the first steps you should consider involves your invoicing — the process you use to get your customers to pay you. With a little planning, your Web site can be turned into a vehicle for the facilitation of swift, hassle-free payments for your services and goods.

E-commerce is a subset of e-business, through which transactions are processed for purchasing, selling, and exchanging of goods and services over computer networks electronically, with the help of the Internet. The three main categories of e-commerce are:

- **Business-to-business (B2B):** Businesses such as manufacturers selling to distributors and wholesalers, who in turn typically sell to retailers.

- **Business-to-consumer (B2C):** Businesses selling to the general public through catalogs and online retailers, using shopping cart software.

- **Consumer-to-consumer (C2C):** Businesses or individuals buying and selling products through online payment systems like PayPal and eBay® and exchanging money online. eBay's auction service is a great example of where person-to-person transactions take place daily.

Paying over the Internet used to be possible only for businesses with specialized merchant bank accounts; now, however, there are many more options available. Bank accounts were once designed to accept credit cards, debit cards, gift cards, and other forms of payment cards, and a "payment gateway" was used to establish the all-important link between the customer's account and the merchant's account. Payment gateways were designed to verify information, transfer requests, and authorize payments. These days, merchant accounts and payment gateways are central to all online payments. Whether you are using a third-party provider like PayPal or your own merchant account capacities, ensuring that you have the ability to accept payments online will be crucial to your business.

When payment gateways were first introduced, credit cards were the only forms of online payment. Today, many different forms of payment are processed online through these gateways, including credit cards, debit cards, eChecks and, of course, PayPal funds.

Most people are familiar with PayPal and the Google Checkout™ feature. PayPal is a special type of account from which individuals can take money to pay for goods and services. Although few companies tend to pay via this method, do not rule it out as an important payment option to offer your customers. PayPal is convenient, quick, and easy to implement. During secure payment transaction processes, information is safely transmitted between the customer's bank account and your Web site, and between your Web site and the customer and merchant accounts. One item you will need to obtain a merchant account is an SSL (Secure Sockets Layer) certificate for your Web site. SSL certificates indicate that good security measures are in place on a particular Web site. They operate through a combination of programs and browser programs like Internet Explorer and Mozilla Firefox.

Among the best-known SSL certificate providers are:

- VeriSign®
- *thawte*®

- InstantSSL®
- Entrust®
- GeoTrust®

Many Web hosting providers supply free shopping cart software with their hosting packages. In most cases, installation is free, and the software itself is not usually difficult to use. Most hosting companies also offer SSL certificates as an add-on service, usually at competitive rates. You can usually expect to spend about $100 per year for an SSL certificate.

Establishing a merchant account is relatively easy, but this may not always suit the purpose of the business. You will have to determine whether a merchant account is right for your Web site business. Depending on the size and type of your business, it may be too expensive and not cost-effective to set up and operate an SSL certificate. You should weigh the pros and cons of having a merchant account versus processing your transactions via a third-party payment processor like PayPal, which has its own merchant account and payment gateway. Third-party payment processors allow individuals and companies to process transactions without having to sign up for their own merchant accounts, and virtually anyone can sign up to use these processors. These are the definite advantages of third-party processes. The major disadvantage is that the third-party processor company makes its money by taking a slice of each transaction processed by your company, eating into your profits. As your sales increase, a merchant account will likely become more cost-effective.

To have a true merchant account, yours must be a business entity; you cannot obtain a true merchant account as an individual. As the business owner, you would only be personally responsible for monitoring the account. A major advantage of having your own merchant account directly with processors like Visa® and MasterCard® is that you are in total control of how your sales are processed. You can process large volumes of sales and add your own personal touch to your online checkout pages with an application programming interface (API). You can also build a professional but personalized look and image on your customers' statements of purchase. Done properly, having a merchant account can be a good way to market your business. Merchant accounts allow you to put your company name — and often your name only — on most of the paperwork and pages associated with the purchasing of your Web site design services and any other products or services you decide to offer your customers.

When a company has a true merchant account, they can also use a separate processing gateway. You are in control of negotiating your own rates for purchases and establishing a unique protocol for each of your sales. One major drawback of getting your own merchant account, particularly for individuals and many small business owners, is the credit check. All true merchant accounts require applicants to undergo a credit check. Because the credit check is likely to be run against the business entity, any business with either low-volume business or bad credit — both of which are more common among small businesses — may not be eligible for the account. True merchant accounts are not for personal use. A high-risk business, generally identified as such by the credit check, is charged a higher rate.

Depending on the background and financial standing of the business, some are also required to sign on to multi-year contracts before their account is approved. Because of the contract element, a true merchant account is one of those business decisions that you have to live with if you decide to go for it. While many businesses benefit from having true merchant accounts, and many businesses need true merchant accounts to make the most of online sales, make sure it is right for your situation before acquiring one. Many businesses start off using a third-party processor, which is quite appropriate. When sales reach a certain point, however, it makes sense to move to a merchant account.

A true merchant account is perfect for businesses with large volumes of sales that need to process many transactions. True merchant accounts do have some additional fees compared to third-party providers. On balance, however, large volume merchants pay less with true merchant accounts. With a large volume to process, merchants receive good discount rates when they maintain their own accounts. The discount rate with third-party providers can be as high as 6 percent per transaction, with an additional transaction fee of $1 applying in most cases. A true merchant account offers rates less than half of what most third-party providers offer. As a merchant's transaction volume rises, the amount of money they save by having their own true merchant account increases.

When you look into automating a business process, focus on defining the process, coordinating the activities required, and facilitating the necessary transactions. If you bring every aspect of your business together properly, it should be clear what parts of your business can be automated and which parts you have to handle yourself. All online payments establish merchant accounts and payment gateways as central elements. It does not matter whether third-party providers like PayPal are being employed or whether merchant facilities are being used; gateways must be used to accept payments over the Internet. These components will always be there, one way or another.

PayPal is a special type of account from which money can be taken to pay for goods and services. To use PayPal to make a payment, a person must already have a PayPal account. For security reasons, PayPal establishes limits on how much a person can spend online without verifying the details of their account (bank account ownership, credit card ownership, or social security number for U.S. citizens and residents). In most cases, however, a person will have deposited funds into his or her account prior to making a purchase. This means that they are then able to pay for goods and services using the PayPal account. When a seller allows PayPal payments, the payee is able to make a payment by simply disclosing his or her PayPal information. In most cases, this is simply an e-mail address and password that are entered as log-in information. PayPal is both a method of payment for customers who have a PayPal account and a third-party payment processor. It can be used for accepting payments made using credit cards, debit cards, eChecks, and PayPal customer accounts. Although many people prefer to have a personalized payment gateway, one that provides a company specific interface, PayPal is an extremely versatile, suitable option.

The history of PayPal has a role in determining the way it is used. eBay users made the system popular as a payment medium. Buyers could deposit and then spend funds. For a long time, PayPal was the only option for individuals without credit cards, and it currently stands as a payment method in its own right and is widely supported as such. It is a measure of the program's success. Even novice Web designers can easily integrate PayPal into their Web sites to accept credit card payments. With PayPal, you do not have to buy software, do not have to buy an SSL certificate, and do not need a special Web hosting account to support e-commerce. Other third-party payment processors include 2CheckOut (2CO) and Google Checkout. These are increasingly popular methods for payment processing.

Providing your customers with safe and secure methods of shopping or purchasing services from your site is critical. Making purchases is often the scariest part of the Internet for people because they will have to share credit card numbers or banking information. According to the Federal Trade Commission (FTC) Web site, **www.ftc.gov/infosecurity**, you need to "take stock of the personal information and files on your business computers or Web sites, scale down the amount of information you store, properly dispose of the information you no longer need, protect what information you have, and design a plan to address any security breaches."

Any good security plan has to begin with identifying who in your company has access to customer data and developing a clear understanding of how this information is transmitted to your company or Web site. The FTC suggests inventorying all computers, laptops, flash drives, disks, home computers, and filing cabinets to learn where all of your company's sensitive data is stored. In the case of running an e-commerce Web site, you also need to be sure that your host server is secure because that is where your data actually lives when transactions occur via an Internet connection. It is not just your Web site that has to be secure; it is every aspect of your site, including your host server. This is another reason to read all the fine print and make sure your server will offer the quality security protection you want for your clients.

Investigate the history of any server you plan to use to host your e-commerce site. Find out if there have been any data breaches to their system and, if so, what additional security measures have they taken to protect your site. The FTC also suggests that, depending on your internal operations, you might want to have a Web site technician run "off-the-shelf security software, or hire an independent professional to conduct a full-scale security audit."

Another important factor when using the Internet to sell products or services is to use encryption when sending a customer's personal information to a third party, when storing any information on your computer network, and even when sending e-mails that contain any personally identifiable information (PII). Set up your anti-virus and anti-spyware software to run daily on in-house computers, and make sure these are also running on your host server, along with good firewalls. When you visit an e-commerce site and decide to buy something, you might see a VeriSign Secured® Seal or similar logo, usually at the bottom of the page.

After you click the "Select" or "Purchase" button to buy the product or service, a dialog box will open that says you are entering a secured area of the site. Sometimes it will say you are entering both a secured and unsecured area, and you have to click the "OK" button to acknowledge that you know this before entering the area where you will provide your credit card number or banking information. You should be looking for the "LOCK" icon in your browser to validate that you have entered a secure session, and the URL should change from **http://** to **https://**.

The FTC says that it is extremely important to "pay particular attention to the security of your Web applications," meaning the software you use to provide and request information from the visitors to your site. They add, "Web applications may be particularly vulnerable to a variety of hacking attacks, and one variation is called an injections attack, where a hacker inserts malicious commands into what looks like a legitimate request for information. Once in your system, the hacker transfers the sensitive data to his or her computer and can then use it for identity theft or fraudulent transactions."

Another aspect to securing information is to also know where the money or credit card information is coming from, because in some instances, the information could already be stolen property. According to the FTC, there are legal statutes in place like the "Gramm-Leach-Bliley Act, the Fair Credit Reporting Act, and the FTC Act" that "may require you to provide reasonable security measures for all sensitive information." You should not request any more information from your customers than is absolutely necessary, and destroy it as soon as possible; once the purchase is finalized and the customer has the product or service completed, you do not need it any longer.

Firewalls are designed to prevent hackers from connecting to your network or computer while it is connected to the Internet. In many instances, businesses and individuals leave their computer systems and networks running 24/7. In the event that your system is breached, the FTC says it is important to have a system in place to catch that breach immediately because if it goes on for any amount of time, the odds are that every sensitive file on your system will be accessed. Design a system in which you are alerted if an outside attempt to enter your network occurs, and make sure it is updated on a regular basis to stay on top of new types of hacking. Another suggestion from the FTC is to monitor all incoming traffic, which you can do by accessing your data logs. Visit the FTC site for OnGuard Online at **www.onguardonline.gov** for additional tips and information regarding the safety of your Web site and the customers you serve.

The Microsoft Web site at **www.microsoft.com/protect/yourself/phishing/spoof.mspx** discusses how some Web site owners and builders might use phishing scams to create a mirror image of a legitimate site. They try to trick you into thinking you are visiting the real site so you will submit your personal information and/or a credit card number. Over the past several years, people have received e-mails telling them their accounts on eBay were suspended for various reasons, and these looked like real eBay e-mails, complete with the logo and official-looking information. These e-mails were immediately recognized as fraudulent for those who did not have eBay accounts, but some did follow the instructions, clicking on the link in the e-mail and going to what appeared to be the login page to reinstate their account. But these e-mails were not from eBay; they were from outside sources who were attempting to obtain the account information, including credit card numbers, of the eBay customers. Microsoft terms these sites as spoofing sites because they are normally used in "conjunction with phishing scams, and the sites are designed to look like the legitimate site." In many instances, they might even have the same URL in the address bar because "there are several ways to get the address bar to display something other than the site you are on," according to Microsoft.

The best way to verify that you are not on a spoofed site is to use the SSL certificate, as discussed earlier. If you enter the secure portion of a site that uses an SSL connection, you can double-click on the padlock icon to display the security certificate that proves the real identity of the Web site. The name on the certificate should match the site you believe you are visiting. Microsoft explains that if the name is different from the one you think it should be, you might be on a spoofed site, so do not leave any personal information. Microsoft has a phishing filter installed in Windows Internet Explorer 7 and Windows Internet Explorer 8.

What is a Shopping Cart?

A shopping cart is a software application that runs on the server where your Web site is hosted and allows customers to browse the products in your store and make purchases on the Internet. Typically, a shopping cart functions similarly to retail shopping: You browse the store online, place items into your shopping cart or basket, and check out, paying with a credit card or another electronic payment system, such as PayPal. A shopping cart is integrated into your Web site so that from any page, a customer can easily find products, view their cart, and proceed to the checkout portion of your store. Shopping carts are written in a variety of programming languages, run on a variety of Web server platforms, and can be basic or advanced in functionality. Many are free, but some are not. In all cases, you will need an SSL certificate to encrypt your Web site and protect customer data, and a merchant account to process credit card payments — unless you utilize another payment processing method, such as PayPal or Yahoo! Store®.

A shopping cart normally includes product details, pricing, and customer data, all stored in a database hosted on the Web server in a very secure location. There are two components to a shopping cart: the storefront and the administration module. The storefront is what your customers see, and the administration module is what you use to add new products or change pricing, shipping costs, and inventory. Shopping carts perform a variety of functions, including shipping and tax calculations, processing secure transactions, and providing e-mail order confirmation. Some may even recognize you upon return and make recommendations for you based on prior purchases. Often they are configured for soft goods downloads, such as purchasing software and downloading it instantly after checking out of the Web store. You can use shopping carts to promote sales, discounts, and coupons.

There are many shopping carts on the market today. If you are paying for Web hosting, your provider will most likely include a shopping cart application at no additional cost. Using the provided and supported cart is a great option because it is usually free, and you have the expertise needed to help you with installation and setup. If, however, you must purchase a shopping cart, it is recommended that you read reviews and narrow down a list of candidates. Review the customer and technical support options available to you, and see if there are any recurring costs to use the cart software.

Check out the shopping carts that interest you at other stores — most shopping cart Web sites have links to see their cart in action. Spend some time online reviewing, testing, and comparing. Some great Web sites to visit for shopping cart reviews include **http://shopping-cart-review. toptenreviews.com, www.seoshoppingcarts.com**, and **www.bestshoppingcartreviews.com**. You may want to network with other designers for recommendations. Chapter 17 of this book contains recommendations as well. In most cases, you can get a free trial to test out the cart software. Above all, make sure to spend the time upfront to ensure you get the cart that will meet your current and future growth needs. It is time-consuming to shift from one cart to another, and in many cases, it is impossible.

PayPal Shopping Cart

PayPal is one of the most recommended shopping carts. PayPal is simple to implement: There is nothing to install and no scripting required, and like other carts, it keeps detailed records of all transactions and generates e-mail notifications. PayPal offers Website Payments Standard and Website Payments Pro, which let you use PayPal within your existing shopping cart. Details on PayPal's cart can be found here: **www.paypal.com/cgi-bin/ Webscr?cmd=p/xcl/rec/sc-intro-outside**. Website Payments Standard is free except for transaction fees per sale, while Website Payments Pro includes a monthly charge along with the transaction fees. There is no need to purchase an SSL certificate, as this is provided through PayPal.

Secure Socket Layer Certificates

SSL technology protects data on your Web site during secure sessions. It protects client data, privacy information, credit card information, and other data. You must have a working SSL certificate installed on your Web server to encrypt your data session. An SSL certificate encrypts sensitive data and contains unique information that identifies the owner of the certificate. An SSL certificate is needed if you have an online store, process credit cards, accept payments, and accept private data. Encryption is key because without it, your data is sent in clear packets and can easily be intercepted and stolen. An SSL certificate has a public key and a private key: The public key encrypts your data, while the private key "unlocks" the encrypted data so it can be read. Your easiest option is to buy this certificate from your Web hosting company, since they will be required to install it anyway. You should compare pricing options, however, as they will vary widely.

Chapter 10

OPTIMIZING YOUR WEB SITE FOR SEARCH ENGINES

To achieve success with major search engines, you must achieve high rankings in search results. Often, the most overlooked factor in Web site development is the optimization of your Web site for search engines. One of the most critical steps in designing and implementing a successful Web site and marketing campaign is to invest in an SEO plan for your Web site to ensure that it is designed to work effectively with all major search engines. SEO should be an ongoing process that you consistently reevaluate on a regular basis. There are more than two billion Web pages on the Internet, meaning that there are many Web sites that are directly competing with yours for potential customers. You need to take realistic, time-proven measures to ensure that your online business gets noticed and obtains search engine rankings that will deliver the results you desire.

SEO consists of a variety of proven techniques that you can use to improve the ranking of your Web site to within your target market on the Internet by using keywords that are relevant and appropriate to the products or services you are selling on your Web site. You should design your site with SEO in mind — building it right is much easier and more effective than building it wrong and having to retrofit it to meet W3C compliance and SEO optimization standards.

The W3C produces the guidelines and standards by which Web pages should be created, constructed, and maintained. Essentially, these are the industry-recognized standards. A W3C-compliant Web site ensures that it is both accessible and navigable; works across multiple browser platforms; can be read by readers, personal digital assistants (PDAs), and mobile devices; and displays properly regardless of monitor size, browser type, resolution, or type of monitor.

Another term you will hear is "Web 2.0." Web 2.0 is not an application or a physical standard. Instead, it is a generalized term to describe the Web "movement," or the latest trends and direction for using technology and Web site design to improve communication sharing, collaboration, and data exchange. Web 2.0 is synonymous with the expansive popularity of YouTube, Orkut™, Facebook, MySpace, and other social networking sites.

When you properly use SEO and optimize your Web site based on sound Web site design principles, you will know that your Web site is ready to be submitted to search engines, and that you will significantly increase its visibility and ranking within the search engines. Focus on the content on each Web page, and strive to include at least 200 content-related words on the pages of your site. Integrate your keywords into the content you place on each page, but be cautious of "keyword stuffing," which is where you overload the pages with keywords. Doing so may result in your site being blacklisted from major search engines.

Google uses PageRank, which measures the quality of a Web page based on the incoming and outgoing links from that page. This has led to a large increase in the emphasis on links to and from Web sites in efforts to increase PageRank scores. Google has since changed its algorithm to eliminate links it deems as being low in quality, lacking Web content, or being irrelevant topically. PageRank is not just based upon the total number of inbound links; it considers some links more important than others. Therefore, all links are not equal. The ranking algorithm for Google is complicated, but in general, a higher PageRank score equates to better search engine placement in the Google search engine — thus, quality inbound links are critical.

You can check out the ranking for any Web site, page, or domain name at **www.prchecker.info/check_page_rank.php**.

Successful Search Engine Optimization

The concepts and actions necessary for successful SEO can sometimes be confusing and hard to grasp when you are first starting out using SEO techniques. There are several steps that need to be followed so that you get the most out of your SEO:

- Making sure that your Web site is designed correctly and set up for optimal SEO.

- Choosing the right keywords that are going to bring the most hits to your Web site.

- Using the right title tags to identify you within search engines.

- Ensuring appropriate content writing on your Web site.

- Using properly formatted meta tags on your Web site.

- Choosing the right search engines to submit your Web site to, and understanding the free and paid listing service options available.

- Having quality inbound links to your Web site.

- Ensuring that every image on your site has an **<alt>** tag.

Once you know which areas to focus on, your ranking in search engines will increase dramatically. The main problem with SEO, and the No. 1 reason most site builders fail to properly ensure a site is optimized, is that it requires significant time investment and patience to obtain high rankings in search engines. SEO will not get you immediate visibility in search engines. You need to be realistic in your expectations — expect it to take months to see tangible results.

Meta Tag Definition and Implementation

Meta tags are a key part of any overall SEO program. There remains controversy surrounding the use of meta tags and whether their inclusion on Web sites truly impacts search engine rankings; however, they are still widely held as an integral part of a sound SEO plan, and some search engines do use these tags in their indexing process. You need to be aware that you are competing against potentially thousands of other Web sites — many of which are promoting similar products, using similar keywords, and employing other SEO techniques — to achieve a top search engine ranking. Meta tags have never guaranteed top rankings on crawler-based search engines, but they may offer a degree of control, and the ability for you to impact how your Web pages are indexed within the search engines.

When it comes to using keywords and key phrases in your meta-keywords tags, use only those keywords and phrases that you have included within the Web content on each of your Web pages. It is also important that you use the plural forms of keywords so that both the singular and the plural will end up in any search that people do in search engines, using specific keywords and key phrases. Other keywords that you should include in your meta-keyword tags are any misspellings of your keywords and phrases, as many people commonly misspell certain words, and you want to make sure that search engines can still find you.

Do not repeat your most important keywords and key phrases more than four to five times in a meta-keyword tag. If your product or service is specific to a certain location geographically, you should mention this location in your meta-keyword tag.

Meta tags comprise formatted information that is inserted into the "head" section of each page on your Web site. To view the head of a Web page, you must view it in HTML mode, rather than in the browser view. In Internet Explorer, you can click on the toolbar on the "View" menu, then click on "Source" to view the source of any individual Web page. If you are using a design tool such as Adobe Dreamweaver CS3, Microsoft SharePoint® Designer 2007, or Microsoft Expression Web, you will need to use the HTML view to edit the source code of your Web pages. You can also use Notepad to edit your HTML source code.

This is a simple basic layout of a standard HTML Web page:

```
<!DOCTYPE HTML PUBLIC "-//W3C//DTD HTML 4.01//EN"
<html>
  <head>
    <title>This is the Title of My Web Page</title>
  </head>
  <body>
    <p>This is my Web page!</p>
  </body>
</html>
```

Every Web page conforms to this basic page layout, and all contain the opening **<head>** and closing **</head>** tags. Meta tags will be inserted between the opening and closing head tags. Other than the page title tag, which is shown above, no other information in the head section of your Web pages is viewed by Web site visitors as they browse your Web pages. The title tag is displayed across the top of the browser window and is used to provide a description of the contents of the Web page displayed. We will discuss each meta tag that may be contained within the head tags in depth.

The Title Tag

This is the first tag a search engine spider will read, so it is critical that the content you put in the title tag accurately represents the content of the corresponding Web page. Whatever text you place in the title tag — between the **<title>** and **</title>** tags — will appear in the reverse bar of an individual's browser when they view your Web page. In the example above, the title of the Web page to the page visitor would read as "This is the Title of My Web Page." Titles should accurately describe the focus of that particular page and might also include your site or business name.

The title tag is also used as the words to describe your page when someone adds it to their "Favorites" list or "Bookmarks" list in popular browsers, such as Internet Explorer or Firefox. The title tag is the single most important tag in regard to search engine rankings. The title tag should be limited to 40 to 60 characters of text between the opening and closing HTML tags. All major Web crawlers will use the text of your title tag as the text for the title of your page in their result listings. Because the title and description tags typically appear in the search results page after completing a keyword search in the Web browser, it is critical that they be clearly and concisely written to attract the attention of site visitors. Not all search engines are alike; some will display the title and description tags in search results, but use page content alone for ranking.

The Description Tag

The description tag enables you to control the description of your individual Web pages when the search engine crawlers index and spider the Web site. The description tag should be no more than 250 characters. This is an important meta tag, as all major search engines use it in some capacity for site indexing. A page's description meta tag gives Google and other search engines a summary of what the page is about. Google Webmaster Tools provides you with a content analysis section, which will notify you if your meta tags are too short, too long, or duplicated too many times.

It is important to understand that search engines are not all the same, and that they index, spider, and display different search results for the same Web site. For example, Google ignores the description tag and generates its own description based on the content of the Web page. Although some major engines may disregard your description tags, it is highly recommended that you include the tag on each Web page, because some search engines do rely on the tag to index your site.

The Keywords Tag

A keyword is simply a word used by Internet users when searching for information on the Internet. But it is also a critical component to developing your pay-per-click campaign, which we will discuss in detail in Chapter 12. The keywords tag is not used much anymore, as it has been heavily abused in the past. Today, page content is critical, while keywords tags are limited or not used at all by spiders indexing your site. However, it is recommended that you at least use the keywords tag in moderation. Using the best keywords to describe your Web site helps Internet users find your site in search engines. The keywords tag allows you to provide relevant text words or word combinations for crawler-based search engines to index.

The keywords tag is only supported by a few Web crawlers. Since most Web crawlers are content-based, meaning they index your site based on the actual page content instead of your meta tags, you need to incorporate as many keywords as possible into the actual content of your Web pages. For the engines that support the description tag, it is beneficial to repeat keywords within the description tag that appear on your actual Web pages — this increases the value of each keyword in relevance to your Web site page content.

The keywords you want to use in the tag **<meta name="keywords" content="..">** should go between the quotation marks after the **"content="** portion of the tag. It is suggested that you include up to 25 words or phrases, with each word or phrase separated by a comma.

To determine which keywords are the best to use on your site, visit **www. wordtracker.com**, a paid service that will walk you through this process. Wordtracker's suggestions are based on more than 300 million keywords and phrases that people have used over the previous 130 days. A free alternative for determining which keywords are best is Google Rankings, which can be found at **http://googlerankings.com/dbkindex.php**.

The Robots Tag

The robots tag lets you specify whether a particular page within your site should or should not be indexed by a search engine, or whether links should or should not be followed by search engine spiders. To keep search engine spiders from indexing a page, add the following text between your tags:

<meta name="robots" content="noindex">

To keep search engine spiders from following links on your page, add the following text between your tags:

<meta name="robots" content="nofollow">

You do not need to use variations of the robots tag to get your pages indexed because your pages will be spidered and indexed by default; however, some Web designers include the following robots tag on all Web pages:

<meta name="robots" content="all">

Other Meta Tags

There are many other meta tags, but most merely provide additional information about a Web site and its owner, and do not have any impact on search engine rankings. Some of these tags may be used by internal corporate divisions. Here are more examples of meta tags from the real estate Web site example from Chapter 3:

<meta name="language" content="en-us">
<meta name="rating" content="SAFE FOR KIDS">
<meta name="distribution" content="GLOBAL">

```
<meta name="contentright" content="(c) 2009 APC Group, Inc">
<meta name="author" content="Gizmo Graphics Web Design">
<meta name="revisit-after" content="30 Days">
<meta http-equiv="reply-to" content="info@crystalriverhouse.com">
<meta name="createdate" content="4/8/2009">
```

You may also use the comment tag, which is primarily used by Web designers as a place to list comments relative to the overall Web site design, mostly to assist other Web developers who may work on the site in the future. A comment tag looks like this:

```
<!--begin body section for Gizmo Graphics Web Design-->
```

ALT Tags

The **<alt>** tag is an HTML tag that provides alternative text when non-textual elements, typically images, cannot be displayed. The **<alt>** tag is not part of the head of a Web page, but proper use of this tag is critically important in SEO. The **<alt>** tags are often left off Web pages, but they can be extremely useful for a variety of reasons:

- They provide detail or text description for an image or the destination of a hyperlinked image.

- They enable and improve access for people with disabilities.

- They provide information for individuals who have graphics turned off when they surf the Internet.

- They improve navigation when a graphics-laden site is viewed over a slow connection, enabling visitors to make navigation choices before graphics are fully rendered in the browser.

Text-based Web content is not the only item that increases your ranking in the search engines; images are just as important, because these images can also include keywords and key phrases that relate to your business. If any visitors to your Web site have the image option off, they will still be able to see the text associated with your images. The **<alt>** tags should be placed anywhere where there is an image on your Web site. It is key to avoid being too wordy when describing your images, but include accurate keywords within the tags. The keywords and key phrases that you use in **<alt>** tags should be the same keywords and phrases that you use in meta description tags, meta keyword tags, title tags, and in the Web content on your Web pages. A brief description of the image, along with one or two accurate keywords and key phrases, is all you need to optimize the images on your Web pages for search engines.

Most major Web design applications include tools to simplify the process of creating **<alt>** tags. For example, in Microsoft Expression Web, right-click on the image and choose "Properties" and the general tab; you can then enter **<alt>** tag text information. Most Web site development applications actually prompt you for **<alt>** tags as you add images. To enter **<alt>** tag information directly into a Web page, go to the HTML view and enter them after the **<img>** tags in the following format:

<img border="0" src="images/cftec.jpg" width="300" height="103" alt= "ChefTec Software helps you save money"></b></font></p>

Optimization of Web Page Content

Web page content is by far the single most important factor that will affect and determine your eventual Web site ranking in search engines. It is extremely important that you have relevant content on your Web pages that is going to increase the status of your Web site in search engine rankings. The content on your Web page is what visitors are going to read when they find your site and start to browse your Web pages, whether they browse to a page directly or via a search engine. You need to optimize your Web site with all the right keywords within the content of each Web page so that you can maximize your rankings within search engines. You can use software tools to find out what keywords people are using when they search for certain products and services on the Internet.

Not only are the visitors to your Web site reading the content on these pages, but search engine spiders and Web crawlers are reading this same content and using it to index your Web site among your competitors. This is why it is important that you have the right content: Search engines should be able to find you and rank you near the top of the listings for similar products. Search engines look for keywords and key phrases to categorize and rank your site; therefore, it is important that you focus on just as many key phrases as you do keywords.

The placement of text content within a Web page can make a significant difference in your eventual search engine rankings. Some search engines will only analyze a limited number of text characters on each page and will not read the rest of the page, regardless of length; therefore, the keywords and phrases you may have loaded into your page may not be read at all by the search engines. Some search engines do index the entire content of Web pages, but they typically give more value, or "weight," to the content that appears closer to the top of the Web page.

How the Google Search Engine Works

All search engines use "spiders" or "crawlers" to index your Web site. They find a page, follow the links to your Web pages, follow links to other pages, and "crawl" the Web in search of all Web pages, indexing each one as they go. This is how your site may be found by Google. You can also submit your URL to Google yourself by visiting **www.google.com/addurl.html** or sign up for Google AdWords, which triggers an indexing of your site. Because higher PageRank equates to better search engine placement in the Google search engine, quality inbound links are critical.

Optimizing Your Web Site

To get the best results from search engines, here are some tips for optimizing your Web site:

- Make sure you have at least 200 words of content on each page. Although you may have some Web pages where it may be difficult to put even close to 200 words, you should try to come as close as you can, as search engines will give better results to pages with more content.

- Make sure that the text content you have on your Web pages contains those important keywords and key phrases that you have researched, that you know will get you competitive rankings, and that are the most common phrases potential customers might use to search for your products or services.

- After incorporating keywords and phrases, make sure that your content is still understandable and readable in plain language. A common mistake is to stuff a Web site full of so many keywords and phrases that the page is no longer understandable or readable to the Web site visitor — a sure way to lose potential customers quickly.

- The keywords and phrases that you use in the content of your Web site should also be included in the tags of your Web site, such as meta tags, **<alt>** tags, head tags, and title tags.

- Add extra pages to your Web site, even if they may not at first seem directly relevant. The more Web pages that you have, the more pages search engines will have to be able to find you and link to. Extra pages can include tips, tutorials, product information, resource information, and any other information or data that is pertinent to the product or service that you are selling.

Optimizing your Web content and Web pages is one of the most important things you can do to ensure the success of your Web site. If you are unable to optimize your Web site yourself, you should hire an expert so that you get the most out of your Web content.

Web Site Optimization Tips, Hints, and Secrets

It is critical that you explore and implement the wide range of suggestions provided in this book to give your Web site the most competitive edge and obtain the highest possible rankings with search engines. The following pages contain various best practices, tips, and secrets:

- It is important to use your keywords heavily on your Web pages. Use key phrases numerous times, placing them close to the top of the page. Place key phrases between head tags in the first two paragraphs of your page and in bold type at least once on each page. Repeat keywords and phrases often to increase density on your pages.

- Design pages so they are easily navigated by search engine spiders and Web crawlers. Search engines prefer text over graphics, and HTML over other page formats.

- Never use frames. Search engines will have difficulty following them, as will your site visitors.

- Limit the use of Flash and other high-end design applications, as most search engines have trouble reading and following them, which will hurt in search engine listings.

- Consider creating a sitemap of all pages within your Web site. While not necessarily the most useful tool to site visitors, it does greatly improve the search engine's capacity to properly index all your Web site pages.

- Many Web sites use a left-hand navigational bar. This is standard on many sites, but the algorithm that many spiders and Web crawlers use will have this read before the main content of your Web site. Make sure you use keywords within the navigation, and if using images for your navigational buttons, use **<alt>** tags loaded with the appropriate keywords.

- Ensure that all Web pages have links back to the home page.

- Use "Copyright" and "About Us" pages.

- Do not try to trick the search engines with hidden or invisible text or other techniques. If you do, the search engines may penalize you.

- Do not list keywords in order within the content of your Web page. It is fine to incorporate keywords into the content of your Web pages, but do not simply cut and paste keywords from your meta tags into the content of your Web pages. This will be viewed as spam by the search engine, and you will be penalized.

- Do not use text on your Web page as the page's background color. This is another way of keyword "stuffing," and all search engines will detect it and penalize you.

- Do not replicate meta tags. In other words, you should only have one meta tag for each type of tag. Using multiple tags, such as more than one title tag, will cause search engines to penalize you.

- Do not submit identical pages with identical content with a different Web page file name.

- Ensure that every Web page is reachable from at least one static text link.

- Ensure that your title and **<alt>** tags are descriptive and accurate.

- Check for broken links and correct HTML.

- Try using a text browser, such as Lynx, to examine your site. Features such as JavaScript, cookies, session IDs, frames, DHTML, or Flash keep search engine spiders from properly crawling your entire Web site.

- Implement the use of the **robots.txt** file on your Web server. This file tells crawlers which directories can or cannot be crawled. You can find out more information on this file by visiting **www.robots txt.org/wc/faq.html**.

- Have other relevant sites link to yours. This is an often overlooked but extremely important way of increasing your search engine rankings, especially with the Google search engine. This is also known as back-linking, and it is critically important to gaining search engine visibility.

- Design Web pages for site visitors, not for search engines.

- Avoid tricks intended to improve search engine rankings. A good rule of thumb is whether you would feel comfortable explaining what you have done to a Web site that competes with you. Another useful test is to ask, "Does this help my users? Would I do this if search engines did not exist?"

- Do not participate in link schemes designed to increase your site's ranking. Do not link to Web spammers, as your own ranking will be negatively affected by those links.

- Do not create multiple pages, sub-domains, or domains with substantially similar content.

- Do not use "doorway" pages created for search engines.

- Consider implementing CSS to control site layout and design. Search engines prefer CSS-based sites and typically score them higher in the search rankings.

Web Design and Optimization Suggestions

Establish links with reputable Web sites

You should try to find quality sites that are compatible and relevant to your Web site's topic, and approach the Webmasters of those sites for link exchanges. This will give you highly targeted traffic and will improve your score with search engines. Your goal is to identify relevant pages that will link to your site, effectively yielding you quality inbound links. However, be wary of creating a "link farm" or "spam link Web site" that offers massive quantities of link exchanges, but with little or no relevant content for your site visitors or the search engines.

Note: Do not link to your competitors.

How to establish a reciprocal link program (back-links)

Begin your link exchange program by developing a title or theme to use as part of your link request invitations. This should be directly relevant to your site's content. Since most sites use your provided title or theme in the link to your Web site, be sure you include relevant keywords that will improve your Web site optimization and search engine rankings. Keep track of your inbound and outbound link requests.

Begin your search for link exchange partners by searching a popular engine, such as Google, and entering key phrases, such as "link with us," "add site," "suggest a site," or "add your link." If these sites are relevant, they are ideal for your reciprocal link program, as they too are actively seeking link partners. Make sure that the Webmasters of other sites actually link back to your site, as it is common that reciprocal links are not completed. If they do not link back to you in a reasonable amount of time, remove your link to them, as you are only helping them with their search engine rankings.

You may want to use **www.linkpopularity.com** as a free Web source for evaluating the total number of Web sites that link to your site.

Establish a Web site privacy policy

Internet users are becoming increasingly concerned with their privacy. You should establish a "Privacy" Web page and let your visitors know exactly how you will be using the information you collect from them.

You may also wish to develop a P3P privacy policy. This may be necessary to solve the common problem of blocked cookies on Web sites, as well as with shopping carts and affiliate programs. Details may be found at **www. w3.org/P3P/usep3p.html**.

This page should include the following information for your potential customers:

- For what purpose do you plan on using their information?

- Will their information be sold or shared with a third party?

- Why do you collect their e-mail addresses?

- Do you track their IP addresses?

- Notify site visitors that you are not responsible for the privacy issues of any Web sites you may be linked to.

- Notify site visitors that you have security measures in place to protect the misuse of their private or personal information.

- Provide site visitors with contact information in the event that they have any questions about your privacy statement.

Establish an "About Us" page

An "About Us" page is an essential part of a professional Web site for a variety of reasons. Your potential customers may want to know exactly who you are, and it is a great opportunity to create a text-laden page for search engine visibility. An "About Us" page should include:

- A personal or professional biography.

- A photograph of yourself or your business.

- A description of you or your company.

- Company objectives or a mission statement.

- Contact information, including your e-mail address.

Establish a "Testimonials" page

Another way to develop credibility and confidence among your potential customers is to include previous customers' testimonials. You need to make sure your testimonials are supportable, so include your customers' names and possibly their place of employment or other contact information, for validation purposes.

Establish a money-back guarantee

Depending on the type of Web site you are operating, you may wish to consider implementing a money-back guarantee to completely eliminate any potential risk to customers in purchasing your products. By providing them with a solid, no-risk guarantee, you build confidence in your company and products with potential clients.

Establish a "Feedback" page

There are many reasons to incorporate a feedback page into your Web site. There are times when potential customers will have questions about your products and services, or may encounter problems with your Web site, and the feedback page is an easy way for them to contact you. Additionally, it allows you to collect data from the site visitor, such as name, e-mail address, or phone number. A timely response to feedback is critical in assuring customers that there is a real person on the other end of the Web site, and this personal service helps increase the likelihood they will continue to do business with you.

Establish a "Copyright" page

You should always display your copyright information at the bottom of each page. You should include both the word "Copyright" and the © symbol. Your copyright should look similar to this:

Copyright © 2009 Bruce C. Brown, LLC.

How Search Engines Work

There are several different types of search engines: crawler-based, human-powered, and mixed. We will discuss how each one works so you can optimize your Web site in preparation for your pay-per-click (PPC) advertising campaign.

Crawler-based search engines

Crawler-based search engines, such as the Google search engine, create their listings automatically. They "crawl" or "spider" the Web and index the data, which is then searchable through Google. Crawler-based search engines will eventually revisit your Web site; therefore, as your content is changed, your search engine ranking may change. A Web site is added to the search engine database when the search engine spider or crawler visits a Web page, reads it, and follows links to other pages within the site. The spider returns to the site on a regular basis, typically once every month, to search for changes. Often, it may take several months for a page that has been spidered to be indexed. Until a Web site is indexed, the results of the spider are not available through the search engines. The search engine then sorts through the millions of indexed pages to find matches to a particular search and rank them in order, based on the formula it uses to find the most relevant results.

Human-powered search directories

Human-powered directories, like the Open Directory, depend on humans for their listings. You must submit a short description to the directory for your entire site. The search directory then looks at your site for matches from your page content to the descriptions you submitted.

Hybrid or mixed search engines

A few years ago, search engines were either crawler-based or human-powered. Today, a mix of both types is common in search engine results.

Using a Search Engine Optimization Company

If you are not up to the challenge of tackling your Web site's SEO needs, it may be to your benefit to hire an SEO company so that the optimization techniques you use are properly implemented and monitored. There are many SEO companies on the Internet that can ensure that your rankings in search engines will increase when you hire them. However, be wary of claims of anyone who can "guarantee" you Top-10 rankings in all major search engines; these claims are baseless. If you have the budget to hire an SEO company, it may be extremely beneficial because you will know that the experts at SEO are taking care of you, and you can focus your energies on other important marketing aspects of your business. To find a good SEO company, follow these basic rules:

- Look at the business reputations of the SEO companies you are considering. Ask the companies for customer references you can check out on your own. You can also contact the Better Business Bureau in each company's city or state to confirm its reputation. To do this, visit **www.bbb.org**.

- Do a search engine check on each company to see where it falls into the rankings of major search engines, such as Yahoo!, Bing, and Google. If the company that you are considering does not rank highly itself in these search engines, you cannot expect it to launch your business to the top of the ranks.

- Choose an SEO company that has *people* working for it, not just computers. While computers are good for generating the algorithms that are needed to use search engine programs, they cannot replace people when it comes to doing the market research that is needed to ensure that the company uses the right keywords and phrases for your business.

- Make sure that the SEO company uses ethical ranking procedures. There are some ranking procedures that are considered to be unethical, and some search engines will ban or penalize your business Web site from their engines if they find out that you — or the SEO company that you have hired — are using these methods. Some of these unethical ranking procedures include doorway pages, cloaking, or hidden text.

- The SEO company you decide to hire should be available to you at all times by phone or e-mail. You want to be able to contact someone when you have a question or a problem.

Once you have decided to hire an SEO company, it is important that you work with the company instead of just handing over all the responsibility to them. How much control over your Web site you should allow your

SEO company is debatable, but because you will be controlling your PPC advertising campaign, you must have control over your SEO efforts. Use these tips to work effectively with your SEO provider:

- Listen carefully to the advice of the SEO account manager. He or she should have expertise and be able to provide factual, supportable recommendations. SEO companies are expected to know what to do to increase your ranking in the search engines; if your chosen company fails to deliver, you need to find another company.

- If you are going to be making any changes to your Web site design, let your SEO account manager know, because any changes you make can have an effect on the already-optimized Web pages. Your rankings in search engines may start to plummet, unless you work with your SEO account manager to optimize any changes to your Web site design that you feel are necessary to make.

- Keep in mind that SEO companies can only work with the data and information that you have on your Web pages. This means that if your Web site has little information, it will be difficult for any SEO company to pull your business up in the search engine rankings. SEO relies on keywords and key phrases that are contained on Web pages filled with as much Web content as possible. This may mean adding two or three pages of Web content that contain tips, resources, or other useful information that is relevant to your product or service.

- Never change any of your meta tags once they have been optimized without the knowledge or advice of your SEO account manager. The SEO company is the professional when it comes to making sure that your meta tags are optimized with the right keywords and phrases needed to increase your search engine ranking. You will not want to change meta tags that have already proved successful.

- Be patient when it comes to seeing the results of SEO. It can take anywhere from 30 to 60 days before you start to see your site pushed into the upper ranks of search engines.

- Keep a close eye on your ranking in search engines, even after you have reached the top ranks. Information on the Internet changes at a moment's notice, and this includes your position in your target market in search engines.

Search Engine Registration

It is possible to submit your Web site for free to major search engines, including Google. When you use paid search engine submission programs, you will find that the process of listing will be faster, but results are often unacceptable, as many search engines reject automated Web submissions. Other than PPC and similar advertising programs, such as Google AdWords, it is not necessary to pay for search engine rankings if you follow the optimization and design tips contained in this book and have patience while the search engine Web-crawling and indexing process takes place. Provided at the end of this chapter is a wealth of tools and methods to submit your Web site to search engines for free. If you do decide to hire a third-party company to register you with search engines, we have provided some basic guidance to ensure you get the most value for your investment.

Submitting to human-powered search directories

If you have a limited advertising budget, you will want to make sure that you have at least enough to cover the price of submitting to the directory at Yahoo!. This is called a "directory" search engine because it uses a compiled directory; it is assembled by human hands, not a computer. For a one-time yearly fee, you will be able to ensure that crawler search engines will be able to find your Web site in the Yahoo! directory. Crawlers consistently use directory search engines to add to their search listings. If you have a large budget put aside for search engine submissions, you might want to list with both directory search engines and crawler search engines. When you first launch your Web site, you may want it to show up immediately in search engines, rather than waiting the allotted time for your listing to appear. If this is the case, you might want to consider using what is called a "paid placement" program. Your PPC advertising campaigns will show up with the top search engine rankings based on your keyword bidding.

Submitting to crawler search engines

Submitting to crawler search engines means that you will likely have several Web pages listed within the search engine. One of the top Internet crawler search engines is, of course, Google. Google is extremely popular because it is not just a search engine; it is also the main source of power and information behind many other search engines, such as AOL. The best thing you can do when getting your Web site listed at Google is to make sure that you have links within your Web site. When you have accurate links on your Web site, you ensure that crawler search engines are able to find you, drill down through your site, and index your pages accordingly.

Using search engine submission software

There are dozens of software applications that can submit your Web site automatically to search engines, the preferred program being Dynamic Submission™. You can find a trial edition at **www.dynamicsubmission. com**. Software programs like Dynamic Submission were developed to offer Web site owners the ability to promote their Web sites to the ever-increasing number of search engines on the Internet without any hassles or complications. These types of software help you submit your Web site to hundreds of major search engines with just a few "clicks," and drive traffic to your Web site.

Because nearly 85 percent of Internet traffic is generated by search engines, submitting your Web site to all the major search engines and getting them to be seen on the search engine list is extremely important, especially in concert with your PPC advertising campaign. It is essential to regularly submit your Web site details to these Web directories and engines. Some search engines de-list you over time, while others automatically re-spider your site.

However, you should be aware that the success of these submission applications has decreased over time, as search engines have begun to reject these "autobot" submissions in favor of human submissions or paid submissions. Google and most other search engines do not recommend the use of products such as WebPosition® Gold or Dynamic Submission, which send automatic or programmatic queries to Google. It is in violation of their terms of use and quality guidelines.

DMOZ

Be sure to manually submit your site to the Open Directory at **www.dmoz.org**, which is free.

Search Engine Optimization Checklist

There are many aspects to SEO that you need to consider to make sure that it works. Though each of these topics has already been covered in this chapter, the following checklist can serve as a helpful reminder to ensure that you have not forgotten any important details along the way.

- **Title tag:** Make sure that your title tag includes keywords and key phrases that are relevant to your product or service.

- **Meta tags:** Make sure that your tags are optimized to ensure a high ranking in search engine lists. This includes meta description tags and meta keyword tags. Your meta description tag should have an accurate description so that people browsing the Internet are interested enough to visit your Web site. Do not forget to use the misspelled and plural forms of words in your meta tags.

- **Alt tag:** Add <alt> tags to all the images that you use on your Web pages.

- **Web content:** Use accurate, rich keywords and key phrases throughout the content of all your Web pages.

- **Density of keywords:** Use a high ratio of keywords and key phrases throughout your Web pages.

- **Links and affiliates:** Make sure that you have used links — and affiliates, if you are using them — effectively for your Web site.

- **Web design:** Make sure that your Web site is fast to load and easy to navigate for visitors. You want to encourage people to stay and read your Web site by making sure that it is clean and looks good.

- **Avoid spamming:** Double-check to make sure that you are not using any spamming offenses on your Web site. This includes cloaking, hidden text, doorway pages, obvious repeated keywords and key phrases, link farms, or mirror pages.

Always be prepared to update and change the look, feel, and design of your Web pages to make sure that you are using SEO techniques wherever and whenever possible.

Free Web Site Search Engine Submission Sites

- **http://dmoz.org**
- **www.trellian.com**
- **www.quickregister.net**
- **www.scrubtheweb.com**
- **www.submitawebsite.com/free_submission_top_engines.htm**
- **www.nexcomp.com/weblaunch/urlsubmission.html**

- **www.submitshop.com/freesubmit/freesubmit.html**
- **www.buildtraffic.com/submit_url.shtml**
- **www.addpro.com/submit30.htm**
- **www.website-submission.com/select.htm**

There are many other free services available on the Internet, and there is no guarantee as to the quality of any of these free services. It is recommended that you create and use a new e-mail account just for search engine submissions, such as search@yourwebsite.com, to avoid spam, which can be prevalent when doing bulk submissions.

Free Web Site Optimization Tools

- **www.websiteoptimization.com/services/analyze:** Contains a free Web site speed test to improve your Web site's performance. This site will calculate page size, composition, and download time. The script calculates the size of individual elements and sums up each type of Web page component. On the basis of these page characteristics, the site then offers advice on how to improve page load time. Slow load time is the No. 1 reason potential customers do not access certain Web sites.

- **www.sitesolutions.com/analysis.asp?F=Form:** A free Web site that analyzes your page content to determine whether you are effectively using meta tags.

- **www.mikes-marketing-tools.com/ranking-reports:** Offers instant online reports of Web site rankings in seven top search engines and the top three Web directories for free.

- **www.keyworddensity.com:** Free, fast, and accurate keyword density analyzer.

- **www.wordtracker.com:** The leading keyword research tool. It is not free, but there is a limited free trial.

- **https://adwords.google.co.uk/select/KeywordToolExternal:** Gives ideas for new keywords associated with your target phrase, but does not indicate relevance or include details on number or frequency of searches.

Web Site Design and Optimization Tools

www.webmastertoolscentral.com: Offers a large variety of tools, guides, and other services for Web design and optimization.

www.htmlbasix.com/meta.shtml: Free site that automatically creates properly formatted HTML meta tags for insertion into your Web pages.

Google's Webmaster Tools

Google's own Webmaster Tools includes powerful applications that help you achieve better and higher rankings in the Google search engine. These tools provide you with a free, easy way to make your site more Google-friendly. The tools show your site from the perspective of Google and let you identify problems, increase visibility, and optimize your site.

To increase your Web site's visibility on Google, you need to learn how their robots crawl and index your site. Webmaster Tools shows you exactly how to do this. Everything you need is available at **www.google.com/Webmasters/tools**.

You can see when your site was last crawled and indexed, view the URLs that Google had problems crawling, and then take corrective action to ensure all of your pages are indexed. You can also see what keywords Google validates and which sites link to yours.

Furthermore, you can see what queries have been performed that are driving traffic to your site and where your site lands in the search engine result for those queries. You can also review how your site is indexed and whether you have any violations that Google is penalizing you for.

To take a closer look at each of these amazing Google tools, first you must sign up with Google and log into your account.

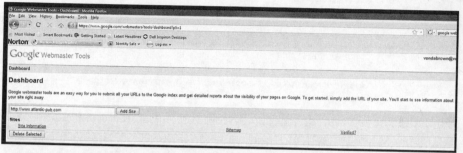

Google screenshots © Google Inc. Used with permission.

Add your URL into the "Add Site" box and click the button.

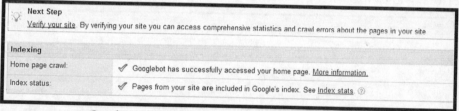

Google screenshots © Google Inc. Used with permission.

Google requires proof that you are the site owner, to prevent you from using the same tools on your competition's site. You can do this by adding a meta tag to your Web site, which Google provides, or by uploading an HTML file. In the example, the meta tag is added to the HTML code in the **index.asp** Web page. Once you add the code, simply click on the "Verify" button to continue.

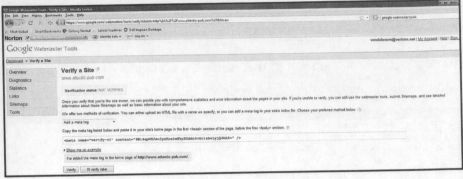

Google screenshots © Google Inc. Used with permission.

Once the site is verified, you can review the status of indexing and Web crawls. As you can see in the following screenshot, the site has been verified and has been included in Google's index. You can look at the index statistics, and you can also submit a sitemap. By examining the Web crawl errors, you can see that the site has 14 URLs not followed.

Google screenshots © Google Inc. Used with permission.

Detailed statistics about the Web crawls are available to you, as is Page-Rank information. This site is ranked "low" in Google PageRank, so there is some work to do.

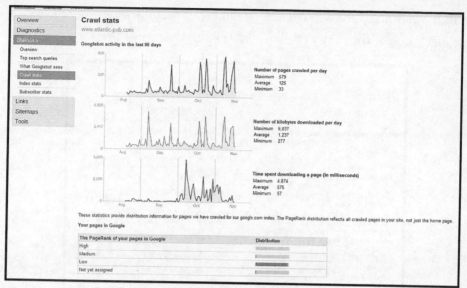

Google screenshots © Google Inc. Used with permission.

You can review your top search queries and the relative position in which your results were ranked on the Google search engine.

Google screenshots © Google Inc. Used with permission.

Spend some quality time with Google Webmaster Tools. They are all simple enough to use and understand as you analyze your site. You can even set up Google Webmaster Tools to monitor your site from your desktop, providing you with constant information about the performance of your site in relation to the Google search engine. The following is a screenshot of just some of the many tools available to analyze your Web site:

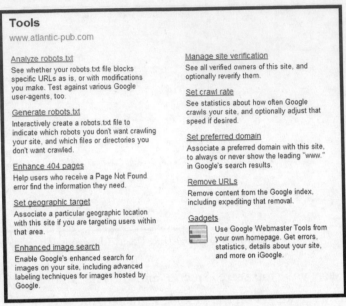

Tools

www.atlantic-pub.com

Analyze robots.txt
See whether your robots.txt file blocks specific URLs as is, or with modifications you make. Test against various Google user-agents, too.

Generate robots.txt
Interactively create a robots.txt file to indicate which robots you don't want crawling your site, and which files or directories you don't want crawled.

Enhance 404 pages
Help users who receive a Page Not Found error find the information they need.

Set geographic target
Associate a particular geographic location with this site if you are targeting users within that area.

Enhanced image search
Enable Google's enhanced search for images on your site, including advanced labeling techniques for images hosted by Google.

Manage site verification
See all verified owners of this site, and optionally reverify them.

Set crawl rate
See statistics about how often Google crawls your site, and optionally adjust that speed if desired.

Set preferred domain
Associate a preferred domain with this site, to always or never show the leading "www." in Google's search results.

Remove URLs
Remove content from the Google index, including expediting that removal.

Gadgets
Use Google Webmaster Tools from your own homepage. Get errors, statistics, details about your site, and more on iGoogle.

Google screenshots © Google Inc. Used with permission.

Remember those 14 URLs that Google reported that they could not follow? Often, this error is caused by a problem with the HTML coding of a page or by a link to a page that does not exist, which is the case with this example. Clearing up this problem is a simple matter of fixing the URLs:

Web crawl
www.atlantic-pub.com

Googlebot crawls sites by following links from page to page. We had problems crawling the pages listed here, and as a result they won't be added to our index and will not appear in search results.

Review the errors below and check any affected page for problems. For example, URLs not followed errors can be a clue that some of your pages contain content (such as rich media files or images) that Googlebot can't easily crawl, or structure is not Google-friendly.

Learn more about crawl errors

Note: Not all errors may be actual problems. For example, you may have chosen to deliberately block crawlers from some pages. If that's the case, there's no need to fix them.

Errors for URLs in Sitemaps (0) | HTTP errors (0) | Not found (0) | URLs not followed (14) | URLs restricted by robots.txt (0) | URLs timed out (0) | Unreachable URLs (0)

URLs not followed

URL	Detail	Problem Detected On
http://www.atlantic-pub.com/TOC/BuySellbook.pdf	Redirect error	Nov 6, 2008
http://www.atlantic-pub.com/TOC/Cateringbook.pdf	Redirect error	Nov 6, 2008
http://www.atlantic-pub.com/TOC/FoodCostsbook.pdf	Redirect error	Nov 16, 2008
http://www.atlantic-pub.com/TOC/Menubook.pdf	Redirect error	Nov 10, 2008
http://www.atlantic-pub.com/TOC/OpCostsbook.pdf	Redirect error	Nov 6, 2008
http://www.atlantic-pub.com/TOC/Publicitybook.pdf	Redirect error	Nov 18, 2008
http://www.atlantic-pub.com/TOC/beveragecosts.pdf	Redirect error	Nov 18, 2008
http://www.atlantic-pub.com/catalogs/2007RealEstate.pdf	Redirect error	Nov 17, 2008
http://www.atlantic-pub.com/catalogs/2008%20Library%20Distributor%20Catalog.pdf	Redirect error	Nov 14, 2008
http://www.atlantic-pub.com/catalogs/Bakery%20cover.pdf	Redirect error	Nov 18, 2008
http://www.atlantic-pub.com/catalogs/Coffeecover.pdf	Redirect error	Nov 15, 2008
http://www.atlantic-pub.com/http://www.chiqulin.com	Redirect error	Nov 8, 2008
http://www.atlantic-pub.com/ncffarn/	Redirect error	Nov 19, 2008
http://www.atlantic-pub.com/www.atlantic-pub.com/http://www.chiqulin.com	Redirect error	Nov 10, 2008

Google screenshots © Google Inc. Used with permission.

Sitemaps & Google

Submitting a sitemap to Google is a critical step toward achieving top rankings in the Google search engine. If you do nothing else with Google Webmaster Tools, submit a sitemap. To do so, first you must log back into Google Webmaster Tools, select the URL you want to work with that you have already verified, and click on the link "Sitemaps." A sitemap is an HTML page listing of all the pages in your site — it tends to be designed to help users navigate your site, and it is especially beneficial if your site is large. In the case of Google, you should create an XML sitemap, which provides Google with information about your site and improves your rankings with Google.

Essentially, a sitemap is an organized list of every page on your Web site. It helps Google know which pages are on your site and ensures that all your pages are discovered and indexed. According to Google, sitemaps are particularly helpful if:

- Your site has dynamic content.

- Your site has pages that are not easily discovered by Googlebot, Google's crawler, during the crawl process.

- Your site is new and has few links to it.

- Your site has a large archive of content pages that are not well-linked to each other, or are not linked at all.

Your sitemap can include additional information about your site, such as how often it is updated, when each page was last modified, and the relative importance of each page. You must create your sitemap and either submit it or an URL to the sitemap to Google. You can create a sitemap in the following three ways:

1. Manually creating it based on the sitemap protocol.

2. Using the Google Webmaster Tools Sitemap Generator. If you have access to your Web server, and it has Python® installed, you can use a Google-provided script to create a sitemap that uses the sitemap protocol.

3. Using a third-party tool.

The easiest way to create an XML sitemap is to use the free tool at **www.xml-sitemaps.com**. This is an incredibly easy site to use; simply type in the URL, and it does the rest for you. You upload the XML file to your Web site, and in the Google Sitemap tool, add the URL for the new file you placed on your Web server. Simply add your sitemap URL into the form, as shown in Google Webmaster Tools in the next screenshot, and click the "Add General Web Sitemap" button.

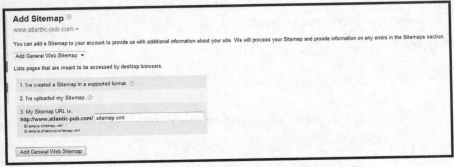

Google screenshots © Google Inc. Used with permission.

Google confirms that your sitemap has been added and will update in several hours. It is important that you check back to ensure that your sitemap has completed processing with no errors. The tool at this site creates an HTML sitemap that you can place on your Web site. It also creates the feed format to submit to Yahoo!, as well as a generic XML format for other major search engines.

Sitemaps
www.atlantic-pub.com ▾

✓ You have added http://www.atlantic-pub.com/sitemap.xml Reports may take several hours to update. Thank you for your patience!

Submit a Sitemap to tell Google about pages on your site we might not otherwise discover. More information about creating and submitting Sitemaps.

Sitemap stats
Total URLs: 0
You have recently submitted one or more Sitemaps for this site. Processing Sitemaps may take some time. Check again later to see if pages from your Sitemaps are included in Google's index.

Add a Sitemap

	Filename	Format	Last Downloaded	Status	URLs submitted	1 – 1 of 1
☐	sitemap.xml	--	--	Pending	--	Details

Delete Selected   Resubmit Selected

⬇ Download this table
⬇ Download data for all sites

Google screenshots © Google Inc. Used with permission.

Creating a sitemap with Google is a must for every Web site, and it is one of the most important actions you can take to improve your site rankings with Google. You will not find a more useful set of applications than you will with Google Webmaster Tools to ensure your site is optimized, error-free, and properly indexed by the Google search engine.

Currently viewing:
http://www.atlantic-pub.com/sitemap.xml

View: sitemap.xml ▾   OK

Sitemap summary
Most sites will not have all of their pages indexed.
Improve how Google crawls and indexes your site. More information.

Property	Status
Sitemap type	Web
Format	Sitemap
Submitted	14 hours ago
Last downloaded by Google	1 hours ago
Status	OK
Total URLs in Sitemap	204
Indexed URLs in Sitemap ⑦	No data available. Please check back soon.

Sitemap errors and warnings
No errors or warnings found.

Google screenshots © Google Inc. Used with permission.

You can view your sitemap results at any time. In the preceding image, you can see that the 204 URLs in the sitemap were indexed properly, and there are no errors or warnings. With Google Webmaster Tools, you can view a wide variety of analytics and statistics.

Snippets

A snippet is simply the text excerpt that appears below a page's title in the Google search engine results and describes the content of the page. Words contained in the snippet are bolded when they appear in the query results. The premise is that these snippets will give the user an idea of whether the content of the page matches what they may be looking for. The description snippet is taken directly from the description meta tag. If no description meta tag is provided, Google may extract a description from the page content. One source Google uses for snippets is the Open Directory Project (ODP). It is possible to tell Google to not use the ODP for generating snippets by using a piece of meta tag code. To do this, use the following code on any Web page you want this rule to apply to:

```
<meta name="googlebot" content="noodp">
```

The Problem with Navigation Bars and Spiders

You already know you need to have excellent navigation menus on your site to ensure that your customers can easily find your products and services. One problem you may face regarding SEO is that your Web site navigation menu, which is commonly on the top or on the left-hand side of each page, is indexed by the search engine and can hurt you in search engine rankings when it indexes words from your menu rather than from your page content. You need to get the search engines to index your content, not your navigation menus. Some advice is to put the navigation menu to the right of each page, which can be effective, although it is non-standard navigation and may turn site visitors off. There are a few options you can use to overcome this challenge if you want to keep your traditional navigation menus. One option is to use CSS to place your navigation menu later in the code, or you can use Web accessibility settings to have the search engine skip over the navigation menu and go right to your Web content.

Breadcrumbs

Breadcrumb navigation is good for user-friendly site navigation and SEO. Essentially, breadcrumbs are a form of text-based navigation that show where the current Web page you are viewing is located in the site hierarchy. It contains shortcuts to the next level of a Web site and lets you jump multiple layers at one time. An example of breadcrumb navigation may be: "Home > Real Estate > Home Inspections > Books." Microsoft Expression Blend features a breadcrumb trail tool, which allows designers to quickly and easily create breadcrumb trails.

Inbound and Outbound Links

Because Google values quality Web links, Google Webmaster Tools includes the ability to search for relevant sites. You can also do this by typing www.yourdomainname.com into the Google search engine. To get links, you often must give out links. Reciprocal links are fine, as long as you link to quality, relevant sites. Create outbound links as text-based links and use keywords in the text. In other words, do not just link to **www.gizWebs. com**; instead, use an embedded hyperlink for the text "Web Design and Search Engine Optimization."

Google TrustRank

Google uses a concept known as TrustRank to give higher search engine rankings to trusted sites, and lower rankings to sites that are not trusted. Exactly how this works remains a bit of a mystery, so use the advice provided here as you strive to optimize your site for Google.

Here are some factors that may affect your TrustRank ratings:

- **Performing routing updates to your site:** Adding content shows your site is maintained and current.

- **Inbound links:** Ensure your site is stacked with quality links from Web sites that have relevant content to your site.

- **Domain name age:** Having an established domain name for several years shows credibility and should give you a benefit over newly established domain names.

- **Use sitemaps:** Use XML sitemaps to ensure that search engine spiders can easily index your Web site.

- **Avoid spam:** This means spam e-mail as well as other techniques designed to trick search engines into giving you higher rankings, such as doorways, landing pages, hidden text, and stuffed keywords.

Submitting Your Site to Other Search Engines

Most Web sites have mechanisms for you to add your Web site to their indexing — for free. For example, go to **www.google.com** and type in "Submit URL," then start going down the list of links. You will find hundreds of excellent links to add your Web site to a variety of search engines. Here are a few to get you started:

- **www.dmoz.org/add.html**

- **www.scrubtheWeb.com/addurl.html**

- **http://siteexplorer.search.yahoo.com/submit**

- **http://addurl.altavista.com/addurl/default**

404 Pages & Search Engine Optimization

Even the best Web designers might, at some point, leave a link to a page that no longer exists. This is known as a 404 Error. Make sure you have a custom 404 page to redirect users back to a page from which they can navigate your site. Often, 404 pages will redirect you to the home page. You may also wish to have links to your most popular pages. An auto-redirect will give site visitors a few seconds to click on a link, and if they take no action, it will bring them to the Web site home page.

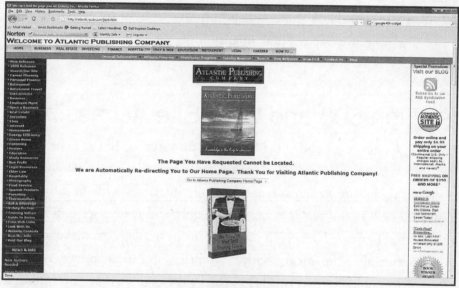

Sample 404 Error Page

Google simplifies the processing of creating 404 pages by providing a Google 404 Widget in Google Webmaster Tools. You can also use the widget to identify which page has the links to the nonexistent page so you can take corrective action.

Other Ways to Generate Web Site Traffic and Inbound Links

Become an expert in your specialty. Post entries into blogs, forums, and discussion groups. Establish yourself as an industry expert by writing and submitting articles to the dozens of free article distribution sites on the Web. You can get started at **www.articlealley.net**. Include your name, URL, and contact information, and you will be amazed at the viral distribution of royalty-free articles throughout the Web. Press releases are another way to publish information about your company while including links and other contact information to drive traffic to your site. Strive to get quality inbound links from .edu or .org domains, or other public, non-profit organizations' sites. These quality links tend to weigh heavier than commercial ones in Google.

Section 508 and Web Site Accessibility

In 1998, Congress amended the Rehabilitation Act to require federal agencies to make their electronic and information technology accessible to people with disabilities. Inaccessible technology interferes with an individual's ability to obtain and use information quickly and easily. Section 508 was enacted to eliminate barriers in information technology, to make available new opportunities for people with disabilities, and to encourage development of technologies that will help achieve these goals. The law applies to all federal agencies when they develop, procure, maintain, or use electronic and information technology. Under Section 508 (29 U.S.C. 794d), agencies must give disabled employees and members of the public access to information that is comparable to the access available to others. You should design Web pages with accessibility in mind, as there are benefits for everyone. While the Section 508 rules are quite involved and apply to much more than Web pages, here are the essential requirements for Web site design:

§ 1194.22 Web-based intranet and Internet information and applications:

- A text equivalent for every non-text element shall be provided.

- Equivalent alternatives for any multimedia presentation shall be synchronized with the presentation.

- Web pages shall be designed so that all information conveyed with color is also available without color; for example, from context or markup.

- Documents shall be organized so they are readable without requiring an associated style sheet.

- Redundant text links shall be provided for each active region of a server-side image map.

- Client-side image maps shall be provided instead of server-side image maps, except where the regions cannot be defined with an available geometric shape.

- Row and column headers shall be identified for data tables.

- Markup shall be used to associate data cells and header cells for data tables that have two or more logical levels of row or column headers.

- Frames shall be titled with text that facilitates frame identification and navigation.

- Pages shall be designed to avoid causing the screen to flicker with a frequency greater than 2 Hz and lower than 55 Hz.

- A text-only page, with equivalent information or functionality, shall be provided to make a Web site comply with the provisions of this part, when compliance cannot be accomplished in any other way; the content of the text-only page shall be updated whenever the primary page changes.

- When pages use scripting languages to display content, or to create interface elements, the information provided by the script shall be identified with functional text that can be read by assistive technology.

- When a Web page requires that an applet, plug-in, or other application be present on the client system to interpret page content, the page must provide a link to a plug-in or applet that complies with §1194.21(a) through (l).

- When electronic forms are designed to be completed on-line, the form shall allow people using assistive technology to access the information, field elements, and functionality required for completion and submission of the form, including all directions and cues.

- A method shall be provided that permits users to skip repetitive navigation links.

- When a timed response is required, the user shall be alerted and given sufficient time to indicate more time is required.

To check out your site for Section 508 compliance, visit **www.content quality.com**.

Google's Quality Guidelines

Google's quality guidelines address most of the common techniques employed to overcome and trick search engines in order to achieve higher rankings. This list is not all-inclusive. Use your time and energy to implement proven Web site design techniques and SEO standards to improve your site in Google's rankings. If you believe another Web site is abusing Google's quality guidelines, you may report it at **www.google.com/ Webmasters/tools/spamreport**.

Here are Google's quality guidelines:

- Make pages primarily for users, not for search engines.

- Avoid tricks intended to improve search engine rankings.

- Do not participate in link schemes designed to increase your site's ranking or PageRank.

- Do not use unauthorized computer programs to submit pages, check rankings, or perform other functions.

- Avoid hidden text or hidden links.

- Do not use cloaking.

- Do not load pages with irrelevant keywords.

- Do not create multiple pages, sub-domains, or domains with duplicate content.

- Do not create pages with malicious behavior, such as phishing or installing viruses or trojans.

- Avoid "doorway" pages created just for search engines.

- If your site participates in an affiliate program, make sure that your site adds value and has content a person would visit based on the content, regardless of whether it has an affiliate program.

Search Engine Optimization Tips and Techniques for Natural Search Engine Indexing and Ranking — by Vickie Acklin

SEO is important, but it is not important that you know everything; all you need to know are the basics. If you are interested in learning more than just the basics, there are hundreds of articles online. Just go to Google and type in, "How can I optimize my Web site?"

You will need to add meta tags and keywords that will help your Web site to be indexed into search engines, then submit your Web site to search engines for indexing. Indexing means that the search engine has placed your Web site in their database. Indexing can take anywhere from three to six weeks. There are millions of Web sites on the Internet, and when you first submit a Web site to a search engine, it has to wait in line behind any that were submitted before yours. Web sites are placed into a queue where they wait to be indexed.

You may wonder, "Will my Web site get on the first page in search engines?" Probably not, unless you are willing to learn about Web site ranking and implement what you learn into your Web site. Getting your Web site listed on the first page in search engine results takes time and work. This is called Web site ranking. Web site ranking is much more advanced than simply putting your meta tags on your Web site pages and getting your Web site submitted to search engines. Web site ranking means to try and get your Web site on the first page of the search results for certain keywords. You can learn everything you need to know to get your Web site a top ranking by following the advice of the experts at **http://searchenginewatch.com**.

The basic meta tags below are important to add to your Web site. These tags are added into the source code of your Web site pages. The source code is the HTML of your Web site pages. Tags are placed at the top of your pages. Below are examples of basic meta tags and where to use them.

Tip: Your title tag is your most important tag. Make sure you use just a few important keywords that describe your Web site. Do not waste this important tag by using something like, "Welcome to my Web site!"

The tag below is a document type tag. It tells the browser what kind of document is loading. There are several document types; the tag below is usually the one to use. This tag is placed at the very top of your HTML Web page before any other code.

<!DOCTYPE HTML PUBLIC "-//W3C//DTD HTML 4.01 Transitional//EN" "http://www.w3.org/TR/html4/loose.dtd">

The title tag below is an example. Change the text to your own. This tag tells the search engine the "title" of your Web site, or what your Web site is about.

<title>Modern Furniture in Your City Name (this is just an example - replace this with your own title)</title>

The description tag is usually the description that comes up in the search results. Many will use exactly what you say here. Make this tag short and descriptive. Use a few important keywords in the sentence you write describing your Web site.

<meta name="description" content="This is what search engines show in the search results so this description should make people want to visit your Web site (replace all of this text with your own description)">

Keywords in the meta tags are only used these days by some of the smaller search engines, but they are still important. Use five to ten keywords that relate directly to your Web site. Try to make sure some of these keywords are used in your title and description tags.

<meta name="keywords" content="Use about five-ten keywords here, each followed by a comma. The keywords must relate directly to your Web site pages and the text that is on those pages">

Here is where to place your tags in your source code:

```
<!DOCTYPE HTML PUBLIC "-//W3C//DTD HTML 4.01 Transitional//EN"
"http://www.w3.org/TR/html4/loose.dtd">
<html>
<head>
```

<title>Modern Furniture in your City Name (this is just an example - replace this with your own title)</title>

<meta name="description" content="This is what search engines show in the search results, so this description should make people want to visit your Web site (replace all of this text with your own description)">

<meta name="keywords" content="Use about five-ten keywords here, each followed by a comma. The keywords must relate directly to your Web site pages and the text that is on those pages">

```
</head>
```

Vickie Acklin is an independent Web site designer and developer who has owned her own business since 1999. She designs for small to medium businesses and has a niche where she offers design packages. You can visit Vickie's Web site online at **www.Websitedesigntexas.com** *and contact her at vickie@Websitedesigntexas.com.*

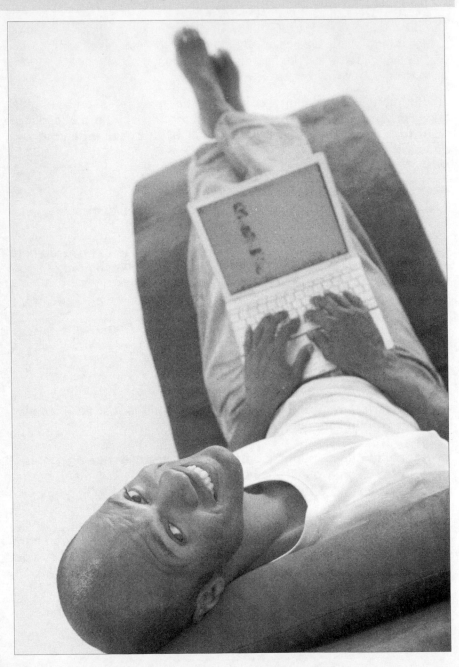

Chapter 11

GENERATING WEB SITE TRAFFIC

One of your primary goals will be to obtain the highest site rankings possible. Web site traffic is determined by the number of visitors and the number of pages they visit. Web sites monitor incoming and outgoing traffic to see which pages of their site are popular and whether there are any apparent trends, such as one specific page being viewed mostly by people in a particular country. Web traffic is measured to see the popularity of Web sites and individual pages or sections within a site. Most quality Web hosting companies provide you with detailed Web statistical analysis and monitoring tools as part of a basic Web hosting package.

Your Web site traffic can be analyzed by viewing the statistics found in the Web server log file or using Web site traffic analysis programs. Any quality Web hosting company will provide free, detailed statistics for Web site traffic. A **hit** is generated when any file is served. The page itself is considered a file, but images are also files; thus, a page with five images could generate six hits — the five images and the page itself. A **page view** is generated when a visitor requests any page within the Web site. A visitor will always generate at least one page view — the home or main page — but could generate many more as they travel through your Web site. There are many ways to increase your Web site traffic, all leading to greater sales and profit potentials. This chapter will discuss a variety of options that will lead to increased Web site traffic.

Businesses: Use Press Releases to Generate Web Site Traffic

An online press release is part of the online medium of communication, and online communication is all about timing. Your press release, whether printed, faxed, or online, is one method of communicating with your customers and your industry. It is up to you to make the most of a press release so that it has as much impact as possible.

Most companies use press releases to alert the public about a new product or service they offer. These press releases, while informative, tend to be somewhat dry, and consumers typically skim over them, sometimes missing the key points. The bottom line is that if it is not newsworthy, then you will not be selected by the media for coverage. That said, a press release promoting specific events, specials, or newsworthy items can be quite effective.

As an alternative to a written press release, you could try a multimedia approach. If you are giving a live press release, you can incorporate the audio or video files onto your Web site, either to complement a written press release or replace it altogether. It is highly recommended that you have a media section on your Web site to serve reporters, columnists, producers, and editors with your latest press release information. Many people find that listening to an audio clip — or, better yet, watching a video clip — is preferable to reading a written press release. There is so much written on the Internet that trying another medium to get your message across could be just the boost your company needs. You should also think of other Web site owners as another form of a media channel, as everyone is looking for fresh content and expert advice.

Consider using an online press release service, such as **www.PRWeb.com**, to generate successful media exposure for your online business. This free service is another tool you can use to distribute your press release information to thousands of potential new customers or clients.

Keep in mind the value of using highly relevant keywords often within the content of your online press release in order to use the benefits of SEO. Including live links within your online press release is another way to ensure increased media coverage. Linking to relevant Web sites increases the credibility and functionality of your online business.

Make sure that you give your customers a reason to visit your site, spend time browsing it, interact with it, and — most importantly — return to it. Offer incentives by showcasing featured products or promotions, and use creative Internet tools, such as video and audio, to create an interactive experience. You can also import video clips from promotional products, CDs/DVDs, or create your own video clips and add them to your Web site.

Publish Testimonials on Your Web Site

Using customer testimonials is a good way to promote the quality and reliability of your Web site and, more importantly, promote your products or services. This is an amazingly effective tactic. The media coverage you get is a subtle, third-party referral to you. However, the strongest, most effective sales assistance comes from direct customer testimonials. It is highly recommended that you use audio and video testimonials as well as printed quotes on your Web site. You should include your customer's name, e-mail address, and Web address with each unsolicited testimonial to increase believability. No matter how flashy or impressive your Web site may look, it is customer service, satisfaction, and reliability that keep customers coming back.

Proven Techniques for Generating Web Site Traffic

The following techniques may be employed to increase Web site traffic. These proven methods will increase your Web site traffic:

- Create a "What's New" or "New Products" page. Site visitors like to see what is new, trendy, or just released. Make it easy for them.

- Establish a promotion program. You can offer free products, trial samples, or discount coupons. Everyone loves a bargain, so give it to them.

- Establish a contest. Create an online contest to promote anything. Be creative; you do not have to market your products in a contest. Atlantic Publishing Company's Top 50 Restaurant Web Site Contest drew tens of thousands of site visitors, ranking the top Web sites of restaurants their site visitors submitted. Winners got a free "Award Winner" image to place on their Web site, which also linked back to Atlantic Publishing Company's Web site. Similar contests cost nothing to create, are simple to manage, and draw visitors.

- Add content-relevant professional articles, news events, press releases, or other topics of interest on a daily basis to draw visitors back to your site.

- Establish a viral marketing campaign, or embed viral marketing techniques into your current advertising programs or e-zines. Viral marketing is when you incorporate such techniques as a "forward to a friend" link within the advertisement. In theory, if many people forward to many more friends, it will spread like a virus and eventually go to many potential customers.

- Use signature files with all e-mail accounts. Signature files are basically business cards through e-mail, so send your business card to all your e-mail recipients. Signature files are included with every e-mail you send out and can contain all contact information, including business name and Web site URL. Signature files can be created in all e-mail applications.

- Start an affiliate program and market it. Include your affiliate information in e-mails, newsletters, e-zines, and on Web sites to promote your program. A successful affiliate program will generate a significant increase in Web site traffic. For an example of a highly effective affiliate campaign, visit **www.atlantic-pub.com/affiliate.htm**.

- Include your Web site URL on everything, such as business cards, letterhead, promotional items, and e-mails.

- Win some awards for your Web site. There are quite a few award sites that are nothing more than link exchange factories, but there are some reputable award sites, such as **www.Webbyawards.com** and **www.100hot.com**.

- Everyone loves search engines, so put Google right on your Web site. Simply visit Google to add a free search feature to your Web site. This is a tool that site visitors will love.

- Implement Google AdSense on your Web site to increase revenue and traffic.

- Implement Google AdWords to increase Web site traffic and generate sales revenue.

- Put your URL into your e-mail signature so you are constantly advertising your Web site.

- Register your site with online directories relevant to your content.

- Write free articles and submit them to other newsletters.

- Post often on content-related forums and message boards, and post your Web site URL with each entry.

- Submit content often to content-relevant e-mail discussion groups on related content, and post your Web site URL with each entry.

- Establish links from other sites to yours. Create a "Links" page or directory on your Web site, and offer your visitors a reciprocal link to your site for adding a link to your site on theirs.

- Develop quality Web site content that is well-organized and captivating.

- List your URL on all offline advertising and printed materials, such as stationery and print advertisements.

Link Exchanges & Web Site Traffic

A link exchange is when two or more Web sites exchange links and point to each other. Be careful here — do not sign up with link farms, which do nothing more than exchange links with thousands of Web sites. Link exchanges can be effective when they are selective, relative, and used in moderation. It is not uncommon for sites to establish a "Link with Us" page, such as the one at **www.atlantic-pub.com/links.htm**. This is often done on a separate Web page on the site, and they are used by individuals and search engines to find the links and follow them to the destination Web site.

Link exchanges can be done manually or automatically, but only the manual method is recommended to ensure strict quality control over who you link with. Be selective, and ensure that you get a quality reciprocal link. For example, if you sell books about how to become a home inspector, linking to the state regulations on home inspection, or Web sites with hurricane standards in the state of Florida, is fine. Also, you may want to link with companies who provide related services and supplies, such as hurricane shutters and roofing. If you link to companies that sell flowers, Web hosting, or shoes, you may be penalized by search engines because these topics are not relevant to your content.

A quick search on the Internet reveals many companies you can use for paid link exchange programs, but it is recommended that you stay away from them all. Yes, manual links take some manual labor to create, and you may only add a link or two a week. This may also require you to initiate the link request with relevant companies you want to exchange links with, but the benefits are well-worth the time investment.

When you initiate a link request, ask for the exchange in a natural-style e-mail; do not use a canned template, which sounds like a robot is asking for the exchange. You will find few responses to this. Links must be to sites of relevant topics, and only high-quality Web sites.

Publishing Articles to Generate Web Site Traffic

Writing articles is amazingly effective for generating Web site traffic and increasing your ranking in search engines because you embed links to your site into articles, which may be published and re-published on several Web sites. The viral effect of this generates quality inbound links, promotes awareness of your Web site, and increases your reputation as an expert in your specialty, because you are publishing articles on the subject. Embed keywords into your article, as well as links to your Web site. Keep your articles fairly short — generally no more than 750 words. If you need to write longer, break the content up into a series of articles. Draw readers to your Web site by giving them enough information to at least instill an interest in visiting your Web site.

For all articles, ensure that you include a biography that includes contact information and information about your experience, education, company, and products, as well as links to your Web site. Establish yourself as an industry expert, and you will be recognized as one by your peers. Below are the most popular free article listing Web sites you can submit to. When you do submit your article, send it to each of the following:

- **www.articlealley.com**

- **www.ezinearticles.com**

- **www.articlecity.com**

- **www.earticlesonline.com**

- **www.articlecache.com**

- **www.goarticles.com**

You must first visit these sites and sign up as an author, which gives you an account login and simple instructions to publish your articles. It could not be easier or more effective. Note that most of these sites have an approval process to ensure that your article meets their content standards.

Using Web Directories to Generate Web Site Traffic

A Web directory is simply an organized cataloging of Web sites by subject. The best examples of this are **www.dmoz.org** and **http://dir.yahoo.com**, which is also the largest human-maintained Web directory. You should submit your Web site to Web directories. Most provide you with a simple "Add URL" link, such as **www.dmoz.org/add.html** and **https://ecom.yahoo.com/dir/submit/intro**.

Although Web directories are often free, some, such as Yahoo!, will charge you for the listing. The following Web site provides you with links to all of the top-ranked Web directories and also provides you with cost information and Google PageRank information. This should be your guide to adding yourself to Web directories: **www.seocompany.ca/directory/top-Web-directories.html**. When adding your Web site to directories, embed keywords or key phrases into your title and description. There are programs that can automate this process for you, such as SubmitEaze, located at **www.submiteaze.com**.

Generating Web Site Traffic
— by Paul Pennel

One of the most important keys to having a successful Web site is to generate traffic. Your Web site can be beautifully designed, your call to action easy to find, and your user experience flawless, but none of this means anything if nobody ever visits your Web site. This article will cover several of the key steps you can follow to generate traffic for your Web site. Some options, like pay-per-click advertising, can be expensive, while others — like back-links, article submission, and message-board posting — cost nothing but time.

Pay-per-click advertising

PPC advertising is a form of advertising in which you only pay money if somebody clicks on your advertisement. Other forms will charge a set price to display your ad in a specific place for a specific amount of time. There are many providers, but I would suggest you use one of the biggest three: Google AdWords, Yahoo! Search Engine Marketing, and Microsoft adCenter®. With each of these, you can set a price you are willing to pay for a keyword(s) and set a monthly budget.

For example, you could target "Individual Taxes," bid 30 cents per click, and state that you are willing to spend $25 per month. Your ad would then show up on searches and Web sites related to your keyword(s). If others have bid more for the same keyword(s), their Web sites will likely be shown instead of yours until they hit their spending limit for the month. Once your account has had enough hits to be charged $25, your ad will not be shown for the rest of the month.

PPC can be a very effective targeted and cost-effective means of advertising. All of the major providers do a good job of only showing your ad on a page with relevant content or a search with relevant content. Therefore, most of the people who click on your advertisement were already looking for a product like yours.

Article writing

One of the best things you can do is write articles. It does not cost anything other than time and can have tremendous benefits. You can post the articles on your Web site to provide relevant content and help establish yourself as an expert in your field. The easiest way to do this is with a blog on your Web site. Write as though you are writing an article you want published in the newspaper, and you will be on the right track. If you decide to create a blog, make sure it is easy to subscribe to so your visitors can keep coming back. A blog with good content will often get linked to from other Web sites that want to reference your good information.

Another method you can use is to publish your article on other Web sites with a short biography and a link to your Web site listed at the bottom of the article. If you are lucky enough to have a relationship with somebody who owns a Web site targeted to your area of expertise that draws a large amount of traffic, send your article to that person and ask him or her to post it. Most people will be happy to do so if it is relevant to their Web site and provides good content.

If you are not lucky enough to know the right person, there is still a great way to get your article published and get traffic. There are several companies, called article repositories, that will publish your article on their Web site and give others permission to do the same. So if somebody is looking for an article on acupuncture and infertility but does not have the knowledge, they can go to one of these article repositories, take a good article, and put it on their Web site. Your biography and Web site are listed at the bottom of the article, and people who read your article and want to know more will likely visit your Web site or contact you. Another benefit is that everywhere your article is placed is another link to your Web site, which makes search engines find your Web site more relevant, in turn moving your sit up their rankings. EzineArticles™ is probably the biggest article repository. They have a nice day-by-day tutorial that walks you through how to write and submit relevant articles that will get noticed to help your business grow.

Message board posting

Another very effective way to be seen as an expert in your area and generate more traffic is to visit relevant message boards and answer posts. Make sure you are providing value and not just advertising your Web site. People will start to know and trust you, thus when you answer a question by directing people to a relevant section of your Web site, they will not question your motives. These answers will not be seen by nearly as many people as other forms of advertising, but the average level of interest in your area of expertise is going to be much higher.

Press releases

Sending out press releases is another great way to generate traffic. This method can range from free to several hundred dollars. It depends on the type of release you want and the type of release you are doing. The cheapest are submissions for use on Web sites. It costs more as you are released to more Web sites, newspapers, and other media outlets. To start, either try doing it on your own, or use a low-cost provider. After doing it a few more times, seeing the results, and knowing what you need to provide, you may want to move up to the pricier providers. Two well-known, free, or low-cost alternatives are **www.pressexposure.com** and **www.pitchengine.com**. Three pricier but more complete alternatives are **www.prnewswire.com**, **www.prWeb. com**, and **www.marketwire.com**.

Help a Reporter Out™

Peter Shankman's brainchild Help a Reporter Out (HARO) is a unique way to generate traffic. If you sign up for his service, you will get three e-mails every business day listing various topics that reporters need information on. Most of these reporters will list some information about you in their articles if they like what you have to say. If you use this, please be patient and wait until you find a request that is right up your alley. Do not waste a reporter's time by responding to topics that you are not really an expert in and are just trying and get your name out there.

Social networking

Web sites like Twitter®, Facebook, and LinkedIn® can all help drive traffic to your Web site. On Facebook, you can create a group and ask your friends to join. Then, when you launch a new product or are setting up a big event, you can let them know about it through Facebook. People go to Facebook to be social, so they do not feel put upon if you post something every week or so that they might read.

LinkedIn is more for professional networking than the other sites. It gives you the option to list your company and post your Web site. LinkedIn is very popular with search engines, so a search of your name or your business is likely to have LinkedIn as one of the top results once you are listed there. Your updates are posted to your LinkedIn network, making this another good way to keep people up-to-date on what you are doing. It keeps you in the forefront of their minds.

Tip sheet

A tip sheet is a single page of targeted information. A good example of an effective tip sheet would be for a green house to provide a tip sheet on how to care for common plants. The tip sheet should consist of eight to 12 bulleted tips. Each tip should have a short bolded description, as well as a sentence or two elaborating on the point. Do not use the tip sheet to advertise your services; instead, use it to advertise yourself as an expert in your field. The only advertising you should have is a sentence or two at the bottom of the tip sheet that gives your company name and Web site. If the tip sheet has enough relevant information, potential customers will hold on to it and refer to it more often than a business card. This will keep your business in the front of their minds.

Traffic frenzy

You can see how easy it would be to spend all your time working on building traffic for your Web site. Most of these activities involve writing about a subject that you are passionate about, so they can be enjoyable. However, do not spend all of your energy doing this, as you are not in business to have a well-trafficked Web site. Instead, take 20 minutes three to five times a week to market your business, then stop once that time is up. You might not get much done at one time, but over time, all those articles and message board answers add up to you having plenty of good content out on the Web that directs potential customers to your Web site.

Make sure you have a reliable way to measure your traffic. Google Analytics is free, easy to set up, and gives you a plethora of relevant information.

Minnow Web Design offers solutions for small businesses or organizations with big ideas. Owner and designer Paul Pennel combines 12 years of information technology experience with a desire to make great Web sites affordable. Paul can be contacted at paul@minnowWebdesign.com or on the Web at **www.minnowWebdesign.com**.

Chapter 12

INTRODUCTION TO PAY-PER-CLICK ADVERTISING

Unlike other paid advertising campaigns in which you pay for the campaign in hopes of generating customers and revenues, with pay-per-click (PPC) marketing, you are not paying for any guarantees or promises of sales, Web site traffic, or increased revenues; you are no longer paying out money in print advertising or other online marketing techniques hoping for a return on your significant investment. Google makes PPC advertising easy, effective, and profitable with Google AdWords, but there several other PPC offerings, including Yahoo! and Microsoft.

Banner advertising was the largest type of advertising on the Internet, and it still holds a small market share, but the main disadvantage of banner advertising is that the ads are embedded within pages. You have to rely on a Web designer to put your banner ad on a page that has similar or complementary content and, of course, it is useless unless someone clicks on it. With PPC advertising, you do not pay to have your advertisement loaded on a Web page or to have your advertisement listed at the top of search engines; you only pay for results. In other words, PPC advertising is entirely no cost — minus potential setup costs — even if your advertisement is viewed by millions of Web site visitors. You only pay when your ad is clicked.

When someone clicks on your AdWords advertisement, Google charges your account based on a formula price. Remember that the "click" in no way guarantees sales; it merely means that someone has clicked on your advertisement and will be routed in the browser to the pre-determined Web page you specified when you created your advertisement. Do not underestimate the importance of having a user-friendly, information-rich Web site to capture the attention of the site visitor and close the deal. Not all PPC campaigns must result in a purchase — many advertisers use PPC advertising to sell products — but many more use them to sell services, promotional material, and news releases, all to build business or disseminate information.

PPC advertising began in 1998. The original concept was that anyone with a brick-and-mortar or online business could manage and determine their own search engine ranking based on pre-selected keywords and how much money they were willing to pay for the resultant "click" on their advertisement. PPC advertising is the fastest-growing form of online marketing today.

You will likely admire the simplicity and functionality of PPC advertising, which allows you to have significant control over your campaign. Before you forge the path toward implementing a Google AdWords PPC marketing plan, it is critical to understand PPC advertising and develop strategies to design an effective campaign, optimize and monitor overall ad performance, and employ sound business principles in the overall management and financial investment of your campaign. To ensure the success of a Google AdWords PPC campaign, you must choose the most effective keywords, design an effective and captivating advertisement, and have a well-designed, information-rich Web site with easy navigation.

Pay-Per-Click Advertising Walkthrough

You pay a specified rate for every visitor who clicks through from the search engine site to your Web site. Every keyword has a "bid" price, depending on the popularity of the keyword in search engines. You set your own budget and financial limitations, and you are done. Here is a step-by-step walkthrough:

- Join Google AdWords and, with a credit card, put money on your account to get started.

- Create your ad as you want it to appear with the selected keywords you wish to target.

- Based on the keyword value, you set how much you are willing to spend on each keyword. More popular keywords are more costly per click than others.

- Upon completion, your ad is ready to appear in the Google search engine.

- When someone searches through Google by using one of your keywords, the advertisement is matched to the keyword query, and the ad is displayed in the Google search engine results.

- If the person clicks on your advertisement, they are navigated to your Web site, and you are charged for the click.

The search engine will return a rank-ordered list of the most popular Web sites matching your search criteria, and it may display your advertisement if it also matches the search criteria and keyword. One of the benefits of Google AdWords PPC advertising is that your advertisement will be placed right up there with the top-ranked Web sites in your search category.

Most PPC search engine applications operate on the same principles: The advertiser with the highest bidder gets top billing in the search engine return. It is a combination of experience, knowledge of the market, and some trial and error that lets you balance keywords and phrases to delivery optimal results, and the tools provided by Google AdWords help you achieve that goal.

Google AdWords Pay-Per-Click Benefits

- It is easy to implement.

- The results are clearly measurable.

- It is cost-effective in comparison to other types of traditional and online advertising programs.

- It is suitable for both large and small businesses.

- It is ideal for testing out market response to new products or services.

- It gives you full control over your budget; you can set systematic budgetary limits to minimize your overall financial risk and investment.

- It is more effective than banner advertising.

- It delivers a higher click-through rate than banner advertising.

- Ads are ideally placed with top search engine results on the most popular search engines.

- It is only delivered to your potential customers when they are searching on keywords related to the products or services contained in your PPC ad.

- Ads are delivered based on keyword searches and are delivered immediately — meaning that the chances of turning one of those potential customers into an actual customer is dramatically increased.

- It allows you to design your ad, which is strategically placed in a prominent location on the Web site.

- Ads can be delivered in search engine results or within the content of a Web page.

This is an example of a Google AdWords PPC advertisement in a Google search results page. The ads are located at the top of the search results, known as "sponsored links," as well as in the column along the right side of the page:

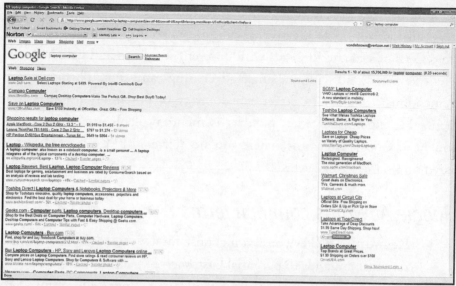

Google screenshots © Google Inc. Used with permission.

In the "Sponsored Links" section on the top right-hand side of the page, you will see the PPC results based on my query "laptop computer." As you can see, Sony® is top shelf, with Toshiba® ranking second. There is no cost to any of these advertisers to have their sponsored links shown in your search engine results. If you were to click on one of those links, you would be taken to their site, and they would be charged a pre-determined amount for that click.

Google screenshots © Google Inc. Used with permission.

Another primary benefit of a Google AdWords PPC campaign is that you have fully customizable advertising solutions in your toolbox. You can create dozens of separate PPC ads with different wordings and based on different keywords, all within a single advertising campaign. This gives you tremendous flexibility to target a wide array of potential customer segments. Having a wide variety of advertisements available is a critical component of Google AdWords, where you are delivered PPC advertisements based on a variety of keywords.

Google AdWords common terms

- **Keyword:** The keywords you choose for a given ad group are used to target your ads to potential customers.
- **Campaign:** A campaign consists of one or more ad groups. The ads in a given campaign share the same daily budget, language and location targeting, end dates, and distribution options.
- **Ad group:** An ad group contains one or more ads targeting one set of keywords. You set the maximum price you want to pay for an ad group keyword list or for individual keywords within the ad group.
- **Impression:** The number of impressions is the number of times an ad is displayed on Google or the Google content network.
- **Keyword matching options:** There are four types of keyword matching: broad matching, exact matching, phrase matching, and negative keywords. These options help you refine your ad targeting on Google search pages.
- **Maximum cost-per-click (CPC):** With keyword-targeted ad campaigns, you choose the maximum cost-per-click (Max CPC) you are willing to pay. AdWords Discounter automatically reduces this amount so that the actual CPC you are charged is just one cent more than the minimum necessary to keep your position on the page.
- **Maximum cost-per-impression (CPM):** With site-targeted ad campaigns, you choose the maximum cost per thousand impressions (Max CPM) you are willing to pay. As with Max CPC, the

AdWords Discounter automatically reduces this amount so that the actual CPM you are charged is the minimum necessary to keep your position on the page.

Cost of Google AdWords Pay-Per-Click Advertising

Google AdWords PPC advertising is, of course, limited by the size of your advertising budget. You will know in advance how much you will pay per click. Most start out with a minimum price per click, such as 10 cents, and can quickly escalate to significantly more money, even as much as $100 per click, depending on the keyword. Essentially, you "bid" with your competitors with the amount you are willing to pay for each click on your advertisement, based on the keywords you choose. It may be cost-prohibitive to be the top bidder, as your advertising budget will be consumed much quicker than if you were a No. 2 or No. 3 bidder, but there are also times when it is more critical to be the No. 1 bidder regardless of the financial impact. Your bid is the maximum amount you are willing to pay for the Web site visitor to click on your advertisement, so be careful when choosing the amount you are willing to bid per click, as you may end up having to pay it.

What is Google AdWords?

Google AdWords is a user-friendly, quick, and simple way to purchase highly targeted CPC or CPM advertising. AdWords ads are displayed along with search results on Google, as well as on search and content sites in the growing Google network, including AOL®, EarthLink®, Ask.com, and Blogger™.

When you create an AdWords site-targeted ad, you choose the exact Google content network sites where your ad will run and specify the maximum amount you are willing to pay for each thousand page views on that site. You pay whenever someone views your ad, whether the viewer clicks or not. It is recommended that you start out with a Google AdWords keyword-targeted ad, and do not allow content matching. There is no minimum monthly charge with Google AdWords, but there is a one-time activation fee for your account. Although your campaign can start in minutes, it is highly recommended that you invest the time to identify the best keywords possible. You can even use text, image, and video formats for your ads. Hundreds of thousands of high-quality Web sites, news pages, and blogs partner with Google to display AdWords ads. The Google content network reaches across the entire Web.

Using the keywords you specify when you create your ad, Google's contextual targeting technology automatically matches your ads to Web sites that are the most relevant in content to your business — this means your ads are displayed only on relevant content sites in relevant content searches. For example, an ad for a laptop hard drive may show up next to an article reviewing the latest notebook computers.

By using the Google Placement Performance report, you can monitor where your ads appear and their performance based on impression, click, cost, and conversion data. You can use this in-depth analysis tool to adjust your campaigns, change content, and remove underperforming ads from your campaign. There is no minimum spending threshold, and you can set your maximum monthly budget for each ad. Google provides you with a wealth of tools and information that will help you choose keywords and stretch your budget to its fullest potential.

Google lets you specify country, state, city, or regions as you create your ads, so they are only served in the markets you choose. This will save your budget from clicks in markets where you have no presence. Your business location will show up on Google Maps™ along with contact information.

How Google AdWords Ranks Ads

Ads are positioned in both search and content pages based on their Ad Rank; the ad with the highest Ad Rank appears in the first position, and so on down the page. If your ad achieves the fourth-highest Ad Rank, your ad will be positioned No. 4 in search engine results.

Here is where it starts to get confusing. While the Ad Rank determines where an ad is placed, the criteria Google uses to determine Ad Rank differs for keyword-targeted ads, depending on whether they appear on Google and the search network, or just on the content network.

How Ad Rank is determined on Google and the search network

A keyword-based ad is ranked on a corresponding search engine result page, based on the matched keyword's CPC bid and Quality Score:

Ad Rank = CPC bid × Quality Score

The Quality Score for Ad Rank on Google and the search network is determined by a number of factors, including:

- Historical click-through rate (CTR) of the keyword and the matched ad on Google

- Account history, measured by the CTR of all the ads and keywords in your Google AdWords account

- Historical CTR of the display URLs in the ad group

- Relevance of the keyword to the ads in its ad group

- Relevance of the keyword and the matched ad to the search query

- Your account's performance in the geographic region where the ad will be shown

Google allows up to three AdWords ads to appear above the search results, as opposed to on the side. It is important to note that only ads that exceed a certain Quality Score and CPC bid threshold may appear in these positions. If the three highest-ranked ads all surpass these thresholds, then they will appear in order above the search results.

The CPC bid threshold is determined by the matched keyword's Quality Score; the higher Quality Score, the lower the CPC threshold.

How Ad Rank is determined on the content network

Your keyword-based ad is positioned on a content page based on the ad group's content bid and Quality Score:

Ad Rank = content bid × Quality Score

The Quality Score related to Ad Rank is determined by:

- The ad's past performance on the site and other similar sites

- Relevance of the ads and keywords to the site

- Landing page quality

How Ad Rank is determined for placement-targeted ads on the content network

If a placement-targeted ad wins a position on a content page, it uses up all the ad space, so no other ads can show on that page. To determine whether your placement-targeted ad will show, Google considers the bid you have made for that ad group or for the individual placement, along with the ad group's Quality Score:

Ad Rank = bid × Quality Score

Google states that the Quality Score for determining whether a placement-targeted ad will appear on a particular site depends on the campaign's bidding option. If the campaign uses CPM bidding, Quality Score is based on:

- The quality of your landing page

If the campaign uses CPC bidding, Quality Score is based on:

- The historical CTR of the ad on this and similar sites

- The quality of your landing page

How to Improve Your Ranking

The bottom line is that relevant keywords, relevant text within your ads, a good CTR on Google, and a high keyword CPC bid all result in a higher position for your ad. The theory is that this system — which is not based entirely on the price you are willing to pay per click — uses well-targeted, relevant ads to ensure that the quality of your ads is factored into placement and helps ensure that your ads can get placed even if you are not the top keyword bidder. The AdWords Discounter monitors other ads and will automatically reduce the CPC for your ads so that you pay the lowest possible price for your ad's position on the search engine results page. One of the main advantages of this system is that you cannot be locked out of the top position — as you would be in a ranking system — based solely on price.

When you have completed the account setup process, you will be required to activate your account through an opt-in e-mail, which is sent to your specified e-mail account. Once this is confirmed, your account is activated and you can log into your new Google AdWords account. At this point, you will be required to enter your billing information. Upon completion of your billing information, your ad often appears within minutes. Google AdWords is set up to operate with three distinct levels: account, campaign, and ad group. In summary:

- Your account is associated with a unique e-mail address, password, and billing information.

- At the campaign level, you choose your daily budget, geographic and language targeting, distribution preferences, and end dates.

- At the ad group level, you create ads and choose keywords. You can also select a maximum CPC for the ad group or for individual keywords.

- Within each ad group, you create one or more ads and select a set of keywords to trigger those ads. Each ad group runs on one set of keywords. If you create multiple ads in an ad group, the ads will rotate for those keywords.

- When you log into your account, you can see the CTRs listed below each of your ads. If a particular ad is not performing as well as the others, you can delete or refine it to improve the overall performance of your ad group.

How Much Google AdWords Will Cost

There are two versions of Google AdWords: the Starter Edition and the Standard Edition. Starter Edition is for those who want to advertise a single product or service and for those who are new to Internet advertising. You can upgrade from the Starter Edition to the Standard Edition at any time. You may pay a small set-up fee to set up your Google AdWords account. Each keyword has a minimum bid that is based on the quality of the keyword specific to your account, and if your keyword or ad group's maximum CPC meets the minimum bid, your ad will be displayed in response to search queries. The following are some key cost factors to remember:

- The position of an ad is based on the maximum CPC and quality.

- The higher the Quality Score, the lower the CPC required to trigger ads, and vice versa.

- There is no minimum spending requirement.

- You set the daily limit on how much you are willing to spend.

- You set how much you are willing to pay per click or per impression.

- You only pay for clicks on your keyword-targeted advertisement.

The Google Keyword Tool generates potential keywords for your PPC campaign and tells you their statistics, including search performance and seasonal trends.

Your CPC will drive your total cost for AdWords, so knowing how much a keyword "costs" is critical in estimating your total monthly costs. Google provides a wide variety of tools to help you establish your account, choose keywords, and manage your budget and your account.

Establishing and Managing Your Google Account

Using the Starter Edition, this section will outline the AdWords process. The first step you must complete is to create a new Google AdWords campaign. To so this, click on the "Create a New Campaign" link on the Google AdWords Campaign Management screen.

Simply answer the questions and follow the steps to walk through the process of creating your account and your first ad. Note that if you do not have a Web site, Google will help create one for you. Make sure you select whether you currently have a Web site. The example below illustrates a user who already has a Web site:

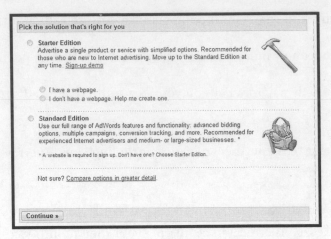

Google screenshots © Google Inc. Used with permission.

In Google AdWords Starter Edition, you choose your customer base, language, and the Web site your ad will direct them to.

Google screenshots © Google Inc. Used with permission.

Next, you will create the actual advertisement that will be displayed in the search engine results page. You simply type in your advertisement as you want it to appear, and Google AdWords formats it for you as you type.

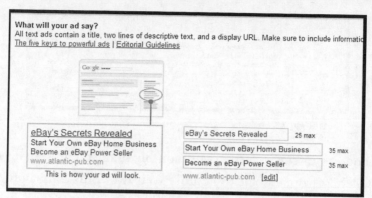

Google screenshots © Google Inc. Used with permission.

The next step is to choose your keywords. Do this using the Google Keyword Tool to ensure your keywords are optimal for your advertising campaign. Simply enter your keywords one at a time, then click "Check My Keywords" to see what Google thinks of your choices. Google also makes recommendations based on keywords or phrases it scans on your Web page as other recommended alternatives.

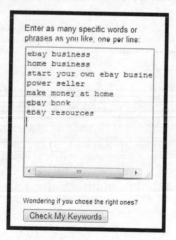

Google screenshots © Google Inc. Used with permission.

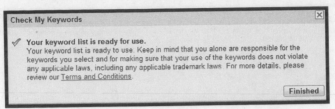

Google screenshots © Google Inc. Used with permission.

Next, choose your currency, set your monthly budget, and sign up for tips and newsletters from Google to improve your AdWords campaign. Set any monthly budget you want, and your ad will be served until you reach this dollar amount, or until it resets the following month or billing cycle.

Google screenshots © Google Inc. Used with permission.

Follow the screen prompts to create your actual account and log into your newly created Google AdWords account. Your ad is not yet running and will not be until you enter your billing information and activate your ad. Then, at this point, you are set. You can activate your ad; monitor your performance through impressions, clicks, or total cost; delete, edit, or add keywords or phrases; and manage your account.

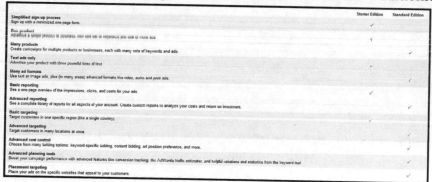

Google screenshots © Google Inc. Used with permission.

How to Graduate to Standard Edition Google AdWords

You can easily move from the Starter Edition to the Standard Edition. It does not cost anything to upgrade, and your account settings and ads will transfer over.

Below is a side-by-side comparison of the Starter and Standard editions:

	Starter Edition	Standard Edition
Simplified sign-up process Sign up with a minimized one-page form.	✓	
One product Advertise a single product or business that uses one set of keywords and one or more ads	✓	
Many products Create campaigns for multiple products or businesses, each with many sets of keywords and ads.		✓
Text ads only Advertise your product with three powerful lines of text	✓	
Many ad formats Use text or image ads, plus (in many areas) advanced formats like video, audio and print ads		✓
Basic reporting See a one-page overview of the impressions, clicks, and costs for your ads.	✓	
Advanced reporting See a complete library of reports for all aspects of your account. Create custom reports to analyze your costs and return on investment.		✓
Basic targeting Target customers in one specific region (like a single country)	✓	
Advanced targeting Target customers in many locations at once		✓
Advanced cost control Choose from many bidding options: keyword-specific bidding, content bidding, ad position preference, and more.		✓
Advanced planning tools Boost your campaign performance with advanced features like conversion tracking, the AdWords traffic estimator, and helpful variations and statistics from the keyword tool		✓
Placement targeting Place your ads on the specific websites that appeal to your customers		✓

Google screenshots © Google Inc. Used with permission.

Standard Edition offers significantly more features over the Starter Edition, including:

- Multiple ad campaigns

- Advanced location targeting

- Access to the complete Google content network and the ability to pick the sites your ad is placed on

- Powerful campaign planning and reporting tools

Creating a Standard Edition Google AdWords Account

The process for creating a Standard Edition account is quite similar to the process using the Starter Edition, except that you do not create your single ad as you create you account. Instead, you establish your account, and all the tools and resources are available to you to create ads and manage your campaigns.

Google screenshots © Google Inc. Used with permission.

Within the Campaign Management module, you can create, edit, and monitor your campaigns and advertisements, as well as run reports, perform analysis, use the tools and the conversion tracking module, and optimize your Web site. This is your command center for Google AdWords. The screenshot above is a real, active Google AdWords account, which will be used to modify and improve each of the under-performing ads.

Google Bidding Strategies

Google now offers a variety of bidding strategies to help you maximize your budget and maintain flexibility in how your ads are placed. The options you may choose are:

- **Manual bidding:** This option sets the highest price you are willing to pay for each click. Use this option if you need maximum control of each bid.

- **Conversion optimizer:** This option sets the highest price you are willing to pay for each conversion. Google will optimize your performance to aim for the best possible return on investment. To use this feature, you must use Google Conversion Tracking.

- **Budget optimizer:** No bids needed; you set a 30-day budget, and Google will manage your bids, trying to earn you the most possible clicks within that budget. This is the best option for simplified bidding and is the best choice for new users.

- **Preferred cost bidding:** This option sets the average price you want to pay for each click and lets Google manage your bids to give you a predictable average CPC.

Google AdWords Tools

Google provides you with a variety of tools to manage and optimize your campaigns with. These include:

- **Campaign optimizer:** Automatically creates a customized proposal for your campaign.

- **Keyword tool:** Builds a list of new keywords for your ad groups and reviews detailed keyword performance statistics, such as advertiser competition and search volume.

- **Edit campaign negative keywords:** Manages your negative keywords and reduces wasted clicks.

- **Site and category exclusion:** Prevents individual Web sites or categories of Web pages from showing your ads.

- **IP exclusion:** Prevents specific IP addresses from seeing your ads.

- **Traffic estimator:** Estimates how well a keyword might perform.

- **Ad creation marketplace:** Finds specialists to help you create multimedia ads.

- **Ads diagnostic tool:** Shows how and if your ads are showing up as the result of a search.

- **Ads preview tool:** Allows you to see your ad on Google without accruing impressions.

- **Disapproved ads:** Lets you review ads that have been disapproved.

- **Conversion tracking:** Shows which ads are your best performers.

- **Web site optimizer:** Helps you to discover the best content for boosting your business.

- **Download AdWords editor:** Enables you to make changes offline and then upload your revised campaigns.

Creating a New Campaign in Google AdWords

At this point, you have created your Standard Google AdWords account, and you are now going to create a new campaign. From your Campaign Summary screen, click on "New Online Campaign," then choose "Start with Keywords."

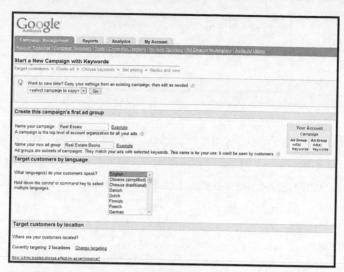

Google screenshots © Google Inc. Used with permission.

Name your campaign and ad group, choose your target language, and target your location; then, create the actual ad. This is done in the same format as the Starter Google AdWords application.

Google screenshots © Google Inc. Used with permission.

Once you complete your ad and click the "Continue" button, your advertisement is validated and checked by Google.

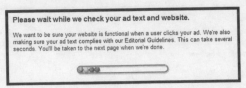

Google screenshots © Google Inc. Used with permission.

Enter your keywords and use the keyword checker to validate them. It will recommend removal of under-performing keywords or those that are too general in nature. Google will also scan your Web site and make recommendations for additional keywords to add.

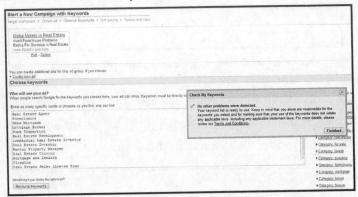

Google screenshots © Google Inc. Used with permission.

Now you must set your daily budget and bidding strategy.

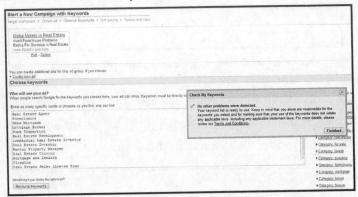

Google screenshots © Google Inc. Used with permission.

Google provides you with help each step of the way. There are always options for advice, detailed information, and guides to improve your campaign. One excellent tool is the Traffic Estimator, which you can use to enter a CPC and see the estimated rank, traffic, and costs for your keywords.

Traffic Estimates
View the ad performance estimates for your selected keywords on the Google Search Network below. Estimates are provided only as a guideline, your actual costs and ad positions for your keywords may vary. Learn more

Your keyword and CPC changes have not been saved.
You may continue making changes and re-calculating estimates below.
When satisfied, please save your changes.

Without budget limitations:
At an average CPC of $0.65 - $1.00 these keywords could potentially generate 8,341 - 12,439 clicks per day (which would cost you $6,680 - $12,489)
▸ Show total potential clicks in the table below

Keywords ▾	Max CPC	Search Volume	Estimated Avg. CPC	Estimated Ad Position
mortgage books (or kw ecutect)			$0.89 - $1.00	
Commercial Real Estate Investor	$1.00		$0.59 - $0.98	1 - 3
Overlaps with: commercial real estate: Real Estate Investor	$1.00			1 - 3
flipping			$0.00	-
Foreclosure	$1.00		$0.55 - $0.82	1 - 3
Home Inspection	$1.90		$0.68 - $1.00	4 - 6
Home Mortgage	$1.00		$0.85 - $0.92	4 - 6
Mortgage Broker	$1.00		$0.56 - $0.99	7 - 10
Mortgage and Lending	$1.00		$0.64 - $0.96	4 - 6
Real Estate Agent	$1.00		$0.50 - $0.75	1 - 3
Overlaps with: real estate agent	$1.00		Not enough data to give estimates.	
Real Estate Closing	$1.00		$0.63 - $0.94	
Real Estate Development	$1.00		$0.63 - $0.94	1 - 3
Real Estate Investor	$1.00		$0.03 - $0.90	1 - 3
Real Estate Sales License Exam	$1.00		$0.67 - $1.00	4 - 6
Rental Property	$1.00		Not enough data to give estimates.	
Rental Property Manager	$1.00		$0.67 - $1.00	1 - 3
Overlaps with: Rental Property	$1.00		$0.03 - $0.97	1 - 3
commercial real estate	$1.00		$0.58 - $1.60	1 - 3
commercial real estate investing real estate investing	$1.00		$0.00	-
investing books	$5.00		$0.36 - $0.84	1 - 3
investment property	$1.00		$0.73 - $1.00	1 - 3
private mortgage insuring	$1.00		$0.66 - $0.97	11 - 15
real estate agent	$1.00		$0.72 - $1.00	1 - 3
real estate books	$4.00		$0.57 - $1.00	1 - 3
real estate broker	$1.90		$0.66 - $0.98	1 - 3
real estate closing	$1.00		Not enough data to give estimates.	
Overlaps with: Real Estate Closing	$1.00			
real estate financing	$1.00		$0.61 - $0.92	4 - 6
real estate investing	$1.00		$0.56 - $1.00	4 - 6
real estate investments	$1.00		$0.69 - $0.99	4 - 6
real estate listings	$1.90		$0.63 - $0.97	1 - 3
reverse mortgage	$1.00		$0.49 - $0.73	4 - 6
second mortgage	$1.00		$0.44 - $0.81	4 - 6

Google screenshots © Google Inc. Used with permission.

Google features multiple advertisement options, which include the following examples:

Text ad:

Luxury Cruise to Mars
Visit the Red Planet in style.
Low-gravity fun for everyone!
www.example.com

Google screenshots © Google Inc. Used with permission.

Image ad:

Google screenshots © Google Inc. Used with permission.

Local business ad: Local business ads are AdWords ads associated with a specific Google Maps business listing. They show on Google Maps with an enhanced location marker. They also show in a text-only format on Google and other sites in the search network.

Mobile business text ad: Your ads will appear when someone uses Google Mobile Search™ on a mobile device.

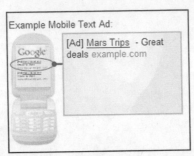

Google screenshots © Google Inc. Used with permission.

Video ad: Video ads are an ad format that will appear on the Google content network. Your video ad will appear as a static image until a user clicks on it and your video is played.

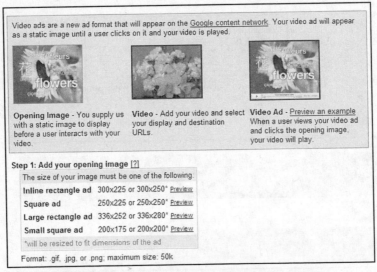

Google screenshots © Google Inc. Used with permission.

Display ad builder: This new feature lets you create display ads as easily as text ads. Once you create your new ad, it will run on Google partner sites based on the target settings you choose.

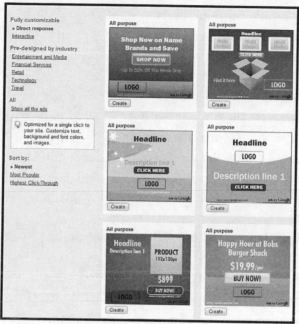

Google screenshots © Google Inc. Used with permission.

You should start out your campaign with a text ad. Google AdWords provides you with a simple form to create your text advertisement. As you enter data into the form, the example is updated with your data. In the screenshot at the end of this section, notice that each keyword is capitalized in every line, and both the display URL and the actual destination URL are provided, as they may be different, depending on your campaign.

You will need to devote some extra time and attention to the wording of your ad. Wording can be tricky because of the limited space you are given on each line of the ad, as well as the restrictions imposed by Google.

It is critical to load the title, or the first line of your ad, with keywords. Your goal is to capture the attention and interest of a potential customer. If you can do that, your ad will be successful. Test multiple versions of an ad to see which works best, and change keywords to help you analyze which is most effective. Review the ads of competitors; you may find they are outperforming you simply because their ad is more well-written, more captivating, or has more customer appeal. The use of words like "free," "rebate," "bonus," and "cash" are perfect for attracting the attention of Web site surfers. Other words that may encourage Web site visitors to click your ad should be used as long as your ad message is concise and clear.

You should also consider the domain name listed in your advertisement, as it may have an effect on your ability to draw in potential customers. Your domain name should be directly related to your products or services, and should be professional in nature. You will find an abundance of companies that offer search engine copywriting services, which is a good option if you are having problems developing successful ad campaigns.

Some recommended sources for copywriting include:

- **www.searchenginewriting.com**
- **www.grantasticdesigns.com/copywriting.html**
- **www.roncastle.com/Web_copywriting.htm**
- **www.futurenettechnologies.com/creative-copywriting.htm**
- **www.tinawrites.com**
- **www.brandidentityguru.com/optimized-copywriting.html**

Search engine copywriting is critical to a successful PPC advertising campaign. Although recommendations of professional services have been provided for this task, it is not overly difficult to achieve yourself if you apply some basic discipline and rules. While the insertion of keywords into an advertisement has been stressed, simply cramming keyword after keyword into your PPC advertisements may be counterproductive. Successful SEO copywriting takes planning, discipline, analysis, and some degree of trial and error. Below are some guidelines for successful SEO copywriting:

- Use no more than four keywords per ad. Four keywords provide a wide keyword variety without saturating the ad with keywords and losing its meaning.

- Use all your allowed characters in each line of the advertisement. There is no incentive for white space.

- Write in natural language. "Natural language" is a popular term used extensively with copywriting. It simply means that the reader should not be able to — or should barely be able to — detect what keywords the ad is targeting. The best ads are written for an individual to read and understand, embedded with subtle keywords, and project a clear message; thus, they read "naturally." The opposite of this is a keyword-crammed ad that is nothing more than a collection of keywords, and is therefore entirely "unnatural" to read.

- Use keywords in the "Title" and "Description" lines, but use common sense so that you do not overload them with keywords.

- Test your ad and analyze your reports and results. Your ad may need tweaking or improvements, or it may be entirely ineffective and may need to be replaced.

Google screenshots © Google Inc. Used with permission.

You may discover that costs can escalate quickly if you do not set daily and monthly budget limitations. Keep in mind that limits on your daily/monthly budgets will also affect your ad performance, as your ad will not be displayed once you hit your budget limits. Google recognizes when your advertisement is bumping against its budget constraints and may suggest you increase your budget amount to increase visibility of your advertisement, as well as subsequent potential customers visiting your Web site, as shown below:

> **Campaign Budget Alert**
> In the last 15 days, your ads missed 46% of impressions for which they were eligible. Increasing your budget could allow your ads to show more often and get more clicks.
> Tell me more | Remove this message

Google screenshots © Google Inc. Used with permission.

The Google Campaign Summary

The Campaign Summary screen is where you will control all your Google AdWords campaigns. At this screen, you will be presented with an overview of each campaign, including campaign name, status, budget, clicks, impressions, click-through ratio, average CPC, and total cost.

To delve further into each campaign, simply click on the campaign name to view a detailed status based on keywords and ad variation performance. This module will help you determine the effectiveness of each keyword and add/remove keywords. Your keywords may be marked "inactive for search" in the "Status" column and stop showing on search results if they do not have a high enough Quality Score and max CPC. This is another way of saying that your keyword or ad group's max CPC does not meet the minimum bid required to trigger ads on Google or its search network partners. This typically occurs when keywords are not as targeted as they could be, and the ads they deliver are not relevant enough to what a user is searching for — which ultimately means you need to refine your keywords or your ad.

Keywords marked "inactive for search" are inactive only for search. They may continue to trigger ads for content sites if you have the Google content network enabled for that campaign. Thus, a keyword marked as inactive for search may continue to generate clicks and charges on the content network. If your keyword is inactive for search, you may increase your keyword's Quality Score by optimizing for relevancy.

Optimization is a technique for improving the quality of your keywords, ad, and campaign to increase your keyword's performance — without raising costs. Try to combine your keyword with two to three other words to create a more specific keyword phrase. This will result in better targeting and, potentially, better performance. You may also increase your keyword's max CPC to the recommended minimum bid. Your keyword's minimum bid is the amount required to trigger ads on Google and is determined by your keyword's Quality Score. When your max CPC falls below the minimum bid, your keyword will be inactive for search. For this reason, you can simply increase your max CPC to the minimum bid to reactivate your keywords. You may also choose to delete all your keywords that are inactive for search.

The "Ad Variations" links allows you to review performance for each ad within a selected campaign. It is common to have multiple ads created for the same, or different, keyword combinations within the same campaign. In the following screenshot, it is clear by the percentages listed that the first ad is served considerably more than the second ad, which is very rarely served. The reasons for this may vary, depending on the keywords chosen or campaign settings.

If you click on the "Edit" link, under the "Actions" column, you can tweak your campaign ads to improve your statistics.

Google screenshots © Google Inc. Used with permission.

For each ad group you create, you can create up to 50 ad variations. The variations can be in any of the formats offered for AdWords, including text, image, and video. When you first sign up for an account, you will be offered the chance to create additional ad variations immediately after you create your first ad. You can also create ad variations later, after your account is running. Sign into your account and choose the ad group you want to work with. Click the "Ad Variations" tab, find the line reading "Create new ad," and select the type of ad you want to create. All ad variations in a single ad group are triggered by the same set of keywords. You may choose to have ads optimized, which would show better-performing ads more often, or to rotate, which shows all ads equally. If you want different ads to appear for different keywords, you can create multiple ad groups or campaigns.

Editing Your Campaign Settings

In the "Edit Campaign Settings" menu, you have the ability to modify your campaign settings, including campaign name, budget options, ad scheduling, keyword bidding, network and bidding, and scheduling and serving.

Google screenshots © Google Inc. Used with permission.

Google AdWords will suggest a recommended budget amount for your campaign if you click on the "View Recommended Budget" link on the Edit Campaign Settings screen, as shown in the following screenshot:

> Based on your current keywords, your recommended budget is $8.00 / day.
>
> If the recommended amount is too high, try raising your budget to a comfortable amount. Or, to make the most of your budget, try refining your ads and keywords.

Google screenshots © Google Inc. Used with permission.

Ad scheduling lets you control the days and times your AdWords campaigns appear. Your AdWords ads normally are available to run 24 hours each day. Ad scheduling allows you to set your campaigns to appear only during certain hours or days of each week. For example, you might set your ads to run only on Tuesdays, or from 3 to 6 p.m. daily. With ad scheduling, a campaign can run all day, every day, or as few as 15 minutes per week.

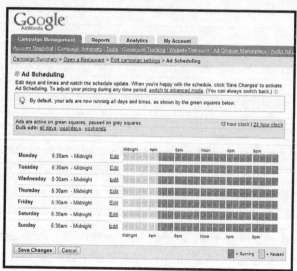

Google screenshots © Google Inc. Used with permission.

To determine when you want your ads to show, you may want to run an hourly report. Ad scheduling can be used with both keyword-targeted and site-targeted AdWords campaigns. If you select the advanced setting, the bid multiplier will apply to both CPC and cost-per-thousand-impressions CPM bids. Ad scheduling will not raise or lower your budget. The Ad-

Words system will try to reach your usual daily budget in whatever number of hours your ad runs each day.

Position preference lets you tell Google where you would prefer your ad to show among all the AdWords ads on a given page. Whenever you run a keyword-targeted ad, your ad is assigned a position based on your CPC bid, your keyword's Quality Score, and other relevant factors. There may be dozens of positions available for a given keyword, spread over several pages of search results. If you find that your ad gets the best results when it is ranked third or fourth among all AdWords ads, you can set a position preference for those spots. AdWords will then try to show your ad whenever it is ranked third or fourth, and avoid showing it when it is ranked higher or lower. If your ad is ranked higher than third for a given keyword, the system will automatically try to lower your bid to place your ad in your preferred position.

You can request that your ad be shown only when it is:

- Higher than a given position
- Lower than a given position
- Within a range of positions
- In a single exact position

Position preference does not mean that your ad will always appear in the position you specify; the usual AdWords ranking and relevance rules apply. If your ad does not qualify for position No. 1, setting a position preference of No. 1 will not move it there. Position preference simply means AdWords will try to show your ad whenever it is ranked in your preferred position, and will avoid showing it when it is not. Position preference also does not affect the overall placement of AdWords ad units on the left, right, top, or bottom of a given page — it only affects your ranking relative to other ads across those units.

Google AdWords allows you to track and measure conversions and ultimately help you identify how effective your AdWords ads and keywords are for you. It works by placing a cookie on a user's computer when he or she clicks on one of your AdWords ads. If the user reaches one of your conversion pages, the cookie is connected to your Web page. When a match is made, Google records a successful conversion for you. Note that the cookie Google adds to a user's computer when he or she clicks on an ad expires in 30 days. This measure, and the fact that Google uses separate servers for conversion tracking and search results, protects the user's privacy.

Demographic Bidding

Demographic bidding allows you to choose your audience by age and gender. Because some publishers on the Google content network know details about their users — such as social networking sites they partake in — they can serve ads based on age and gender. Google AdSense can display your AdWords ads to the demographic groups that you select, or block them from groups you do not want to reach.

Google AdWords Reports

Google provides full statistical, conversion, and financial reporting for the Google AdWords program. You can view all your account reports online 24 hours a day, and you can also have them set up to be e-mailed to you on a scheduled basis.

The AdWords Report Center allows you to easily create customized performance reports to help you track and manage multiple facets of your AdWords campaigns. There are dozens of highly customized options available for you to choose, all of which are simple and easy to generate.

Key features include:

- Quick report generation in categories such as site/keyword performance, URL performance, campaign performance, ad group performance, and account performance

- The ability to select individual campaigns and/or ad groups for report

- Customizable report columns to focus only on the data you need

- Performance filters screen for the most relevant information in categories such as cost, impressions, clicks, and CTR

- Scheduling for automatic report generation and delivery

- E-mailing option for multiple recipients

- Saved templates for reusable reports

Impressions 2,626,900	Clicks 36,300	CTR 1.38%	Avg CPC $0.21	Cost $7,678.84

Google screenshots © Google Inc. Used with permission.

Impressions 2,626,900	Clicks 36,300	CTR 1.38%	Avg CPC $0.21	Cost $7,678.84	Avg Position 3.74

Google screenshots © Google Inc. Used with permission.

Google AdWords Ads Diagnostic Tool

One of the best features of Google AdWords is the Ads Diagnostic Tool, which helps you find out why your ads may not be showing on the first page of search results for a certain keyword.

Ads Diagnostic Tool
Choose one of the two options below to find out why your ads may not be showing on the first page of search results for a certain keyword.

Option 1: Search Terms and Parameters
Use this option if you're concerned about all ads within your account that should be appearing for a specific search term. For example, you could check your ad status for the phrase-matched keyword "Hawaiian cruises," targeted to California users.

Keyword:	
Google domain:	www.google.com << ex: froogle.google.com, www.google.co.uk
Display language:	English
User location:	⦿ Geographic: United States
	All regions within this country
	○ IP address: Format: xxx.xxx.xxx.xxx

Continue >>

Option 2: Search Results Page URL
Use this option if you're concerned about a particular search results page that you believe should be showing one of your ads. Copy and paste the URL from the address bar on the search results page where your ad should be showing.

Search results page URL:

Continue >>

Google screenshots © Google Inc. Used with permission.

Tips, Tricks, & Secrets for Google AdWords Pay-Per-Click Advertising

Here are some tips that will help you develop and manage a highly effective Google AdWords campaign, which in turn will generate higher CTRs, lower your CPC, and obtain conversions:

- Design Google AdWords ads so they target potential customers who are ready to buy. Rarely will banner ads or PPC ads draw in the curious Web site browser and result in a sale.

- Ensure your Google AdWords ad is specific in nature.

- Target one product for each Google AdWords ad if possible, instead of using a generic ad that targets a large market segment.

- Make your ad link directly to the product page with a link to buy the product on that page, instead of to a generic page or the Web site home page.

- If your Google AdWords ad targets a specific product, you may see a reduction in clicks because your advertising segment is narrow. However, those clicks are most likely extremely profitable because you are only getting clicks from individuals seeking information on your specific product — this means your advertising cost may actually be reduced, while your sales go up.

- Be willing to bid for a good position. If you do not want to spend much money or are willing to settle for the bottom of the bids, no one is going to see your ad.

- Bid enough to gain the exposure you need, but balance exposure to stretch your advertising budget. It is rarely worth the cost to have the No. 1 bid.

- Being the No. 1 listing on search engines may not be all it is cracked up to be. The top listing is the one that is clicked the most often, but it also has the worst percentage of converting clicks into actual sales. Many "click-happy" people click on the top listing without ever converting a sale. Those clicks will quickly eat up your advertising budget. You may have better luck by being below the No. 1 listing, as you have the potential to garner better clicks.

- Use the provided tracking tools to monitor performance and adjust keywords/bidding as necessary.

- Lower your overall costs while increasing the potential conversion rate by choosing multiple highly targeted words or phrases instead of generic terms.

- Use capital letters for each word in the "Title" and "Description" fields of your PPC ad.

- Use demographic and geographic targeting with your Google AdWords ad.

- Use the Google Keyword Suggestion Tool to help you determine which keywords are most effective for your campaign.

- Keep an eye out for fraud. Although Google has fraud detection and prevention, if you suspect your competition is clicking on your ads, you may want to invest in additional protection. An example of this is **www.whosclickingwho.com**.

- Check the spelling in your Google AdWords ad to ensure it is correct.

- Embed keywords within your actual Google AdWords PPC ad.

- Define your target audience and narrow the scope of your ad to potential customers.

- Develop multiple advertisements for each campaign, and run them at the same time. You will quickly determine which is effective and which is not. Do not be afraid to tweak advertisements or replace poorly performing advertisements.

- Monitor and use Google Reports by tracking your costs, rate of return, and the click-through rate for each ad.

- Include targeted keywords in the "Headline" and "Description" lines of your ad. Keywords stand out in search engine results, help to attract the attention of potential customers, and increase your overall advertisement effectiveness. Be quite specific in your keywords.

- Include words that stand out and grab the attention of potential customers, such as "New" and "Limited Offer."

- Do not just link to the home page of your Web site. Link directly to the relevant landing page for your specific product or service. This will help you convert the visit to a sale.

- Free may not be good for you. If your advertisement says "free," then you can expect considerable traffic from folks who just want the free products and will never buy anything, which will just increase your costs. Consider limiting the use of "free" to cut back on traffic that will never culminate in a sale.

Chapter 13

INCREASE PROFITS & GENERATE INCOME WITH GOOGLE ADSENSE

Google AdSense lets you place advertisements on your Web pages, earning money for each click by site visitors. You do not pay for Google AdSense; instead, you give up some real estate on your Web site to "host" advertisements, with content relevant to your Web site, placed by Google. Instead of paying per click, you actually earn revenue per click, just for hosting the advertisements on your Web site. The bottom line is that AdSense is simple to use, costs nothing, and can generate significant amounts of residual monthly income for you. There is minimal effort to implement; all you have to do is sign up and place a small bit of code on your Web page. Google AdSense can be used on business or personal Web sites.

The concept of Google AdSense is simple: You earn revenue potential by displaying Google ads on your Web site. Essentially, you become the host site for someone else's pay-per-click advertising. Because Google puts relevant ads through the same auction and lets them compete against one another, the auction for the advertisement takes place instantaneously, and Google AdSense subsequently displays a text or image ad that will generate the maximum revenue for you.

There are three basic types of AdSense products you can use:

1. **AdSense for content:** Crawls the content of your Web pages and delivers text and image ads that are relevant to your audience and your site content.

2. **AdSense for search:** Enables Web site owners to provide Google Web and site search to their visitors and to earn money from clicks on Google ads on the search results pages.

3. **AdSense for mobile content:** Earn money from your content with a simple, integrated solution for mobile-device-compatible Web sites.

Becoming an AdSense publisher is simple. You must fill out a brief application form online at **www.google.com/AdSense**, which requires your Web site to be reviewed before your application is approved. Once it has been approved, Google will e-mail you HTML code for you to place on your Web pages. When the HTML code is saved onto your Web page, it activates immediately, and targeted ads will be displayed on your Web site.

You must choose an advertisement category to ensure that only relevant, targeted advertisements are portrayed on your Web site. Google has ads for all categories of businesses and for practically all types of content, no matter how broad or specialized. The AdSense program represents advertisers ranging from large global brands to small, local companies. Ads are also targeted by geography, so global businesses can display local advertising with no additional effort. Google AdSense supports multiple languages.

You can also earn revenue for your business by placing a Google search box on your Web site — literally being paid for search results. This service may help keep traffic on your site longer because site visitors can search directly from your site; it is also available at no cost and is simple to implement.

Google states that their "ad review process ensures that the ads you serve are not only family-friendly, but also comply with our strict editorial guidelines." They "combine sensitive language filters, your input, and a team of linguists with good common sense to automatically filter out ads that may be inappropriate for your content." Additionally, you can customize the appearance of your ads, choosing from a wide range of colors and templates. This is also the case with Google's search results page. Google also provides you with an arsenal of tools to track your advertising campaign and revenue.

How to Set Up Your Google AdSense Campaign

The first step is to complete the simple application form, which is located on the Web at **www.google.com/AdSense/g-app-single-1**. It is critical that you carefully review the terms of service. In particular, you must agree that you will:

- Not click on the Google ads you are serving through AdSense

- Not place ads on sites that include incentives to click on ads

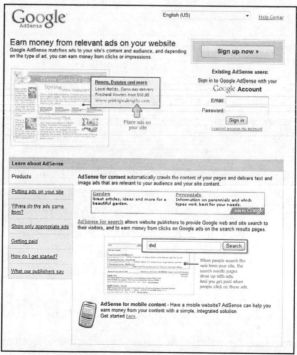

Google screenshots © Google Inc. Used with permission.

You cannot click on your ads, have others click on your ads, or place text on your Web site asking anyone to click on your advertisements. The reason for this is simple: You cannot click on — or have anyone else click on — your own advertisements to generate revenue.

Google screenshots © Google Inc. Used with permission.

When your Web site is reviewed and your account is approved, which tends to take a day or two, you will receive an e-mail indicating approval that will provide detailed instructions to set up AdSense.

Google AdSense Program Policies

Publishers participating in the AdSense program are required to adhere to the following policies. If you fail to comply with these policies, Google may disable ad serving to your site and/or disable your AdSense account. Program policies are strictly enforced and are available on the Google Ad-Sense Web site for review.

Setting Up Google AdSense on Your Web Site

To set up your initial AdSense account, click on the "My Account" tab. Because Google will be paying you, you will be required to complete several steps before your account is activated, such as providing W-9 tax data and choosing your form of payment.

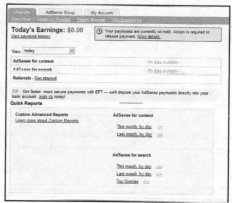

Google screenshots © Google Inc. Used with permission.

Click on "Account Setup" to begin setting up your ads. The following screen will be displayed:

AdSense Setup

Choose the product you'd like to add to your site.

AdSense for content
Display ads that are targeted to your site's unique content.

AdSense for search
Offer your users web search while earning revenue from ads relevant to their search terms.

Referrals
Earn more by referring users to useful products and services.

Google screenshots © Google Inc. Used with permission.

Choose which product you would like to add to your Web site. You may select AdSense for content, AdSense for search, or referrals. Following the example, set up a Google AdSense for content ad on your Web site. You will now choose your ad type: ad unit or link unit. To choose the ad unit, use the drop-down menu to choose text and image ads, text-only ads, or image-only ads. The ad unit with text and images is the default — and recommended — setting. The link unit displays a list of topics relevant to your Web page. Click on "Ad unit" to continue.

AdSense for Content

Choose Ad Type > Choose Ad Format and Colors > Get Ad Code

Wizard | Single page

Google AdSense program policies allow you to place up to three ad units and one link unit on any page.

Ad unit   Text and image ads (default)
Ad units contain either text ads, image ads, or both. The ads are targeted to the content of your page using contextual and site targeting.

Link unit
Each link unit displays a list of topics that are relevant to your page. When users click a topic, they're brought to a page of related ads. Learn more.

Google screenshots © Google Inc. Used with permission.

You will be presented with several options to choose from, including unit format and colors. Choose your desired options using the drop-down menus. This is not the actual ad that will be displayed on your Web site; it is merely a sample of how it may appear. AdSense lets you customize the appearance of ads to match the look and feel of your Web site. You can also customize the style of your AdSense for search boxes and search results pages.

AdSense for Content

Choose Ad Type » Choose Ad Format and Colors » Get Ad Code

Wizard | Single page

You can customize your ads to fit in with your pages. Use the options below to specify ad size, style, and more.

Format

Ad units come in a variety of sizes - view all the options on our Ad Formats page.

728 x 90 Leaderboard

Colors

Choose from one of our pre-designed color palettes, or create your own palette. Tips

* Some options apply to text ads only.

Sample
Linked Title
Advertiser's ad text here
www.advertiser-url.com
Ads by Google

Palettes — Default Google palette — Edit palettes

Border   # FFFFFF
Title   # 0000FF
Background   # FFFFFF
Text   # 000000
URL   # 008000

More options

Custom channel
Specify a custom channel to track the performance of these ads. Learn more.

No channel selected
Add new channel | Manage channels.

Alternate ads or colors
Choose what to display if no relevant ads are available. Learn more.

- Show public service ads
- Show ads from another URL
- Fill space with a solid color

Google screenshots © Google Inc. Used with permission.

You may use "More options" to enable custom channels or elect to alternative ads or colors, including the option to show public service ads if there is no advertisement ready to be displayed on your Web site. After making your selections, you will be provided with HTML code, which simply needs to be placed in the HTML code on your Web site. You are free to place the code on one or many Web pages within your site.

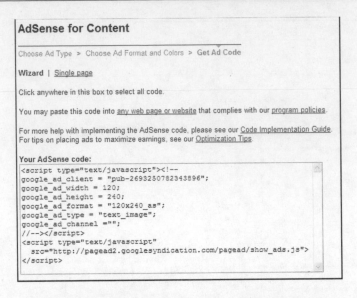

Google screenshots © Google Inc. Used with permission.

When you insert the HTML code into your Web site, your campaign is activated, and advertisements are immediately served to your site. Because you cannot click on your advertisements at any time, even to "test" them, Google provides a preview mode for testing. Google's AdWords technology matches the most relevant, highest performing AdWords ads to your Web site. You can bid on ads on a per-click or per-impression basis. Depending on the type of ad appearing on your site, you will be paid for valid clicks and impressions. You also have the option of monthly payment via check or Electronic Fund Transfer (EFT). How much you earn depends on a number of factors, including how much an advertiser bids on your site, but you will receive a portion of what the advertiser pays.

The following ad was created and set up on our Web site in under five minutes:

Google screenshots © Google Inc. Used with permission.

You can expand your AdSense account well beyond traditional Web pages. They can be implemented successfully into blogs and feeds. In 2008, Google implemented "AdSense for Feeds," which lets you place ads into RSS feeds, allowing you to increase the reach of your content while earning revenue.

How to Set Up Your Google Referrals

Google AdSense program policies allow you to place one referral per product, for a total of up to four referrals, on any page. You simple click on the referral link to choose your referrals.

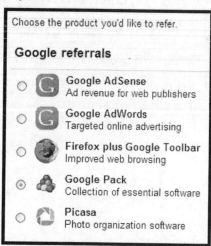

Google screenshots © Google Inc. Used with permission.

Google AdSense will generate the HTML code for your Web site. Once the code is placed on your Web pages, your referral will be activated and displayed on your Web site, as shown in the following screenshot. You have a variety of options in size, color, and wording to choose from and are free to change your referral ads at any time.

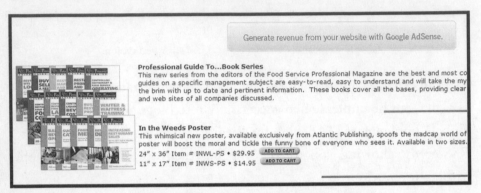

Google screenshots © Google Inc. Used with permission.

Google AdSense is simple to implement, non-intrusive to your Web site, and allows you to open channels to earning potential revenue for your business.

Hints & Tips for Maximizing Google AdSense on Your Web Site

Google AdSense is an outstanding way to generate Web site traffic, attract advertisers, and create a revenue stream for your business. Use these hints and tips to maximize your earning potential:

- Always follow the Google AdSense guidelines.

- Do not modify or change the Google AdSense HTML code you place on your Web site.

- Do not use colored backgrounds on the Google AdSense ads. If you have a Web site with a colored background, modify the advertisement to match your background.

- Place your ads so they are visible. If someone needs to scroll down to see your ads, you will likely not get any clicks on them. Play with the placement to maximize visibility.

- Do not place ads in pop-up windows.

- Do not buy an "AdSense Template Web site," which is readily available on eBay and other online marketplaces. These get-rich types of "click" campaigns are against Google's policies and do not make money.

- Text ads tend to perform better than image ads. If you insist on using image ads, keep them at a reasonable size.

- You can modify the URL link color in the ad through the Google AdSense account panel to make it stand out among your ads and attract the eye of the site visitor.

- If you have a blog, have others place ads there. Google will need to approve your blog.

- If your Web site has articles on it that you wish to embed ads in, use these guidelines:

  - For short articles, place the ad above the article.

  - For long articles, embed the ad within the content of the article.

- Wider-format ads are more successful. The paying ad format is the "large rectangle."

- Distribute ads on each Web page. Combine ads with referrals and search boxes so your Web site does not look like a giant billboard.

- Put the Google search box near the top right-hand corner of your Web page.

- If your ads are based on content, the first lines of the Web page determine your site content for ad-serving purposes.

- Set the Google AdSense search box results window so that it opens in a new window, as this will keep your browser open and users will not navigate away from your Web site.

- Google AdSense allows Webmasters to customize their Google Ad-Sense ads. Because of this, you can actually customize the links, borders, and color themes of your ads. Borderless AdSense Web banners tend to produce more clicks.

Chapter 14

GENERATING INCOME WITH AFFILIATE MARKETING

Affiliate marketing is simply defined as a Web-based marketing practice — often using automated systems or specialized software — in which a business rewards their affiliate for each visitor, customer, or sale that is brought about as a result of the affiliate's marketing efforts. In most cases, the reward is monetary, in the form of a monthly commission check. Most well-designed affiliate programs are easy to implement, require little or no setup, are free, and can instantly generate a new source of revenue for you. If you have products to sell, establishing your own affiliate marketing program will let you dramatically increase your marketplace. Instead of your selling your product on your Web site, hundreds or thousands of others can sell your products through their Web sites, bringing you the potential for significantly increased sales.

You can easily join an affiliate program or network and sell products on your Web site, earning revenue on your Web site as you convert sales through your affiliate links. If you sell your own products on your Web site, you may even consider starting your own affiliate program, letting others sell your products on their Web sites and dramatically increasing the number of outlets where your products are sold throughout the world. While affiliate marketing may not be something you want to consider until you establish your Web site and are happy with its appearance and performance in search engines, it is certainly a method you should eventually look into as an extra revenue stream for your business.

Affiliate Marketing Options

Essentially, you have two affiliate marketing options:

- Host an affiliate program on your Web site so others can join your affiliate network and sell your products on their Web sites — they will earn a commission for each sale, and you will sell more products through them. This is the ultimate solution for those who have products to sell; imagine your products advertised for free on thousands of Web sites across the world.

- Join an affiliate network and sell other products on your Web site; in doing so, you will earn a commission for each sale. You do nothing and pay nothing. The setup is simple, and all you do is keep the content updated with what you want to advertise on your Web site and cash the monthly commission check.

Think about the basic philosophy and principles of an affiliate marketing program: You can sell other people's products on your Web site for free, and they pay you a commission to do it. You do not ever touch the products and are not responsible for the sale, packaging, shipping, customer service, customer complaints, problem resolution, returns, or headaches — and for your simple act of allowing their products to be sold on your Web site, you receive a monthly commission check.

Alternatively, if you establish your own affiliate marketing campaign for your products, you are implementing a program that allows others to sell your products for you while you pay them a commission fee. Instead of your products being sold only on your Web site, they can be sold on dozens, hundreds, or thousand of other high-traffic sites. The increases in sales and profits more than offset the commission fees you will pay, and you still have full control over the affiliates; can approve who is allowed to participate in your program; and still retain administrative control of your products, pricing, inventory, sales, and recordkeeping. Affiliate marketing can be powerful, lucrative, and profitable. That said, as with many aspects on the Web, if it were that simple, why is not everyone making millions through affiliate marketing? The truth is that affiliate marketing still takes some experience, knowledge, understanding, determination, and hard work. Another critical factor is that you have to sell products people want to buy, or you have to join affiliate networks offering products people want to buy.

Crash Course in Affiliate Marketing

Affiliate marketing allows merchants to dramatically increase their marketplace by paying their affiliates to promote their products on a commission formula, based on a sale or sales lead. Affiliate marketing is not always about selling products; it can also be used simply for impressions, or "per action." For example, driving traffic from your Web site to the affiliate owner's site may qualify for an affiliate payment. In most cases, affiliate networks are created to sell products and expand the marketplace. In all cases, the concept is to drive traffic back to the merchant Web site. Even if you are an affiliate of someone else and feature their products on your Web site, when someone clicks on the link to order or view information about the product, they are driven back to the merchant Web site to complete the sale or transaction.

Typically, upon completion of the sale, you are given a commission. Simply put, if the visitor to your Web site clicks on something that is an "affiliate" item and they go to the merchant Web site to purchase this item, then when the visitor completes the transaction on the merchant Web site, you get paid the referral or commission. Some affiliate programs are on a cost-per-click (CPC) basis, and some are strictly sales-based. With CPC programs, the affiliates get credit based on the number of clicks on ads or banners on their Web sites, while in cost-per-action (CPA) programs, affiliates only get credit when the site visitor completes a purchase or other transaction on the affiliate merchant's Web site.

Affiliate Marketing Principles

Affiliate marketing has grown in the past decade and has exploded in both popularity and profitability. It has expanded into every aspect of the Web and has the potential to be one of the more lucrative ways of generating both sales and revenue. The basic principles of affiliate marketing are sound and have stood the test of time. Simply, "You promote my stuff on your Web site, and I will pay you commission for each sale," *or* "I will promote your stuff on my Web site, and you pay me a commission for each sale." Usually, any commercial link on any Web site is tied to affiliate or pay-per-click marketing in some form or another.

Here is a more in-depth summary of the two primary affiliate marketing methods covered in this book:

- **Joining an affiliate program or network:** This means that you have your own Web site, and you join an affiliate program or network selling other products. Let us say that you have a Web site or blog about running. To increase your revenue, you join the affiliate network of a large running shoe merchant. This is free to you, and after joining, they provide you with the information to add their products to your Web site. Keep in mind that they will provide you with special URLs that uniquely identify that the sales originated from your Web site. You can encourage your site visitors to buy the running shoes by following the image and other information you place on your Web site, and when they click the ad, they are taken to the merchant's site and can then place the order. Once the order is processed and completed, you are typically notified of the sale and of your commission amount. Typically, you have access to an online account to monitor your statistics, revenue, and other vital information. You can switch out products as often as you want to keep your Web site ever-changing and interesting. You do not process the sale, handle the merchandise, ship the merchandise, or provide customer service. Once the transaction is completed, you have earned your commission. The merchant must do the rest.

- **Creating or managing your own in-house affiliate program:** This means that you have your own Web site and have products to sell.

You want to expand your marketplace beyond your Web site and leverage the power of thousands of other sites to promote and sell your products. Those who promote these products for you on their Web sites are your affiliates, and they fall into the category above. They place your products and material on their Web site; if someone visits their site and clicks on your products, their unique affiliate link takes the visitor to your Web site, where you complete the transaction. You now have the luxury of featuring and promoting your products on Web sites all over the world, at no cost to you, and reaching millions of people you could not previously reach. As each sale is completed, they earn a commission.

At the end of each month, you must pay your affiliates their commission on the sales. Although this does mean you have to give part of your profits to your affiliates, theoretically you are also selling more products than you could have before. You must maintain your affiliate account status, generate monthly checks, and administer your affiliates, thus there is some overhead and work on your part; however, this work is typically minimal. As you add new products to your inventory, you can add them to your affiliate program so that your affiliates can instantly start promoting them. Here, you process the sale, handle the merchandise, ship the merchandise, provide customer service, and handle the transactions.

There are several choices in the types of affiliate marketing software available to you if you wish to build your own affiliate network or install an affiliate program on your Web site. Here are the general options you have:

- **Affiliate network:** In this case, the software is provided and hosted by the affiliate network provider. You simply join the existing network and offer your products for sale to other members of the affiliate network. They handle the program administration, reporting, and commission payments.

- **Hosted affiliate network software:** The software is not provided to you or installed on your Web server; rather, the software provider hosts it on their servers, and you pay a fee — usually monthly — for support and maintenance. All you typically have on your Web site is a small piece of tracking code, so your work is minimal. Because they own and host the software, you instantly benefit from software upgrades, patches, and enhancements. They are also responsible for the servers, backups, and reliability. Technical support is included with the package.

- **Affiliate network software (standalone):** You buy the software package outright, and you own the license to use it as you see fit. This is a one-time fee, and it can be expensive. You install it on your Web server — although often this is included for free or for a small fee — and you integrate it with your shopping cart or inventory management system. This software is typically very robust and packed with features, and there are usually no recurring fees, unless you want to sign up for upgrades.

However, the world of affiliate traffic is one full of misconceptions. Here are some of the realities of affiliate marketing:

- Setting up an effective affiliate traffic program is not necessarily easy and will take an investment of time and money, but it can return large dividends.

- Affiliate marketing does not automatically mean a huge increase in Web site traffic. Setting up or joining an affiliate program or network alone will not necessarily bring you any noticeable increase in traffic. You will still have to promote your program through other means in order to make it effective.

- You must avoid over-hype. Build credibility in your Web site and your products.

- Some Web surfers are reluctant to click an affiliate link/banner. The nice aspect is that many affiliate programs have built-in methods to help combat this. It all goes back to credibility; if they trust you, this is a non-issue.

- There are no shortcuts. Affiliate traffic is one of the most labor-intensive techniques available, but is also potentially one of the most effective.

It is also important to realize that affiliate marketing is perhaps one of the most effective tools that you have at your disposal to generate traffic and sales, but again, only when used in conjunction with other traffic generation methods. In traditional affiliate marketing, the traffic generated is only a side issue; the main focus is on the sales figure. The traffic you might get can be relatively low, but the conversion to sales can be fantastic.

Affiliate Links & How to Deal with Them

A major problem you will face when dealing with affiliate links is the reluctance that people have to follow an affiliate link. Whether you want to start an affiliate program on your Web site or join other affiliate programs or networks, you need to realize that there is reluctance to click on affiliate links and banner advertisements. To combat this, ROIAdvantage (ROIA) from TrackingSoft, found at **www.trackingsoft.net**, uses clean links, meaning there is no "affiliate" code in the affiliate links.

In a traditional tracking solution, links provided to the affiliate program contain code where the requisite tracking data is captured before the visitor is forwarded on to your domain. The visitor is instantaneously redirected to your site, but the link may point to the affiliate host. This is a functional solution for affiliate marketing programs and is the standard. In this case, you should be straightforward and acknowledge that the link presented is of the affiliate type. If your visitors are familiar with what affiliate marketing is and are all right with it, there is nothing wrong with this option — although there is a price to pay in regard to SEO.

For those who want to reinforce brand name recognition and increase SEO, direct linking offers a cost-effective solution. In a direct linking model, traffic flows uninterrupted from a partner's Web site to your domain through a link to your Web site with tracking information appended at the end. Once the visitor arrives, a special, invisible code captures the tracking information and forwards it to the affiliate host, while the visitor remains at your site the entire time. This eliminates the issue of people not wanting to click a link because it directs them to a third-party Web site they are not familiar with.

Google and other major search engines use complex algorithms to determine the order in which sites appear when a given term is searched for. One of the major factors in this algorithm is how many other sites link to yours. In traditional tracking, those links point to the affiliate marketing server that, while very effective, do not help your search engine rankings. In direct linking, you have affiliate links pointing at your domain, which counts toward this search engine popularity. There are still tracking parameters present in the link, which may still prevent you from receiving full credit for the incoming link.

Promoting Your Affiliate Program

Starting up a new Web site is like opening a store in the middle of the Sahara Desert. Land is plentiful and cheap, but no one is shopping in the middle of the desert. You can build it, but do not expect instant Web site traffic. This is true for any new Web site — not just affiliate ones. This means that your quest for traffic should never end. You should also employ a diverse array of traffic-gathering techniques.

Affiliate Program Payment Methods

Affiliate programs use different ways to determine the payment method. Each can be successful in its own way, but there are slight differences between each. The three most common methods of payment are as follows:

- **Pay-per-click:** If you enter into this type of method, you will be paying your affiliates a total price that is determined by the number of Web visitors who click on a link on the affiliate Web page to arrive at your business Web site. These Web visitors are not required to buy anything; all they have to do is visit your Web site through the affiliate link.

- **Pay-per-lead:** If you use this type of method, you will be paying your affiliates an amount that is determined by the number of Web visitors that leave information at your Web site. All the Web visitor needs to do is fill out a form on your Web site, which you can then use as a lead to further sales and communication with the potential customer. Your goal is to make a sale and obtain the visitor as a repeat customer so that you can increase your client database and overall sales performance.

- **Pay-per-sale:** If you are using this type of method with your affiliates, you pay a total that is determined by the number of sales you make from the Web visitors who click on the affiliate links and make a purchase. The amount you pay is based on a predetermined amount that is fixed ahead of time for each sale — known as a flat rate — or a percentage of each sale.

Essentially, by using an affiliate program, you are promoting your Web site and products or services across hundreds or thousands of other Web sites throughout the world, dramatically increasing the exposure and potential sales for your profits — all at little or no cost.

The Challenges of Managing Affiliate Marketing

If you decide to develop your own in-house affiliate program, your first choice is to decide what software to use. While ROIA is recommended, this section will go through the process so you can make your own choices. Building an affiliate program from the ground-up is in itself a challenging task; it requires a great deal of effort and promotion. But it also has some important benefits that are unique to managing your own program — namely, total control over all aspects of the operation.

The first hurdle you will encounter is the affiliate platform development. Here, you have several choices:

- **Develop the software program yourself:** This requires good software development skills and a great deal of time. It is not recommended that you choose this option.

- **Outsource the development process:** If you truly cannot find a software solution on the commercial market and wish to develop your own, but lack the time or skills to do so, you can contract this work out. However, it will be expensive and time-consuming as you test the development work, fix bugs, and deploy and manage the process. It is not recommended that you choose this option.

- **Use a free/open-source affiliate software:** Free affiliate scripts can be found all over the Web. The problem is they are typically incomplete, have no support, are bug-filled, and usually require customization. The advantage is that they are free to use. The best place to find free/open-source scripts is at Hot Scripts, found at **www.hotscripts. com**. They have hundreds of free PHP affiliate scripts available.

- **Buy affiliate software:** Although this is the most expensive option, it is also the most reliable because it includes support and thoroughly tested applications. These applications also come with upgrades, which are typically free. Most software includes free installation and setup, and you can use hosting in-house or hosting on the affiliate company's Web site, as with ROIA; this means there is very little customization to your site other than the code that is placed on your Web site.

Tiered Affiliate Marketing

While straight, non-tiered affiliate marketing is simple and effective, you may choose a tiered affiliate marketing program. If you choose to use multi-level tiers, do not go beyond two-tier approaches. The basic affiliate structure falls in one of the two categories:

- **Single-tier affiliate structure:** The simplest approach of the two, this means that you pay a commission for every sale or lead that your affiliates will generate. Your affiliates will only be promoting and selling *your* product.

- **Two-tier affiliate structure:** A more complex model, this structure separates your affiliates into two categories: those who attract other affiliates, and those who actually sell. The first tier earns a percentage of what the affiliates signed under them sell, while the second tier comprises those doing the grunt work and selling. This can be expanded to multiple tiers.

Each of the approaches presented above is equally valid. The first works best if you have access to a large pool of potential affiliates and you want to keep it simple, and the second works best if you only have access to a few, but very active, affiliate marketers — and you do not mind some extra complexity. This will be covered later in this chapter in more detail, but it is recommended that you start out with single-tier marketing to keep it simple.

Cross-Selling and Up-Selling

A higher commission percentage means that you will have more affiliates, although a smaller one brings more profit per sale. As you will find, this is a careful balancing act between offering the maximum commission while ensuring you are profitable when paying out that commission.

You need to implement creative strategies to increase your overall sales volume. One great way to do this is through up-selling and cross-selling. Up-selling simply means that at the moment you convert a sale, you capture details from the customer, such as an e-mail address, so you can use this in your e-mail marketing campaigns. Cross-selling means at the time of a purchase, you obtain various details from the customer such as past purchases so you can offer them similar or related products. Amazon does a great job of this by suggesting products based on your past purchases and offering additional items you might like to consider at the time of a purchase. The PDG Shopping Cart, available at **www.pdgsoft.com**, has an attractive feature you can use to manage cross-selling at the time of a customer purchase.

How to Attract Affiliates

Once you have a fully functional affiliate program and are ready to start adding affiliates to your network, the next challenge is how to convince online entrepreneurs that they should join your network, become your affiliates, and promote and sell your products. The following sections will guide you through the options.

Hiring an Affiliate Manager

The easy choice — and the most expensive — is to hire an affiliate manager. An affiliate manager is someone with significant experience who can propel your program to its maximum potential. One major caveat here is that this option will not be cheap. In most cases, you will not be hiring an affiliate manager due to the prohibitive cost. However, an affiliate manager is a great option if money is not an issue. Affiliate managers possess the know-how and have the contacts to have your affiliate program producing profit in a much shorter period than you could possibly achieve on your own.

Promoting Your Affiliate Program on Your Own

No matter what, you must promote your affiliate program somehow, and you can certainly do this yourself. You will first need to get to know your market. Identify where potential affiliates may congregate — forums and online groups, for instance. This is critical as you spread the word of your affiliate program. Do not discount the use of blogs; they are very powerful tools, and because they ping the search engines after each new posting, they are very search-engine friendly.

Your affiliate program has to be enticing to a potential affiliate. It needs to be easy to understand, easy to sign up for, and easy to manage. The registration process should be quick, and your marketing materials should be diverse and effective. Use this checklist to make sure you meet the minimum requirements for an effective promotion:

- The affiliate link to join the program should be very visible.

- The registration process should be quick and painless, capturing the minimum required information with a solid affiliate agreement and e-mail confirmation.

- The marketing materials you use should be wide-ranging, from banner ads to articles and sales copy. Atlantic Publishing Company has had success with allowing authors of books to sign up as affiliates, earning up to 40 percent commission while promoting their own books. In this case, the book cover and copy is readily available to them to use in the affiliate program. The easier it is on an affiliate to integrate your content into their Web site, the more consistent the CTR will be. You will also attract more affiliates since you have substantially decreased the work necessary for them to join and manage the program.

Here are some ideas to help promote your affiliate program:

- Ask your friends and online neighbors to start a topic and ask questions in a forum thread so you can interject your affiliate program into the discussion. This definitely needs to read as a natural conversation, not a canned sales pitch specifically meant to promote your affiliate program — even though that is basically what it is.

- Offer promotional incentives to new affiliates, such as advertising that your first 50 affiliates will receive a 50 percent commission for the first six months.

- Buy endorsements or listings in blogs, forums, and Web sites promoting your affiliate program. Of course, you can also list your affiliate program with affiliate directories for free. This will be discussed in detail later in Chapter 14.

The goal with any promotional program is to ensure that it grows and prospers.

How to Make Your Affiliates More Effective

Do not count on your affiliates being Internet-savvy, experienced with affiliate marketing concepts, or technically savvy. Expect them to ask for help, and be ready to deliver it. Even software applications that appear to be very simple to you may be challenging to others. In many cases, your affiliates may need help integrating your products into their Web sites. If this is too challenging for them, they may sign on as an affiliate and never complete the integration.

Arm your affiliates with the information they need to succeed. Providing them with affiliate marketing articles or a resource center is a great way to inspire ideas. Giving them a copy of this book or other marketing guides may pay dividends many times over in return. Communicate with your affiliates often through e-mail to promote two-way communication.

Increasing Your Affiliate Numbers

Promoting your affiliate program never stops. It should be a constant process that you use to expand your affiliate network, draw in new affiliates, and promote sales conversion. It is critical that you earn credibility and gain exposure through forums, blogs, and Web sites.

Once you establish your affiliate program, be on the constant lookout for new products. In the case of Atlantic Publishing, this is easy because they produce 75 or more new books each year; for others, however, it may not be so simple. If you are not adding products, you might be surprised how shortly a certain product can last on the market before it becomes obsolete. Once you establish a solid, reputable affiliate program, you have a significant advantage you did not have earlier, should you wish to start another affiliate program on a new Web site. Here are some of those advantages:

- You already have a list of potential affiliates who trust you and who will likely join your program.

- You already have a list of potential customers who may be interested in your new products.

Cookies and Affiliates

It is important that you understand the concept of cookies and how they affect your affiliate commissions. A cookie is a text file that a Web site puts on your computer to remember something about you for a predetermined period of time, such as 90 days. This is very important to you as an affiliate because the cookie "remembers" your affiliate ID for this predetermined period of time. In other words, if a customer visits your Web site, your cookie is "served" to them. This cookie contains your affiliate ID information, which ensures that you get credit for future sales conversions. If customers browse your Web site, click through to the affiliate Web site, and buy something, you get the conversion and commission. However, if they do not buy anything right away and are just comparison-shopping, but decide to come back and make the purchase later, they may very well bypass your Web site and go directly to the affiliate host Web site. In this case, because they have your cookie on their computer, your affiliate ID is recognized, and even though they did not click through your Web site for this purchase, you are given credit for the conversion because of the cookie. Once a cookie expires, the memory of your affiliate information also expires, so if a cookie is set to 30 days and they make their purchase on day 35, you will not get credit for the conversion. It is important when joining an affiliate program to check how long a cookie is valid; a good rule of thumb is a minimum of 60 days.

Another feature of ROIA, at **www.trackingsoft.net**, is its "cookieless" technology. Cookieless tracking lets you track sales and leads without the need to place a cookie in the visitor's browser. With people becoming more conscious of their surfing habits and deleting cookies regularly, cookieless tracking provides another solution for successfully tracking traffic.

Multi-Tier Marketing and Commissions

It is important to understand the basic principles of multi-tier marketing. Just as in a traditional affiliate concept, you get a publisher to sign up, and he or she earns a percentage commission for each sale referred and converted. If he or she signs up other affiliates, the new "second-tier" affiliate earns a percentage of the commission, as does the first-level affiliate. The concept is similar to pyramid marketing schemes: If you get enough second-tier affiliates under you, they all generate revenue for you with no work on your part. For the affiliate program owner, muti-tier systems are harder to manage and cost more money in commissions. They are typically not effective and, in fact, will turn off many potential affiliates from joining. It is recommended that you do not engage in multi-tier marketing.

Affiliate Networks

An affiliate network is defined as a network that consists of a group of merchants and affiliates. Merchants will join this network so that affiliates will join and promote their products. The advantage for merchants is that their products are advertised across the network of affiliates and through a variety of means, potentially including Web site advertisement, rich media, and e-mail marketing. This ultimately lowers their overall advertising budgets. As with a traditional affiliate marketing program, the affiliates are paid based on commission from the merchants they feature. Typically, the commission is based not on individual merchant performance by each affiliate, but on the aggregate total of merchants belonging to that affiliate network. In other words, if you join the network as an affiliate and sign up with 10 merchants, your overall performance and commissions are generally based on the performance of all the merchants as a whole, not on an individual merchant basis.

As a merchant, you are provided with an administrative control panel, reporting tools, tracking, and payment processing. Of course, the greatest benefit is that you have access to a large pool of potential affiliates. As an affiliate, you get one control panel, integrated reports, simplified integration, and one-stop shopping. And as an affiliate, the networks are free to join. As a merchant, you have to pay a fee — typically monthly. In most cases there is a sign-up or setup fee, followed by monthly recurring maintenance or support fees to maintain active membership as a merchant in the affiliate network. In many cases, instead of a flat fee, your monthly costs are based on a total percentage of your affiliate sales; therefore, if you are highly successful with your affiliate marketing, your costs can increase. This is a factor you need to consider when setting your affiliate payout percentages.

If you are willing to have advertisements on your site, affiliate networks provide a simple and convenient means to raise revenue for your Web site. An affiliate network acts as the "broker" between the merchant and the affiliates. In this model, you can be the merchant or the affiliate. If you have products to sell but do not want to invest the money, time, and overhead to start your own affiliate program on your Web site, then joining an affiliate network is a great option. However, keep in mind that it is not free. If you wish to offer products from multiple companies as an affiliate, then an affiliate network may be the best choice for you as well. If you know companies who have the product you want and you are confident in their quality, service, and reputation, you may find that higher commission percentages can be achieved by joining their affiliate program directly versus through an affiliate network. Typically, companies who have their own affiliate programs are not part of a larger affiliate network, so if you want to become an affiliate with particular companies, you may want to look into this prior to joining an affiliate network.

As a merchant, it is recommended that you consider establishing your own affiliate program on your Web site. Although the cost to establish one is typically a few hundred dollars and, potentially, some monthly recurring maintenance fees, you have full control of the program. An affiliate network is a great option if you do not want to commit to the support and administration of an affiliate program. There are many outstanding affiliate programs you can install on your Web site. Designing and developing a program from scratch is not cost-effective given the variety of great programs available on the market today.

Here are some existing affiliate networks you may wish to consider:

- 15 Days Cash: **www.15dayscash.com**
- Ad Communal.com: **www.adcommunal.net**
- Google AdSense: **www.google.com/adsense**
- Affiliate Window: **www.affiliatewindow.com**

- TradeDoubler®: **www.tradedoubler.com**
- Commission Junction: **www.cj.com**
- Clash-Media®: **www.clash-media.com**
- ClickBank®: **www.clickbank.com**
- Clickbooth®: **www.clickbooth.com**
- Copeac®: **www.copeac.com**
- adperio: **www.adperio.com**
- clixGalore®: **www.clixgalore.com**
- Profitistic: **www.profitistic.co.uk**
- CX Digital Media (formerly IncentaClick): **www.cxdigitalmedia.com**
- IncentReward: **www.incentreward.com**
- Motive Interactive: **www.motiveinteractive.com**
- Pepperjam Network: **www.pepperjamnetwork.com**

There are many others to choose from; these samples merely provide a starting point.

Become an Affiliate of Others

If you do not have products to sell, only offer services through your Web site, or do not feel that your products would be profitable through an affiliate program, you may want to consider becoming an affiliate of others. This option is free, easy to implement, requires minimal Web HTML coding on your Web site, and — once established — runs itself. You just monitor your performance and wait for the check in the mail.

At this point, you have two basic options: Join an affiliate network, or sign up with an individual company's affiliate program, typically through their Web site. An affiliate network has some advantages in that there is typically no cost, and you can select multiple vendors to become an affiliate for. There is one control panel you will use to monitor performance and results, whereas if you sign up with individual companies and join multiple affiliate programs, you will have separate control and administrative panels for each. Another advantage of an affiliate network is that you get one single check per month versus many.

Though affiliate networks are easy to use and provide the ability to add a wide variety of affiliate products to your site effortlessly, do not get carried away. Adding products to your site does not equal sales or profits; do not flood your Web site with page after page of links and banner ads. Find your market niche, concentrate on it, and drive customers to your affiliate links — but keep it focused and relevant to your Web site. For an example, if your Web site is about Boston terrier puppies, there is little likelihood of success through adding computers and automotive supplies to your Web site because they are not related to your content; on the other hand, custom grooming items, dog collars, and shampoos may be highly profitable for you.

Establishing Your Own Affiliate Program

If you have niche products to sell or those that are highly desired, you may consider starting your own affiliate program on your Web site. This provides you with the greatest flexibility, control, and administration over your program, affiliates, and products. Do not attempt to design and develop your own affiliate software; it is not worth the effort, cost, or time. Think of the advantage of starting an affiliate program. You have full control over every aspect of the program, you can save on other marketing and advertisement costs, and you can advertise your program through your blog and e-mail marketing. Once established, businesses and individuals will seek you out wanting to join your program. Here are some of the basic benefits of establishing an affiliate program:

- Other businesses, Web sites, and blogs advertise your products for you.

- Your products, banner advertisements, text, and other promotional material are on other Web sites and blogs throughout the world, driving traffic to your site.

- You can easily establish your presence in an often unstable Internet world and earn brand name recognition, appeal, and customer satisfaction.

- You dramatically increase sales volume.

Here are some general rules of thumb to follow when choosing which affiliate to join:

- Choose a solid company that has been in business for at least two or more years.
- Commissions should be paid on time.
- Their affiliate program should be well-established.
- They should use feature-rich affiliate software.
- It is helpful if you know someone who recommends their program.
- They should have minimal product returns or disputes.
- They should provide customer and technical support.

Each affiliate operates on different terms and uses a wide variety of software, but essentially the process is nearly identical. You can monitor your progress, track how much you are owed, and track when checks are issued to you. If you have products to sell, you may consider implementing an affiliate program on your Web site. This can be done quickly, easily, and at little or no cost to you. As an alternative, selling products on your site as an affiliate is also free and offers tremendous profit potential.

Chapter 15

HARNESSING THE POWER OF BLOGS

A blog is an ideal alternative to a Web site. You can set up a blog for free in minutes. Blogs offer a wide variety of pre-designed templates, the ability to customize to suit your needs, and are excellent for search engine visibility. Of course, you need to know and understand what a blog is, how it functions, what it does and does not do, and how it can help you achieve your personal or business goals.

What is a Blog?

The word "blog" is a combination of the words "Web" and "log." A blog is a Web site in which short entries or "postings" are made in an abbreviated style format, and they are displayed in reverse chronological order. Blogs can consist of numerous items, from a personal standpoint to a political or business collaborative that discusses specific topics, products, or services. Blogs can also be used as a news-style of publication; this is something that a lot of journalists are beginning to utilize to publish their thoughts and perspectives on a variety of issues, or to get the word out instantly about a breaking news item of concern to a local community.

Blogs can be about any subject, including politics, news, world events, public opinion, and cooking. There are also many personal blogs from celebrities, world leaders, and aspiring political candidates, for a few examples. If you can think of a topic, there is most likely a blog related to it. Personal blogs are often considered online versions of a diary or journal. Although this is a pretty good comparison, they are far different from paper-based diaries or journals because they offer interactivity you cannot get with these more traditional forms, or even with a static HTML-based Web page diary or journal.

A blog uses a combination of text, graphics, images, and hyperlinks to other blogs, Web sites, Web pages, and multimedia content such as movie or audio clips. One of the features associated with blogging is that blog visitors can leave comments on the blog, thus creating a collaborative dialogue between you and potential customers, donors, or others you may wish to interact with. A blog opens the door to two-way communications between yourself and millions of people on the Internet. A blog can be used as a Web site or in place of a Web site.

Everything on a blog, especially if it is a news-oriented project, must be consistently and constantly updated, including the answers to your visitors' comments and questions. Unlike a Web site where visitors can post a comment on a news article and you can respond if you choose, blogs require a more in-depth commitment because your visitors expect you to answer their comments and questions, which can be time-consuming if you are trying to update your site several times a day to keep it active.

If you are going to build a blog, you also have to remember that blogs become outdated much faster than a regular Web site. The need to update is continuous because if you do not, visitors will disappear much quicker than if you were hosting a normal Web site. People visiting a Web site expect it to be updated regularly, but if you miss a day, you do not necessarily lose all of your visitors. In contrast, if you miss a day or two updating your blog, your visitors may move on to someone new who updates his or her blog more regularly.

A blog is an ongoing journal of events, news, or opinions offered for others to interact with and respond to, creating an ongoing dialogue between the blogger and the reader. The key difference between a Web page and a blog is that the Web page is static content — you can read the page, but not interact with it — while the blog is interactive. Another major difference between static Web pages and blogs is that blogs can be syndicated using RSS or Atom feeds. Syndicated blogs allow subscribers to "join" the blog and receive updates automatically.

If you write a blog, you are a blogger. There are millions of blogs, thus millions of bloggers, and the numbers grow every day as blogging continues to gain popularity. The majority of blogs are personal blogs, but there is a growing trend for businesses and organizations to produce blogs for their company, products, and services. The prevalence is especially clear in news media and politics, where blogging is a part of the culture and an integral form of accepted communications.

Blogging is all about linking. As with Web sites, links can help raise visibility with search engines. Links to and from blogs to other blogs and Web sites are directly relevant to the popularity, overall visibility, and ranking of blogs. A blog is an invitation for customers to look into your company and allows you to develop trust, two-way communication, and, ultimately, increased sales.

The Construction of a Blog

There are many tools available to help you write and publish blogs. Many are retail software, but there is also a wealth of free products to simplify the process. Before delving into a discussion about writing blogs, however, you first need to understand how a blog is constructed.

Every blog essentially consists of the following:

- **Title:** The title of the blog. This provides the blog reader an overall idea of what the blog is about.

- **Date:** The date of the blog's most recent update or post. Blogs are displayed in reverse chronological order, so the most recent post is at the top of the blog.
- **Post title:** The title of each blog post.
- **Blog text:** This is the actual text of each blog post.
- **Blog post information:** This is information about the individual or business who actually wrote the blog. Sometimes this contains contact information as well.
- **Blogger comments:** This is an area for the readers of a blog to place comments, responses, opinions, or reactions to a blog post. However, this is not a mandatory field; if your intent is only to push information via your blog, you do not have to accept comments.
- **Previous blog posts:** This is the reverse chronological listing of previous blog posts from most recent to oldest.
- **Archived posts:** Even the best blogs get unwieldy; it is not uncommon to archive old posts after a preset period of time.
- **Blogroll:** A list of links to other related sites.
- **Advertising:** This is a common sight in the world of blogging. Many advertisements are prominently featured, typically in free blogging applications. In some cases, you can generate revenue through the use of advertising, but often these are third-party advertisements you allow for the use of blogging software.
- **Feeds:** Feeds to push blogs posts automatically to subscribers, either in RSS or Atom form.

What Do I Need to Create My Own Blog?

You need two critical elements to create your own blog. These are:

- Blogging software
- Web hosting

Blog Software & Blog Hosting Options

Essentially, you have four choices when deciding how to publish your blog:

- **Free blog software with free blog hosting:** This option is of no cost to you. However, you must often allow paid advertisements to be placed within or on your blog pages. These paid advertisements are typically obtrusive and will not generate any residual income for you as they might through Google AdSense. Also, free blogging software typically has some reduced functionality compared to paid software. But there are two outstanding, advertisement-free options available to you. Both Blogger (**www.blogger.com**) and WordPress (**www.wordpress.com**) produce professional blogs and are powerful, customizable through templates, and easy to use. Blogger even lets you switch between a hosted application and publishing directly to your Web server via FTP.

- **Free blog software with paid blog hosting:** You pay for the domain name and/or hosting space with the hosting company, and the blog software is provided at no cost to you. This is very common with many Web hosting companies; as part of the hosting package, you get "free" blog software. While you do not have advertising on your blog, the software may have reduced functionality compared to commercial software. In most instances, this is an attractive option since your blog is usually hosted under your own domain name; however, some providers charge you an extra monthly fee for the blogging service. If this is the case, you will most likely do better to use Blogger or WordPress for free. However, if you wish to use your own domain name and want to use the blog software your hosting company provides, this may be an option to consider. Because your hosting company is providing the blog software, you are stuck with the brand they use. They take care of the installation and maintenance, which is one major plus.

- **Paid blog software with paid blog hosting:** This means you buy the full-featured software and also pay for the hosting service through a service provider. This is a great option if you need very powerful blog or CMS software and a very large hosting account under your own domain name.

- **Paid blog software hosted on your own Web servers:** This means you buy the full-featured software and install and host it on your own servers — you must physically own or lease the servers; this is not just a shared hosting space. This is a good option if you do not want to use open-source or free software but already have Web servers, meaning you do not need to pay for hosting commercially.

The free options may not offer all the functionality you desire, but both Blogger and WordPress will meet the needs of most small businesses and individuals, making these the perfect option for a small budget. Even with free blog hosting, do not forget the power of hyperlinks. You can easily establish a blog on a commercial hosting provider, and link or integrate that blog into your own Web site, even though it is not physically hosted on your own Web servers and does not use the same URL as your company's Web site. This practice is very common. Blogger allows you to host under your domain name as part of their built-in functionality, and WordPress allows you to export your blog if you with to move it to a new domain. The only real factor in deciding whether you want to host your blog under your own name may appear years down the road if you outgrow the free products and want to move to a new domain name. Your audience will already know the old domain name, so it may be hard to move your blog without losing them.

The following sections will provide a more detailed look at the five options and compare them.

Free Blog Software with Free Blog Hosting

While you may find this option to offer limited features — including limited functionality, limited access, and limited control over design, colors, and presentation — this option will cost you nothing. Blogger and WordPress are the recommended options because both offer advertisement-free, hosted blogging solutions, and both are customizable, rich in features, and easy to use.

One of the main advantages of having your own Web site is that you own the domain name, so you can choose a domain name that is directly related to your company or corporate image. With free hosting, you have no control over your domain name. In fact, you will most likely be hosted under another domain name and utilize a subdomain name. A subdomain is a domain name that is part of another domain name, such as www.yourfree-blog.brucecbrown.com. This might not be bad if your blog is hosted on your corporate Web site; however, if it is hosted by another free hosting provider, your blog domain name may be very lengthy and not at all related to your company name or profile.

The primary advantage to this option is that there is no cost involved. This is a great way to start blogging because you can try it out to see if it is something you will truly enjoy. If you find it is not your kind of hobby, you have not wasted any money. If you become an avid blogger, you can move to a better option in the future if you choose.

Free Blog Software with Paid Blog Hosting

This option may be the ideal solution if you already own a Web site and have it hosted with a provider that provides you with blog software for free on its servers. The main advantage is that you are ensuring that your blog is advertisement-free and is hosted under your domain name. The downside is that you are stuck with whatever blog software they provide, which may be subpar, and you often have to pay an extra fee to use the blogging features.

As in the first option, free software may have reduced features or functionality, which will limit your control over the look and feel of your blog and may not have all of the features you seek. In addition to free software, there are numerous "shareware" versions of blogging software that are both reliable and widely used. The primary disadvantage of this type of software is that many hosting services will not allow it to be installed on their servers. A common theme with Web hosts is the exclusion of third-party software on their sites to protect themselves from security breaches as well as performance hits by allowing you to run bandwidth-hungry software on their servers.

If your current Web hosting provider allows you to install third-party blog software on their servers, this is also a possible option, especially if you already have a Web site and domain name. Be sure to check with your current Web hosting provider; they most likely already offer free blog software to you as part of the hosting package.

Paid Blog Software with Paid Blog Hosting

This is a good option if you want to get feature-rich, fully functional software, do not want to hassle with hosting or software setup, and require reliable technical support for both hardware and software. The tradeoff is that, obviously, you have to pay for it. In this case, the hosting is provided by the reseller of the blog software, sometimes on their domain, but typically hosted under your domain name. There is usually no installation fee, no setup, and one monthly payment; however, sometimes you pay for the software and hosting separately, depending on which software package you buy.

This is considered an all-in-one solution that provides the most feature-rich blog software with hosting services dedicated to support Web and blog servers. Software installation is not an issue because the service provider usually installs and configures the software and hosting. It is also one of the more expensive options. You may also be charge based on the volume of blog traffic, so as your blog popularity grows, so do your costs. One of the main advantages with this option is that you have full control over the look of your blog and can mimic your main Web site branding, unless the hosting provider limits your options. Typically, though, you have full design control.

One advantage of a dedicated blog hosting account is that the rates are typically flat, meaning they do not change based on the volume of blog traffic. From the technical support perspective, multiple accounts and multiple hosting providers typically equal multiple headaches when it comes to support and troubleshooting. Although the software and hosting is supported by the commercial provider, that does not mean you will not have a degree of tech support and troubleshooting headaches of your own if the service is unreliable.

Paid Blog Software Hosted on Your Own Web Servers

This is an ideal solution if you want to get feature-rich, fully functional software, and you already own or lease your owner-dedicated Web servers. If you own or lease them, you might as well use them if you can install the blog software and configure it to operate on your Web server under your own domain name.

One of the main advantages with this option is that you have full control over the look of your blog and can mimic your main Web site branding, and because you own the servers, the cost for hosting is non-existent. Additionally, you have full control over your hardware and server maintenance. With leased servers, although you are leasing a dedicated machine, you will still rely on the service provider to perform installations and hardware maintenance, so you will need to check to be sure that your provider will support the blog software installation and other requirements.

Who Blogs?

Obviously, a critical component to the success of any blog is who will participate in the blog. A blog is nothing without participation from subscribers, readers, customers, and potential customers. Whether you are a business, organization, or cause will determine your target blog audience.

Bloggers come from every walk of life, including professionals, executives, blue-collar workers, housewives, and techno-geeks. Blogging has exploded in popularity and is considered a communications method of the future. Blogging is much more than simply a journal, as it was when it was first invented. Blogging is a marketing tool, allowing you to communicate and interact directly with your bloggers. The beauty of blogging is that it is very simple to do. Not only is it easy to establish a blog site, but it is very easy to become an active blogger. You do not need any technical knowledge, special skills, or training to establish a highly effective blog site or become an expert blogger.

Instead of publishing static information, you are engaging your visitors in an online conversation on a blog. You want bloggers to talk to you and with each other, discussing your company and products and/or services. Ultimately, if you can engage current and potential customers through conversation, you will successfully promote your products and services through blogs. Anyone on the Internet can read and join your blogs, and they are searchable. You will quickly discover that your blogs are a primary source for promoting, marketing, and building brand-name reputation and recognition.

Blog versus Content Management Systems

Blogs and Content Management System software are distinctively different, although related. Blog software simply provides you with the features and functionality to create, maintain, and manage your blog. A CMS typically has a built-in blogging module, but it provides significantly more features and functionality across all spectrums of content management than blog publishing software.

Understanding Pings and Trackbacks

The most unique feature of blogging is comments. Comments create the two-way communication between you and your blog readers. Bloggers read your blog and post comments, questions, opinions, and concerns. This dialogue is what makes blogging unique. Your readers can also link directly to your blog posts and recommend your blog to others. This is known as trackbacks and pingbacks.

Trackbacks are simply a notification method between blogs. It allows a blog reader to send a notice to someone else that the blog might be something they would have an interest in reading. Here is an example:

1. You publish something in your blog.
2. One of your blog readers sees this blog post and decides to leave a comment. In addition to having other blog readers see what they have posted, the commenter also wants to allow any fellow readers to comment on his or her blog.
3. The blog reader posts something on his or her own blog and sends a trackback to your blog.
4. You receive the trackback and display it in the form of a comment on your blog along with the link back to the blog reader's post.
5. Anyone who reads this blog can follow the trackback to your blog, and vice versa.

This illustrates how blogging is unique from Web sites and discussion forums. The theory is that blog readers from both your blog and the commenting reader's blog can read the blog posts, and ultimately more people will join in the blog discussion. The idea is to encourage blog readers to click on the trackback link and visit the other blog. As you can see, the number of blog posts and trackback links can grow exponentially. The problem with trackbacks is that they can be spammed easily, and there is no real authentication process to ensure that a trackback is valid.

Pingbacks are a method for Web authors to request notification when somebody links to one of their documents. Typically, Web publishing software will automatically inform the relevant parties on behalf of the user, allowing for the possibility of automatically creating links to referring documents. A detailed description of pingbacks can be found at **www.hixie.ch/ specs/pingback/pingback**. Here is an example:

1. You publish something in your blog.
2. One of your blog readers sees this blog post and decides to leave a comment. In addition to having other blog readers see what they have posted, the commenter also wants to allow any fellow readers to comment on his or her blog.
3. The blog reader posts something on his or her blog and links back to your blog.
4. The blog reader's blogging software automatically sends a notification telling you that your blog has been linked to and automatically includes this information about the link in your blog.

Although they are very similar, there are differences:

- They use different technologies to communicate.
- Pingbacks are automated, while trackbacks are manual; pingbacks will automatically find hyperlinks within a blog posting and try to communicate with those URLs, whereas trackbacks require you to manually enter the URL that the trackback needs to be sent to.
- Trackbacks send the comments while pingbacks do not. Trackbacks typically send only part of your comments to entice the reader into following the actual links to read the entire blog or blog entries.
- Pingbacks appear as links only. Trackbacks appear as links with content or comments.

- Trackbacks can be faked, spoofed, and spammed. Pingbacks are not easily faked.
- Trackbacks provide the reader with a preview of the content on the blog, whereas pingbacks do not.

Blogging & Spam

Just as spam is a huge problem for e-mail, it is a growing problem for blogs. There are two major categories of blog spam. They are:

- **Bogus blogs**, or spam blogs. These are designed purely for spamming purposes by launching spam attacks through viral methods.
- **Comment spam**, in which spam comments are inserted into legitimate blogs.

Spam blogs are also referred to as "splogs," a combination of the two words. According to Blogger's help pages, spam blogs "cause various problems, beyond simply wasting a few seconds of your time when you happen to come across one. They can clog up search engines, making it difficult to find real content on the subjects that interest you. They may scrape content from other sites on the Web, using other people's writing to make it look as though they have useful information of their own. And if an automated system is creating spam posts at an extremely high rate, it can impact the speed and quality of the service for other, legitimate users." The spam blog problem has continued to grow despite efforts to stop it through IP blocking and word verification fields.

Comment spam contains links to one or more Web sites, which are usually also irrelevant, inappropriate, or purely spam-centric Web sites. Combating spam blog entries is time-consuming, frustrating, and a growing problem. While most blog software has built-in tools to combat comment spam, they are not foolproof. Spammers use automated software applications, robots, auto-responders, and other techniques to spread spam throughout the blogosphere. The secret to defeating — or at least minimizing — spam in your blog is to employ the tools of your blog software and host to their fullest potential. Just like with e-mail, you may not stop all content spam, but you can certainly minimize it. Spam is not a reason to quit blogging; it is simply an annoyance you will have to deal with.

Blog Software Comparison and Reviews

You will need blog software to establish your blog. To assist you in the decision-making process, the following sections contain reviews of the most popular blog software applications available.

Full-Service Blog Providers

- **TypePad® (www.typepad.com):** Probably the most recognizable full-service blog provider. Typepad is fully featured, easy to use, and an industry leader. TypePad offers a free 14-day trial if you wish to give this route a try. For most users, the basic or plus level of service are more than adequate. TypePad offers a wide variety of features:
  - Use the professionally designed blog templates or build your own.
  - Customize the layout of your blog with drag-and-drop tools.
  - TypePad generates XHTML-compliant pages and uses CSS for layout and design, which makes it easy to customize and extend your blog.
  - Enjoy the WYSIWYG ("what you see is what you get") editing environment.
  - Edit the HTML of individual posts.
  - Categorize your posts and create automatic archives.
  - Insert photos into your posts quickly with automatic resizing and thumbnails.
  - Schedule future posts for automatic publication, so you do not have to be at your computer every time you need to publish.

- Invite multiple authors to collaborate.
- Send posts and photos via e-mail, and TypePad will automatically post them to your blog.
- TypePad Mobile offers powerful posting and editing features for smartphone users.
- Point your domain to your TypePad blog at the Plus and Pro levels.
- Add content and functionality from dozens of third-party sites, including Google, CafePress, ProStores, Skype, Sitemeter, Technorati, Pandora, Sphere, Rollyo and more to your blog through TypePad Widgets.
- Google, Technorati, and other blog search engines are instantly notified about new content.
- Send ping notices to **http://blo.gs** and **http://Weblogs.com** when you update your site.
- Send trackbacks to sites you read when you write about them.
- Track blog visitors with TypePad's statistics functionality.

• **Blogware (home.blogware.com):** Blogware is an enormously popular online application that is sold and hosted through retailers' Web servers. The obvious advantage to this is you can select whom your blog hosting provider will be. With Blogware, there is no HTML to learn and no new software to download and install. Blogware is an easy-to-use, feature-heavy, secure blogging tool.

Blogware was created to meet the needs of both retailers looking to sell a blogging service and you, the blogger. Blogware's features include photo albums, visitor interaction, privacy, rich text editor (RTE), statistics, and the ability to syndicate.

Here are some of the major features of Blogware:

- Interfaces make blogging simple. Posts are created in an RTE with a WSYWYG environment. You can preview and edit your entries and photos before you publish them.

- With Blogware's security model, you can control who sees what content.
- You have the ability to post content from your cell phone or an e-mail application.
- You can create custom templates or components for your blog.

Blogware lets you choose which retailer to purchase from; most offer free trials. If you need a reliable hosting service that offers Blogware, consider **www.blogging.com** or **www.blogharbor.com**.

- **Squarespace®** (**www.squarespace.com**) — Squarespace is a full-feature software package for managing Web sites and blogs. Squarespace helps you build stylish, state-of-the-art blogs. The Squarespace Journal, which can represent either a piece of your Web site or the entirety of your site, is an ideal way to create a professional blog. Squarespace's professional-grade blogging tools feature spell checking, Atom and RSS feed auto-discovery, XML-RRC pinging, comment management, member registration, and timed publishing dates.

Squarespace offers a free 14-day trial and is very simple to use. Both the Web site design and the blog design feature integrated publishing software, so there is nothing else to buy. All the tools you need are provided in the package.

Independent Blog Software

There are dozens of good blog software products for purchase, which you can install and customize on your Web server. Here are some of the best, which I have reviewed.

- **Movable Type®** (**www.movabletype.com**) — Movable Type is free for personal use. Movable Type has a loyal following and is powerful, user-friendly blog software. Features of Movable Type 4 include:

  - A redesigned user interface.

- Easy to install and easy to get started.
- At-a-glance summary of your blogging activity from content to contributors on the new dashboard.
- Easily insert text, photos, and files with WYSIWYG editing.
- Built-in asset, photo, and file management.
- Support for creating standalone pages that automatically inherit your blog's design.
- Built-in member registration system for reader and comment authentication.
- Aggregate posts from multiple blogs into a single blog.
- Expanded options for archiving and displaying content.

With Movable Type, you can publish an unlimited number of blogs with one installation and manage hundreds of users with customizable user groups and roles.

- **ExpressionEngine®** (**http://expressionengine.com**) — Arguably the most powerful CMS application on the market, this is blogging software and significantly more. A summary of the numerous features of ExpressionEngine is available at **http://expressionengine. com/overview/features**. ExpressionEngine offers Web publishing, blog publishing, built-in templates, a mailing list manager, built-in searching, and group/member management. While there is a free 30-day trial period, the software license is expensive, and installation will tack on another $50. But there is a long list of testimonials at **http://expressionengine.com/sales/testimonials**.

- **MiniWeb 2.0 Blog Writer** (**www.miniWeb2.com**) — MiniWeb 2.0 is actually a suite of products available for download and installation on your Web server. The suite of 10 products includes a blogging software application called Blog Writer. One of the great benefits of MiniWeb 2.0 is that installation on your Web server is free. Intesync technicians install the application directly onto your

Web server in minutes, and then your blog is up and running. You can see a working demo of the product at **www.miniWeb2.com/ moduledemo/blogwriter**.

Free Blog Software

There are two major players who offer free blogging software. They are Blogger and WordPress. Here is a close look at each:

- **Blogger (www.blogger.com):** Blogger is entirely free. It is a very basic but effective way to start a blog. Blogger is simple to use and works nicely for a basic blog. Blogger, which was started in 1999, was recently bought by Google, so you can assume it will continue to be supported and improved upon.

  Blogger uses standard templates to get you started with an attractive site right away without the need to learn HTML. It also allows you to edit your blog's HTML code whenever you want, and you can use custom colors and fonts to modify the appearance of your blog. The simple drag-and-drop system lets you easily decide exactly where your posts, profiles, archives, and other parts of your blog should live on the page. Blogger also allows you to upload photos and embed them in your blog.

  Blogger Mobile lets you send photos and text straight to your blog while you are on the go. All you need to do is send a message to go@blogger.com from your phone. You do not even need a Blogger account. The message itself is enough to create a brand new blog and post whatever photo and text you have sent.

  An example of how to use Blogger to create your own blog is included later in this chapter. You will not find a simpler free option for creating a blog than Blogger. It is perfect for casual bloggers or personal blogs; however, if you want to use your blog for business, you may wish to choose WordPress or invest in blog software that you can host on your site.

- **WordPress (www.wordpress.org):** WordPress is a free, open-source blogging application. It is fully featured and fairly simple to install. If you prefer, you can have it hosted on the WordPress servers for free. WordPress boasts outstanding features that will give you control over most aspects of your blog without being overcomplicated and difficult to use.

WordPress has features for user management, dynamic page generation, RSS and Atom feeds, customizable templates and themes, password protection, the availability of plugins to enhance functionality, scheduled postings, multi-page posts, file and picture uploads, categories, and e-mail blog updates. It is as powerful and feature-rich as most commercially available blogging applications. You should install it on your existing Web servers if they can support it, but as an alternative, you can host it free on WordPress.

How to Write a Great Blog

There is an art to blogging effectively, though you really do not need to have any special skills in writing to write blogs. You do need some education if you wish to create and write effective blogs. You are not writing the next great novel, but neither is it an e-mail. Lose your audience, and your blog is useless. In this chapter the best time-proven techniques for writing effective blogs have been compiled for you.

This list is certainly not complete, and is in fact dynamic, based on the type of blog, topic of the blog, target audience, and the "attitude" of the bloggers who are posting comments on the blog. That said, this is a helpful compilation of the best techniques to help you write effective blogs and become a master blogger.

How Important is Your Blog Content?

Your blog content is the most important factor in your blog. Of course, the key question is, how do you determine what good content is? There is not a simple answer, as it depends on the type of blog, the intention of the blog, the target audience, and the experience of the bloggers. A good blog entertains, enlightens, captures interest, fascinates, sparks debate, and inspires conversation. A blog needs to be unique, invigorating, and useful. There are many blogs in the blogosphere; you need to be unique or create your own market niche in order to gain an audience.

You need to define what your target audience is after, design it with content that addresses what your target audience wants, communicate it effectively, and reach out to your readers. Give them what they want, and they will be back. A little research on your target audience can go a long way. Seek feedback and make changes to your blog accordingly. Your readers know what they want, so deliver it to them. One of your challenges will be to establish a unique blog when using free blog software such as Blogger, as it is not as customizable as some of the higher-end commercial products.

Guidelines for Writing Blogs

Your blog needs to be relevant and on topic. Keeping your blog on topic is critical in preventing you from going in directions that may cause you to lose your core audience. Keep your main point intact, and make sure it is lively and interesting.

A blog is a compilation of opinions. What draws in the audience initially is the topic. Keep the topic on track, and encourage others to share opinions, thoughts, and opposing views where possible to keep the blog engaging and interesting. Interject humor and wit when you can.

Here are some guidelines to help you establish your blog:

- Inform your readers. You must convey knowledge about what you are posting. Be factual, accurate, and professional. Ensure that your blog is clearly written, and there are no glaring spelling or grammar errors.

- Differentiate between fact and opinion. If your post is based on fact, then clearly present the fact. If it is your opinion, be sure to make it clear that it is your opinion only, and is not based entirely on fact or corporate policy.

- Be timely. Blogging can be time-consuming, but you need to present timely information for it to be of value. Dated information will indicate that your blog is not timely, and it will ultimately become irrelevant.

- Punctuality is important. You need to have periodic blog updates, and you need to stick to that schedule. As your blog grows in readership, your audience will look forward to your scheduled blog posts. Do not disappoint them by failing to stick to your schedule. Be realistic with that schedule; do not announce daily updates if you cannot stick to it. Do not lose your audience because your communication is lacking.

- Be straightforward and simplistic in your blog entries. Keep them clear, easy to read, and easy to understand.

- Keywords drive search engine rankings, so if you want to have your blog visible, you need to insert keywords into your blog posts. Include related keywords in both the title and content post of your blog entries. Do not overload your keywords to the point that your blog post becomes nothing more than a string of unreadable keywords. Use them in natural sentences.

- To increase your visibility, you need to develop thorough content that is keyword-enriched and captures the both the reader and the search engines.

- The frequency of your blog posts also affects search engine rankings and visibility. Update your blog on a regular, frequent basis.

This not only develops and increases your audience, but it also helps you with search engine rankings.

- Spelling counts. It reflects professionalism and attention to detail. Make sure you read what you post before you publish.

- RSS expands your blog like a spider Web by pushing your blog out to your subscribers as you post entries.

- Be patient. You may think your blog is exciting, but it takes time for people to find it, and even more time to cultivate your audience.

- Blogging is all about opinions. Although you do need to be careful about posting your blog opinions, your audience wants your personality, thoughts, and feelings — so express them.

- Links are critical. Link where possible to other Web pages that are relevant to your blog post. Link to Web sites, other blogs, books, articles, and news.

- Keep it brief, but not too brief. Get your point across quickly using a minimal number of words. Long posts can lose your readers and get off-topic. Short blog posts may not contain enough information to be of value. Learn the magic length for your blog and try to stick to it. You may have more success keeping your blog posts shorter and breaking them into multiple posts to capture increased readership through your RSS feeds and in search engines.

- Titles attract attention. Make them capture the essence of your blog post. Good titles also drive your overall readership. Most people scan Web pages and only stop when something catches their eyes. If your titles do not draw people in, you will lose potential blog readership.

- Organize your posts for clear readability. Keep sentences short, and use spacing or bullets to organize thoughts. Use bullets and white space to maintain easy readability.

- Consistency is important, especially as you win over audiences by adding your unique personality or interjections into your blog posts. Keeping your posts consistent is important in sustaining audiences.

- Blogging is not an art form. It does not require a graduate-level education. Try not to over-think it; keep a sense of humor and do not patronize your readers.

- Write something that you would actually want to read. If your blog is boring and contains no useful or interesting information, do not write it. No one will read it, anyway.

- You are not writing a term paper. Do not get hung up on grammar rules. Yes, spell correctly. Beyond that, keep it simple and clear, but do not spend hours worrying about perfect grammar. You will not be receiving a grade on it.

- Bullets are great for organization. Use them in your blogs to help with readability and to present key topics/ideas.

- Bold and italics are good for emphasizing keywords, phrases, and ideas.

- Jargon and acronyms are bad. Do not use them. You may understand them, but others may not.

- Write in clear, captivating, and descriptive tones. While following the length rules, give enough verbal signals in your descriptive words to "paint the picture" in the readers mind. By providing enough detail to capture the imagination, you draw in interest and avoid monotone, colorless, one-line entries.

- Take a risk. Write outside of your comfort zone about topics you have an interest in, want more information about, want to learn about, or want to offer your opinion on. If you only write about your specialty, you may get bored, and your blogs might get boring and one-dimensional.

- Be humorous or witty when you can. It makes for a fun read, and captures audience attention.

- Give readers the details they crave. Few things are more disappointing than headlines that capture your interest, only to find the blog posts have no substance and are boring.

- Be tough. Your opinions and blog posts may be your opinion, or your company position on issues, but there will be opposing thoughts and opinions. Do not take them personally, and do not worry about negativity. It comes with the territory.

- Topic and content are what make or break a blog. You have to have a topic someone is interested in, and the content needs to support the topic.

How to Write Comments on a Blog

The best bloggers out there are known by reputation for their blogs and blog comments, and several have written articles on blogging. There are some specific guidelines you can follow when posting comments that will help you build a reputation and improve your professionalism as a blogger. Write respectfully and intelligently, and support your comments. In the blogosphere, reputation is everything.

Your blogs will be read by a wide variety of individuals. Some will seek you out for potential partnerships, to purchase products, and for marketing ventures. You never know who will read your blog, so follow the guidelines of professionalism. This is critical for corporate blogging.

The key is to provide useful, factual information so that, over time, it becomes clear to other readers of the blogs to which you post that you know what you are talking about. In general, it is a good idea to keep your posts short and on-point.

Guidelines for Blog Comments

- Keep your comments short and simple.
- Keep your comments relevant, professional, and on-topic. Blog administrators will purge offensive material, personal flames, and other inappropriate content. When using someone else's material, give them the appropriate attribution.
- Sign your comments. Include your e-mail address, Web site URL, and blog URL.

- Provide quality comments that add substance and meaning. Fluff or generalized two-word entries are of no value.
- Promote your blog, business, and Web site in your blog posts by providing a URL and brief description, or embedding it naturally into the blog comment so readers can have the option to follow your link if they wish to visit your site and obtain more information relative to your blog comment.
- If you have nothing useful to add to a blog, do not add anything.

Blogger

Blogger started out as a small, independent company in the late 1990s. In 2002, Blogger was bought out by Google. While you go to Blogger to create your blog, you will be using your Google account login information to access your blog.

The following example will show you how to create a blog using Blogger. As shown below, navigate in your browser to **www.blogger.com**:

Google screenshots © Google Inc. Used with permission.

Click on the "Create Your Blog Now" arrow to continue. If you already have a blog with Blogger, you simply log in to access your account.

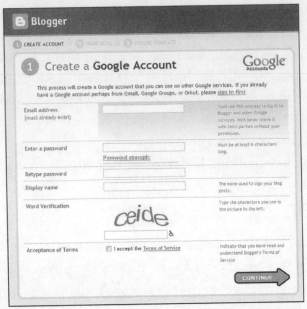

Google screenshots © Google Inc. Used with permission.

Because Blogger is owned by Google, you must have a Google account to access your blog or create a new blog. Follow the instructions to create a blog, or log in if you already have an account.

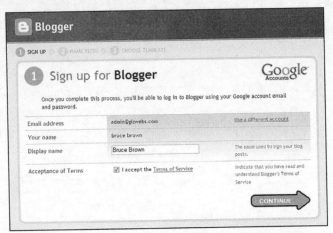

Google screenshots © Google Inc. Used with permission.

After you log in or create an account, you will see the "Sign up for Blogger" screen. You must specify your display name, which is the name you will use to sign your blog posts, and you must check that you accept the terms of service. Click the "Continue" button.

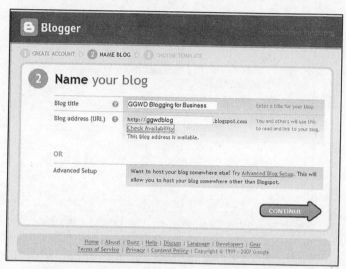

Google screenshots © Google Inc. Used with permission.

Enter the desired title of your blog. This example will create a blog for this book. You have the option to choose which blog address, or URL, you want to use. Note that your chosen title may already be in use, so you must click on "Check Availability" to ensure it is available; it will either tell you that the blog address is available or recommend alternatives if it is already in use. The first example will use the basic setup; the advanced setup will be shown in a later example.

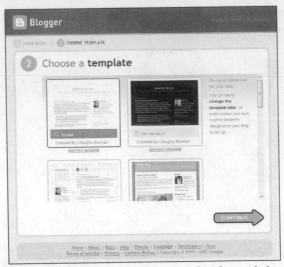

Google screenshots © Google Inc. Used with permission.

Choose one of multiple template formats for your blog. With Blogger, you do lose some control over the look and feel of your blog. Blogger does compensate for this by offering a multitude of attractive templates to choose from. Click the "Continue" button after you have chosen your template.

Google screenshots © Google Inc. Used with permission.

You are now done; your blog is ready for you to start posting. Click the "Start Posting" button to navigate to your blog.

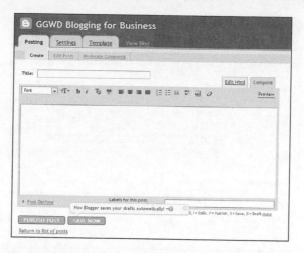

Google screenshots © Google Inc. Used with permission.

In this screen, you can create and publish new blog posts, edit your posts, moderate comments, and compose and save draft blog posts. You can also edit your settings and template design.

On the top right-hand side of each page, you will see a link to the "Dashboard." This is the central control panel for your blog. It is also where you edit your settings and profile, manage your blog, and read news and features from Blogger.

Google screenshots © Google Inc. Used with permission.

Now you will edit the settings of your blog. Click on the "Settings" link and go through each section to customize your preferences:

Google screenshots © Google Inc. Used with permission.

Most of the setting features are self-explanatory and are based on your personal preferences. The "BlogSend Address" is an e-mail address to send your blog when it is published, and the "Mail-to-Blogger Address" is an address you can use to e-mail posts directly to your blog without having to access it.

Google screenshots © Google Inc. Used with permission.

The permissions page lets you specify blog authors and who can read your blog.

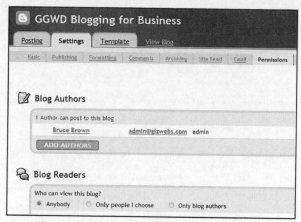

Google screenshots © Google Inc. Used with permission.

The "Template" link lets you edit and format your template. Although you have limited control over your template, you do have options.

Google screenshots © Google Inc. Used with permission.

You can customize quite a few elements and add page elements, images, links, and text. Blogger is configured to add page elements automatically by clicking the "Add a Page Element" link. Page elements are items such as Google AdSense accounts, labels, pictures, and text, as well as a profile of yourself, which can easily be plugged into your blog.

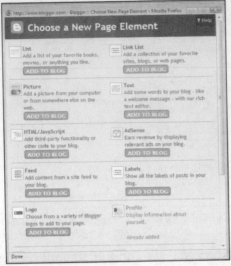

Google screenshots © Google Inc. Used with permission.

You can also change your template with the click of a button.

Google screenshots © Google Inc. Used with permission.

You have now completed your blog and customized it. You are ready to publish your first post.

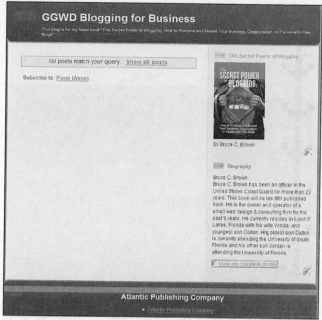

Google screenshots © Google Inc. Used with permission.

Navigate back to the "Posting" tab of your Blogger site to create your first blog post. Simply type in the title and post content, and you are ready to publish.

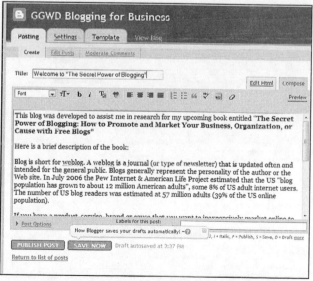

Google screenshots © Google Inc. Used with permission.

Click the "Publish Post" button to publish your new post, or click the "Save Now" button if you wish to save it for editing or posting at a later time. Once you publish your post, you will receive a confirmation from Blogger.

Google screenshots © Google Inc. Used with permission.

You may now view your blog. Since Blogger automates the ping process for you, the notification service is kicked off each time a blog post occurs.

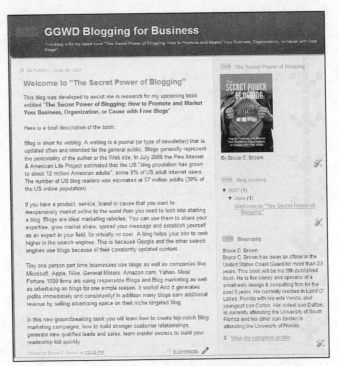

Google screenshots © Google Inc. Used with permission.

Because you have enabled e-mail notification of each post in the "Settings" section, you will receive an e-mail after each blog post is published.

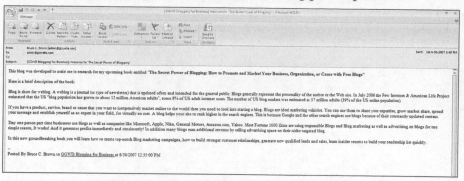

Google screenshots © Google Inc. Used with permission.

You can also e-mail blog posts to Blogger. You are provided with the e-mail address. Simply create the e-mail and send it; your post will automatically publish to your blog.

The e-mail blog entry is created within seconds of receipt at Blogger, and you will receive an e-mail confirmation of the published blog.

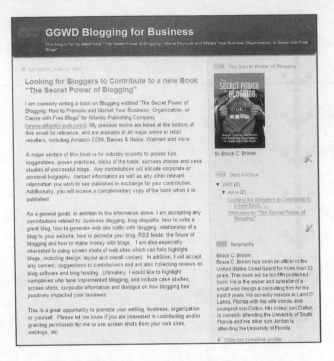

Google screenshots © Google Inc. Used with permission.

At this point, you have created a blog, published several posts, and have customized your blog. Blogger is completely free, easy to use, and does not include any advertising on your blog pages. You have dozens of templates to choose from, and although you do not have total control over your blog, it is a great way to get started. Make sure to link your blog to your Web site and place the URL on your business cards, e-mail signatures, company literature, and e-mail newsletters.

Blogger supports syndication feeds for your Web site. Syndication means that when you publish your blog, Blogger automatically generates a machine-readable representation of your blog that can be picked up and displayed on other Web sites and information aggregation tools. The setup within Blogger is very simple; you should click on the "Site Feed" link to specify your feed parameters. You can specify "full" or "short" to syndicate the full blog text, or truncate the first 255 characters.

Blogger supports Atom, which is a syndication format or "feed" for your blog. When a regularly updated site such as a blog has a feed, people can subscribe to it using software for reading syndicated content called a "newsreader." People like using readers for blogs because it allows them to catch up on all their favorites at once and avoid navigating to multiple Web sites, and it is delivered spam-free. There are many newsreaders that support Atom, including News Monster, NewzCrawler, NewsGator™, NetNews-Wire™, Shrook, RSSOwl, and BottomFeeder.

Spend the time to customize your blog through the settings control panel. Some features you will want to turn on and customize may be under the "Comments" tab, which lets you specify whether to turn backlinks and word verification on or off. Allowing word verification is a critical step in preventing spam posts from hitting your blog through automated blog systems.

Help is readily available by clicking the "Help" link in the upper right-hand corner of any page.

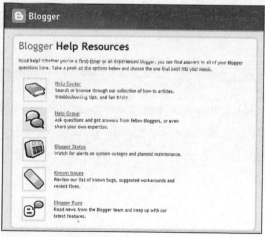

Google screenshots © Google Inc. Used with permission.

Hosting a Blogger Blog on Your Own Web Server

The next example will show you how to configure Blogger using the advanced setup to host the blog on your own Web servers or hosted Web account.

With an existing blog at Blogger, you may switch, at any time, from the hosted blogging Web site to your own Web site. To do this, click on the "Publishing" link and switch to a custom domain link.

Google screenshots © Google Inc. Used with permission.

Simply enter the URL for your blog, and blog readers will be re-directed to your hosted URL. The "missing files host" allows Blogger to redirect to your original blog URL in the event it cannot find files at your hosted site.

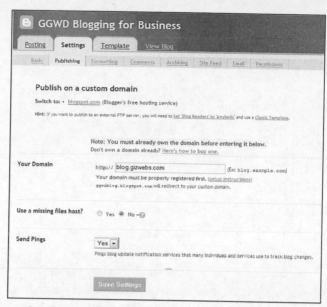

Google screenshots © Google Inc. Used with permission.

To set up a blog from scratch and host it on your own Web site, navigate in your browser to **www.blogger.com** and create your account, or log in with your existing account.

Instead of choosing the basic setup option, this time click on the "Advanced Blog Setup" link to access the advanced setup screen. At this screen, you will enter your blog title, listing options, and detailed server information. You will also need to enter your FTP server information, blog filename, and FTP access information.

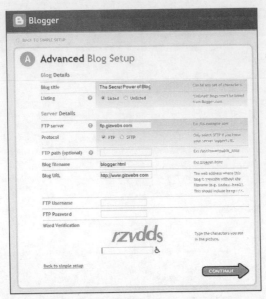

Google screenshots © Google Inc. Used with permission.

Once this is completed, you are ready to customize any other settings and publish your blog.

Google screenshots © Google Inc. Used with permission.

You will be given a confirmation if your FTP publishing update is successful, and you can click the "View Blog" link to view your blog. All of the other features are available to you, giving you control over the template, style, and settings, as well as the ability to publish posts via e-mail to your own Web server. The best part is you do not need to have a new Web site or domain name for your blog; you can host it right alongside your main Web site.

Google screenshots © Google Inc. Used with permission.

In the image below, you will see that the sample blog was created via the FTP publishing feature and is hosted on the main domain URL. For businesses or organizations who wish to maintain a professional Web site, it is best to host the blog on the company's URL instead of on Blogger or another free hosting service. Because you own the domain name and Web server/hosting, you have ultimate control over access to the data. You may have multiple blogs with Blogger; some may be hosted on Blogger, and some may be hosted by yourself, but all are managed within the main control panel.

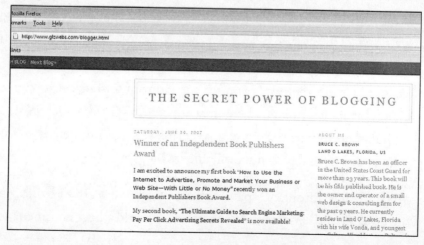

WordPress

WordPress is immensely popular within the blogging community. It is by far the most powerful and customizable application with many available plug-ins. Just as with Blogger, WordPress is simple to set up.

Features of WordPress

WordPress has a wide variety of built-in features. This includes pre-designed blog templates that let you change the look of your blog with dozens of professionally designed themes. You can switch between themes instantly with just a click of a button, as with Blogger. WordPress also lets you customize your blog code using CSS, and it includes a system that allows you to categorize and tag your posts while you write them — this is another feature shared with Blogger.

WordPress also includes a spell check option, previews, autosave, photos, and videos. You can upload your own photos or easily include images from other services such as Flickr® or Photobucket®. You can also embed videos from places like YouTube or Google. An inline spell checker makes it easy to proof your posts. As with Blogger, you have the ability to preview your blog post before you publish it, and your draft posts are automatically backed up while you write.

Just as with Blogger, WordPress allows you to have a completely public blog; a blog that is public but not included in search engines; or a private blog only members can access. WordPress also provides you with an integrated stats system that gives you up-to-the-minute stats on how many people are visiting your blog, where they are coming from, which posts are most popular, and which search engine terms are sending people to your blog. This is a feature that is not available in Blogger.

You will find that automatic spam protection is one of the best features of WordPress. WordPress uses Akismet™, the world's best comment and trackback spam technology, to block spammers from leaving spam comments on your blog.

If you grow tired of using Blogger or are ready for more features, you can actually import your entire blog from sites like Blogger, TypePad, and Live-Journal™. You can also easily track follow-ups to your comments — WordPress created a special page that notifies you so you can track these follow-up comments, even if they are on other blogs. What sets WordPress apart from Blogger and most other blog applications is the availability and ease of adding widgets to your site. WordPress defines widgets as "tools or content that you can add, arrange, and remove from the sidebars of your blog." You can add widgets to your sidebar by simply dragging and dropping. Widgets add functionality, design, and interactivity. With WordPress, you can also create Web pages, not just blog pages. You can even create an entire Web site, using your blog as one of the pages on your site.

All WordPress blogs support RSS, while Blogger supports Atom. WordPress creates feeds in RSS format and allows people to subscribe to updates on your blog using services like My Yahoo! or Bloglines™.

Establishing a WordPress Account

The following example will guide you through the process of setting up a WordPress Blog. This example will use Atlantic Publishing Company, which would like to use a blog to promote its new book releases and publish related news and information. To start, navigate to **www.wordpress. com** and click on the "Start Your Free WordPress Blog" link.

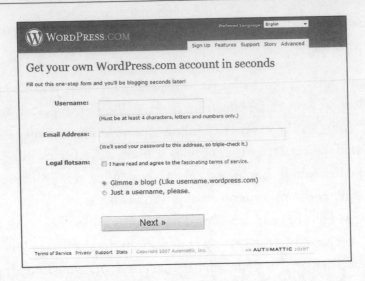

You will need to establish a user name, enter your e-mail address, comply with the terms and conditions, and then click the "Next" button.

WordPress will use your user name as part of your domain name; in the example, this would be **atlanticpub.worldpress.com**. Enter your blog title and language; then click the "Privacy" box to allow your blog to be publicized to search engines such as Google and Technorati™. You will be directed to the confirmation screen, which tells you that an e-mail has been sent to you to confirm your account.

Once you confirm your login through the e-mail activation process, you may use the provided password and your user name to log into the blog site. Your basic blog is now completed and published.

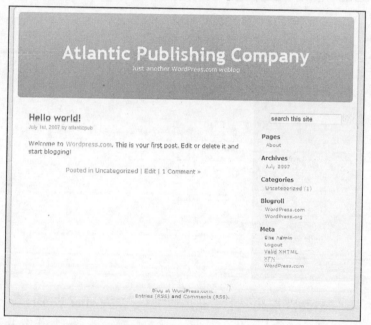

You will receive a confirmation e-mail that contains your account information along with helpful links, frequently asked questions, and other information to help you access, update, and publish to your blog.

Begin by clicking on the "My Account" link and the "Edit Profile" option to start customizing your account. Update the basic information such as name, profile, and password.

You are now ready to start customizing your blog. Although it takes only a few minutes to actually create the blog, it most likely does not yet have the look and feel you desire.

Customizing Your WordPress Blog

Begin by click on the "Options" link in your WordPress account to begin customizing your blog. This allows you to update your general settings and customize most other publishing options.

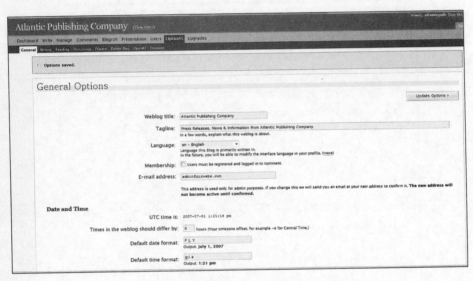

Under the "Privacy" link, you will want to ensure that you have selected the options for your blog to appear in search engines and public listings in WordPress to ensure maximum visibility.

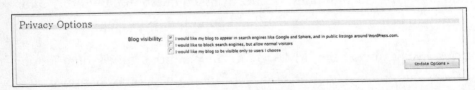

Click on the "Presentation" tab to begin the process of selecting a site template and adding widgets and extras to your blog.

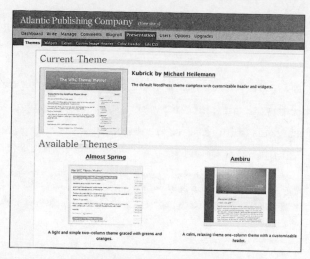

Go through each tab to customize your blog to your desired settings. You have a great degree of flexibility in choosing the final appearance of your blog. Simply drag and drop your desired widgets into the sidebar of your blog. For widgets that require customization, click on the blue customization tab within the widget in your sidebar to modify the settings and preferences.

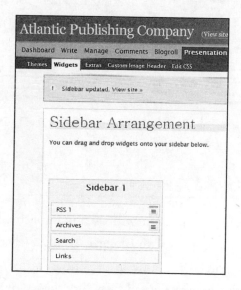

The "Write" link is where you will post your blog entries. The "Manage" link lets you manage your blogs, uploads, imports, and exports and delete individual posts. The "Comments" tab allows you to search, view, edit, and delete comments from your blog.

The blogroll is where you can add your favorite blogs or relevant blogs that have content your audience may be interested in. Maintaining your blogroll is a great way to increase your audience. As you can see below, this process is very simple.

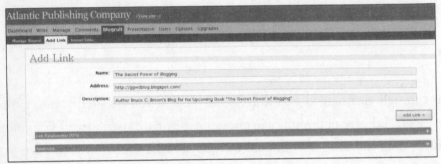

You can also create and indicate which specific categories each blogroll listing should be listed under by selecting it when you add the new blog listing. If you need to change anything later, just click the "Edit" link to change any of your information, links, or category selections.

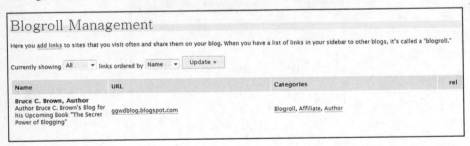

The "Write" feature is what you will use to publish blog posts. This is much more robust in features than Blogger. You can use pre-edited HTML formatted text or format on the fly in the entry form. You can attach images, include trackbacks, and upload files, slideshows, or videos. WordPress saves every 60 seconds, and you can also save drafts for later publishing to the blog.

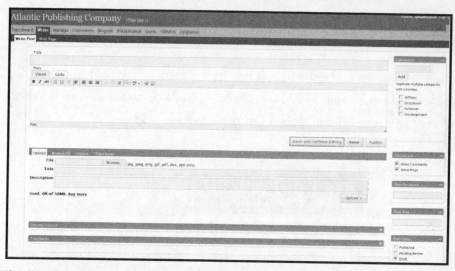

The "Dashboard" is the main control panel for your blog. You can publish posts, view comments, edit your site, change preferences, and edit your template, layout, widgets, and extras.

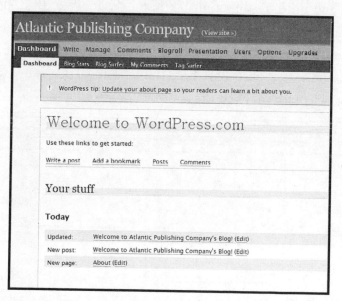

You should always turn on the RSS syndication feature. You will then want to clearly publicize the link for readers to subscribe to your feed on both your blog and your Web page. To do this, grab the RSS image icon and save it to your Web server or Web host. Drag a text widget to your sidebar and open it by clicking the blue lines. Type in the following code:

`<a href="http://atlanticpub.wordpress.com/feed"> <img src="http://www.atlantic-pub.com/rss.png">`

Save the changes and your RSS subscription feed will appear on your blog. You can use the same HTML code on your Web site. RSS feeds will be covered in greater detail later on in this chapter.

It is recommended that you spend some time on the discussion forums, help files, and other readily available resources for WordPad. There is a wealth of information available, as well as an abundance of widgets you can use to customize and enhance your blog. At this point, your blog has been published, and several posts have been published. All that is needed now is to link the blog with the Web site and start promoting it.

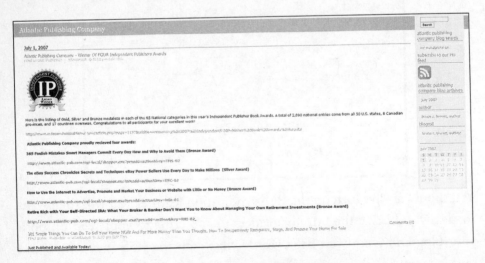

Office 2007 and Blog Posts

If you use Office 2007, you will find that Word 2007 has bult-in support for blogging, and it supports most major blog products on the market. To use this feature, simply open Word 2007, click on "New," then click on "Blog Post."

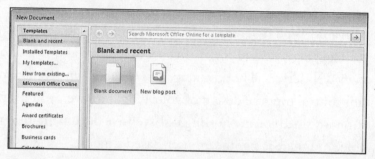

Click on the icon labeled "New Blog Post." You will be given a drop-down menu of options to configure the first time you use this feature in Word 2007:

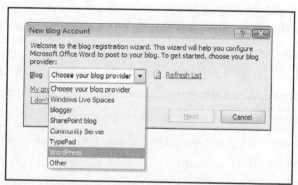

As you can see, Word supports Blogger, Windows Live, TypePad, WordPress, and others. You will need to set up your account information, user name, and password; you can then publish to your blog directly from Word:

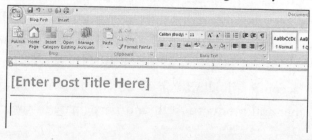

Other Free Blogging Applications

There are many other free blogging applications you can use as an alternative to Blogger and WordPad. A detailed listing is available at **http://asymptomatic.net/blogbreakdown.htm**. The following list contains some of the best in the blogosphere:

- **Movable Type (www.movabletype.org):** Movable Type is powerful blogging software that is free to download and install on your own Web servers. The advantage of Movable Type is that you have full control over the design of your blog; however, you provide the support, since you are hosting it. Extensive documentation is available, and there is significant user-based support.

- **LiveJournal (www.livejournal.com):** You can use LiveJournal in many different ways: as a private journal, a blog, a discussion forum, and a social network. It is not recommended in use for a business, organization, or cause.

- **ClearBlogs (http://clearblogs.com):** Free, but you will have advertising on your blogs.

- **SoulCast™ (www.soulcast.com):** At SoulCast, you can blog about anything without the constraints of society, friends, or family. Great for personal use, but not so much for business use.

- **Blog.com (http://blog.com):** Also free, and this platform is supported by advertisements.

- **ExpressionEngine (http://expressionengine.com):** You will also find this listed under the "commercial" section below. ExpressionEngine is an outstanding and robust product, and a free version with reduced capabilities is available for personal use only.

- **TeamPage5 (www.tractionsoftware.com):** Traction®TeamPage5™ is a free version of Traction's TeamPage™ software. TeamPage5 supports up to five projects and five named user accounts. Your personal account will allow you to download software updates, read customer and product FAQs, and participate in the customer forum. For the free download, visit **https://tractionserver.com/trac-tion/post?type=newprofile**.

TeamPage5 is easy to download, install, and manage. All TeamPage products are pure Java standalone server applications. Full requirements and an extensive list of features are listed at **www.traction software.com**. TeamPage is fully featured, and the free download is an incredible deal. There is also a more robust version also available for purchase. To use this product, you must have your own Web server to host it.

Introduction to RSS Feeds, Atom, and Syndication

RSS and Atom are XML-based file formats that provide you with an easy way to syndicate your blogs to your readers. These feeds provide your readers with all recent content posted to your blog, with links to each content page. By subscribing to feeds, your customers are automatically notified whenever new content is posted. They can also use newsreaders to read your updated content along with any other feeds they may subscribe to, all in one place.

RSS- and Atom-powered blogs are the most effective way to keep the lines of communication open with your audience and site visitors. They will support all of your goals, such as customer interaction, acquiring new customers, improving customer relations, selling products, and promoting your goods, services, or business/organizational philosophy.

E-mail can be time-consuming, ineffective, and challenging due to spam blockers and filters that prevent even legitimate subscriber e-mails from reaching their intended targets. Syndication helps generate new business by effectively marketing directly to your subscribers. It is free and simple to use.

Both of the free blog applications featured in this book, Blogger and Word-Pad, automatically include the capability to create RSS or Atom feeds.

The concept is very simple. You publish blog posts on a regular basis, and people want to read your blog posts. It may be time-consuming for individuals to navigate to blog after blog to read the latest post. To simplify things for your readers, you can syndicate your blog posts to everyone who has subscribed. As you publish blog posts, they appear on your blog and are also sent out in an XML formatted file — either RSS or ATOM — to your subscriber or syndication list, and they are automatically delivered to your subscribers' "readers."

Typically the reader is an e-mail application, or it is built into the Web browser. To find a free reader to download, browse the list at **http://blog space.com/rss/readers**. As you publish new posts, they are automatically sent to the subscribers. The subscribers then open your feed in their reader and browse your new blog posts. They do not even need to be online to do this. A perfect example is for individuals who travel often for work or pleasure. They subscribe to various blog RSS or Atom feeds, and the information is delivered to them as soon as it is published. They can then browse, read, and reply to these new blog posts offline and maximize the use of their time when they do not have Internet connectivity, such as during air travel.

Web feeds eliminate all of the concern with e-mail subscription-based delivery. With RSS or Atom, there is no spam, no viruses, no phishing, no identify theft, and no opt-out process. They are safe and simple to establish, send, and receive.

You must have a reader in order to subscribe to a feed. Bloglines, located at **www.bloglines.com**, is a great free source for blogs, feeds, and podcasts, and it includes a reader. Both Internet Explorer and Firefox include the ability to accept feeds. Google Blog Search, found at **http://blogsearch. google.com**, is a great tool for searching blogs, and since it is Google, it is the most widely known.

There are many free RSS or Atom feeds you can subscribe to. Think of a topic, it has an RSS or Atom feed. Since your blog software creates the feed for you, there is no reason not to have your own RSS feed. Although there are dozens of readers and syndication services to choose from, you can stick with what you know, and use your e-mail client or your browser as your reader.

When you subscribe to feeds, you are usually asked how you want them delivered, such as in the example below, where you can choose from Mozilla Firefox "Live Bookmarks," Outlook, Yahoo!, and Bloglines. In this example, "Live Bookmarks" is chosen.

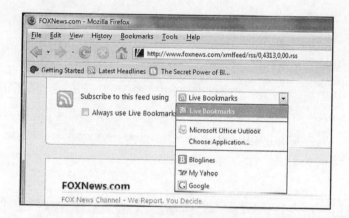

You are asked how you want to store the data from the subscription:

Your subscription to the feed is effective immediately, and it brings in all the recent posts you have subscribed to for you to review. You simply pick which ones are of interest, and you can view them. In this example, there is a subscription to the headline stories from **www.FOXNews.com**. You would click on this "Live Bookmark" to obtain the latest top news stories from this site.

You can find RSS or Atom feeds in directories and search listings and through search engines. You can even specify parameters in your subscriptions to deliver only content that has keywords relative to your search parameters.

Creating an RSS Feed in WordPress

Establishing an RSS feed with WordPress is simple. Navigate to your dashboard, click on the "Presentation" link, then click on the "Widgets" tab. Drag one of the "Text" widgets to your sidebar and double-click on the blue lines in the text box to open the parameters feature.

In the parameters, enter your title and RSS link in the format below. Replace **yourblog.wordpress.com** with your actual blog address, such as **atlantic pub.wordpress.com**, and replace **imagelocation.com** with the location of your RSS image icon:

<a href="http://yourblog.wordpress.com/feed"> <img src="http:// www.imagelocation.com/rss.png">

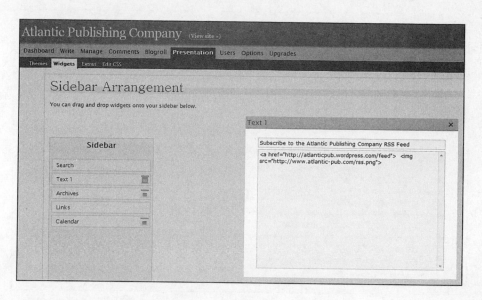

When it is saved, your RSS syndication feed is then displayed on your blog, as shown in the image below:

When a visitor clicks on this link, he or she will be presented with the subscription form, options on how to subscribe to the feed, and a listing of recent blog posts. In the example, Microsoft Outlook is used.

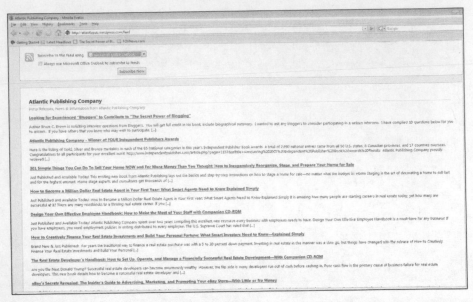

When you look in Microsoft Outlook under the RSS Feeds, you can now see your subscription to Atlantic Publishing, including nine new entries.

You can look in the preview pane of Outlook to read each item, or you can double-click it to open it, as if it were an e-mail.

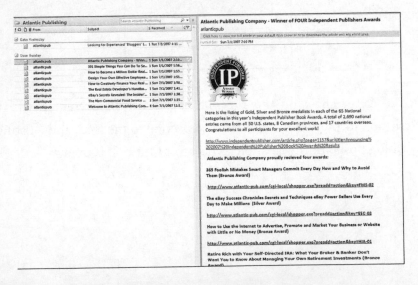

The last thing you will want to do is add your RSS feed image and link to your Web site to allow individuals to subscribe from both your blog and your Web site.

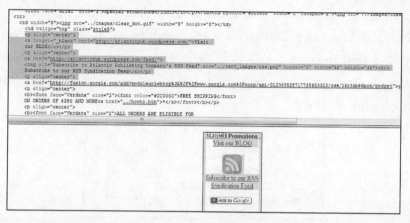

Creating an Atom Feed in Blogger

To create the Atom feed in Blogger, simply log into your Blogger dashboard. Click on "Settings," then "Site Feed." Here, you can turn your site feed settings to off, short, or full. With new Blogger accounts and templates, your feed is automatically displayed on your blog unless you turn it off. If you have turned it on, but are not seeing it displayed in your blog, follow the manual procedures located at **http://help.blogger.com/bin/answer.py?answer=42663**.

Microsoft provides a nice guide to setting up an RSS feed in Outlook, which is available at **http://office.microsoft.com/en-us/outlook/HA10159 5391033.asp**. Also, if you are using Microsoft Internet Explorer 7 or 8, or Firefox 2.0, the browser will automatically detect and notify you of any feeds available on the Web pages you are browsing. If you want to offer your RSS feed through a variety of free readers, visit **www.toprankblog. com/tools/rss-buttons**, which creates buttons automatically for you to place on your Web site.

Feedburner™

As you read the expert advice at the end of this book, you will notice that Feedburner is often recommended. Feedburner, a service of Google, is the leading provider of syndication services for blogs and RSS feeds. There is a free version of Feedburner and a professional version, which you must pay for.

To use Feedburner, you simply type in your blog URL and follow the on-screen prompts. You set up your feed, and it provides you with your Feed-burner URL, and can enable tracking and statistics options on the feed. A step-by-step walkthrough is provided to insert the code on your Blogger blog, and you can add the code as a text widget in WordPress. If you up-grade to the full self-hosted version of WordPress, a plug-in is available to simplify the process.

One of the nice features of Feedburner is the statistics it provides. It also presents the subscriber with a variety of options as far as which reader to choose from.

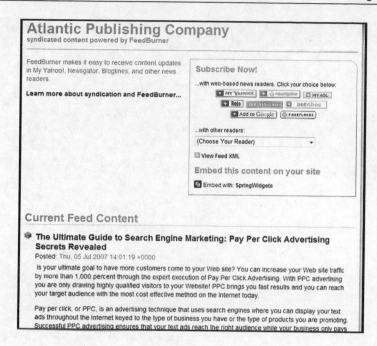

There is no reason not to create an RSS or Atom feed; it will help you increase your audience base and allow you to consistently send all blog posts to your subscribers. Best of all, the process is completely automated, seamless, and free.

Chapter 16

SOCIAL NETWORKING

Social networking focuses on building online communities of people who share similar interests and/or activities. Most social network services are Web-based and provide a variety of ways for users to interact. Social networking has become tremendously popular, and its membership grows daily and at an exponential rate. The potential marketing and networking power of using social networks to promote your business and products cannot be understated, and in many cases, it is the perfect substitute for personal Web pages or blogs.

Here are some of the benefits to using a social networking service:

- **Meet new people:** With just a few clicks, you can meet new people from all over the world, or focus on making certain types of friends.
- **Find old friends:** You can find friends with whom you have lost contact. These could be friends from high school or people you used to work with.
- **Join interest group:** Many social networking services offer specific groups called "communities." These groups can be based on anything. If there is not a group you like, you are permitted to create your own and invite others to join and share.
- **Create photo albums and share photos:** You can create photo albums to share with friends and relatives.

- **Add videos:** Some social networking sites will allow you to add your own videos to the network, while others only let you upload your video to your profile.

- **Get advice and help others:** Whether on forums or in interest groups or communities, you can always find and give advice.

- **No cost:** These services are absolutely free.

Social networking has grown tremendously in popularity in the last few years and is an incredibly powerful marketing and networking tool. Do not assume that social networking is just for teenagers. Social networking sites not only aid in keeping in touch with relatives and friends, but they also help to find new friends and establish new networking opportunities. These services allow people to be close even if separated by continents, and the viral effect of social networking means that you can build large networks effortlessly and quickly.

With the ever-increasing number of people who use the Internet on a regular basis, these social Web sites have become a must, as these are some of the best and the easiest ways for people to get connected with each other and stay in touch.

Social Networking Sites

- **Orkut (www.orkut.com)** is a popular social networking site owned by Google. This social networking site has millions of users: 63 percent of Orkut traffic originates from Brazil, followed by India with 19.2 percent. Like other sites such as Facebook, Orkut permits the creation of groups known as "communities" based on a designated subject and allows other people to join the communities. Orkut is an online community designed to make your social life more active and stimulating. Unlike other social networking Web sites that prevent users from viewing your profile if they are not on your "Friends" list, Orkut has no such restriction. Anyone can view anyone else's profile. However, there is also an "Ignore List," where members can list people they want to restrict from viewing their profile or sending them messages.

- **Facebook (www.facebook.com)** is the leading social networking site, with more than 300 million active users at the time of publication. Initially, Facebook was developed to connect university students, but over time, the site became available publicly, and its popularity exploded. The majority of users on Facebook used to be college and high school students, but this trend is shifting rapidly to people of all ages and backgrounds. On Facebook, it is extremely easy to add friends, send messages, and create communities or event invitations. To discover Facebook, you must create a free account. Once you have created an account and answered a few questions about where you work, where you went to school, and where you live, Facebook will generate a profile for you. Facebook is a great place to share information and stay in contact with friends, family, and coworkers.

- **MySpace (www.myspace.com)** is a social networking Web site that offers an interactive platform for all its users. It allows the sharing of files, pictures, and even music videos. You can view the profiles of your friends, relatives, and any other users; you can also create and share blogs with each other. Users often compare Facebook to MySpace, but one major difference between the two Web sites is the level of customization. MySpace is a large social networking site that allows users to decorate their profiles using HTML and CSS, while Facebook only allows plain text. The most prominent feature that makes MySpace unique among other sites is its affiliate program. If the affiliate product you are selling has a broad appeal, you may want consider using MySpace to market your product, as you will be able to reach a large crowd quickly.

- **YouTube (www.youtube.com)** is another social networking site owned by Google. To become a member of YouTube, go to the "Signup" page, choose a user name and password, enter your information, and click the "Signup" button. YouTube is the largest video sharing network site in the world, and it is a great place to do viral video marketing.

- **Digg™ (www.digg.com)** is a place to discover and share content from around the Web, from the smallest blog to major news outlets. Digg is unique compared to other social networking sites because it allows you to directly network with people and directly sell products. Once a post is submitted, it appears on a list in the selected category. From there, it will either fall in ranking or rise in raking, depending on how people vote. Digg is actually what is known as a "social bookmarking" site. You submit your content to Digg, and other Digg users — known as Diggers — will review and rate it. Once it is rated high enough, your content may get posted on the home page of Digg, which gets thousands of visitors a day, potentially driving tons of traffic to your Web site or blog.

- **Twitter (www.twitter.com)** is different from other social networking sites, and the popularity of Twitter has grown at an amazing rate. Instead of having to sit down at the computer to update your status such as with MySpace, with Twitter, you can let your friends know what you are doing throughout the day right from your phone, although you can also update through the Web. When you sign up with Twitter, you can use the service to post and receive messages with your Twitter account, and the service distributes it to your "followers," who are your subscribers. In turn, you receive all the messages sent from those you wish to follow, including friends, family, and even celebrities. In essence, Twitter is a cell phone texting-based social network, and it is known as a "microblogging" tool.

- **Flickr (www.flickr.com)** is a photo and video sharing Web site that lets you organize and store your photos online. You can upload from your desktop, send by e-mail, or use your camera phone. It has features to get rid of red eye, crop a photo, or get creative with fonts and effects. Google Picasa™ is another great photo-sharing and storing application.

- **Friendster** had 110 million members worldwide at the time of publication and is a place where you can set up dates and develop new friendships or business contacts. However, this site has lost a substantial number of users since the popularity of other social networking sites has increased.

Using Social Networks to Expand Your Web Presence

The main objective of social network is to allow members who have the same interests to interact and exchange information. Members of social networking sites are numerous, which creates an excellent opportunity for an individual to expand and promote their business without having to pay for advertising. With social networking, you can build an image and develop your customer base. To increase their Web site traffic, many site owners are quickly realizing the value social networking sites have in drawing new customers. Here are some ideas on how to use social networking site to generate Web site traffic:

- Link from your Web site to your social network profile.
- Use social bookmarking to increase your Web site's exposure on social networking sites.
- Create and share videos and photos on Flickr and YouTube describing your business, products, and services.
- Use social networking forums to promote your business, Web site, and blog.

- Promote your business through your profile, with links to your home page.

You can use the power of social networking sites to promote your Web site by sending messages, leaving notes, and creating communities. You can establish yourself as an industry expert and promote your business services or products through the established networks. Once you gain credibility, you gain popularity; once you gain these, you can increase Web site traffic.

Social networking sites can be fun for personal use, but they can also be beneficial for your Web site. It may surprise you how many people who visit your Web site will take the time to take a peek at your Facebook site and ask to be your friend so they can look at your Facebook content and share information. As your network grows, you will quickly find that you have established a powerful business network that will help you maintain relationships and increase your Web site traffic dramatically. Spend some time researching and using social bookmark sites; they can generate a great deal of Web site traffic for you. The focus of your social networking activities is to increase the popularity of your Web site or blog, so target those communities that have mutual interests.

Chapter 17

INTERVIEWS WITH WEB DESIGN EXPERTS

This chapter contains interviews with dozens of industry-recognized Web design and Web development experts, as well as a few novices who have achieved success by building their own Web sites and achieving their goals. The goal of the interviews is to provide you, the reader, with tangible information you can readily apply to your Web design efforts and to help you learn from industry experts. Their sage guidance and insight is an invaluable addition to this book; you will surely find these interviews inspiring and full of practical, useful advice.

Interview with Stephane Grenier

1. How does someone begin the process of determining what they should put on their Web site, what design elements it should have, how navigation should function, and what the overall appearance should be? When starting with a blank HTML document, what steps or techniques would you recommend to get to a finished product?

The very first step is to clearly define your goal. Is it to sell a product? Is it to sell many different products? Is it to create leads for your company? Is it to spread your views? Is it to get the biggest readership possible? Is it to create interest for your consulting business? Is it to advance in your career? Is it just for fun? There are many Web sites with different goals, and each has to be designed around its specific goal.

For example, a Web site that sells a product should have a very different design than a Web site built to advance your career. A single-item Web store will try to keep the focus on why the product is so great. The main page will be designed to the draw the visitor to purchase the product. It should have clear benefits as to why the product is better. Most likely, you will find a picture of the product on the main page. Not only that, but almost all the critical information will be designed to be above the fold — above where you will need to scroll down the page.

On the other hand, a Web site designed to advance your career will be focused on showcasing your knowledge as related to your career. Most likely it will take the format of a blog, or something very close. It will consist of articles and posts about your field. It might contain a picture of you, which may or may not be prominent — a visual picture is not as critical; it is only used to confirm that the Web site is yours. Having elements above the fold will be less important, since it is about your total knowledge.

Once you have a goal, then you can start to ask yourself what elements need to be where on your Web site. Which elements need to be on the FrontPage? Which elements need to be the most visible? Once you have determined this, the rest of the Web site generally seems to follow. Because you cannot fit everything in one page, breaking it down to the basics forces you to start assigning values and importance to every element. If it cannot be on the main page, how far away can it be? How easy should it be to find from the first page? What is the most obvious route to get to it?

As well, I strongly recommend you look at similar Web sites, or even your competitors, if you have any. Do not necessarily look at what you find nice and pretty; look at what gets your attention to perform the desired action. For example, let us say you are a lawyer, and you want to build a Web site for your law firm; pretend you are looking to hire a lawyer for yourself. Why would you contact one lawyer over another? Look at the elements that attracted you. Do not try to copy their Web site, because if you do, it most likely will not work; every Web site has to fit their owner. Instead, look at what it is specifically that made you want to contact and hire them. Emulate those parts that called you to action: Contact the lawyer, buy the product, or hire the person.

As an extra quick tip, design your Web site according to how people will naturally interact with your Web site, not how you think they should interact with it.

2. *There are many Web design products available, such as Microsoft FrontPage, Microsoft Expression Web, and Adobe Creative Suite. For a beginner who wants to have a professional Web site, yet use a fairly simple-to-use Web design product, what would you recommend and why?*

In all honesty, I would generally recommend learning HTML itself. It is actually not that complicated once you get the hang of it, and learning it will mean that you are no longer tool-dependent. It will also mean that you will be able to do amazing things that some tools cannot. And it will give you a better appreciation for how much a professional Web designer should charge to build your Web site in the future.

But if you are going to use a tool, I would recommend going with the simplest possible. I recommend Nvu (**www.net2.com/nvu**). It is a completely free tool, and it is very easy to learn and use.

After that, surprisingly, I would suggest Microsoft Word. This is because most people are familiar with using Word, so the learning curve is lower. The downside is that managing a Web site that is more than a few pages will start to get pretty complex fast. And the HTML code generated from Word is not exactly the best.

Following Word, you are very likely going to get into Fireworks® from Adobe. Although it is really meant to be a Web site prototyping software, it is pretty handy to get good-looking Web sites out fast. It is also good because it does not require that much knowledge.

If you really want to get a professional Web site out, and you want to use a tool, the next step is to move up to Dreamweaver from Adobe (previously Macromedia). However, the issue with Dreamweaver is that it takes almost as much time to learn and use as it does to learn HTML for anything more than the basics.

3. *What type of image format do you recommend using on Web sites? There are several different formats, such as GIF, JPEG, and PNG — is there a difference? Is one better than the other?*

GIF, if you can get away with it, because the file sizes are generally very small. The only downside is that they are limited in terms of how many colors they can use and, therefore, how good the image will look. GIFs are great for simple images or buttons.

If you are going to include images, then you generally end up with JPEGs because they are not limited in the number of colors and can compress an image very well. The downside with JPEGs is that they are a lossy compression. A lossy compression means that some data can be loss every time you save/compress the data. For pictures, the average person will not notice the difference for a few times, but after enough edits, a JPEG image can get pretty bad.

I generally do not recommend PNG because most people just do not use it. It is a great format to save images; it is loss-less (the data is perfectly saved every time); it compresses very well; it offers a full range of colors; and so on. The only thing is that I have heard some browsers are not fully compliant — do not forget, there are also mobile/cell phone browsers — with the PNG file format. Of course, this is changing, but it goes back to either you go with what is fully supported or with what is guaranteed to be supported. Every browser I have ever heard of supports GIF and JPEG, but not everyone supports PNG. This is quickly changing, but it is not a mainstream image file format yet, even if it should be.

4. How much should someone spend on Web site hosting? Is there a Web hosting platform or other features we should specifically be looking for? If you were to recommend a Web hosting provider, who would it be?

It really depends on what your Web site is about. How important is it to have your Web site available all the time? Does it really matter if it goes down for a few hours? Does it really matter if the Web site is slow to load sometimes? Is security important? For example, if your Web site only contains articles showcasing your knowledge in regard to your career, then security is not as important when compared to a Web site that processes credit cards.

If you can live with some downtime and a slower Web site, and if security is not a big concern, then you can probably get away with paying under $10 per month right now. The only thing is that at that price, do not expect to get any hand-holding to get your Web site up. The tech support is very likely to be lackluster at best. The reality is that you just cannot afford to pay someone of any quality to answer and respond to phone calls when you only make them $5 to $10 per month. The cost of one call will cost more than the cost of several months. And they still have to pay for their computers and their bandwidth.

If you expect a decent amount of traffic, and you want to guarantee your resources — that is, how much computer power you can have — then you should consider VPS hosting. VPS hosting stands for Virtual Private Server. With VPS hosting, each account gets its own virtual instance of a server. In VPS hosting, they take a computer and give each person a guaranteed cut of that computer, with the unused resources passed on to whomever needs them. The key is that you are guaranteed a minimum level of computing power. For these, you can expect to pay anywhere from $20 per month to several hundred dollars a month. Some VPS packages offer multiples — more computing power than a normal home computer. For $20 per month, do not expect much; you are still dealing with the bottom of the barrel. So support is going to be sketchy at best. At the high end, things generally get better.

If that is not enough for you, then I would recommend a dedicated server (your very own computer). Here, you have full control of the computer; it is all yours. This is great if you are processing credit cards directly on your computer — rather than through a third-party service — or if you are managing sensitive and/or important data. Not only that, but you get full control over the machine, which means you can install anything or do anything on the machine. Dedicated servers rarely go for less than $100 per month and can climb to more than $1,000 per month. Dedicated servers will also often require a setup fee that is anywhere from half a month to two months' worth of services.

Something to note is that once you get into the level of dedicated servers, you can either go with a managed solution or not. With a managed solution, the hosting company will provide the operating system upgrades for you, as well as many of the core software upgrades. They will also, as requested, perform some of the software upgrades for you — for example, if your Web site is PHP-based, they may be able to upgrade the PHP version for you. There are, of course, more options beyond this, but if you get to that stage, you will very likely need some professional IT assistance.

As well, a great resource to research individual hosting companies is Web-HostingTalk® (**www.Webhostingtalk.com**). It is a discussion forum where many people go and comment on the different hosting companies. Unless the company is very small, I have rarely not been able to find a hosting company discussed on that Web site.

5. *What low- or no-cost options would you recommend for selling products on a Web site, such as PayPal integration or other shopping carts? Is all shopping cart software essentially the same? For a Web site with hundreds of products, what shopping cart software would you recommend? What do you recommend for SSL?*

If you want to keep your costs to an absolute minimum, I would recommend using PayPal in conjunction with E-junkie™ — PayPal as the payment processor and E-junkie for the shopping cart. For those not familiar with E-junkie, it is a third-party service that will set up a shopping cart for you that connects to your PayPal account (though they support other payment processors above PayPal). For only $5 per month, E-junkie will make setting up a shopping cart incredibly easy. I cannot even begin to say how easy it is. For the amount of time and hassle you save, it is beyond worth it. I sell my own e-book through E-junkie/PayPal.

I would strongly recommend SSL if you are processing credit cards yourself, or if you have to transmit any sensitive data, such as user accounts. It is crucial. If you do not use SSL, you are asking for trouble. SSL is what encrypts the data from the Web browser to your Web site. Without that, anyone can potentially intercept the data and look at it, including the credit card numbers, user names, and passwords.

SSL costs very little; you can get an SSL certificate for as little as $100. It is worth it, as many people, myself included, refuse to buy from a Web site without a valid SSL certificate. But even more than that, have you seen the scary messages from Mozilla Firefox, Internet Explorer, and Google Chrome if you do not have a valid SSL certificate? Talk about how to get people to abandon their shopping carts and move on to another Web site.

6. There are dozens of companies that you can buy domain names from. Is there any company in particular that is better than the others, and why? Is there any advantage to buying several domain name types for my domain, such as .com, .biz, .us, and .net?

Any company that charges more than $20 per domain, I would question. In the old days, it used to be limited to three companies, and they would charge a lot. Because of this, there is still some legacy perception and branding. For example, some people who have been on the Internet longer still perceive Network Solutions® to be the "safer" solution, but it is no longer necessarily true. They just had a monopoly, and people still recognize the brand because that is whom they bought their domain from 10 years ago.

One thing I would strongly recommend is to avoid buying your domain from the same place you host your Web site. Yes, it is easier because it is all in one place, but there have been stories of Web sites keeping a domain ransom. For example, they will not allow you to transfer hosting services or a domain without a gargantuan amount of effort. Why? Because if you cannot transfer it, then you have to keep hosting with them. By buying and hosting at two different locations, you guarantee this will never be an issue.

Another thing I have seen reports of is domain registrars that will temporarily lock up a domain after you do a search for the domain on their Web site. So for example, you go to Bob's Domains — unknown to you, he is a less than reputable domain registrar — and check to see if the domain MyFavoriteDomain.com is taken. "Great," you think, "it is not taken." But for whatever reason, you decide not to buy it today and just leave things be. Then, a day later, you go to another domain registrar — maybe they have a better price, but for whatever the reason, the domain is no longer available. However, if you go back to Bob's Domains, it is still available. How can this be? What is happened is that Bob locked the domain for a few days. And if Bob is of the even less reputable type, he might put up a parking page (a page of just ads) to see how well it does due to type-in traffic — people just typing in the domain in their browser. If it generates more than the cost of the domain, he might just keep it for himself. If you do not think this happens, think again: It does. And not just from less-reputable domain registrars — some bigger players have been caught doing this.

When you buy a domain, be careful to check whose name the domain will actually be under. Some less reputable domains will keep the ownership under their name instead of yours. I have seen this more from companies that try to get you to host and register your domain from them — not all companies are bad, but why take the risk if you do not have to? If they own the domain, you are stuck.

The thing to realize is that domains are a low-margin business. When you sell a domain at $10 per year, you are not going to make a large profit. The profits generally come from selling add-ons, like private registration and so on. So expect to be up-sold a lot. Unless you knew you needed it ahead of time, odds are you do not need it at the time of your purchase. If you really think you do, double- and triple-check before you buy any domain add-ons.

7. When designing a Web site, we want to ensure compatibility with major Web browsers, such as Microsoft Internet Explorer, Mozilla Firefox, Google Chrome, and others. Do you have recommendations for how to design the site to ensure maximum compatibility and user functionality?

I really hate to say this, but the more bleeding-edge your CSS, the more issues you are going to have when it comes to cross-browser support. The browser support is just not mature enough, although it really should be.

If you are going to use JavaScript/Ajax, then use a library like ExtJS, Dojo, or Prototype. It will save you an incredible amount of time; they deal with many of the cross-browser issues for you.

Having developed many sites, I generally recommend developing the Web site first in Firefox, then making the adjustments for the other browsers. The reason for this is that Firefox has lots of great development tools that significantly simplify your development efforts. I cannot imagine developing a Web site without the Firebug and Web Developer plug-ins for Firefox, not just for JavaScript, but for CSS or isolating sections of the Web site. They are great little tools.

8. *What is a useful CSS technique that you use often? What is the most common font you use when designing Web pages? What advice can you give regarding Web site navigation?*

Carefully define your body. If you do it right, it makes the rest a lot easier. As well, if you encounter any issues with your CSS, break it down right away. Keep it simple. And definitely use a tool like Firebug or Web Developer to figure out exactly which CSS definition is being applied to what element. Sometimes it is surprising what is inherited by what.

For fonts, always assume the bare minimum. I know it is not exactly conducive to great design, but the reality is that most people do not add fonts to their computers. And if you want to maintain control over the real look, then expect only the default fonts.

If you need complex fonts for headers or logos, then convert the text to images. It is the only way you can absolutely guarantee the quality of a font on a Web browser.

That being said, there is a new JavaScript engine (**http://typeface.neocracy.org**) out there that is supposed to render the fonts for you on the fly, without requiring the browser's computer to have the font installed. I do not know how cross-browser it is, or how many fonts it supports, but it is an option. Also, remember that rendering the font on your client's computer means that you have to send them extra JavaScript code (how to render the font), as well as have their computer process the font. Not everyone has faster computers; many people are still using computers from years ago.

In regard to Web site navigation, the biggest tip I can offer is to try to keep all pages accessible within three clicks. It does not mean you cannot have some pages embedded with links 10 deep; it just means that there should be at least one path within three clicks. Preferably, all pages will be within three clicks, but that is not always possible.

The three-click rule is for two reasons. Firstly, most people will only go three-clicks deep to find something. There is a reason why 90-plus percent of all people will only click on search results from the first page of a search engine like Google. By the third page, you pretty much do not exist. But secondly — and this is just as important — it is for SEO purposes. Most search engines will not crawl Web sites farther than three links deep. So if you really want to help increase the odds that your page will be crawled by search engines like Google, then keep your navigation to three links deep.

Which also leads me to my next point — unless there is a really compelling reason, avoid implementing your navigation through JavaScript or other pretty and dynamic menu-generating libraries. Yes, it might not be as fancy (multi-level menus that pop up as your mouse goes over them), but they can still look pretty amazing. But much more importantly, you will be in the search engines.

9. A challenge of any new Web site is obtaining search engine rankings. What practical advice can you give to someone with a new Web site to achieve visibility in major search engines?

I sell my own e-book, *How to Generate Traffic to Your Website*; it is full of advice on how to achieve search engine rankings and can be found here: **www.followsteph.com/how-to-generate-traffic-to-your-Website.html**.

10. If you could only give three pieces of advice, what would you tell a business or individual as they attempt to build and/or establish a viable Web presence?

1. Absolutely define your goals, first and foremost.

2. Keep it simple. Not all Web sites need to be Web 2.0. Sure, it is nice to have Ajax widgets and beautiful menus that interact with your visitor, but is it necessary? Especially if you are trying to in- crease your search engine rankings on Google, because in many cases, this will only reduce your SEO effectiveness.

3. A great design is not a Web site. Many companies assume that if they build a great-looking Web site, they are done. That is not true. Like the saying, if a tree falls in a forest, does it make a sound if no one is there to hear it? The same is true for a Web site. Designing your Web site is only part of the effort; you need to get people to know you exist. I cannot tell you how much this is true, especially after having interviewed 40 high-profile bloggers for my book *Blog Blazers*.

*Stephane Grenier is the nationally known founder and CEO of LandlordMax Software Inc., a longtime builder and promoter of numerous blogs (including his own, **www.followsteph.com**), a seminar speaker for "Website Promotion and Traffic Generation," and the author of the critically acclaimed e-book,* How to Generate Traffic to Your Website. *His passion for helping business-people maximize the power of their blogs and Web sites is the driving force behind* Blog Blazers, *compiling the best proven practices of the most successful bloggers in the world. He can be contacted at steph@followsteph.com.*

Interview with Dr. Robert Worstell

1. How does someone begin the process of determining what they should put on their Web site, what design elements it should have, how navigation should function, and what the overall appearance should be? When starting with a blank HTML document, what steps or techniques would you recommend to get to a finished product?

You have to look at what you want and what you like to see in others' sites. What you want determines what lengths you have to go to in order to get it. If you want to be a premium video-review blogger, you will have a different look and different features than someone who wants to post pictures of their family for relatives to view easily.

As you browse the Web, you will find many different aspects that you like, and more that you do not like. If you bookmark the ones you like, then you can come back to them to see what is personally appealing to you about them. As you build your site, you will be able to ⸱ ke the best elements of these sites and put them into play on your own. This follows the idea that "you get as good as you give," meaning that if you build a site that you like, you will attract people with similar tastes and interests. These are potential clients and potential returning visitors.

But you really have to put up a site that will be interesting enough for you to keep at it. Constantly updated content is what search engines are looking for. So whatever you build, you need to really, really want to do this from here on out. Otherwise, build it, get traffic to it, and then sell it off.

Page building sequence:

1. The sequence of building a page starts with the idea. Usually you have been researching something for a while, and then get an idea for a great piece that you can put up on your site.

2. You have chosen your design platform, and this will tell you a lot of what you have to do first. You will have a site template — or templates for sections of your site — which pre-determine the look and feel.

3. Generally, start with the keyword and put it in the title to have something there.

4. Flesh out the text. Add in one or more images, like a Creative Commons picture from Flickr.

5. Then go back to your title and make it something really catchy.

6. Finally, do all your SEO work in creating a page title, assigning tags and categories, and making a catchy description or excerpt.

7. And then preview it and tweak any points that need it — especially correcting spelling errors — before you upload it.

2. There are many Web design products available, such as Microsoft FrontPage, Microsoft Expression Web, and Adobe Creative Suite. For a beginner who wants to have a professional Web site, yet use a fairly simple-to-use Web design product, what would you recommend and why?

WordPress. This is really a beginner's paradise that still continues to be a joy when you are a pro at it. Everything is already laid out. You can change the template as many times as you want, as there are thousands of these available for free. And you quickly learn the essentials of putting a Web page together and can instantly see the result.

WordPress is really being touted now by some of these search engine optimization specialists as the best way to get rankings on Google.

I have used almost every one of these site-builder software programs and can say that they are all good and all have drawbacks. The chief one is that you have to build it locally and then upload it. Many, like FrontPage, are so proprietary they will give you headaches if you try to convert the pages to anything else.

This is where WordPress shines, since it has probably the largest community out there for any blog or Web site building software. And it is supported everywhere, because it is so popular and easy on Web hosts. The great part is that most good Web hosts come with cPanel®, which is a control panel that has various free scripts that come with it. So you can install WordPress yourself and also learn all the back-end operations that need to occur with any hosting. Web hosts that do not have cPanel will usually also have an option for installing WordPress, just due to its popularity.

But with the good, you have to know that it is a resource hog if you get cheap hosting. Every time you tweak something, it is calling a lot of resources from your host. I was kicked off one host (at least for that domain name) simply because I was creating a lot of pages there and they could not handle the traffic.

Now, another great solution down this line is in the fact that WordPress allows you to export a blog to anywhere else. So you can set up your blog with WordPress, or Blogetery, or Blogsome, or any other free WordPress hosting, and get it just the way you want it. Then go get your own hosting with the domain name you want and simply transfer it there. You can also download WordPress for free and do a local installation to test things and then upload it just like the others. I prefer the free hosting, as you can see it under the regular bandwidth stress a site will be under.

3. What type of image format do you recommend using on Web sites? There are several different formats, such as GIF, JPEG, and PNG — is there a difference? Is one better than the other?

I try to use PNG when I can. Reason is that it is now supported commonly and has loss-less compression, meaning you do not have all these little squiggly bits showing up when you want to edit it. JPEG format loses some quality every time you compress it, so you have to keep the original file around when you want to change something. But if your original is a JPEG, then you are going to have to run it through some filters in Photoshop or some other editor to get it looking nice before you make any changes. PNG simply gives you the best quality with a decently small file size. As well, it supports transparency, which is the main reason GIFs were used. Let the background come through.

Now, GIFs are ideal for buttons, because you can make them extremely small in size by limiting the colors in them. But frankly, buttons are becoming less common these days, because the more images you have on a page, the easier it is to have some missing. A lot of what used to be done with buttons can now be done with CSS, which looks nearly identical on different browsers.

I use JPEGs when I have to, but generally try to replace them with PNGs every chance I get.

4. How much should someone spend on Web site hosting? Is there a Web hosting platform or other features we should specifically be

looking for? If you were to recommend a Web hosting provider, who would it be?

"You get what you pay for" is true. I have used cheap hosting for years and have only run into problems when I wanted to scale up and they could not handle the bandwidth. As well, their customer service was iffy. Good thing their servers ran regardless.

HostGator comes highly recommended from the pros I have dealt with. GoDaddy has as many detractors as supporters. But there are so many options out there, the key point is always to keep local backups of all your data and be able to switch to another provider when you find one that is actually better.

Since Web hosting is fairly inexpensive these days — and you really should look hard if you are being asked to spend more than $10 per month — you can actually check out various hosts for a few months and see how they do. But always do your homework by checking out forums first. They give you the best reviews, because they have been using it and can tell you specifically what they did and did not like — not just, "These guys suck."

Spend plenty of time doing your homework, but know you are not stuck if your host does not work for you. It is really a buyers' market out there.

5. *What low- or no-cost options would you recommend for selling products on a Web site, such as PayPal integration or other shopping carts? Is all shopping cart software essentially the same? For a Web site with hundreds of products, what shopping cart software would you recommend? What do you recommend for SSL?*

Now, I recommend WordPress for anyone starting out in e-commerce. There are now probably a dozen good plug-ins that will enable you to convert your site to an e-commerce shop in a few hours of work, and most of that is uploading the products and descriptions.

If you are doing a professional business, the actual best way to go is to hire someone who sets up these sites professionally. I have recently run across **www.visible.net®**, which sells you a decent package and will even call you back on the phone. And they have started a free WordPress hosting service so people can blog and drive traffic to their e-commerce: **www.storeblogs.com**.

The e-commerce engines I have worked with are osCommerce and Zen Cart. Both are professional-quality engines and are customizable. They will scale nicely and also accept a wide variety of payment options. And both are free with any Web hosting that uses the cPanel interface, so you can try them both out. They work best with tangible products, but reportedly can be used with digital downloads as well.

But if you are publishing books, host them with print-on-demand publisher Lulu.com — then your e-commerce backend is set. You will only have to concentrate on promoting the books. Wil Wheaton (who was a teenage star on *Star Trek*) has several good-selling books published this way. Lulu® is also free to upload and host your books.

6. There are dozens of companies that you can buy domain names from. Is there any company in particular that is better than the others, and why? Is there any advantage to buying several domain name types for my domain, such as .com, .biz, .us, and .net?

Branding and trademarks are the key point here. The **.com** is the most popular and easiest for most people to find, so grab it if you can. If you really want to set your trademark, grab the **.net** and **.info** as well. Otherwise, you can skip it. Some people have tried to come in with a different suffix and then sue the earlier one for trademark infringement, but it usually does not work.

Selecting a domain name is part of your original business plan homework and research. You can name a company anything, but the trick is to get something that people can remember. Yahoo!, AOL, and Google still do not make sense to most people as names themselves; it is the amount of content and service they have provided that actually developed their brand.

7. When designing a Web site, we want to ensure compatibility with major Web browsers, such as Microsoft Internet Explorer, Mozilla Firefox, Google Chrome, and others. Do you have recommendations for how to design the site to ensure maximum compatibility and user functionality?

Do not use the currently popular trick stuff. Stick to simply providing great content that is styled with simple CSS. Some sites warp way out when you have certain features that are only really supported by Internet Explorer. While more people surf with that browser, it is not smart to just design for that platform.

Again, I tell people to use WordPress to design their sites, as it renders straight across all browsers. Stay away from Flash pages and plug-ins, excepting only videos — but use the code that the video host provides — and use their bandwidth as well. That keeps it simple.

I used to worry about this when I was designing static pages with straight HTML, but if you simply use CSS standards for your headings and body text, then most of the browsers will render it just fine. If you start specifying oddball spacings and typefaces, you are going to break your presentation sooner or later.

When in doubt, load several browsers on your machine and view the same page in all of them.

8. What is a useful CSS technique that you use often? What is the most common font you use when designing Web pages? What advice can you give regarding Web site navigation?

Common usage is to have a sans-serif font as a heading and serif font for the text, or vice-versa. If you stick to the default settings on browsers, it is easier for them. Helvetica®, Arial, Verdana, Tahoma are all good sans-serif fonts. Georgia® is a font for serif that was designed specifically for easy reading online.

One trick is to look for the default fonts that come with operating systems and then use them. Palatino® used to be the default serif font on Macs, for instance. So when you design, be sure you have those default fonts listed as options in your CSS, and they will be readable most anywhere.

A current trend is to use sans-serif fonts for everything, because they will scale smaller than serif fonts. But it is a matter of what you want to present and how readable it looks when you are designing it. Again, check your result in various and multiple browsers to make sure that it looks most of the time what you intended. The name of the font you use is secondary to what it looks like.

9. A challenge of any new Web site is obtaining search engine rankings. What practical advice can you give to someone with a new Web site to achieve visibility in major search engines?

There are basic search engine optimization techniques that are employed only in your Web design itself:

- Keywords in title of page
- Keyword in headings (H1 and H2, as well as bold and italic text)
- Keywords in ALT tags for images
- Keywords in page descriptions
- Body of the content should use synonyms and related materials to your keywords

The other SEO techniques mainly deal with off-site links, which is beyond this discussion.

Another tip, which has fallen out of use due to earlier abuse, is having your meta tags also include your keywords. While many search engines ignore these, you will also see more that do not. So it is worthwhile including these.

But do not stuff your keywords. Many experts in this field have the keyword in the page title, headers, and once or twice in the text body, but use that text body to define what your keywords mean. Google can only tell the difference between "Tiger Woods" and "Bengal Tiger" by the text on the page. Mentioning the word "Tiger" for more than 3 percent of your total text will not help your case.

Give good, descriptive content and it will do more on more levels for you than anything else.

10. If you could only give three pieces of advice, what would you tell a business or individual as they attempt to build and/or establish a viable Web presence?

1. **Do your homework thoroughly.** Make sure you know your clientele and what their habits are, what they really need and want. Spend some time on social media and find out what they are talking about and what sites are popular with them before you design anything.

2. **Plan your work and work your plan.** Lay out exactly what you want it to look like and then execute that plan. Make sure you have all the legal pages for your site as part of that design (a privacy policy and a trademark and copyright notice, for example). Lay it all out on a piece of paper what the pages are and how these should look. Then design it just that way. Do not tweak it until after you have had a few hundred people look at it. Then you will be able to see from your server logs what people are looking at, what browsers they are using, what search engines are bringing you traffic, and what search terms are being used to find your site.

3. **Test, test, test, test**. This also includes testing out various templates on free blog hosts so you can try out what looks better and provides better service to your potential clients. But do not just try something and then change it right off. Set something up and test that for a few hundred viewers for a few months and see what is bringing you traffic and what pages are not. Then study these to improve them. Always consider your site a work in progress, but "do not fix what ain't broken." In many cases, you might be better getting another domain name and setting up a completely new site to test something, rather than making drastic changes and then accidentally "throwing the baby out with the bathwater."

*Dr. Robert Worstell has been professionally designing Web sites since the late 1990s and has worked with nearly every type of operating system and design software produced between then and now. Currently he works as an independent researcher/consultant and freelances design on the side. While Dr. Worstell has published several papers on wireless computer networking, his name comes up more frequently for his prolific writing output: more than four dozen books published on Lulu.com and more than two dozen blogs maintained on as many subjects. His interest in e-commerce and social media stems from the research he has needed to do in promoting those books. Dr. Worstell can be contacted through any of his blogs: **http://robertworstell.com**, **http://stop-telemarketers.midwestjournalpress.com**, and **http://gothunkyourself.com**.*

Interview with Richard Villasana

1. How does someone begin the process of determining what they should put on their Web site, what design elements it should have, how navigation should function, and what the overall appearance should be? When starting with a blank HTML document, what steps or techniques would you recommend to get to a finished product?

A lot has to do with the purpose of the Web site. There are several types of Web pages. The cheapest Web sites are those you can create through **www.**

blogger.com and through Google. You can sign up for a Google account and get a free Web page. Depending on your skill level, you could have your Web page up and running in minutes. However, below are the types of sites people most often see on the Internet.

The first type is a branding site. This is the most common Web site type seen on the Internet. An example is **www.themexicoguru.com**. This site has links to products and services and provides information about the company. This is not, however, a site positioned to generate high sales on products and services on the Internet. There are too many choices for a visitor. They can choose to read information, buy a product, or sign up for updates and newsletters.

This type of Web site is also the most costly. People will spend months, even years, working on their branding site. Companies such as radio stations, car dealerships, and Internet companies will spend incredible amounts of money on their Web site. When you want to create a Web site, you absolutely do not want to try to copy a Web site such as **www.att.com**. Most of us simply cannot afford the upkeep. Because the focus is on setting up a Web site for little or no money, you want to look at ways to get your message out or convert visitors to buyers. There are cheaper ways to do this than with a branding site.

When your goal is to generate sales, then you may want a site that has just a sales page. Such sites have a singular focus, to sell a product or service. An example is **www.iamnotapoodle.com**. This site was developed to promote anything and everything about Bichons and to sell products to people who love Bichons.

Finally, there is the "squeeze page" site, also referred to as an opt-in page. This site usually only has a few pages, and few or no links. A visitor has one choice — to sign up to get information, or leave; that is it. When they sign up, they may be directed to other pages with product and service offerings or a branding site.

A site with either a squeeze page or a sales page can be a very low-cost way to create a Web site that can bring in a lot of money. Although the concept is simple, it is just not that easy to put up a site that generates money without investing a little on marketing knowledge. A great strategy for creating a Web site on the cheap is to purchase a template. This way, you bypass the expensive costs of having someone design a banner, doing the layout of the site, and adding lots of extras you do not need — and that really do not help you sell.

Some sites offer a package of templates so you get three pages with the same banner, color scheme, and design. Prices can be below $100 for a set of templates with many variations and color schemes; all you have to do is put in the HTML code. This is very helpful because with some training, you can learn how to add text or change the size of headlines.

You want to be careful about companies that claim to provide quick Web sites using templates. One company charges $750 for their templates along with their service, and this company's Web page is one of the worst I have ever seen. After seeing the template they used for their own site, I urge all my clients to be very careful about such companies. Another limitation is that the templates offered by some companies can be restrictive on what you can add or how you can format the look of the Web page. One associate spent more than $1,000 for a template Web site. For her purposes, the template was seriously inadequate. She finally had to get away from the template and start all over.

Do not get me wrong: There are companies out there that are working hard to provide a simple and easy way for people to get online without spending hundreds of dollars. You just have to devote the time to research a company before you invest your time, energy, and money.

To get up and running fast, stay away from graphic designers offering the latest technology. Once you get into JavaScript, CSS files, Flash, and any customization, you are setting yourself up for a lot of maintenance costs and possibly serious limitations on what you can do with your Web site, especially if your IT person leaves. One of our techs is so talented that he sets up Internet radio stations in his spare time. He used a lot of Flash and the sites looked incredible. But he confided that after a while, the sites started to have maintenance issues, so now he has cut back on his use of Flash. He is always up on the latest new graphic trends, but this does not mean they are necessary or even desirable for most Web sites.

The type of site you set up really depends on the purpose of the site. Unless you are planning to create an online presence like Microsoft or Yahoo!, you can accomplish a lot for cheap with templates, some HTML code, or a simple blog. You could have a blog site up in about 30 minutes. When you are planning to put up a site for business purposes, my recommendation is to invest a little on quality advice so you set up your site right to move you toward your goal.

2. What type of image format do you recommend using on Web sites? There are several different formats, such as GIF, JPEG, and PNG — is there a difference? Is one better than the other?

My company works mainly with JPEGs for the images on Web sites. We have not noticed much of a difference between GIF and JPEG.

3. How much should someone spend on Web site hosting? Is there a Web hosting platform or other features we should specifically be looking for? If you were to recommend a Web hosting provider, who would it be?

The question of whom you should get Web site hosting with depends on what you plan to do with your Web site. When you want a Web site that will provide just the basics and allow you to post information, you can use a service such as GoDaddy. They are quite cheap, with costs under $8 per month. An excellent hosting company is 1&1® at **www.1and1. com**, also with service at under $8. This company has tech support 24/7 and is geared toward people who want to add e-commerce components to their Web site.

If you are planning to use FrontPage, then you will probably have to get a Windows platform. This is good to determine before you start your service. Otherwise, you could sign up for an inexpensive Linux or Unix platform and then find that you have to move your site to a Microsoft platform. Another recent consideration is that some Web hosting companies do not support FrontPage. Check with your Web hosting company to be sure they can meet your needs.

4. *What low- or no-cost options would you recommend for selling products on a Web site, such as PayPal integration or other shopping carts? Is all shopping cart software essentially the same? For a Web site with hundreds of products, what shopping cart software would you recommend? What do you recommend for SSL?*

When it comes to selling products online, you want to decide your needs. If you want to be up fast and selling by this afternoon, PayPal is a great way to go. There is no upfront investment, and setup is relatively easy. You may want to go through some verifications if you will be collecting money. Although not advised, you can even use a personal account to get started. If you are planning on doing business online, you want to set up a business account.

You will, however, need a shopping cart program, even with PayPal. A very good one is **www.1shoppingcart.com**. Once you have your shopping cart program, you can set up your PayPal account, hook it up, and be selling products. PayPal takes their fee every time they process a charge, so there is no monthly statement or extra costs.

All shopping cart software is not the same. One of my Internet companies has a Daisy shopping cart. What is that, you ask? It is a very old shopping cart system. We have not changed it because it works and would be a lot of time and cost to change over to a new system.

One of the downsides to this shopping cart system is that our company cannot integrate an autoresponder. This means we cannot automate the process of building a database of buyers and later sending them messages about new products and services. The benefit of this shopping cart is that it is part of the Web hosting service we have through **www.myhosting. com**. You may find other Web hosting companies that have a shopping cart feature included. You want to go with a reliable company. A good way to select a shopping cart is to ask someone who processes a lot of orders online, such as someone you know through eBay.

There are some great shopping carts out there, but some can cost more than $250 per month. Most people will not ever need this much power, so **www.1shoppingcart.com** (at about $30 per month) and similar programs will work just fine.

5. *There are dozens of companies that you can buy domain names from. Is there any company in particular that is better than the others, and why? Is there any advantage to buying several domain name types for my domain, such as .com, .biz, .us, and .net?*

Many Internet marketers like and use GoDaddy to buy domain names for the simple reason that they are cheap. When getting a domain name, you want a company that will answer the phone with a live person. Do not laugh: I once used a company where no one ever answered the phone. They looked great online, but it was a scam company that had all calls routed to an answering machine. The people at GoDaddy are very polite, and they are available 24/7.

The other quality you want is a company that will auto-renew your domain names. This is critical if you are in business. The last thing you want is to develop a great Web site and brand and then lose it because you let the domain registration expire. There are companies that are hunting for Web sites that already have traffic; they are just waiting for your registration to expire so they can grab your domain name.

I have worked with companies that charge $25 and more. Honestly, I get very little benefit from those companies such as **www.register.com** compared to GoDaddy or 1&1 at **www.1and1.com**, which is another great place to register your domain. You cannot go wrong with either company.

The advantage with 1&1 is that they have great Web hosting services that work very well for people who want to expand into doing sales online — what we call e-commerce.

Someone brought it to my attention recently that they had received an e-mail from China warning them that someone wanted to get their domain with the domain type .cn. I have also received such e-mails about my Web sites. It may sound serious, but .com is still the gold standard for domain names. My Chinese is non-existent, so I am not too concerned if someone wants to have a similar domain name with .cn. Most marketing experts agree that you really want a .com. If you cannot think of a great domain name that is not already taken, then .biz will work. Do not think that all the great names have been taken. One associate just got the domain **www.the winningentrepreneur.com**. That is a great domain name for a business.

I have not invested in all the variations. What is more important is to get variations of a .com. For instance, one of my sites is **www.themexicoguru.com**. I had to go with that domain name because someone already has **www.mexicoguru.com**. As a strategy, what I did was register **www. themexicanguru.com** and **www.mexicanguru.com**. Many people will write me at **www.mexicanguru.com,** even though this site redirects them to my main **www.themexicoguru.com** Web site. There is so much similarity between "Mexico" and "Mexican" that having these domains allows me to protect my brand as best as possible. You do want to be aware of the domain name you get. If you have a site such as **www.borntoshop.org**, you may want to get **www.born2shop.org** because some people — especially those texting like there is no tomorrow — are used to abbreviations and might put in a "2" instead of "to." If you do not cover yourself, someone could get a domain name variation that outperforms your site.

6. What is a useful CSS technique that you use often? What is the most common font you use when designing Web pages? What advice can you give regarding Web site navigation?

The most common fonts I use are Arial, Verdana, and Times New Roman.

My recommendation for Web site navigation is not to get too fancy. One company has their navigation on a left panel, but the problem is that the links are vertical, making it more difficult to read the link text. A simple rule to follow in Web design is to keep it simple. Simple does not mean boring or ugly; it means you leave out the spinning football and the blinking lights.

Although I like a fancy Web site, as do most people, you want your visitors to move around easily. If they have to work hard at all, most will leave in seconds. Remember that, statistically, most new visitors will leave your site within seven seconds, so you do not want to have your navigation as an obstacle.

7. A challenge of any new Web site is obtaining search engine rankings. What practical advice can you give to someone with a new Web site to achieve visibility in major search engines?

Everyone wants to achieve visibility of their Web site; otherwise, no one is ever going to see your message or learn about your product or service. One strategy is to think of terms that describe what you do. One company wanted to promote their service to help people in the U.S. find their relatives in Mexico. Many people would use terms such as "relatives" or "Mexico." These terms are so common that it would be almost impossible for anyone to do a search and find the company.

Instead, they used a better strategy by focusing on better, more specific terms. They used phrases such as "find relatives in Mexico," "find father in Mexico," and others in their meta tags and title section of their Web site. These are more restrictive and limiting terms, but here are what you have to ask yourself: Do you want to attract everyone in the world, or is there a specific group of people you want to have come to your site? In the case of this company, they want people who are searching for a relative in Mexico, not people who want to vacation in Mexico. If you go to Google and put in the term "find father in Mexico," their site is actually No. 1 organically. This means they do not pay to advertise on Google and yet come up first for that search term.

The next thing you want is to have these phrases in the body of your Web site. When you want someone to find a relative in Mexico, then use that term, such as, "To find relatives in Mexico, you want to…" This way the search engines can see that there is relevancy between what you have in the meta tags and what you have on your page.

You do not, however, want to "stuff" your page with these terms or try to put every phrase possible on one page. You want to use specific terms on specific pages. This will help give each page a high ranking. For instance, some of my company's other pages rank high because they focus on one specific term, such as "social security identity theft" instead of just using "identity theft." Note that I am using quotes only to identify the keyword phrases.

8. If you could only give three pieces of advice, what you would tell a business or individual as they attempt to build and/or establish a viable Web presence?

- **Keep your Web site simple.** It should look nice graphically, but forget the fancy Flash at the start of your site, unless yours is a graphic design company.
- **Know what you want from your Web site.** Know if you want to build a list (use a squeeze page), sell products (a sales page) or just share information (a blog or a free Google Web site could work just fine).
- **Get someone who not only knows the tech side of a Web site, but who also offers marketing advice.** You want a company that

knows what e-commerce is all about, uses those features, and can guide you as you grow — not sell you a lot of costly and needless graphic designs that will leave your wallet empty, and a site that does not generate sales and profits.

Richard Villasana is the CEO and Principal of All Media Marketing Solutions, a company that provides consulting to businesses wanting to grow their company through marketing and e-commerce. He provides consulting to service providers such as attorneys, physicians, realtors, and Internet marketers. His company provides expert help and Internet marketing services. Richard has been interviewed by NBC and appeared on ABC. He has been profiled and interviewed by BusinessWeek, San Diego Business Journal, *and trade publications such as* CRM Magazine. *He is the top-selling author of* Insider Secrets for Doing Business in Mexico *and an international speaker. He can be contacted at rvillasana@AllMediaMarketingSolutions.com.*

Interview with Paul Pennel

1. How does someone begin the process of determining what they should put on their Web site, what design elements it should have, how navigation should function, and what the overall appearance should be? When starting with a blank HTML document, what steps or techniques would you recommend to get to a finished product?

First, go ahead and browse Web sites that you like. Take some time to note what you do and do not like on each Web site. If you are creating a Web site for the first time, you should stick to the basics. Use only the programming languages HTML and CSS to create your Web site. There are many other useful tools, but until you learn about the more complex aspects, such as SEO, browser compatibility, and other Web design options, it is best to be simple. Put your navigation either at the top or the left side of the page. List your company name and contact information at the top of the page. Make the look of each page of the Web site the same.

If you are staring at a blank HTML document, the first thing I would do is search out a template to help you get started. There are many free templates out there. Depending on how much control you want, you can either find a template that gives you a basic structure, or one that gives you a specific look. A basic structure template will handle the layout of the page and allow you to fill in the style and content. The basic structure templates almost always have a header and footer and one, two, or three columns in between.

2. There are many Web design products available, such as Microsoft FrontPage, Microsoft Expression Web, and Adobe Creative Suite. For a beginner who wants to have a professional Web site, yet use a fairly simple to use Web design product, what would you recommend and why?

I use Adobe Creative Suite, which is an excellent suite of tools for Web designers. If you are trying to build an inexpensive Web site, then Adobe Creative Suite is not the way to go, as the price tag is quite expensive. If you are willing to spend a couple hundred dollars, Adobe's Dreamweaver is a pleasure to use. Dreamweaver has two very nice tools for beginners. There is a WYSIWYG editor that allows you to make updates in a Word document-type view instead of using HTML. It also makes it very easy to transfer files from your computer to the Web site you are building.

3. What type of image format do you recommend using on Web sites? There are several different formats, such as GIF, JPEG, and PNG — is there a difference? Is one better than the other?

I do not believe there is a one-size-fits-all format for images. The general rule I would recommend is to use the format that gives you the look you desire and keeps the size as small as possible. The size is more important, as larger images make the page take longer to load, even for people with high-speed connections. If one page has several large images, it will load so slowly that most people will leave before it finishes loading.

4. How much should someone spend on Web site hosting? Is there a Web hosting platform or other features we should specifically be looking for? If you were to recommend a Web hosting provider, who would it be?

This answer depends on how much traffic you plan to have to your Web site. If you are creating a Web site for a small business or for personal use, you probably will not have more than a couple hundred visitors a day, and then one of the cheaper hosts is more than enough for your needs. I would recommend that the host you go with has cPanel, which is an easy-to-use interface that allows you to install things like a calendar, blog, or photo gallery with a click of a button. It also handles basic changes that you may need to make to your Web server without having to know a scripting language. I would also look for a company that has been around for several years and has good support. If you are planning on creating another Web site, make sure you get a provider that allows you to host multiple Web sites for the same price. I personally chose HostMonster for most of my Web hosting because they qualify for everything mentioned above, and all of their support calls are handled by people in the United States, which eliminates any language barriers.

5. What low- or no-cost options would you recommend for selling products on a Web site, such as PayPal integration or other shopping carts? Is all shopping cart software essentially the same? For a Web site with hundreds of products, what shopping cart software would you recommend? What do you recommend for SSL?

If you are going low-cost, then PayPal is probably the best option. PayPal takes a small percentage, but it works effectively, and is well-known and trusted. Not all shopping carts are the same, but there are several free and open-source versions that should be good enough for your needs. I personally find Zen Cart the easiest to use. As for SSL, the most simple way is to go through your hosting company. They do it all the time and can handle it without you having to know much about how they are doing it.

6. There are dozens of companies that you can buy domain names from. Is there any company in particular that is better than the others, and why? Is there any advantage to buying several domain name types for my domain, such as .com, .biz, .us, and .net?

I have not noticed any major difference among companies that you buy domain names from. The only time it probably makes a difference is if you need to transfer your domain to another hosting company. The good companies make this process easy, while some of the cheaper ones appear to be hiding this ability so they do not lose current customers. With persistence, though, you can even get these transferred.

7. When designing a Web site, we want to ensure compatibility with major Web browsers, such as Microsoft Internet Explorer, Mozilla Firefox, Google Chrome, and others. Do you have recommendations for how to design the site to ensure maximum compatibility and user functionality?

This is probably the toughest part of Web design. All of the major browsers work off the same standards, so you would expect everything to look the same on every browser. Unfortunately, this is not the case. I have spent many hours pulling my hair out trying to fix a Web site that looks great in Firefox and Safari but is unusable in Internet Explorer 6.

Here are a couple of techniques that I use to deal with browser incompatibility that I could not live without. Earlier I mentioned starting with a template; most of the publicly available templates have been tested with every major browser, but before you start using it, test it in all browsers. That way, you are starting with a solid base. I cannot stress this next point enough — write in Firefox, then go back and make fixes for Internet Explorer. This is because Firefox has some great tools that every Web developer needs. The two most important ones are Firebug and the Web Developer Toolbar. Both are free plug-ins for Firefox. With Firebug, you can make changes to the page within Firebug and see the changes in real time. This is invaluable for those times you are trying to get something pixel-perfect. Web Developer Toolbar has several useful shortcuts, like changing the size of your browser window to any size in order to mimic different screen resolutions that you find on different computer screens.

Another great trick is to add a style sheet (CSS) that is only used in Internet Explorer. To do this, add the following just before your **</head>** tag:

```
<!--[if IE]>
    <link rel="stylesheet" type="text/css" href="includes/myiehacks.css" />
  <![endif]-->
```

Then create the myiehacks.css style sheet and add only the styles that you want IE to do differently. This is very useful because there are several styles that work in all of the browsers except IE. In this method, you can code it the correct way in your main style sheet and do it IE's way in the hack style sheet. This makes it easier to achieve the look you are going for in all browsers.

It is all right to add functionality that current browsers support but older ones do not — as long as you leave a way for people using the older browsers to accomplish the same thing. It can be as simple as applying rounder corners in newer browsers that are squared in older browsers, to something more complicated — like an Ajax application that can also be used in the old HTTP request/response way of working as well. This important idea is known as progressive enhancement.

Lastly, there is one very important point: Do not try and get all browsers to look exactly the same. It is important that your Web site looks good and is usable in all browsers, but it does not have to match pixel by pixel. If you try living up to that expectation, you will drive yourself crazy.

8. *What is a useful CSS technique that you use often? What is the most common font you use when designing Web pages? What advice can you give regarding Web site navigation?*

The IE hack I previously mentioned is probably the most useful CSS technique that I use. I have read several articles about which fonts are best for readability on the Web. While there is some debate on both sides, most agree that sans-serif fonts are easiest to read. So I often use a serif font for the navigation and a sans-serif font for the majority of the content. This is another area that can be a pain between browsers and even between computers. There are only a couple of fonts that you can safely assume are viewable on all of your users' computers. Because of this, I usually use Verdana for my main content. It is important to note that if you use more than one font on a Web site that you use a font that is clearly different from your other font so that it creates a contrast rather than discord. If two fonts are used on one page and they look very similar but not quite the same, it then gives the user an uneasy feeling about what they are seeing. If it is clear that the two fonts were meant to be different to showcase different sections of the page, it is much more pleasing to the eye.

Web site navigation is very important. The basic rule of thumb is to never have a page more than three levels deep, so it does not take more than three clicks to get to any single Web page. I feel this is too deep for most Web sites. I think using drop-down menus at the top of your page that shows all of your pages, or at least all of the important ones, is vital for navigation of your Web site.

Another important idea is to know ahead of time where you want most users to go when they first visit your Web site and guide them to that location. For instance, on **www.getfirebug.com**, there is a large download button that your eye is drawn to when you first enter the page. Most people who are going there want to download this Firefox plug-in and are very happy to find such easy navigation. For users who do not want to download, there is still other content and navigations options, which are more in the background of the Web page.

9. A challenge of any new Web site is obtaining search engine rankings. What practical advice can you give to someone with a new Web site to achieve visibility in major search engines?

First, run the other way from any company promising you top-10 ranking in Google. Think about how many Web sites are out there already, and most of them are doing their best to achieve high search engine rankings. If there was a magic formula that always got you high rankings, then its inventor would be rich. However, there are some basic ideas that you can follow and will help your rankings.

Submit your Web site to all of the major search engines as soon as you have it up and running. If Google does not know you exist, none of the rest of this matters.

Content is king. You must have good content that is viable to search engines to get a good ranking. Also, pick a couple of keywords that you really want to capture, and make sure to list them prominently on your Web site. If you are an attorney and want to be listed in the top 10 when somebody searches "attorney" in Google, you are probably out of luck. But if instead you want to be listed near the top for the search "divorce attorney Kansas City Missouri," you can structure your content in a way that you will be listed well. Make sure you have your location listed in several places on your Web site. If you are near a larger city, make sure to mention it as well. Something like, "…located in Creve Coeur, Mo., 20 minutes from downtown St. Louis" should do the trick. It allows search engines to find you both for searches on "Creve Coeur" and "St. Louis."

List your most important keywords in the title of all of your pages. Also, use the header (H1, H2) tags on your Web site and put your keywords in these as well. Search engines recognize that the title and your headers most likely have the most relevant information about your Web site.

Back-links are also very important. Back-links are links from other Web sites to your Web site. The more highly ranked the other Web site is, the more relevant the link back to your Web site is. The longer your Web site exists, the better off you are. Search engines are more likely to list a Web site that has been around longer than a year higher than one that is only a month old. While you cannot control this particular factor, being aware of this might help you with patience and realistic expectations.

10. If you could only give three pieces of advice, what would you tell a business or individual as they attempt to build and/or establish a viable Web presence?

- Take 10 to 15 minutes a couple of times a week to market your Web site. This can be as simple as working on getting more backlinks or going to a forum related to your field and commenting on people's posts. In your responses, you can direct people to your Web site in order for them to find more information on a relevant topic.
- Keep your Web site updated. If a customer goes to your Web site in May and sees information about Christmas sales, they will assume the Web site is no longer active and will leave.
- Have patience. It takes a lot of hard work and time to build a solid Web presence, but it is attainable and well-worth the rewards. As more and more people visit your Web site, you will see an increase in your business as a result.

*Minnow Web Design offers solutions for small businesses or organizations with big ideas. Just because you are working with a shoestring budget does not mean that your Web site cannot be professional, well-designed, and user-friendly. Owner and designer Paul Pennel combines 12 years of information technology experience with a desire to make great Web sites affordable. That means that you can finally join the online business community, where advertising is inexpensive and returns are considerable. Paul can be contacted at paul@minnowWeb design.com, or on the Web at **www.minnowWebdesign.com**.*

Interview with Pablo Solomon

1. How does someone begin the process of determining what they should put on their Web site, what design elements it should have, how navigation should function, and what the overall appearance should be? When starting with a blank HTML document, what steps or techniques would you recommend to get to a finished product?

The most important thing is to decide what image that you want to project. What about yourself and what you do is what you want the world to see — forever? You should make your site as visually balanced as possible, and stick to a color scheme that you want to be part of your "label." Navigation should be as clear and easy as possible. Also keep in mind that much of the world, including my ranch, is still on Internet dial-up at extremely slow load speeds, so make your photo files small so that they will load up fast, even at 28k dial-up. Make sketches ahead of time to get an idea of what you want to achieve. Create a file on your computer with all photos cropped and at a small file size to load up. Also, write your text on Word and edit it.

2. There are many Web design products available, such as Microsoft FrontPage, Microsoft Expression Web, and Adobe Creative Suite. For a beginner who wants to have a professional Web site, yet use a fairly simple-to-use Web design product, what would you recommend and why?

The only ones I have used are Dreamweaver — too complicated — and Trellix® — excellent for those of us with no tech skills.

3. What type of image format do you recommend using on Web sites? There are several different formats, such as GIF, JPEG, and PNG — is there a difference?

Stick to JPEG. Most fill-in-the-blank sites require it. Also, label your photo files Joegoes.jpg as opposed to Joe Goes to Town, one run-on word; this way, all computers and design templates can read it.

4. *How much should someone spend on Web site hosting? Is there a Web hosting platform or other features we should specifically be looking for? If you were to recommend a Web hosting provider, who would it be?*

As little as possible. Keep in mind that your Web site is just one of many advertising and promotional tools. I like EarthLink® because they provide a site and Trellix for free, and they have good Web support.

5. *What low- or no-cost options would you recommend for selling products on a Web site, such as PayPal integration or other shopping carts? Is all shopping cart software essentially the same? For a Web site with hundreds of products, what shopping cart software would you recommend? What do you recommend for SSL?*

PayPal seems to be most universal. Of course, all providers will sell you as much "help" as you have money. Do not overdo it. Just so you can get money into your account from a customer with as much online security for you and the customer is the important thing.

6. *There are dozens of companies that you can buy domain names from. Is there any company in particular that is better than the others, and why? Is there any advantage to buying several domain name types for my domain, such as .com, .biz, .us, and .net?*

All are about the same. Only buy other domain names to keep someone else from getting a similar site name. For example, if you register as Art. com, someone else might get Art.net, which could be confusing.

7. *When designing a Web site, we want to ensure compatibility with major Web browsers, such as Microsoft Internet Explorer, Mozilla Firefox, Google Chrome, and others. Do you have recommendations*

for how to design the site to ensure maximum compatibility and user functionality?

That is why I use Trellix — it is up to the software provider to do all that.

8. *What is a useful CSS technique that you use often? What is the most common font you use when designing Web pages? What advice can you give regarding Web site navigation?*

Verdana is good, as is Times New Roman; just what you like. Do not use anything that is too script-looking, as people who do not read English well have a hard time.

9. *A challenge of any new Web site is obtaining search engine rankings. What practical advice can you give to someone with a new Web site to achieve visibility in major search engines?*

Do not fall for the various companies that promise to keep you at the top of the list. The only way you can do this is to pay Google or whatever other search engine a lot of money. Otherwise, use good keywords and hope a lot of people go to your site. Rankings are on either bribes or number of hits.

10. *If you could only give three pieces of advice, what would you tell a business or individual as they attempt to build and/or establish a viable Web presence?*

- Plan your image well.
- Remember, what you publish is in cyberspace forever.
- The same advice I give people taking my figure drawing classes: A good eraser is more valuable than 50 good pencils.

*Pablo Solomon is an internationally recognized artist known primarily for drawings and sculptures of dancers. He has been featured in books, magazines, newspapers, radio, TV, and film. Currently he lives and work with his wife, Beverly, on their historic 1856 ranch north of Austin, Texas. You can see his work at **www.pablosolomon.com**.*

Interview with Mikel Bruce

1. How does someone begin the process of determining what they should put on their Web site, what design elements it should have, how navigation should function, and what the overall appearance should be? When starting with a blank HTML document, what steps or techniques would you recommend to get to a finished product?

Start by looking for designs that you like on the Web and use them as a point of reference. It is always best to get a professional opinion when choosing design elements. I would suggest either purchasing a professional template versus starting with blank HTML and having the template built out by a designer.

2. There are many Web design products available, such as Microsoft FrontPage, Microsoft Expression Web, and Adobe Creative Suite. For a beginner who wants to have a professional Web site, yet use a fairly simple-to-use Web design product, what would you recommend and why?

If someone wants a professional design, they should go with a designer. It does not have to be custom. It could be using a template. I would avoid the cheap/free build-your-own Web site templates like Yahoo! SiteBuilder. A Web site is much like a double edged sword — it can be powerful or can cause more harm than good. It is in many cases the first thing people see of your business, and it has to represent you in the best way possible. If someone does not have Web design skills, they should not be building their own site if they want it to be a quality site.

3. What type of image format do you recommend using on Web sites? There are several different formats, such as GIF, JPEG, and PNG — is there a difference? Is one better than the other?

It does not really matter. A PNG is important if it needs to be a transparent image. JPEG is typically the standard and, in most cases, is fine.

4. *How much should someone spend on Web site hosting? Is there a Web hosting platform or other features we should specifically be looking for? If you were to recommend a Web hosting provider, who would it be?*

Hosting should cost about $10 to $30 per month. Some of the higher-priced systems with a CMS built into the design can be worth the extra few dollars.

5. *What low- or no-cost options would you recommend for selling products on a Web site, such as PayPal integration or other shopping carts? Is all shopping cart software essentially the same? For a Web site with hundreds of products, what shopping cart software would you recommend? What do you recommend for SSL?*

PayPal is great for a few products, but an actual in-line shopping cart is best for multiple items. There are not any no-cost options worth recommending, but there are several shopping cart companies that have good options. I would recommend hiring a designer to implement a self-managed shopping cart like **www.litecommerce.com** into the site. It may cost a few hundred dollars to get it implemented and some hosting fees, but it is the best long-term, low-cost option if ease of shopping and quality are important.

6. *There are dozens of companies that you can buy domain names from. Is there any company in particular that is better than the others, and why? Is there any advantage to buying several domain name types for my domain, such as .com, .biz, .us, and .net?*

GoDaddy is good because they have good prices and great service, and if one is buying multiple domains, they have a program for that.

7. *When designing a Web site, we want to ensure compatibility with major Web browsers, such as Microsoft Internet Explorer, Mozilla Firefox, Google Chrome, and others. Do you have recommendations*

for how to design the site to ensure maximum compatibility and user functionality?

This is one of the reasons a designer is critical. Most build-your-own software or Web-based programs make it difficult to achieve compliances, and this is very important as more people are using many different browsers.

8. What is a useful CSS technique that you use often? What is the most common font you use when designing Web pages? What advice can you give regarding Web site navigation?

The average user probably cannot implement CSS on their own. Verdana is probably the best Web font. Centralized navigation with all links on one navigation bar is critically important. The average site visitor will not take the time to bounce around once they get lost.

9. A challenge of any new Web site is obtaining search engine rankings. What practical advice can you give to someone with a new Web site to achieve visibility in major search engines?

Take the time to do a good keyword analysis and to implement meta tags correctly. If a term is not very competitive, one may have results with minimal effort.

10. If you could only give three pieces of advice, what would you tell a business or individual as they attempt to build and/or establish a viable Web presence?

- Use a designer at least at some point when implementing a design. Probably the cheapest way to go while maintaining quality is purchasing a template and having a designer implement the template.
- Be patient — it always take longer than expected to get a site up and to achieve success in the search engines. Come up with a three-part plan for Web marketing.
- Definitely use e-mail marketing, as it is probably the most cost-effective form of marketing that has ever existed.

Mikel Bruce is the founder of WebFlexor Technologies and has been in market-ing since 1991. WebFlexor is a privately held, San Diego-based Web design and hosting company that has been in business since 2002. Their Web sites are known in the industry for having one of the easiest to use CMS programs, the Flex-Edit system. WebFlexor gives their clients control over their Web sites by al-lowing them to act as their own Webmasters. WebFlexor also has Green Hosting status, and every WebFlexor Web site they offer is powered by renewable energy. This commitment is certified through Green Mountain Energy®. Mikel can be contacted at mikel@Webflexor.com.

Interview with Michael Silverman

1. How does someone begin the process of determining what they should put on their Web site, what design elements it should have, how navigation should function, and what the overall appearance should be? When starting with a blank HTML document, what steps or techniques would you recommend to get to a finished product?

The first question that they should ask themselves is: What is the point of the Web site they are putting up? Are they trying to increase brand aware-ness (more active), simply create an online presence (more passive), have a dialogue with their customers, or expand their market for their product line? The key is knowing precisely what you want on your Web site and why you want it. This will guide most of your choices in terms of content. In terms of design, if you keep it simple, your customers will appreciate it. For example, in my case, as a student my goals were to promote my current work, illustrate my past projects, advertise my biographical information and promote myself as a brand, and — perhaps most importantly — create an online presence that was positive and that I could control.

In terms of navigation, a set of four or five key items at the top of the page is a solid foundation to build upon. I started out with a home page, an "About Me" page, a blog page, a page dedicated to my projects, and a page dedicated to my photography. You can then have drop-down menus that illustrate different aspects or projects in those four or five categories at the top.

In terms of overall appearance, your brand may dictate what your color scheme should be, but in my case, I was building a brand from scratch. As my projects and interests were concerned with the environment and sustainable development, and I was choosing to brand myself as a "student of sustainability," I decided I wanted a color scheme with an eco-theme of sorts. The best way to figure out a color scheme is to utilize one of the many color scheme pickers online. Adobe Kuler is a fantastic resource and is how I ended up with my color scheme of green, beige, and dark grey. Utilizing one of these tools ensures that your colors will match and will not look like you simply picked colors at random. If you get one thing right, it should be the color scheme. Take your time with this step. It may take you many variations (it took me 20) to get just the right feel for it.

2. There are many Web design products available, such as Microsoft FrontPage, Microsoft Expression Web, and Adobe Creative Suite. For a beginner who wants to have a professional Web site, yet use a fairly simple-to-use Web design product, what would you recommend and why?

My advice is to skip them entirely. The Internet has changed a great deal, and while it used to be a requirement for one to possess Web design software to create a professional-looking Web page, this is simply not true anymore. There are Web-based hosting/publishing platforms that will do most of the work for you and allow you to have a professional Web site at the same time. For an extremely busy individual, learning HTML and the necessary background knowledge in terms of security software, quality Web site hosting, and CSS design is simply not possible — nor efficient.

I had a limited amount of time to create an online presence, hence not enough time to learn all the HTML that I would need to create what I desired. So I turned first to Weebly™, the best free Web site creation Web-based tool out there. It is a perfect way to start out with Web design, as it is well-designed, requires no HTML knowledge, and is entirely free. This is where I started building my online presence.

However, as good as Weebly is to start out with, it is not yet a complex enough tool to handle the customization you most likely desire. This led me to seek out another platform with greater complexity. And this led me to Squarespace, which you can visit at **www.squarespace.com/?assoc iateTag=michaelsilverman**. Squarespace will give you as much or as little freedom as you desire. They have amazing pre-designed templates that you can then customize to your heart's content, right down to the colors, fonts, and link-hovering effects. They have a no-risk, no-credit-card-required trial that I heartily recommend. If you do decide to host with them, their prices start at $14 a month. I am available as an independent Squarespace consultant, should you need help getting your site off the ground.

3. What type of image format do you recommend using on Web sites? There are several different formats, such as GIF, JPEG, and PNG — is there a difference? Is one better than the other?

As far as imaging goes, I would recommend utilizing JPEG images simply for the fact that I have never had a problem with a JPEG image displaying properly. Be sure to utilize a compression program, such as Photoshop, to reduce the size of your images. Otherwise, you will be wasting precious and often costly bandwidth.

On a side note, should you need to implement a lot of photography on your Web site, or if that is one of your primary hobbies, like it is mine, I would recommend setting up an alternative photo Web site, as this will take one of the largest bandwidth drains off of your primary Web site account. I use **www.zenfolio.com**, which offers unlimited bandwidth for an unlimited amount of photos for $40 per year. This will end up being much cheaper than hosting all of your photos on your primary Web hosts account (use promo code EV7-ZAC-5HZ).

4. How much should someone spend on Web site hosting? Is there a Web hosting platform or other features we should specifically be looking for? If you were to recommend a Web hosting provider, who would it be?

Quality hosting will cost you approximately $100 to $200 per year. This includes the purchase of a domain name, which you will absolutely need. Again, I heartily recommend Squarespace in this case. Their support is fantastic; they will literally contact you within 15 minutes of your e-mailed question; and my Web site is hosted on the same servers as their Web site is. If my site goes down, they go down as well. I have never had any down time whatsoever at Squarespace, or Zenfolio, for that matter. They are both fantastic options.

5. There are dozens of companies that you can buy domain names from. Is there any company in particular that is better than the others, and why? Is there any advantage to buying several domain name types for my domain, such as .com, .biz, .us, and .net?

I again would heartily recommend **www.1and1.com**. They are one of the largest registrars on the net. They have been around forever and have some of the best prices among all registrars. They have amazing customer service and do not engage in some of the tricks that other domain name companies can/will do. You can use this link: **www.1and1.com/?k_id=17078631**.

As far as purchasing different domain types goes, I would recommend buying the top three for your company name if they are available. For example, for my site, I have **www.michaelwsilverman.com** and **www.michaelsilverman.net** for my photography site. I did not buy .org because I felt it would be a waste of money for my own needs. However, if your name is Best Baked Goods, if they are available, I would recommend purchasing the .com, .net, and .org variants of the domain name, just in case.

An important item to note is that the importance of the domain is waning as search engines become the primary avenue for finding businesses. While a good domain name is important, content should be your primary focus.

6. When designing a Web site, we want to ensure compatibility with major Web browsers, such as Microsoft Internet Explorer, Mozilla Firefox, Google Chrome, and others. Do you have recommendations for how to design the site to ensure maximum compatibility and user functionality?

Yes, use Squarespace. All of their pages are already optimized for search engines and are compatible with all browsers, without any effort on your part. The advantage of using Squarespace is you do not have to worry about most of the technical stuff and can simply concentrate on building your brand via quality content.

7. What is a useful CSS technique that you use often? What is the most common font you use when designing Web pages? What advice can you give regarding Web site navigation?

One piece of advice is to keep it simple. Less is often more in terms of Web site design.

8. A challenge of any new Web site is obtaining search engine rankings. What practical advice can you give to someone with a new Web site to achieve visibility in major search engines?

While my advice may run counter to a lot of the SEO books out there, what I am about to tell you is what truly works: Build quality content and update it frequently; that is it. Have a blog. Even if you do not think it is important, in terms of search engine visibility, it is invaluable. The more often that your content is updated, the higher you will eventually rank. Do not try any of the gimmicks, such as link building. These will hurt your ranking in the long run, and besides, your goal is a long-term, quality presence — not a short-lived spot at No. 1 on Google.

9. If you could only give three pieces of advice, what would you tell a business or individual as they attempt to build and/or establish a viable Web presence?

- Building a quality online presence will take time. You need not only time to figure out what you want on your presence, but also for search engines to pick up on how good your content is and why you are worth indexing. Do not worry if you are not at No. 1 on Google in the first three months or even later. This stuff takes time.

- Do not try and go the cheap route on hosting. I have heard horror stories of fly-by-night hosting operations that have cheated customers and stolen data. Spend some money on a quality Web host; the alternative is just not worth the $5 you will save every month.

- Google is your friend. If you do not know how to do something, look it up. The Internet is an amazing resource for learning about Web design. One more rule: Have fun with your site. If you enjoy posting and updating your site, your customers will most likely enjoy reading it.

Michael Silverman has been studying sustainability for close to a decade and continues to do so at Stanford University. In addition to being featured in both the Arizona Republic *and the* Paradise Valley Independent *for his work on behalf of the environment, Michael was also awarded the American Solar Electric Sunny Community Blue Diamond Award for his environmental leadership within the Greater Phoenix community. He has been publishing his work on the Web for close to half a decade, and is continuously expanding his knowledge of Web site design and virtual collaboration via his Web site,* **www.michaelwsilverman.com**. *Michael is a published photographer as well, having had his work published in* PC Magazine, Physics Today, *and the campaign literature for the mayor of Paradise Valley. He has been exploring photography for nearly a decade and continues to publish his work on* **www.michaelsilverman.net**. *You can contact Michael at mws@michaelsilverman.com.*

Interview with Susan Whitehead

1. How does someone begin the process of determining what they should put on their Web site, what design elements it should have, how navigation should function, and what the overall appearance should be? When starting with a blank HTML document, what steps or techniques would you recommend to get to a finished product?

When beginning the process of creating a Web site, I actually prefer to use something other than a standard HTML site. My content management system of choice is WordPress. It allows for simple content updating without having to deal with the headaches of HTML templates. WordPress lets you choose from thousands of different themes that you can install with very little effort, and changing themes does not affect existing content. This is a huge plus in my book.

2. There are many Web design products available, such as Microsoft FrontPage, Microsoft Expression Web, and Adobe Creative Suite. For a beginner who wants to have a professional Web site, yet use a fairly simple-to-use Web design product, what would you recommend and why?

WordPress is my product preference. It allows a beginner to create a very professional-looking site without having to know any HTML or PHP.

3. What type of image format do you recommend using on Web sites? There are several different formats, such as GIF, JPEG, and PNG — is there a difference? Is one better than the other?

I use JPEG, but do not have a reason.

4. How much should someone spend on Web site hosting? Is there a Web hosting platform or other features we should specifically be looking for? If you were to recommend a Web hosting provider, who would it be?

Web site hosting should be around $100 a year or so. The most important feature to look for in any hosting company is whether the hosting comes with cPanel. Stay away from hosting that does not include cPanel. If you ever end up working with a Web designer, it will make his or her life a lot easier if you have cPanel. My preferred Web site host is **www.mediaserve. com**. I have used them for more than five years and have been very pleased with their support and uptimes.

5. *What low- or no-cost options would you recommend for selling products on a Web site, such as PayPal integration or other shopping carts? Is all shopping cart software essentially the same? For a Web site with hundreds of products, what shopping cart software would you recommend? What do you recommend for SSL?*

I personally use PayPal for its ease.

6. *There are dozens of companies that you can buy domain names from. Is there any company in particular that is better than the others, and why? Is there any advantage to buying several domain name types for my domain, such as .com, .biz, .us, and .net?*

I buy my domains through MEDIASERVE™, but have purchased through **www.godaddy.com** when they have sales. I have not seen a need to buy different types of domains for myself or for any of my clients. The one we always try to go for are the "dot-coms" and nothing else. If the .com we want is not available, we will use keywords to try to get one that works.

7. *When designing a Web site, we want to ensure compatibility with major Web browsers, such as Microsoft Internet Explorer, Mozilla Firefox, Google Chrome, and others. Do you have recommendations for how to design the site to ensure maximum compatibility and user functionality?*

I just check the site with other browsers.

8. What is a useful CSS technique that you use often? What is the most common font you use when designing Web pages? What advice can you give regarding Web site navigation?

The most popular font I use is Arial. As for navigation, I think most users are used to left navigation, but for a blog, many people are used to top or right-hand navigation. It just depends on the feel of the site.

9. A challenge of any new Web site is obtaining search engine rankings. What practical advice can you give to someone with a new Web site to achieve visibility in major search engines?

Search engine placement is part art, part science, and is not something that can be described in a short paragraph. The biggest thing to consider is the way your site is designed. If the site is designed in Flash or another language that the search engines cannot read, you are going to have an up-hill battle to show up in search engines. WordPress is easily read by all the search engines. It also includes plug-ins that allow you to tweak content to maximize your search engine marketing efforts. Outside of "on-site" search engine optimization, you will need to regularly get other Web sites to link to yours to boost your rankings. Again, it is not an instant process; it takes time to build.

10. If you could only give three pieces of advice, what would you tell a business or individual as they attempt to build and/or establish a viable Web presence?

The key before building a Web site is to consider what your goals are for the site. Do you want a Web site just for credibility's sake? Or do you want your site to make you money or bring traffic to your business? Depending on what your goals are, your approach to the site should be different. Do not buy into the idea that "if you build it, they will come," because it will not happen — not unless you are very lucky. Do your research, choose a keyword-rich domain name, and market your site using video, social media, and articles. Come up with a plan on how to market your Web site after you build it so your efforts will be rewarded.

*Susan Whitehead has been marketing online for more than 10 years. Her expertise is in lead generation using eBay and video and e-mail marketing to drive highly targeted traffic to her clients' Web sites. She currently works with her husband, Michael, providing custom Internet marketing solutions to small to medium-sized businesses. Susan and her husband live in rural eastern North Carolina, and she enjoys teaching entrepreneurial skills to their five children. Susan can be contacted at susan@marketingwake.com and **www.marketingwake.com**.*

Interview with Jason Corgiat

1. How does someone begin the process of determining what they should put on their Web site, what design elements it should have, how navigation should function, and what the overall appearance should be? When starting with a blank HTML document, what steps or techniques would you recommend to get to a finished product?

Designing your own Web site can be extremely difficult — or a fun, exciting process. It all depends on how you start. Before jumping into the design, you need to visualize your project flow. To make it easier, let us consider this the same way a general contractor would consider a building project. First, what are you building? A cozy single-family home, or a multi-level commercial building? Next, think about the steps needed to get to the final outcome. For most people, the fun part is picking out the paint and carpet — but do not start there. If you do, you will end up with a poorly constructed home built on a shaky foundation.

Start with a blank piece of paper. You need to first start with your sitemap and design layouts. These are your Web site blueprints. What pages are you going to need? What do your visitors want to see? Ask people who do not know much about your subject matter what would they want to find. Based on your findings, you may realize that your Web site should or should not contain certain elements. These are factors you will want to take into consideration in the design phase. Once you have got your pages figured out, now think about consolidation. Perhaps your "Widget Info," "Widget Pricing," and "Widget Comparison" could all go under a page called "Widgets." Make sure your sitemap makes sense and is easy to follow.

Once you have got your sitemap finalized, get yourself another blank piece of paper (do not worry, you will be on the computer lots later.) Draw out your vision on a piece of paper. First, think about the top section of your site, also known as the header. Most likely it will contain your logo and a menu bar. Then start with the main body. If this is your first Web site, or you are not a creative genius (I am certainly not!), keep a simple two-thirds rule in mind. This means that the page is split using a sidebar or column to the right or left of the main content. A tip: If you want the search engines to get to your main content first, put your sidebar on the right side. This will put your main content higher up in the code that makes up your page and therefore search engines will give it more importance when indexing your page. Your side column can contain additional links, advertisements, or other helpful information.

Once you have drawn up a few concepts, let us create a blueprint on our computer. Now you can go ahead and fire up your favorite Web site building software, but I like to head over to **www.jumpchart.com**. This is a Web-based software — with a free account option — that allows you to start visualizing your Web site. It is easy to use, and within minutes you will have your online blueprint built. You can then easily make revisions or share your idea with other people. This will at least allow you to play around with your layout without spending hours redesigning your pages. There are other options Jumpchart has to offer, but you can find that out for yourself.

2. There are many Web design products available, such as Microsoft FrontPage, Microsoft Expression Web, and Adobe Creative Suite. For a beginner, who wants to have a professional Web site yet use a fairly simple-to-use Web design product, what would you recommend and why?

To be honest, I am not a big fan of any desktop publishing software. First, because it costs money. Second, because it costs more money. It seems every time we update our Web design firm workstations, a new version has come out, and we can upgrade for a nominal fee. If you are not planning on getting into the design business, I would recommend finding a Web host that allows you to easily install Web-based software on your hosting account. In particular, I am a huge fan of WordPress and Joomla! WordPress is a blogging software that one can easily build a site from, and Joomla! is a content management software with a bit of a learning curve but endless possibilities. If you are more of a desktop software kind of person, then I would recommend something like CoffeeCup Visual Site Designer. For $50, you can have a software that helps you make Web pages with no HTML knowledge. Most of the software that claims you can build a site with no HTML knowledge is not worth messing with, but CoffeeCup has been around a long time and has a vast selection of easy-to-use, worthwhile products.

3. What type of image format do you recommend using on Web sites? There are several different formats, such as GIF, JPEG, and PNG — is there a difference? Is one better than the other?

When saving images for the Web, there are a few formats, all with pros and cons. To keep it short, GIF images can be set as transparent (great for colored backgrounds), can be animated, and are usually a smaller file size. To achieve this smaller file size, a GIF is only made up of 256 colors, thus you would not want to save an image with soft edges or gradients as a GIF. For photographs or images with lots of color and contrast, you will want to save them as a JPEG. A JPEG, while being a bit larger file size, will preserve color, gradients, and texture much better than a GIF. A PNG, the newest format of images for Web, has all the benefits — minus animation — of a GIF with all the benefits of a JPEG. Some older browsers may have issues with the proper rendering of PNG files, so keep your audience in mind when saving PNG files. To find out more about these files, check out a great article at **www.sitepoint.com/article/GIF-JPEG-PNG-whats-difference**.

4. How much should someone spend on Web site hosting? Is there a Web hosting platform or other features we should specifically be looking for? If you were to recommend a Web hosting provider, who would it be?

Web hosting is probably one of the most confusing subjects when starting your own Web site. What is the difference between the $7.99 per-month host and the $89.99 per-month host? What is a dedicated server? Do I need a static IP? There could easily be — and I am sure have been — many books written on this subject alone. However, for the sake of keeping it simple, I am going to recommend one of my favorites. They have excellent pricing, an 800-number for support, and great reliability. They also allow you to install a ton of different software very easily right from your control panel. Visit **www.HostGator.com** to host unlimited sites for $7.95 per month with HostGator.

5. What low- or no-cost options would you recommend for selling products on a Web site, such as PayPal integration or other shopping carts? Is all shopping cart software essentially the same? For a Web site with hundreds of products, what shopping cart software would you recommend? What do you recommend for SSL?

Regarding taking payment on the Web, I recommend PayPal and Google Checkout. Neither has monthly fees associated, and the per-transaction fees are reasonable.

If you want to take credit cards yourself, I recommend North American Bancard — **www.nabmerchantaccounts.com** — or First Data — **www.firstdata.com**.

If you do decide to take credit cards yourself, you will want to get yourself an SSL certificate to ensure your transactions are secure. Pricing can be all over the board on SSL certificates, and even as a Web professional, figuring out who needs what can be tricky at times. It is best to do your research and try not to overpay for your SSL certificate. As a rule of thumb, you should be able to get a decent SSL certificate from a reliable company for under $100 per year.

Shopping cart software is another one of those subjects that the options are limitless and comparisons are tough. So, here are a few I am familiar with: X-Cart — for a couple hundred dollars, you can have one of the most powerful shopping carts out there. It will take some time to learn the administration area, but once you do, your options are endless. Whether you are going to sell ten or 10,000 products, I have yet to find an e-commerce need that X-Cart could not fill.

My other favorite is ASPDotNetStorefront™. It is a bit pricey, but I have heard lots of good things about it. Of course, if you have decided to build your site on Joomla!, make sure you check out VirtueMart. It is a plug-in that will make your Joomla! site e-commerce ready. While I have not had much experience with it personally, I have heard many good things about it. Best of all, it is free just like Joomla! Speaking of free, probably the most popular free shopping cart out there is osCommerce. I have heard some say they had great success and others say it was a real pain. Use at your own risk. A tip: Changing e-commerce software after you have built up a store is a nightmare. Take your time analyzing and playing with inline demos before making your decision. It is an important one.

6. There are dozens of companies that you can buy domain names from. Is there any company in particular that is better than the others, and

why? Is there any advantage to buying several domain name types for my domain, such as .com, .biz, .us, and .net?

Like my father always said, "a domain name is a domain name is a domain name." OK, he never said that, but if he were around today, he probably would. Why do some companies charge $9.95 and others charge $35? It is all about their marketing. If you have ever been to GoDaddy's Web site to check out their unbelievable pricing on domain names, you probably know that getting through the checkout without purchasing anything else is like trying to navigate your way through a thick jungle with a butter knife. Maybe you want those extra services, but if you do not, just keep looking for the "no thanks" button and keep an eye on your total. Whatever you do, just make sure you are dealing with a big-name company like GoDaddy, Network Solutions, eNom®, or Register.com. Do not try to save a couple bucks by registering with "Bob's Discount Domain Warehouse." You might just end up finding out what limited options you have when they will not return your calls. Oh, and do not let anyone — like a Web design firm — register the domain name for you. I cannot tell you how many times we get a new client that is looking to move away from their previous company, and when we want to move the domain name, it just so happens to be in the name of their previous company, and not the client themselves. This is a total nightmare, especially when the relationship with the previous company is strained. Take the time and set up the account yourself and register the domain name. Trust me, it is well worth the effort.

7. When designing a Web site, we want to ensure compatibility with major Web browsers, such as Microsoft Internet Explorer, Mozilla Firefox, Google Chrome, and others. Do you have recommendations for how to design the site to ensure maximum compatibility and user functionality?

When you start with software like Joomla! or WordPress, all these things are taken into consideration already. However, if you make modifications or want to design your own site, take a moment and check the compatibility on sites like **http://browsershots.org** and **http://validator.w3.org**.

8. *What is a useful CSS technique that you use often? What is the most common font you use when designing Web pages? What advice can you give regarding Web site navigation?*

CSS has really taken off recently. If done well, you can make your Web site load fast, look great, and get rid of all the junk code that search engines do not like. Done simply, CSS keeps your formatting consistent across your Web site. Simple little things like rollover highlighting can make your Web site stand out from the rest.

We usually stick to four main fonts when designing sites: Arial, Verdana, Tahoma, and Helvetica. Times New Roman is making a comeback, but I am not crazy about it personally. A tip: When using fonts, the visitor needs to have the font installed on their computer to see it correctly. Do not buy a really cool font and use it everywhere on your site. Chances are your visitors will not see it, and your Web site will not look the way you intended.

9. *A challenge of any new Web site is obtaining search engine rankings. What practical advice can you give to someone with a new Web site to achieve visibility in major search engines?*

"Content is king" — that is good advice. However, that does not mean, "If you write it, they will come." You need to keep your visitor in mind, not the search engines. Your visitor wants lots of content, organized well; a clean, functional site; and easy-to-follow navigation. Guess what? That is what the search engines want, too. If you are in a competitive industry, then your best bet is to go after regional key phrases. If you offer widget repair, instead of "widget repair," try "widget repair Los Angeles." This will greatly increase your chances of getting ranked for some relevant keywords and start building your chances at eventually getting ranked for that coveted "widget repair" keyword. Another tip: quality over quantity. If you offer local widget repair, spending your waking hours trying to get ranked for "widgets," you may bring lots of traffic, but not many conversions. Go after less competitive but more targeted key phrases.

10. If you could only give three pieces of advice, what would you tell a business or individual as they attempt to build and/or establish a viable Web presence?

1. Do not be afraid. Technology has a way of freaking people out. Do not worry; the information is out there. Take your time and learn what it all means and how everything works together. You can do this. Before you know it, you will be talking about technology to your friends and family and watching them stare at you with blank expressions. Welcome to the club.

2. Pick brains and learn from some else's mistakes. I do not know a Web development specialist or programmer who does not like talking to someone that is truly interested in what they are saying (note the point above). Do not be afraid to ask questions, post to message boards, and talk to successful people. And everyone who has a success story has a few failure stories as well. Make sure you listen to those, too.

3. Track your efforts. You just made a sale. How did they find your Web site? Was it the newspaper ad or the search engine? What did they type in to find you? The more you know about your visitors, the better you will do. Do not rely on the small percentage that you actually talk to; install stats-tracking software on your Web site. I recommend Google Analytics. Not only does it provide amazing stats about everything you ever wanted to know, but it is free.

4. Bonus — Pick a niche. I just could not leave this out. Do not try and compete with established businesses with deep pockets. Find something unique, or put a different spin on your offering to make it original. My first Web site was an online limousine directory.

Jason Corgiat is the owner of the Web site development company, ***www.Leap-Go.com***. *Jason started his first Web site,* ***USALimos.com***, *with no formal Web design knowledge in 2000. Shortly thereafter, he started doing Web sites for other businesses on the side. Being 100-percent self-taught, he now runs a very successful Web site development business and utilizes his real-world experience when working with clients. Jason has been featured in various magazines and news articles and loves being an entrepreneur. Jason can be contacted at* ***www.leapgo.com***, *by phone at 1-800-211-7619 ext. 4, and by e-mail at jcorgiat@gmail.com.*

Interview with Lauren Krause

1. How does someone begin the process of determining what they should put on their Web site, what design elements it should have, how navigation should function, and what the overall appearance should be? When starting with a blank HTML document, what steps or techniques would you recommend to get to a finished product?

The first step should be written-down details about what it is you want your Web site to do, like who your target audience is and what you want them to do when they come to your site. It may also be helpful to write down what you want your Web site to say about your company: Are you professional, playful, kooky, serious?

Web design is not as simple as going from blank document to finished product in six easy steps. There is a design-aesthetics side as well as a technical side, and both are equally as important. I would not recommend starting with a blank document if you are unsure what you are doing. It is far too overwhelming.

I suggest going to **www.wordpress.org** and downloading and installing WordPress. Then, you can visit free theme sites and pick what you like, or premium theme sites if you want to have higher quality themes. There are also many Web designers who work on WordPress themes if you want them to customize an existing theme or build you a custom one from scratch.

WordPress started as a blogging platform, but it is far more powerful than that. I have built entire Web sites off it. And it is open-source, which is better than free. Open-source means it is supported by a wide community of passionate users who are always improving it and offering free plug-ins for functionality, as well as free themes to customize the look of the site. There are also people who sell plug-ins and themes, and user support can often be included in these; at the very least, they are usually better products than the free ones.

And pictures are worth a thousand words, right? There are plenty of professional-quality free images out there from sites like Flickr and Stock. XCHNG® (**http://sxc.hu**). When you use Flickr in particular, go to the advanced search options and choose the Creative Commons License option.

Recommended free theme sites:
http://wordpress.org/extend/themes

Recommended premium theme sites:
www.studiopress.com
www.woothemes.com

Recommended sites for design theory:
http://creativecurio.com
http://inspirationbit.com
http://graphicdesign.about.com
http://Webdesign.about.com

Recommended free stock photo sites:
http://flickr.com
http://sxc.hu

2. There are many Web design products available, such as Microsoft FrontPage, Microsoft Expression Web, and Adobe Creative Suite.

For a beginner who wants to have a professional Web site, yet use a fairly simple-to-use Web design product, what would you recommend and why?

Actually, you can edit HTML or PHP with Notepad; you really do not need a complex Web design or development program. That said, I prefer Adobe Dreamweaver, which you can buy separately from the Creative Suite bundle for about $400 (or buy the previous version for about half that).

3. What type of image format do you recommend using on Web sites? There are several different formats, such as GIF, JPEG, and PNG — is there a difference? Is one better than the other?

Yes, there are differences between the Web graphics formats. A general guideline would be:

- GIF for solid colors like logos; supports transparency, but only if the pixel is "on" or "off" — in other words, no 50 percent transparencies.
- JPEG for photos or images with gradients (colors fading smoothly from one to the other). Does not support transparency and has the potential to become very pixelated.
- PNG is a "loss-less" format, meaning there are no compression artifacts like you can have with a JPEG. The problem with the PNG format is that they can turn into very large files. This format also supports alpha transparencies, or having something be halfway transparent.

If you would like more information, I wrote an article about this here: **http://creativecurio.com/2007/10/file-formats-for-images**

If you really like to edit your own graphics for the site, I would suggest Adobe Photoshop Elements (about $100). Or, for some good open-source (free) alternatives, there is GIMP (open-source Photoshop alternative), or

Inkscape (open-source Illustrator alternative), which can both be downloaded online at **www.gimp.org** and **http://inkscape.org**, respectively.

4. *How much should someone spend on Web site hosting? Is there a Web hosting platform or other features we should specifically be looking for? If you were to recommend a Web hosting provider, who would it be?*

If you are not going to have a Web site generating thousands of visits a day, you can use a shared hosting plan as opposed to a dedicated or cloud server. Shared hosting plans usually run about $4.95 to $6.95 per month, and you often pay for a year or more in advance.

Especially if you want to run WordPress, you will need to make sure your server supports at least one MySQL database and runs on a Linux platform instead of Windows — if the features say it has PHP capabilities, it is a Linux host. You also want to make sure it has the latest version of mySQL and PHP. You can ask the sales team for the host you are considering about that — check their answers against **http://dev.mysql.com/downloads** and **www.php.net/downloads.php**; just look at the latest stable version number on those pages and do not worry about anything else.

I personally use **www.BlueHost.com** and have been thrilled with their services. Their customer service call center is based in the U.S., too. Being able to talk to a live person is actually becoming a paid-for add-on for hosting services. Not so for BlueHost; it is included in their very reasonable monthly fee. I have heard good things about DreamHost® and HostGator as well. There are many hosting services that even have one-click installs for WordPress, including BlueHost.

5. *What low- or no-cost options would you recommend for selling products on a Web site, such as PayPal integration or other shopping carts? Is all shopping cart software essentially the same? For a Web site with hundreds of products, what shopping cart software would you recommend? What do you recommend for SSL?*

Online stores and e-commerce is tricky because you are dealing with credit cards and other sensitive information. I recommend you go with a third-party-developed and -hosted solution like a PayPal store or CartManager™ so that this information is stored on another company's secure server instead of your own host.

6. *There are dozens of companies that you can buy domain names from. Is there any company in particular that is better than the others, and why? Is there any advantage to buying several domain name types for my domain, such as .com, .biz, .us, and .net?*

GoDaddy is my No. 1 choice for domain registration. Their rates are reasonable, and the service is easy to use, but they have good customer service just in case, and they have been around a long time, so you can be sure your domain is safe. David Airey, a good friend and fellow designer, had his domain stolen and GoDaddy went well out of their way to help him get it back; how is that for customer service?

I know many hosting services will register a free domain for you, but it is best to have your domain separate from your hosting service in case you ever need to change hosts. You do not want to have the problem of not being able to unlock your domain from your host.

Unless you plan on using other domains or really think a competitor will try to hijack your name on another suffix, I would just stick to the .com version. If you do get the other versions, be sure to redirect them to your main site.

7. *When designing a Web site, we want to ensure compatibility with major Web browsers, such as Microsoft Internet Explorer, Mozilla Firefox, Google Chrome, and others. Do you have recommendations for how to design the site to ensure maximum compatibility and user functionality?*

You are absolutely right that cross-browser compatibility is paramount to good Web design. This is going to be one of those services that you will automatically receive when hiring a professional Web designer. Truth be told, browser testing can be a harrowing and time-consuming issue, and without years of experience or training, it is unlikely that someone would be able to figure out, first, what the problem really is, and second, the hacks and work-arounds required to fix it.

This is just one of the reasons it is of great benefit for business owners to hire a professional Web designer; you leave what he or she does best to him or her (building Web sites), and you do what you do best, which is run your business. Think about the long-term benefits: all those new clients and customers you will reap from a professionally designed and built site.

8. *What is a useful CSS technique that you use often? What is the most common font you use when designing Web pages? What advice can you give regarding Web site navigation?*

Floats are probably the most common element used for structuring Web sites with CSS. They are a difficult concept to understand, and I suggest visiting this site for the best explanations:
http://css.maxdesign.com.au/floatutorial

There are a limited number of fonts you can use on the Web because in order for others to see it, they have to have that font on their computer — you cannot host them on a Web server. For sans-serif fonts, which I recommend for regular text, stick to Arial, Verdana, Trebuchet®, and Century Gothic™. For serif fonts, which I recommend for headlines and maybe navigation, Times New Roman, Georgia, Palatino®, and Book Antiqua™ are safe bets.

Web site navigation should be clear and concise. Use as few words as possible and try not to use any flashy JavaScript menus.

Recommended CSS sites:

http://css-tricks.com
http://cssplay.co.uk

9. A challenge of any new Web site is obtaining search engine rankings. What practical advice can you give to someone with a new Web site to achieve visibility in major search engines?

Register your business with Google Local Business Center. Blogs, because they are frequently updated, can be a great way to gain traffic in long-tail keywords, which are detailed search terms people type in, like "DIY green wedding invitations" instead of a more competitive term like simply "wedding invitations" that you are unlikely to rank well for. When writing, make sure to repeat your desired search terms several times on the page, and use the Keyword Tool from Google (free) to look at what alternatives people have searched for in the past. Also consider your page titles, because those are an important part of a search algorithm figuring out what the page is about. Google is also loving video updates right now, so if you can have an introduction to the site/company by the owner, that would be big points.

If you are extremely concerned with ranking on the first page of a search, you might try using a pay-per-click marketing strategy like Google Ad-Words. But beware — the costs can be extreme for popular keywords.

And track what people are doing on your site and how they found your site with Google Analytics (free and quick to set up).

If you do not have much time to write copy or you want to delegate it to someone inexpensive, try local colleges and universities. Offer to pay a small fee per article, and let the career services department know you would like to hire a journalism student to write copy for you.

Recommended sites for Web copywriting:
http://copyblogger.com
http://www.michelfortin.com

http://www.remarkable-communication.com
http://menwithpens.ca

Recommended sites for SEO and SEM:
http://seomoz.com
www.seobook.com/blog

10. If you could only give three pieces of advice, what would you tell a business or individual as they attempt to build and/or establish a viable Web presence?

- Build a Web site around your organization's goals (drive sales, capture e-mails, and sell products or services) and have your contact information easily accessible from anywhere on the site.

- Be prepared for it to be a time-consuming process and something that will need some dedicated time to maintain and keep up-to-date.

- Your Web site can be a huge source of income and new leads for your company if it is designed properly, and after you have evaluated your goals, it may be worth it to hire a professional designer. Compare the value of a new lead/client/customer to the one-time cost of a professional Web site.

Lauren Krause is a creative consultant and graphic/Web designer whose passion is helping businesses tell their stories better visually and, more importantly, to the right people. She is also the author of a popular graphic design Web site, **http://creativecurio.com***, where she publishes her insights into what makes good design and enjoys sharing her industry experiences with visitors. Lauren has brought value to business owners in international corporations, local small businesses, and non-profit organizations with a wide range of work, including large-format tradeshow graphics, banners, brochures, direct mail campaigns, identity systems, and Web sites. Her work has previously been published in* The Big Book of Green Design, *a compendium showcasing excellence in environmentally conscious design. Lauren may be contacted at* **http://creativecurio. com** *or lauren@creativecurio.com.*

Interview with Kent Lewis

1. How does someone begin the process of determining what they should put on their Web site, what design elements it should have, how navigation should function, and what the overall appearance should be? When starting with a blank HTML document, what steps or techniques would you recommend to get to a finished product?

We always recommend starting the Web development process by setting tiered objectives with associated metrics and benchmarks. The second step is to research the target audience needs and desires, ideally with focus groups, surveys, and card sorts. The next step is to create a site wireframe — how the site will function, where content will be placed, and how the navigation will work. At this stage, we typically assess the current Web site — if available — and that of top-tier competitors in order to determine what the new site needs to do in terms of navigation, content, and functionality. Design should be based both on the brand style guide and search engine optimization best practices, assuming being visible in search results is desirable. Typically, designers produce site templates that then need to be produced into HTML, while programmers develop any back-end functionality like e-commerce, databases, or CMS capabilities. Once the site is in pre-launch (functional HTML, final template design, and copy), each page should be optimized for search results (including title and meta tags) as well as be thoroughly quality-assurance tested to iron out any kinks.

2. There are many Web design products available, such as Microsoft FrontPage, Microsoft Expression Web, and Adobe Creative Suite. For a beginner who wants to have a professional Web site, yet use a fairly simple-to-use Web design product, what would you recommend and why?

Although I am not a Web developer per se, my teams have had the best success with Adobe Dreamweaver (Creative Suite) and WordPress. They are relatively intuitive, flexible, and powerful. WordPress is particularly search-engine friendly as a CMS.

3. *What type of image format do you recommend using on Web sites? There are several different formats, such as GIF, JPEG, and PNG — is there a difference? Is one better than the other?*

As a search engine marketer, I always recommend the cleanest code possible (W3C-compliant), like HTML elements such as CSS, with minimal strategic use of imagery, Flash, and JavaScript, as those elements are not easily indexed or weighted by Google and other search engines.

4. *How much should someone spend on Web site hosting? Is there a Web hosting platform or other features we should specifically be looking for? If you were to recommend a Web hosting provider, who would it be?*

Hosting in general is a commodity. Ensure that the ISP has the bandwidth, security, and redundancy to maximize uptime and accessibility. Also make sure the servers are located in a safe and reliable location, and do not host spam-related sites than can injure your credibility with search engines and corporate firewalls. I recommend EasyStreet®, as they meet the criteria listed above.

5. *What low- or no-cost options would you recommend for selling products on a Web site, such as PayPal integration or other shopping carts? Is all shopping cart software essentially the same? For a Web site with hundreds of products, what shopping cart software would you recommend? What do you recommend for SSL?*

Low-cost e-commerce solutions include Yahoo! Stores, Google Checkout, and PayPal. SSL encryption options are fairly standardized and readily available when setting up a cart. For WordPress, I recommend WP e-Commerce by Instinct.

6. *There are dozens of companies that you can buy domain names from. Is there any company in particular that is better than the others, and*

why? Is there any advantage to buying several domain name types for my domain, such as .com, .biz, .us, and .net?

Like hosting, domain name registration is a commodity business. I recommend GoDaddy, Dotster®, and NameBoy, as they are well-established and reliable. When purchasing domains, a .com is most desirable, and I only recommend purchasing alternative TLDs (.biz or .net, for instance) to protect trademarks and brand names.

7. When designing a Web site, we want to ensure compatibility with major Web browsers, such as Microsoft Internet Explorer, Mozilla Firefox, Google Chrome, and others. Do you have recommendations for how to design the site to ensure maximum compatibility and user functionality?

By designing for the lowest common denominator (W3C-compliant HTML code), you are ensuring optimal compatibility across browsers. Opting for CSS over more advanced languages and scripting is desirable; otherwise, you end up in QA for a longer period of time, and the site is more difficult to manage on an ongoing basis.

8. What is a useful CSS technique that you use often? What is the most common font you use when designing Web pages? What advice can you give regarding Web site navigation?

We recommend HTML for better readability by search engines, and always incorporating basic elements like "Home," "Contact," and "Sitemap."

9. A challenge of any new Web site is obtaining search engine rankings. What practical advice can you give to someone with a new Web site to achieve visibility in major search engines?

The simple answer to achieving visibility in search results for desired terms is to follow the 3 C's of SEO: content, code, and credibility. Start by incorporating keywords into unique and valuable content; designing the site in W3C-compliant code (CSS); maximizing credibility by encouraging inbound links, citations (mentions); and creating an internal link structure that maximizes index ability by search engines. Make sure that your site is hosted on a friendly IP block (ISP) and that you have registered your domain to expire in at least five to 10 years out.

10. If you could only give three pieces of advice, what would you tell a business or individual as they attempt to build and/or establish a viable Web presence?

My advice to a business or individual building a Web presence is to:

- Design the site for the end user (target audience) based on research and customer insights.
- Design the site to be search-engine friendly, following the 3Cs of SEO.
- Maintain and market the site. Keep content fresh and augment organic search visibility with pay-per-click advertising and social media marketing.

As President of Anvil Media, Inc., Kent Lewis is responsible for managing operations, marketing, and business development to achieve the search engine marketing agency's mission: to build Anvil into the one of the most respected search engine marketing agencies in the world. He is also founder and acting President of Formic Media, an SEM agency focusing on the small business market. Kent is also co-founder and former President of SEMpdx, a trade organization for SEM professionals based in Portland, Oregon. In 2001, Kent created pdxMindShare, an online career community and Portland-area networking event. He is also an adjunct professor at Portland State University, where he teaches e-marketing and SEM workshops. Kent is a member of EO, a global organization for entrepreneurs, and is a recipient of Portland Business Journal's Top 40 Under 40 Award. Kent can be contacted at kent@anvilmediainc.com or www.anvilmedia.com.

Interview with Joy Brazelle

1. How does someone begin the process of determining what they should put on their Web site, what design elements it should have, how navigation should function, and what the overall appearance should be? When starting with a blank HTML document, what steps or techniques would you recommend to get to a finished product?

Before starting with the HTML document, think about what the goals of the Web site are. Do a competitive scan to see what is out there. Create a list of pages you think you can create for the site's initial launch, as well as a long-term plan to grow your site and enhance content. From that, group the pages into logical categories and create a sitemap. You can draw the sitemap on paper, or use Word or Visio to create an electronic version. Once you have the sitemap complete, create wireframes, which are simply visual representations (no creativity is necessary) that show all of the elements on the page.

2. There are many Web design products available, such as Microsoft FrontPage, Microsoft Expression Web, and Adobe Creative Suite. For a beginner who wants to have a professional Web site, yet use a fairly simple-to-use Web design product, what would you recommend and why?

Dreamweaver seems to have the most robust functionality to build a professional-looking Web site. However, regardless which tool you select, you will have to have some basic (to more advanced) HTML skills, or at least HTML resources. All WYSIWYG tools have shortcomings. Tables get messed up, formatting gets broken. The only way to fix these issues will be to look in the HTML code, find what is wrong, and fix the bad HTML. A good resource that has been around for a long time is **http://htmlgoodies.earthWeb.com**.

3. *What type of image format do you recommend using on Web sites? There are several different formats, such as GIF, JPEG, and PNG — is there a difference? Is one better than the other?*

I would recommend using JPEG for most images. The formats PNG and GIF are good for situations in which you need higher-resolution images. Often, files that someone would download (a property map or company logo, for example) are in the higher-resolution formats.

4. *How much should someone spend on Web site hosting? Is there a Web hosting platform or other features we should specifically be looking for? If you were to recommend a Web hosting provider, who would it be?*

There is not a need to spend a lot of money on hosting unless you receive a lot of traffic, need almost 100-percent uptime, or have security concerns beyond the normal e-commerce type site. That said, you get what you pay for. For less than $10 (often less than $5) per month, you can get decent hosting with companies like GoDaddy.com. I personally am wary of free hosting sites because in my experience, there is always some catch. One company got blacklisted from Google because their "free" hosting company engaged in black hat SEO, which refers to tricks designed to fool the search engines into ranking their sites higher than they should be.

5. *What low- or no-cost options would you recommend for selling products on a Web site, such as PayPal integration or other shopping carts? Is all shopping cart software essentially the same? For a Web site with hundreds of products, what shopping cart software would you recommend? What do you recommend for SSL?*

If a company is spending money on marketing online and they want to offer their clients a great checkout experience (one page), Volusion® is the company that I would recommend. Their solution price ranges from $30 per month to $200 per month, depending on how many products you have, and bandwidth. There is a discount on the first month and a onetime set-up fee. There are other less expensive (and possibly free, like osCommerce) options, but the user — or shopper — experience is not as good; most can be quite clunky, some do not offer tech support, and their tracking capabilities are often lacking.

For SSL, I would recommend acquiring that through GoDaddy.com. One note about getting an SSL certificate — it is always more legwork in the initial process than one would expect. You need very specific business documentation. Make sure to allow a few days, at least, to gather all the necessary documents and information; do not wait until the day before your site goes live to think about getting an SSL certificate.

6. There are dozens of companies that you can buy domain names from. Is there any company in particular that is better than the others, and why? Is there any advantage to buying several domain name types for my domain, such as .com, .biz, .us, and .net?

GoDaddy.com is where I have purchased domains over the last few years. I would highly recommend it. Their domain management tools are very easy to use. You receive reminders when domains are expiring, or you can set them to auto renew. Their technical support service is beyond compare. It is actually a pleasure dealing with their support staff, which is saying a lot. My only complaint — and it is a non-issue, really — is that they run pay-per-click ads on domains that are parked with them, but do not give the domain owners any of the profits from these sites.

If you can get the .com or .net version of the URL, that is generally the best — for users as well as for SEO purposes. It will be interesting to see if the flexibility of any top-level domain (such as www.yoursite.yourcompany) will actually come to pass.

7. When designing a Web site, we want to ensure compatibility with major Web browsers, such as Microsoft Internet Explorer, Mozilla Firefox, Google Chrome, and others. Do you have recommendations

for how to design the site to ensure maximum compatibility and user functionality?

The key to ensuring maximum cross-browser compatibility is to ensure your HTML code is well-written and properly formatted. Bad, malformed HTML will almost always break in other browsers. Historically, IE was the most forgiving for badly coded sites, but it is less forgiving now — or maybe there are just a lot more poorly coded sites out there. Also, important to note is that not all visitors are as sophisticated as you would expect (or hope). Bells and whistles are less important than good design for usability. Also, do not assume that everyone has the highest resolution screens available. Do homework to see which resolutions are the most popular: **www. w3schools.com/browsers/browsers_display.asp**.

8. *What is a useful CSS technique that you use often? What is the most common font you use when designing Web pages? What advice can you give regarding Web site navigation?*

Although I do not have extensive experience with CSS, I would recommend keeping the font definition big, simple, and sans-serif, such as Arial or Helvetica. Do not assume that people can read small text — make it at least an 11-point font. Navigation should be obvious, with links blue and underlined. Web site navigation should be above the fold, consistent, and easy to use. Flash and DHTML navigation can be hard for some visitors to use. Pages should not link back to themselves — your logo should link to your home page on every page except your home page.

9. *A challenge of any new Web site is obtaining search engine rankings. What practical advice can you give to someone with a new Web site to achieve visibility in major search engines?*

The best advice I ever heard for SEO was, "What is good for human experience is good for the search engine spiders." Make your Web site easy for a non-technical, non-savvy visitor to navigate, and you will reap the rewards with the search engines. Have meaningful content on each page. Each page should have a limited number of keywords that appear often enough in the content to be relevant, but not so much that it makes the content confusing or hard to read. One of the biggest helps for a new site is to sign up for the Webmaster tools (Google and Bing™) and take advantage of the tools and advice they offer.

10. If you could only give three pieces of advice, what would you tell a business or individual as they attempt to build and/or establish a viable Web presence?

- Do not assume your visitors will be as Web-savvy or as interested in you or your company as you might think. Make your site easy to navigate, quick to load, interesting, and visually appealing.

- Pay attention to Web analytics. Google Analytics offers a wealth of great knowledge for free. Use the reports to get a handle on what is working and what is not.

- Web sites are always a work-in-progress. Once you launch your site, the job is not done. You need to keep the content updated, promote your site, and continually improve it based on what you find in your Web analytics.

Joy Brazelle is currently Director of Product Marketing and Client Services at ClearSaleing, an advertising analytic software company. As such, she gets to spend her days with her two professional passions — analytics and helping customers spend money more wisely by making informed decisions. She has made analytics her priority over 10 years, helping clients build and improve their online presence. Joy has been a member of the Web Analytics Association since its launch in May 2006. Joy can be contacted at jbrazelle@gmail.com.

Interview with Joe DiDomenico

1. How does someone begin the process of determining what they should put on their Web site, what design elements it should have, how navigation should function, and what the overall appearance should be?

When starting with a blank HTML document, what steps or techniques would you recommend to get to a finished product?

The first thing you need to do is form an objective. What do you want your Web site to do? The overall appearance depends on your objective. For example, if you are an artist, your Web site should reflect your particular genre and style and have lots of cool imagery. Or, if you are offering information for research, then you should probably avoid the fluff and get straight to the point. Once you have your objective and basic appearance guidelines, then you can get started laying out your page.

To begin your page layout, I recommend creating a simple page using HTML tables and cells with plain text inside the cells. Most of us Web designers now design for a screen resolution of 1024 x 768. This is currently the most popular screen resolution. This means your HTML document should be no wider than 975 pixels across to accommodate for the scroll bars and have a little bit of a margin. Never make your viewers scroll from side to side.

Keep your page simple and familiar. By this, I mean put your navigation in an area that folks are familiar with. They will be more apt to click around if they do not have to think about how to do that. Do not put your navigation in a place that is hard to find. I recommend using the header and/or left side of the page for navigation. You should think about your Web page as having four sections: header, navigation, body, and footer. Keep it simple, and your viewers will appreciate it.

I highly recommend learning the Adobe Creative Suite, especially Photoshop. You would be surprised at how much you can do in Photoshop alone. It will even write the HTML for you, then you can manually edit it. Make sure you keep image file sizes to a minimum for fast load time. You do not want to keep your visitors waiting for pictures to download. Remember, there are still a lot of folks still using dial-up connections.

2. There are many Web design products available, such as Microsoft FrontPage, Microsoft Expression Web, and Adobe Creative Suite. For a beginner who wants to have a professional Web site, yet use a fairly simple-to-use Web design product, what would you recommend and why?

You can create a Web site using products that are already installed on most computers today. Any word processing program like Notepad will do the trick. However, this method requires you to know how to write HTML from scratch. I highly recommend learning the basics of HTML and have the ability to write from scratch. Then, progress to using an HTML editor that has color-coding and code validation. Color-coding makes it easy to find different elements inside your code. Code validation assures you of having valid HTML, which is a great start to having an SEO-friendly Web page.

And again, I highly recommend using Photoshop for most, if not all, of your Web site designing. It will do almost anything you want it to and is not difficult to learn. You can cut up your design into slices and export it as a Web page. It writes clean HTML, and you have all kinds of choices of image compression. The downside is it is a little pricey. I use it exclusively for my images. I export the HTML and then manually edit it for proper display on all browsers and, of course, use proper SEO techniques and CSS.

I use a great HTML editor called HomeSite, which is now an Adobe product. It used to be a Macromedia product, and I still use their version. I love it for the color-coding, automatic tag insight, and excellent code validation. It even has FTP ability, so you can work on your site directly on the server. It also comes bundled with TopStyle Lite, which is a great CSS tool.

Never use Microsoft Word to create a Web page. This is absolutely the worst way to create Web pages. It writes terrible HTML, and the size of your HTML files will increase tenfold, making your site very slow to load.

Let us quickly talk about Flash. This is an awesome program that is very powerful. However, I never recommend building a site completely in Flash. Unless you are a Flash guru, this makes editing your Web site much more difficult. And, the search engines are still not very good at indexing Flash. I recommend using Flash animations in strategic places on your site. Make sure the animations are subtle and add to your design. Do not make your animations a distraction, and make sure the file size is small so your viewers are not waiting for it to load. And never create an "Intro" page. This not only annoys the heck out of me, but it has been proved to be ineffective and chases people away from your Web site.

3. What type of image format do you recommend using on Web sites? There are several different formats, such as GIF, JPEG, and PNG — is there a difference? Is one better than the other?

It is quite easy to determine which image file format to choose for each image you want to display. You basically have three image formats, and here are some simple guidelines to follow. I am all about keeping it simple:

1. GIF should be used for an image that contains solid colors only. This format will handle transparencies, but not very well. Stick to the solid color images when using this format.

2. JPEG should be used for images that are not solid and use lots of colors, such as photographs. There are different levels of compression that can be used to make sure the file size is reasonable. Each graphics program has its own compressions settings. Test a few images before deciding which ratio of compression versus file size looks best to you. Most images in JPEG format can be kept below 100k in size. Ideally, you should keep each image below 50k. If you have images that are more than 100k, you should rethink how you are saving your file. Make sure you are using a good level of compression — use 72 DPI and RGB format (not CMYK).

3. In my opinion, PNG files should only be used if the image you are displaying requires transparency for one reason or another. PNG files handle transparencies very well, but the file sizes can get large if you are not careful.

4. How much should someone spend on Web site hosting? Is there a Web hosting platform or other features we should specifically be looking for? If you were to recommend a Web hosting provider, who would it be?

This really depends on your objective, but for the context of this book I would recommend using a shared server on any one of many reputable Web hosts such as GoDaddy, Yahoo!, Lunarpages, or HostGator. For the most part, they all offer the same basics: disk space, bandwidth, e-mail addresses, domain registration, and SSL.

If you are building an e-commerce Web site, I recommend going with a plan that includes Linux, MySQL, and PHP because they are the most economical, and there are lots of great free open-source products written for this configuration. Most Web hosts will include shopping carts on this platform for free. I do not recommend using a Microsoft server for several reasons:

1. Web hosting plans are more expensive.
2. Shopping cart software is expensive.
3. Hackers love to hack Microsoft servers.

5. What low- or no-cost options would you recommend for selling products on a Web site, such as PayPal integration or other shopping carts? Is all shopping cart software essentially the same? For a Web site with hundreds of products, what shopping cart software would you recommend? What do you recommend for SSL?

Here is a great way to get started with e-commerce:

1. Purchase a Web hosting plan from GoDaddy with Linux, MySQL, PHP, and SSL. (No, I am not a GoDaddy reseller. I have had good results and good support from these folks for the past few years and my clients seem to like them.) If you want better service with faster server speed, they have good virtual server plans for business that start around $150 per month.

2. Install the free shopping cart software called Zen Cart and learn how to use it. Install a template and customize it. Populate it with your products. You can easily add and edit an unlimited amount of products (including product images), categories, and sub-categories.

3. Offer two methods of payment for your customers: PayPal and a standard credit card method. You will need to purchase a payment gateway service that handles the credit card transactions and makes the deposits to your business bank account. I recommend using Authorize.Net. They are the most popular, and their support is very good. PayPal is rapidly becoming the payment method of choice for many customers. If you do not offer this method, you are losing a lot of sales. Zen Cart easily integrates with all of the above and more. Test, test, test using a real credit card, and get used to the process before going live with your Web site.

4. Look through the "Free Software Add-Ons" section of the Zen Cart Web site for any special features you want to add. There are many contributions I am sure you will want to add. Make sure you add features that keep with your objective. Do not add too much fluff, as it will only cause you problems. I love Zen Cart because you can always add more features to your site as it grows, and there are lots of resources on their forum and lots of great programmers willing to help you.

6. There are dozens of companies that you can buy domain names from. Is there any company in particular that is better than the others, and

why? Is there any advantage to buying several domain name types for my domain, such as .com, .biz, .us, and .net?

I always recommend purchasing your domain through the company you choose to host your Web site; this makes life a lot easier. But make sure you do not fall for the tricks of some of those not-so-recognizable Web hosts. Some will actually purchase the domain in their name, and you never actually own it. Stick with the known brands such as the companies I mentioned above. They are ridiculously cheap, so to try and save a measly $50 per year is simply not worth the risk. Let us use the GoDaddy example. They charge less than $10 per year for domains, and less than $10 per month for Web hosting. That is less than $100 per year for your Web site. Why would you want to risk going with an unknown if your fee is just $100 per year?

As far as purchasing other top-level domains (.biz or .tv, for instance), I think it is only necessary if you think your Web site will become so popular that someone else will purchase your domain with these TLDs. If you are a small local business, there is no need to purchase these, in my opinion. I would always try to stick with a .com address, as this is the most popular and most folks automatically use .com when typing a Web site URL.

7. When designing a Web site, we want to ensure compatibility with major Web browsers, such as Microsoft Internet Explorer, Mozilla Firefox, Google Chrome, and others. Do you have recommendations for how to design the site to ensure maximum compatibility and user functionality?

If you use a quality HTML editor with code validation and proper CSS, your Web site should look relatively the same across these browsers. Each browser has its own nuances, and I highly recommend installing and testing your Web site on all these browsers. The browsers are getting much better at rendering things similarly, but you may be surprised at how some of your pages may look completely different, especially if you use fancy CSS in your pages. If you have installed a shopping cart like Zen Cart, you really will not have to worry too much about the browsers rendering your pages differently because most of the templates have already been tested in each browser before being offered.

If you wrote the HTML yourself, I highly recommend using CSS, as it makes it much easier to deal with fonts. If you start getting fancy with the CSS, then you will need to pay closer attention to testing in the different browsers. Some may not render certain elements properly, and you may need to add additional lines or "hacks" to the CSS code.

8. *What is a useful CSS technique that you use often? What is the most common font you use when designing Web pages? What advice can you give regarding Web site navigation?*

First, let me answer the question about type of font: Use Verdana and/or Arial, period. Do not ever use any fancy-looking font. The fonts used on HTML pages are being pulled from the viewer's machine. So, chances are they do not have the same fancy font as you do, and their computer will automatically choose another font. You never want that. Verdana and Arial are installed on every personal computer, and they have been proved to be the most legible and easiest on the eyes when reading on a computer monitor. I never recommend using a serif font like Times; this font is better suited for print.

CSS is perfect for managing fonts and great for creating navigation because it eliminates the need to create images for rollovers, for example. And, it makes it much easier to add and/or edit your navigation because you are editing text rather than images. I like to use CSS to create drop-down menus that use the HTML **<ul>** and **<li>** tags. You can really make them look great across all browsers. Do some research on this and have some fun making your own.

9. *A challenge of any new Web site is obtaining search engine rankings. What practical advice can you give to someone with a new Web site to achieve visibility in major search engines?*

Ah, the search engines. Is there a magic pill? No. I always start by telling my clients that Google updated their search algorithm more than 400 times in 2008. That is more than once per day, so do not fall for the false guarantees of the so-called SEO companies. If you build your site using proper HTML and do not use any tricks to try to get better search engine placement, you are off to a good start.

The old phrase "content is king" still applies. The more quality content and pages you have on your Web site, the better your SEO. Make sure you have quality content, and you are not filling your pages with text just to have content. If you are not a good writer, I recommend using a service like Amazon Mechanical Turk. You can get some very well-written content at very cheap prices.

Here are some simple tips when writing your own HTML for proper SEO: Always use a well-written **<title>** and closely matched **<h1>** tag on each page. Below is an example. Notice how they are not exactly the same but very close.

Example title tag:
<title> Hardwood floor repair & restoration, Orlando, FL</title>

Example H1 tag:
<H1> ABC Hardwood - hardwood floor repair & restoration</H1>

Do not get too wordy, and make sure you use keywords that you think your audience will use to search for you. Try to use a maximum of 50 to 60 characters in these. The rest of the textural content should be wrapped in a **<p>** tag. Again, make sure you are using good keywords in the copy. Try to have at least one, preferably two, paragraphs of well-written, keyword-rich text on your home page. This is a good foundation to start from.

Some other simple ways to improve SEO is to add **<alt>** tags to all your images with well-written descriptions. Try to use keywords in your navigation links. Use bulleted lists when possible to highlight areas of importance; search engines like bulleted lists when they are written using proper HTML. Link appropriate keywords in your copy and bulleted lists to other pages on your Web site.

I see a lot of Web sites that have a ton of text content on their home page that scrolls forever. They may get good SEO placement, but I think it turns a lot of people off when there is too much information on one page. I think you should strategically create as many pages as you can to house your content, and make sure all of the pages are linked from your home page somewhere. This way you can be assured that search engines will index all your pages.

Of course, do not forget to submit your site to the search engines. Most search engines allow you to submit your site for free. Do not worry: If you submit your site to Google only, most of the other engines will find you sooner or later.

Here is a tip. Most of the time, your business will be focusing on a general demographic area, such as a large city you live in or near, or maybe an entire state or tri-state area. You get my point. Make sure you use these keywords on your pages. Most folks looking for local businesses will use the local town, city, or state in their searches. This also makes your SEO work a little easier, because you have now substantially reduced your search engine competition.

10. *If you could only give three pieces of advice, what would you tell a business or individual as they attempt to build and/or establish a viable Web presence?*

- Make sure you go with a reputable Web host.
- Make sure your HTML is written properly.
- Make sure your site is easy to navigate.

Start with this foundation. As you get more experience, you can add more sophisticated methods, including content writing, affiliate marketing, or search engine advertising.

And always stay on-track with your objective.

*Joe DiDomenico started designing Web sites in 1997 for a startup dot-com company called Internet Products International. In 2002, he became the Webmaster for the parent company, AH&LA. Joe started his company Embryo Design in 1997 as a part-time hobby to make some extra cash. He decided to give it a go on his own in 2007 and has not looked back. Joe recently partnered with Pet Nutrition Products (**www.petnutritionproducts.com**). Since he became their Webmaster, they have seen a 300 percent growth in revenue in about 18 months and continue to grow at a steady rate. Joe's specialty is helping small startup companies design professional, easy-to-use, SEO-friendly Web sites. You can view his portfolio online at **www.embryodesign.com**, and you can contact him at joed@embryodesign.com.*

Interview with Jeff Davis

1. How does someone begin the process of determining what they should put on their Web site, what design elements it should have, how navigation should function, and what the overall appearance should be? When starting with a blank HTML document, what steps or techniques would you recommend to get to a finished product?

Before any consideration of look and feel, the first step in designing a Web site is to ask yourself, "Why do I want a Web site?" Is it to reach a larger audience for your product or service? Is it to better inform new or existing clients about you? The answer can consist of multiple reasons, but whatever it is, it should lead you to identifying your target audience. Your site must be designed to appeal to that audience.

The trick is to divorce yourself from the idea that the site is for you; to be effective, it needs to be designed for the audience you want to attract. Ask your existing customers, or those you think might fit into your chosen demographic, what they expect and what makes a good Web experience for them. Most likely, you will hear the following over and over: easy-to-understand navigation, not too cluttered, and common practices followed — if it is underlined, it should be a link. Whatever you discover, keep those points in mind when you write your site.

It is the content on your site that matters most, so write your site — every page, every word. You then design your site to fit and accentuate the content. Too often, people have a specific look in mind, and they try to cram the necessary content into that format. Write it down on paper. It is much less frustrating to go through a notebook, crossing things out or tearing out pages, than it is to try and code a page off the top of your head.

Once you have a plan, it is time to design it. Consistency is key, and each page should look like it belongs with the rest of the site. The home page is your front door, among millions of other front doors, so knowing what your audience wants and expects is critical to getting them to choose yours.

Some basic ideas to consider are:

- Red means action, passion, excitement — but too much of it can be scary.
- Pastels are good to calm and soothe — great for enticing people to read or choose from a large set of items.
- Warm colors are great for products like foods and wines.
- Cool colors are great for clinical or professional services.
- Your logo is important for brand identity, but not more important than the person looking at it.
- If you want people to view your catalog, make sure the link to it says "Catalog." People are busy, and they will not spend time trying to figure out a convoluted description.

2. There are many Web design products available, such as Microsoft FrontPage, Microsoft Expression Web, and Adobe Creative Suite.

For a beginner who wants to have a professional Web site, yet use a fairly simple-to-use Web design product, what would you recommend and why?

For many folks who are used to working in a word processor or office suite of tools, Microsoft FrontPage is a good first Web tool. It works like what you are used to using and will help guide you as you learn. Like most MS products, it tries to help too much and adds a lot of unnecessary elements to your HTML code.

Adobe Dreamweaver is the end goal. Rich and robust, with a comprehensive set of tools and supporting programs, Dreamweaver will give you the opportunity to find the keys to the kingdom without bloating your code.

3. *What type of image format do you recommend using on Web sites? There are several different formats, such as GIF, JPEG, and PNG — is there a difference? Is one better than the other?*

Graphic image formats can be confusing. Just remember that each format has its best uses. Images that are in the GIF format are created to display flat, solid color areas, like cartoons and illustrations. Images that are in the JPEG format are images that allow for colors to blend across each pixel, resulting in a smoother transition between colors, which are great for photos and faces, provided that the quality settings are not too low. The coolest thing about PNG images is that they bring with them an alpha channel, which allows for transparency within the image. This will alleviate the rectangular constraint of images on a page and allow the background to show through the transparent areas.

4. *How much should someone spend on Web site hosting? Is there a Web hosting platform or other features we should specifically be looking for? If you were to recommend a Web hosting provider, who would it be?*

The prices for hosting packages range from free on sites like GoDaddy, to hundreds of dollars a year for enterprise-sized solutions. Research is your friend here. Determine what you need in the way of server storage space — HTML is tiny, but video and imagery can get big fast — and functionality. Most hosting companies offer a range of price plans, and most give you way more tools than you will ever need. The hidden cost is downtime. If the server is down, your site does not work — and that costs you money in lost sales. Look for the hosting companies that proudly display their uptime.

5. *What low- or no-cost options would you recommend for selling products on a Web site, such as PayPal integration or other shopping carts? Is all shopping cart software essentially the same? For a Web site with hundreds of products, what shopping cart software would you recommend? What do you recommend for SSL?*

When you are just starting out, PayPal, Yahoo! Shopping, and Amazon Z-Shop can all be a good solution for your shopping cart needs. They handle the security and processing and are pretty good about offering the tools you will need. You will pay a percentage on each sale, but that will be true with just about any service you use. You can code a shopping cart widget into your site and password-protect it, but really, do you want to?

6. *There are dozens of companies that you can buy domain names from. Is there any company in particular that is better than the others, and why? Is there any advantage to buying several domain name types for my domain, such as .com, .biz, .us, and .net?*

The hosting company you choose will most likely offer you a domain name with your package. They are all simply brokers. Domain names are regulated by InterNIC, the international consortium that controls the master lists of domains. No matter where you buy it, that is who you are buying it from. You should be able to get a domain name for free, or nearly free, as part of your hosting package.

If your name or service is really distinct, you may want to snap up the other extensions to avoid confusion, but right now, .com is king.

7. When designing a Web site, we want to ensure compatibility with major Web browsers, such as Microsoft Internet Explorer, Mozilla Firefox, Google Chrome, and others. Do you have recommendations for how to design the site to ensure maximum compatibility and user functionality?

Test, test, test. When building your site, test each page on as many platforms as possible. Most Web browsers will work running on all the popular operating systems, so download them and run them all. Test your color choices, table structure, and images in each of them, and identify those features that work well across the board. Of all the major browsers, IE has the most trouble working and playing well with others, but about 40 percent of the users on the planet are looking at your Web site with Microsoft Internet Explorer, so suck it up and make sure your site works when viewed with it.

8. What is a useful CSS technique that you use often? What is the most common font you use when designing Web pages? What advice can you give regarding Web site navigation?

CSS allows you to use a common set of rules for multiple pages regarding fonts, spacing, and colors. It can be tricky when you are just starting out, but its usefulness cannot be ignored, especially on a large site with many common elements. There are tons of user forums and code example sites on the Web (Google lists more than 95 million returns on "CSS help"), chock-full of people who know this stuff inside and out, and they are usually more than happy to help with a problem or question. With a little tweaking, their code can become your code.

When you are choosing fonts, there are two things to consider: readability and usability.

The easiest text for humans to read is a black serif font on a white background (500 years of book printing bears this out) for large blocks of text, and sans-serif fonts for headlines and headers. The farther away you go from this by adding background colors or wacky fonts, the harder it becomes to read until you get to full reversed text, which is white words on a black page. Seems easy at first glance, but your viewers' eyes will get tired long before they come to the end of your text.

The second thing to remember is usability. Your audience uses a browser to build your Web page when it is served from the host server. That means that their computer rebuilds the page, element by element. If you use a font that they do not have on their computer, the user's computer will substitute its own default font. On most Windows systems, this is Courier™, the most ugly font there is. Your carefully crafted Web site will be at the mercy of an overly large, badly spaced, table-structure-destroying letter set that will make your site look like, well...just do not go there.

Stick to the basics: Times New Roman, Georgia, Verdana, or Arial. These have equivalents on most computers and will retain your page's look and feel.

9. A challenge of any new Web site is obtaining search engine rankings. What practical advice can you give to someone with a new Web site to achieve visibility in major search engines?

SEO is a business that has sprung up around the idea that if your site does not show up on a search engine's first page of returns, then you cannot reach your customers. There is a valid argument for this thinking, but take heart: There are other ways to achieve your goals. You can hire a company or use a service that will generate AdWords and meta tags to help your rankings, but this may not be the approach your business needs. If your company provides a local service (one that places a geographical limitation on your customers), they will search your name or company name and find you anyway. If I need a tree service, for example, where they rank in a Google search is far less important than their ranking in a local directory.

Reach out to the many local and regional directories in your area, and get your link placed there. Network with others in your field or in complimentary businesses, and agree to link to each other's site. The more reciprocal links your site has, the better your traffic flow will be.

10. If you could only give three pieces of advice, what would you tell a business or individual as they attempt to build and/or establish a viable Web presence?

- Understand your customers' needs.
- Build your site for them, not you.
- Three clicks to the money. If your site sells a product or in any way drives a customer to a sale, get them to page where they pay you in three clicks or less.

As an Art Director for IBM's Internet/Multimedia center in Southbury, Connecticut, Jeff had the good fortune to work with some of the brightest people in the new media business at a time when the Internet and the World Wide Web were first being embraced by some of the world's best-known companies. In 2002, Jeff began his freelance career as a Web designer and multimedia producer. Today, JD Savage Productions has many clients in both the commercial and municipal sectors in the areas of Web development, new media, broadcasting, and video content production. You can contact Jeff at jd@jdsavage.com.

Interview with Deborah Gallant

1. How does someone begin the process of determining what they should put on their Web site, what design elements it should have, how navigation should function, and what the overall appearance should be? When starting with a blank HTML document, what steps or techniques would you recommend to get to a finished product?

I take exception to the question. You cannot build a Web site unless you are dead-clear on what the business is all about and the goals of the Web site. The call to action for a site that is intended to sell something to a Web visitor would be substantially different than what you would need if you were a service professional — like an accountant or chiropractor — where your goal is to interest a site visitor enough to pick up the phone and call.

2. There are many Web design products available, such as Microsoft FrontPage, Microsoft Expression Web, and Adobe Creative Suite. For a beginner who wants to have a professional Web site, yet use a fairly simple-to-use Web design product, what would you recommend and why?

I am biased on this one. My company sells a Web site builder that was designed for a novice with no technical ability to build and maintain their own Web site. The company is currently re-branding itself, but it has been known to date as Web Power Tools. If you have enough technical ability to write a document in Word or send an e-mail, you have all the ability and knowledge you need to create your own professional Web site.

3. What type of image format do you recommend using on Web sites? There are several different formats, such as GIF, JPEG, and PNG — is there a difference? Is one better than the other?

Our system uses JPEGs.

4. How much should someone spend on Web site hosting? Is there a Web hosting platform or other features we should specifically be looking for? If you were to recommend a Web hosting provider, who would it be?

Web hosting should be bundled with your package. Our system is $99 per year for hosting, maintenance, and support.

5. What low- or no-cost options would you recommend for selling products on a Web site, such as PayPal integration or other shopping carts? Is all shopping cart software essentially the same? For a Web site with hundreds of products, what shopping cart software would you recommend? What do you recommend for SSL?

For rank beginners, using PayPal as both your merchant account (so you can accept credit cards) and your shopping cart is probably all right. I work closely with a firm called Practice Pay Solutions (**www.practice paysolutions.com**) that sets up merchant accounts for solo professionals and is a reseller of 1ShoppingCart, which I recommend to my clients. One of the reasons I like it is that it is expandable, and you can get more features as the complexity of your business grows.

6. *There are dozens of companies that you can buy domain names from. Is there any company in particular that is better than the others, and why? Is there any advantage to buying several domain name types for my domain, such as .com, .biz, .us, and .net?*

I like GoDaddy and am an authorized reseller for them. I recommend getting a .com address if at all possible; it is still the gold standard. If you want to protect your name, you can buy the other variations to try to protect yourself, but it is not always necessary.

7. *When designing a Web site, we want to ensure compatibility with major Web browsers, such as Microsoft Internet Explorer, Mozilla Firefox, Google Chrome, and others. Do you have recommendations for how to design the site to ensure maximum compatibility and user functionality?*

Test, test, test. Ask your provider if they are compatible.

8. *What is a useful CSS technique that you use often? What is the most common font you use when designing Web pages? What advice can you give regarding Web site navigation?*

Do not use CSS; it is built right into the system. Tahoma is my personal favorite, but some people prefer traditional serif fonts like Times New Roman. And regarding site navigation: Think like your site visitors and put things in an orderly, logical naming convention that makes sense to them.

9. A challenge of any new Web site is obtaining search engine rankings. What practical advice can you give to someone with a new Web site to achieve visibility in major search engines?

Patience. If you do all the right things — solid, changing content; good keywords that people are searching for; and links into and out of your site, along with a submitted sitemap — you just need to let the Internet do its magic. You should think long and hard before paying anyone for a search campaign and make sure you can justify it monetarily.

10. If you could only give three pieces of advice, what would you tell a business or individual as they attempt to build and/or establish a viable Web presence?

- Be clear on what your business is and why you are building your Web site. All the other decisions flow from that.
- If at all possible, keep control of your Web site so that you are not held "hostage" by your Web designer, and so that your Internet marketing can keep up-to-date with the changes and evolution of your business.
- Get a good enough Web site. In most cases, a small business owner is still going to make the majority of his/her income from their traditional lines of business, so it does not make sense to spend thousands of dollars on a too-fancy Web site that does not create paying customers.

Bold Business Works was launched in early 2009 when Deborah Gallant integrated her many business ventures under one powerful brand. By combining her coaching practice (known as Lifework Catalyst) with her do-it-yourself Web site builder (Web Power Tools), entrepreneurs can now find all the training, support, and tools for success in one place. Deborah was an early Internet pioneer, starting Journal Square Interactive (JSQ), *a division of Advance Publications, and then working for a startup (FamilyPoint) that was subsequently acquired by iVillage, the women's Web site. In 2001, Berkley Books published Deborah's book,* Internet Jobs For the Rest of Us, *a book about adapting job* *skills and knowledge to the Internet industry. Deborah was awarded the Education Advocate of the Year award by the National Association of Women Business Owners in 2005. You can contact Deborah at info@boldbusinessworks.com or **www.Webpowertools.com**.*

Interview with David Gadarian

1. How does someone begin the process of determining what they should put on their Web site, what design elements it should have, how navigation should function, and what the overall appearance should be? When starting with a blank HTML document, what steps or techniques would you recommend to get to a finished product?

The first place to start is from a place of passion or necessity — either you are really into something, or you have a pre-existing business that is in need of a Web presence. There is a ton of work involved, and it at times has been very frustrating. Without the passion, I would have been hard-pressed to see **www.MostMost.net** through to the stage I have taken it to.

Start out with a series of diagrams — draw out the site once, then spend time thinking about how the navigation works, where you want people to go, and what you want them to do once they have gotten there; then, draw it out again. There is a pretty good book called *Don't Make Me Think!* by Steve Krug. This book did a great job of really orienting my mind to the task at hand — building a site with the end user in mind. Again though, before diving in, make sure you have a good wireframe to work from.

Additionally, in my case I was not familiar with HTML, so there was a great learning curve I had to overcome. But before diving into that, another great book I eventually found was *Creating a Website* by Matthew MacDonald. I wish I had found this book much earlier as it explained really basic things like what an FTP is and how to actually get an FTP to work — I use FileZilla, which is open-source and free to use.

In terms of design, I would suggest spending time looking at other sites to get a sense of what is interesting to people, but many of the Web 2.0-looking sites will be hard to achieve without outsourcing, and I do not think I would sacrifice functionality for design. Also, make sure the load time of your site is not too long, as this will encourage people to leave before they ever actually make it to your site.

WordPress is another great resource, and in addition to helping to maintain control over your content with a solid CMS, WordPress also has a huge list of pre-existing free templates and plug-ins to help enhance your site. WordPress is also free, but you can hire other developers to help build a WordPress site. Most importantly, there is a huge community surrounding WordPress, and they are very active in helping one another out.

2. There are many Web design products available, such as Microsoft FrontPage, Microsoft Expression Web, and Adobe Creative Suite. For a beginner who wants to have a professional Web site, yet use a fairly simple-to-use Web design product, what would you recommend and why?

KompoZer is what I use. Unlike the one you mentioned, KompoZer has — from what I gather — most, if not all, of the above functionality, but it is also open-source, free to use, and has a fairly active community helping to maintain it.

One great attribute of this tool is you can pull down existing sites and go beyond simply "view page source" to get a really good sense of the design of places you like — in terms of learning how to do things, this is very helpful. Another free tool is GIMP, which is an open-source photo editing tool in the vein of Photoshop.

3. How much should someone spend on Web site hosting? Is there a Web hosting platform or other features we should specifically be looking for? If you were to recommend a Web hosting provider, who would it be?

I use GoDaddy, and to be honest, I have never had reason to go elsewhere. As my site ramps up, we will see if my existing hosting package is still sufficient, but I have a shared hosting plan for $7 per month.

In addition, every time I have called them, they have been exceptionally helpful. I know some more Web-savvy people have had less nice things to say about GoDaddy, but I have had a really good experience with them so far, and given how little I know about things, I have had plenty of occasion to call them as a result of my own lack of understanding.

4. There are dozens of companies that you can buy domain names from. Is there any company in particular that is better than the others, and why? Is there any advantage to buying several domain name types for my domain, such as .com, .biz, .us, and .net?

In theory, the reason to buy multiple domain names is if you get to be a big success, you are protecting your initial investment. I tried to buy MostMost.net a while back, and it just was not a realistic conversation. In terms of companies, I have only bought domain names through GoDaddy, and I have been happy with the experience. I believe I got MostMost for something like $12, and then $7 a year — I recall $84 being the total to have the site registered in my name for the next 10 years.

5. When designing a Web site, we want to ensure compatibility with major Web browsers, such as Microsoft Internet Explorer, Mozilla Firefox, Google Chrome, and others. Do you have recommendations for how to design the site to ensure maximum compatibility and user functionality?

The way I have done it is by downloading the browsers and going to my site using them. I am sure there are better ways to do this. If you outsource your design, you should make sure that part of the final delivery includes cross browser compatibility, and it is pretty standard. Also, if you outsource, you might consider adding mobile compatibility to the list of final deliverables — there might be an added charge, but mobile seems to be gaining steam.

6. *What is a useful CSS technique that you use often? What is the most common font you use when designing Web pages? What advice can you give regarding Web site navigation?*

http://matthewjamestaylor.com/blog/equal-height-columns-cross-browser-css-no-hacks

Matthew James Taylor has some of the best and most useful tutorials that I have found in terms of using CSS to make sure your site formats correctly.

7. *A challenge of any new Web site is obtaining search engine rankings. What practical advice can you give to someone with a new Web site to achieve visibility in major search engines?*

Still too soon to tell, but it is all challenging. WordPress offers up a number of free plug-ins to help with SEO, but from what I have gathered, the key elements are inbound links and relevant content.

The most practical advice would be to not be too focused on SEO initially and instead to concentrate on building the site and putting together specifically relevant content.

8. *If you could only give three pieces of advice, what would you tell a business or individual as they attempt to build and/or establish a viable Web presence?*

The best advice I read was from Jason Calacanis, and he quoted someone else in saying something to the effect of, "Launch early and update often, rather than focusing on getting it absolutely perfect out of the gate." Once I internalized this, I felt much more at ease letting my site go live.

Spend lots of time reading, especially if you are doing the design yourself — there are tons of blog posts out there and user groups within a number of social networks that will have very specific info and answers to your questions.

The downside of creating my own site was there was — and still is — so much to learn, but some of the upside is that it cost me my time but not my money. More importantly, I know where the bodies are buried on my site, which has allowed me to feel much more comfortable with the back end, and as the site continues to evolve, I will be in much better shape to confront new challenges and to adjust the site accordingly.

*David Gadarian founded and runs MostMost, a site dedicated to providing a digital snapshot of each day from a broad range of sources. MostMost represents David's first foray as a Web-based entrepreneur. David headed the television series department at Parkchester Pictures since its inception in August 2003 through 2008. While working with Parkchester, David set up more than 20 scripted projects for development for buyers, including CBS, NBC, The CW, TBS, Showtime, and FX. From February 2008 through May 2008, concurrent with his duties at Parkchester Pictures, David also served as Director of Business Development at **www.LiquidGeneration.com**, a leading animation Web site featuring irreverent humor geared to young adults, overseeing deals with partners including Yahoo! and MySpace. David can be reached at davidgadarian@mostmost.net; additionally, you can view MostMost at **www.mostmost.net**.*

Interview with Maria Pia Celestino

1. How does someone begin the process of determining what they should put on their Web site, what design elements it should have, how navigation should function, and what the overall appearance should be? When starting with a blank HTML document, what steps or techniques would you recommend to get to a finished product?

Gathering information is, to some, the first step to building their Web site, but really, the first step is to find out the information your clients and prospects want to find on your Web site. Once this information is targeted, gathering may begin.

In order to define the look and feel of their Web site, a company must have a professional logo and corporate image. If they do not, then this would be the first step. If you are not a designer yourself, you may be better off hiring a professional for this one; you will be stuck with your logo for a long time, so you need to make sure it makes your company look relevant and important. No matter the size of the business, when I am structuring and designing a Web site for my clients, I recommend them to look at the biggest guys in their industry, such as what colors, styles, and type of pictures they use, what their content is. What is their approach?

Then, we begin taking what is best from each and create our own concept. As far as actually designing the Web site, we create the concepts in Photoshop and then create the HTML using CSS and HTML. But this process can be tedious for a non-Web-savvy person, so in some cases, less is more. For my clients who have no knowledge at all, I would recommend to skip the Photoshop part and create something simpler directly in the HTML editor such as Dreamweaver or FrontPage, or use a template or customized blog to create their Web sites. The important point is that whatever you choose to do, the site is clean, organized, and current.

2. There are many Web design products available, such as Microsoft FrontPage, Microsoft Expression Web, and Adobe Creative Suite. For a beginner who wants to have a professional Web site, yet use a fairly simple-to-use Web design product, what would you recommend and why?

Adobe is the industry standard used by professionals. Even though it may sound intimidating, I find it more organized and easier to use for the average user.

3. What type of image format do you recommend using on Web sites? There are several different formats, such as GIF, JPEG, and PNG — is there a difference? Is one better than the other?

It depends. JPEGs are the most used because their compression rate is very good and they tend to keep really high quality, even at high compressions rates. JPEGs cannot have transparent backgrounds.

GIFs are used when you need movement or transparent backgrounds. GIFs are compatible with all Internet browsers, and their compression rate is great, but sometimes their quality is a bit grainy and cannot be used for higher-quality images.

PNGs are used when you need high-quality and transparent backgrounds. PNGs have an issue with Internet Explorer 7 where their transparent areas show cyan, so they need a fix on the CSS to appear correctly. The fix can be found online, but it is an extra complication.

4. How much should someone spend on Web site hosting? Is there a Web hosting platform or other features we should specifically be looking for? If you were to recommend a Web hosting provider, who would it be?

Web hosting can go from $5 to $10, $25, and more; again, it depends on the type of Web site. Most personal and small business sites will be all right with $5 to $10 hosting.

I recommend hosting with Linux cPanel only because the administration is very user-friendly, so the users can add e-mail accounts, check stats, install SSL certificates, and more.

5. What low- or no-cost options would you recommend for selling products on a Web site, such as PayPal integration or other shopping carts? Is all shopping cart software essentially the same? For a Web site with hundreds of products, what shopping cart software would you recommend? What do you recommend for SSL?

The most cost-effective option is to set up a page with your products and a link to PayPal on your own Web site. There are Web sites online that generate and customize the PayPal buttons for you.

Instead, if what you need is a store with customer and order databases, then you must know that all shopping carts are not created equal. There are as many options as you can think of, but the important points are that your cart is search-engine friendly, user friendly, versatile, that it has some type of marketing tool, is versatile, and that it has a good system to control your orders and customers. Many shopping carts lack a good administration of orders, turning obsolete when your business grows and needs to process tens, hundreds, or thousands of orders per day.

Preferably choose a shopping cart provider that will give you access to the files; you will soon find out that there is no perfect system and you will want to make changes to it. The cheapest shopping carts, like the ones from GoDaddy or Yahoo!, are like a lease; you will not have access to making changes the files. For this you will need to purchase your shopping cart.

It is always good to test drive a shopping cart before making your final choice.

6. *There are dozens of companies that you can buy domain names from. Is there any company in particular that is better than the others, and why? Is there any advantage to buying several domain name types for my domain, such as .com, .biz, .us, and .net?*

GoDaddy is my top option; the price and service is pretty much the same on all companies, but GoDaddy excels in customer support for domain name registration (not so much for hosting, though). You can call GoDaddy at any time of the day, and they will have qualified personnel to help and guide you. Most of the time, they will do stuff for you like changing name servers or updating your information.

7. When designing a Web site, we want to ensure compatibility with major Web browsers, such as Microsoft Internet Explorer, Mozilla Firefox, Google Chrome, and others. Do you have recommendations for how to design the site to ensure maximum compatibility and user functionality?

Always design for Firefox, as it is the browser that respects standards the most. Then, after building your Web site under the standards, you will need to check browser by browser and tweak whatever fix you may need to do. Hopefully, if you have done everything right and designed a simple Web site, you may not need to fix much.

8. What is a useful CSS technique that you use often? What is the most common font you use when designing Web pages? What advice can you give regarding Web site navigation?

We use CSS to build our Web sites; a few techniques we use usually are: DIVs and CSS, pure CSS menus (great for SEO), customization of forms, CSS bar graphs, and CSS lists.

The most common font we use is Arial, but lately we have been using Tahoma or Verdana.

The Web site navigation must always be intuitive of the content you will find and must be always visible. Visitors get annoyed when they do not know how to get back to a page.

9. A challenge of any new Web site is obtaining search engine rankings. What practical advice can you give to someone with a new Web site to achieve visibility in major search engines?

Search engine optimization depends on two things: relevancy and popularity. If you are building a Web site, make sure that you are relevant to your important keywords; be repetitive and even redundant. Have your keywords everywhere. When your site is finished it will be relevant, so you will only need to worry about marketing your site to make it popular. With these two ingredients combined, your Web site will be found in the first results of search engines.

10. *If you could only give three pieces of advice, what you would tell a business or individual as they attempt to build and/or establish a viable Web presence.*

- Before you do anything, make sure your corporate image is professional. This is the base of the perception others will have about your business. Save on everything except corporate image; you will be glad you hired a professional.
- If you cannot hire a professional to build your Web site and decided to build it by yourself, check what the big companies on your area are doing. It will help you design your own site and keep it professional.
- On your free time, post free ads with links to your Web site. It will help people find you online and create links back to enhance your search engine optimization. If your site is not No. 1 in Google yet, your ad may show up and drive you traffic.

*Maria Pia Celestino founded **www.Crea7ive.com** in June 2006. With almost 10 years of experience designing Web sites and an impressive portfolio, she is currently the head project manager and designer at the company. Crea7ive.com has been internationally recognized by the high quality, originality, and versatility of its work, being awarded by different organizations and ranking as the second-best Web design company in the country by the top independent search engine optimization authority, **www.topseos.com**, in April and May 2009. Crea7ive.com provides custom solutions for corporate branding, high-end Web design, 3D, motion graphics, and organic SEO. Maria can be contacted at info@crea7ive.com.*

Interview with Aaron Guldberg

1. How does someone begin the process of determining what they should put on their Web site, what design elements it should have, how navigation should function, and what the overall appearance should be? When starting with a blank HTML document, what steps or techniques would you recommend to get to a finished product?

What we do at the very beginning of our engagement with our clients is find out why they want a Web site, what the purpose is behind having it built, and what goal or goals they think having a Web site helps them achieve. We also try to get them to define what success would look like with their site in six months and in a few years. We do this because a Web site is not something you check off the list — it evolves as your business evolves.

Doing this helps you focus on what you need to have as a part of your site today and think about what you may add later to the site, so that as you implement version one of your site, you have a plan for the future and can build your Web site and navigation structure in a way that will support it when you are ready.

Once you know that, it is about organizing the content in a manner that is easy and logical for a person to find. One of the best ways to go about doing this is to use a silo approach. The term "siloing" originated as a way to group related information into distinct sections of a Web site. Much like the chapters in a book, a silo represents a group of themed or subject-specific content on your Web site. This approach works well, as grouping your content together in this manner creates relevancy in the search engine's eyes and additionally makes it easier for people to navigate and find the information they are looking for on your Web site.

When it comes to how to lay out your navigation and the look of your Web site itself, keep it simple. Visitors expect to find navigation either at the top or on the left side of the site — this is something you do not want to vary from, or users will have potential customers finding their way through your Web site. Most people who start a new Web site use some sort of template design for their site, and there is nothing wrong with that, as long as you personalize it to fit your purpose. The goal is to pick a design that reinforces the brand you are starting to build and does not distract your potential customer from learning more about what you have to offer and take the next desired step, whether that is downloading a white paper, contacting you through your contact page, or purchasing your product from your Web site.

2. There are many Web design products available, such as Microsoft FrontPage, Microsoft Expression Web, and Adobe Creative Suite. For a beginner who wants to have a professional Web site, yet use a fairly simple-to-use Web design product, what would you recommend and why?

It really depends on what type of budget and time a person had to invest in building their site. FrontPage, Expression Web, and Adobe Dreamweaver are three products that all have WYSIWYG editors that can effectively build a Web site if you plan out your site ahead of time. I do not believe FrontPage is offered anymore, as it was replaced by Expression Web recently, which just improved upon the existing FrontPage product. Dreamweaver is a good product as well but is geared a little more toward developers versus someone just starting out to build their first Web site, in my opinion. If money matters, Dreamweaver is a more expensive product as well, so you need to keep that in mind. In addition, individuals who are already familiar with Microsoft Office will have a little less of a learning curve with Expression Web. Thus, for someone starting out, I think Expression Web would be a better choice.

3. What type of image format do you recommend using on Web sites? There are several different formats, such as GIF, JPEG, and PNG — is there a difference? Is one better than the other?

The two image formats I mainly use when designing Web sites are GIF and JPEG files.

The GIF format is one of the most popular formats on the Internet. Not only is the format excellent at compressing areas of images with large areas of the same color, but it is also the only option for putting animation online — unless you want to use Flash or other vector-based animation formats, which typically cost more.

GIF files support a maximum of 256 colors, which makes them practical for almost all graphics, including logos, line drawings, and icons. Avoid using it for photographic images and graphics that have long stretches of continuous tone in them.

The JPEG format, with its support for 16.7 million colors, is primarily intended for photographic images. As a rule, the JPEG format should be used on photographic images and images that do not look as good with only 256 colors.

The PNG format is supposed to bridge the gap between these two other formats, but to my knowledge is not fully supported at this point — thus we do not use it with our clients.

4. How much should someone spend on Web site hosting? Is there a Web hosting platform or other features we should specifically be looking for? If you were to recommend a Web hosting provider, who would it be?

How much you should spend on your Web site really is a product of what capabilities you need to implement your Web site. If you are building a personal Web site, you might consider trying to find the cheapest host out there, because if there is a little downtime, it is not the end of the world. However, if you are running a business Web site, especially one that offers e-commerce, it needs to be up 24/7, and I would want great customer support that I can get a hold of at the drop of a hat that can fix my problem.

You will find hosts that offer Windows plans and Linux plans. If you are just using HTML, JavaScript, and CSS files, you can actually use either type. Linux tends to run a little less expensive than Windows-hosted plans.

However, if you have any programming done, such as a contact form that e-mails you information, you need to look a little more closely at the file extension of the files that perform that functionality, as .php files only run on Linux-hosted plans and .aspx files only run on Windows-hosted plans. In addition, if you are using anything that needs FrontPage extensions, you need to be on a Windows-hosted plan.

Other factors to consider as you are selecting a host are your future needs and if your host can support you if you decide that later on you want to add a database, need increased bandwidth, or want to add shopping cart capabilities to your site down the road. It is pretty painful to switch from one host to another, and has to be done in a very specific order to avoid significant downtime for your Web site in this process. Thus, you only want to do this when you absolutely have to.

As far as who do we recommend, we work a lot with HostMySite (**www. hostmysite.com**) for hosting the majority of our clients, as they are well–set up for not only people who are just starting up; they have plans and solutions that allow you to continue to grow as your business does, have great customer support that have given us great advice as needed, and have helped us through a number of issues throughout the years.

5. *What low- or no-cost options would you recommend for selling products on a Web site, such as PayPal integration or other shopping carts? Is all shopping cart software essentially the same? For a Web site with hundreds of products, what shopping cart software would you recommend? What do you recommend for SSL?*

If I was going to sell products through a Web site and was just starting out, I would definitely recommend utilizing PayPal as using their Web site payments standard solution. Normally when you set up e-commerce on your site, you have to get a merchant account (basically a bank account), have a payment processor to process the credit cards, a gateway to send the funds to your bank account once paid, and an SSL certificate to make sure that this entire transaction was safe. To set this up, you are normally dealing with a number of different companies, all of which have either annual fees or monthly minimums and transaction fees so you are in the hole without ever knowing if your product will even sell.

PayPal is a payment processor, and by creating an account with them, upon verifying your identity through a number of checks, it lets you link an existing bank account with them at no charge, thus fulfilling the merchant account and gateway need. Any funds received will sit in your PayPal account, and you can transfer them to your normal bank account without any additional charge. With their Web site payment standard solution, whenever someone adds something to a shopping cart, buys now, or views the cart, they are redirected from your site to PayPal using PayPal's SSL certificate; thus, you do not have to have a certificate on your Web site, which is another cost savings. The only thing you pay for is a transaction fee of around 3 to 4 percent when someone completes an order, but there is no monthly overhead of having this capability on your Web site.

The downside to this is it obviously is not as smooth as having it all on your own Web site, and while they do offer a little bit of customizing to make it look a little more branded with your Web site, it is quite clear you have left and are on PayPal's site. The good news is PayPal is recognized and trusted throughout the globe, so it does not hurt the confidence of those who are there to complete the order.

If you go down this road, you need to create a business account, which is free to do. A personal account will not have all the functionality you need.

PayPal does offer a Web site Payments Pro version that has a monthly fee in addition to a little cheaper transaction fee. The main difference in this version is it allows you to host the entire shopping experience from the user's perspective on your Web site, which is a good goal to strive toward once you have proven your product has a market and are getting predictable traffic and sales through your Web site to make that investment worthwhile.

As far as other shopping carts, they all come in different shapes and sizes, and it really depends on what you need it to do for your site. Some are more focused with delivering electronic goods, where others are better at handling physical products and backend inventory and reporting. The one I hear is good is a company called 1ShoppingCart (**www.1shoppingcart. com**), but I know there are a lot of players in this space, including some open-source options, so you will want to do some research. It is a good idea to try to get a demo or a free look to make sure they will fit your specific need before committing your business to a specific shopping cart solution.

If you are going to process credit cards directly on your Web site, you definitely need an SSL certificate on your site. Some hosting companies will offer the option to buy an SSL certificate through whom they have an arrangement with. You will need to weigh if that is a viable alternative for what you need versus getting one through a company like VeriSign, whom everyone knows and trusts.

6. There are dozens of companies that you can buy domain names from. Is there any company in particular that is better than the others, and why? Is there any advantage to buying several domain name types for my domain, such as .com, .biz, .us, and .net?

You really can get a domain name from a number of sources. You can get them from Register.com or GoDaddy, and a lot of the hosting companies will allow you to register a domain name at the same time you are securing hosting. In my experience, Register.com is more expensive than other places you can get the same domain name. With GoDaddy, you have to be careful as you are going through their registration process, or you may inadvertently have some additional fees added to your cart for what should be just a simple domain name registration. If you decide to register your domain name with your hosting company, just make sure your information is on the domain name itself and not the hosting company so you do not have any issues transferring the domain to another location should you have issues with the host. The last thing you want is to have a hosting company hold your domain name hostage. The best practice is to keep the domain name with a different company than the hosting. The downside is you then have to not only keep track of your hosting bill, but also your domain name, and you will have to make the changes to point your domain name to your hosting company if you keep them separate. Thus, it is not really that one is necessarily better than another — it is more about your comfort level.

As far as how many types of a domain name to buy, we recommend, at a minimum, registering the .com, .net, .org, and .biz versions of your domain name once you find a domain name that works for your company. It is more about protecting your potential brand with the mainstream extensions. The last thing you want to do is find out six months down the road someone is now promoting a competing product using the your company. net domain name that you could have simply prevented by spending an extra $10.

7. When designing a Web site, we want to ensure compatibility with major Web browsers, such as Microsoft Internet Explorer, Mozilla Firefox, Google Chrome, and others. Do you have recommendations for how to design the site to ensure maximum compatibility and user functionality?

The easiest way is just to follow HTML and CSS standards. Expression Web actually has some of that compliance checking within it. In addition, you can download the latest Firefox and Google Chrome to make sure everything looks relatively the same. They do all act slightly different, especially when you look at your site in older versions of Internet Explorer. There are free places online that you can view snapshots of a given page on various browsers so you do not have to have a bunch of machines lying around with different Internet browsers installed on them.

8. What is a useful CSS technique that you use often? What is the most common font you use when designing Web pages? What advice can you give regarding Web site navigation?

Best tip I have with CSS is there is a plug-in for Firefox called Firebug that will let you inspect and change CSS on a given page on the fly, which is extremely handy when troubleshooting alignment or display issues.

Fonts are really client-specific — I try to lean them to either Arial, Times New Roman, or Verdana because all machines (both Mac and PC) have these fonts installed as a part of their OS. There are a few others that are cross-platform, but those three have the best readability of the approximately eight fonts that come standard on both Macs and PCs. Although I think I covered this in a previous question, the best advice I have for navigation is to keep it simple.

9. A challenge of any new Web site is obtaining search engine rankings. What practical advice can you give to someone with a new Web site to achieve visibility in major search engines?

Assuming the Web site has been architected correctly, you need to start a link-building campaign to build links to your Web site.

Visibility takes time, and Google is not the only way to get traffic to your Web site — start promoting your Web site using both online and offline channels so people know that it now exists.

10. If you could only give three pieces of advice, what would you tell a business or individual as they attempt to build and/or establish a viable Web presence?

- A Web site is not something you do and check off a list. To do it right, it is an investment, and it will continually evolve as the business does.
- Once your site launches, put Google Analytics — it is free — on your Web site so you can gather data on your Web site traffic

and make educated decisions on how to improve your site. Your visitors will tell you what is wrong with your site by how they interact with it.

- For a business site, focus on building traffic and conversions, not rankings. I have yet to meet a search engine that had a credit card, so focus on getting people to your Web site and continually improving your sales funnel to generate more leads and sales via your Web site.

*Over the last 10 years, Aaron Guldberg has developed a passion for designing effective Web sites. In that time, he has amassed an impressive number of Web solutions for individual Web sites, corporate intranets, and business-to-business applications, as well as consumer e-commerce objectives. Having had the opportunity to work on a number of artist Web sites, startups, and small businesses over the years, Aaron realized that no one is really focused on helping these clients succeed online. Critical Exposure was formed to address this market need and specializes in working with such clients to achieve their goals by not only building and improving upon their Web sites, but also providing them with sound advice on how to better market their products and services online. Aaron may be contacted at info@criticalexposure.com and **www.criticalexposure.com**.*

Interview with Frank Moten

1. How does someone begin the process of determining what they should put on their Web site, what design elements it should have, how navigation should function, and what the overall appearance should be? When starting with a blank HTML document, what steps or techniques would you recommend to get to a finished product?

Your starting point should be to consider that you are presenting, selling, or bragging.

1. Less is more, especially when you are new.

2. Focus directly on the goal — think getting dressed for an interview or cleaning house for a guest.

3. Look at some other sites of people or companies you admire.

If you find your skills, software, or time fall short, just appreciate the navigation and where they go with content.

2. There are many Web design products available, such as Microsoft FrontPage, Microsoft Expression Web, and Adobe Creative Suite. For a beginner who wants to have a professional Web site, yet use a fairly simple-to-use Web design product, what would you recommend and why?

Of the major products today, Expression Web 3 is by far the best. The Adobe design products have always been more complicated and difficult to publish than they should be. The only concern could be cost; in that case, really any editor (such as CoffeeCup) can get you started and through your first years.

3. What type of image format do you recommend using on Web sites? There are several different formats, such as GIF, JPEG, and PNG — is there a difference? Is one better than the other?

This question requires care. If you have a quality image editor such as Photoshop or the more affordable Photoshop Elements, follow these rules: Photos should be JPEGs at 72 DPI, and use the Photoshop "save for Web" option, saving at the lowest percentage that the image still looks perfect to your eyes. A pixelated image is a loser in any industry. Graphics and logos should be in GIFs started at about 100 DPI. If you are using the software for a digital camera, just try to keep them clean and less than 150k.

4. How much should someone spend on Web site hosting? Is there a Web hosting platform or other features we should specifically be looking for? If you were to recommend a Web hosting provider, who would it be?

Well, if I did not run a Web hosting company, I would want to spend $7 to $10 as an individual or a new business. The best OS is Unix; variations from that would really only come from applications like e-mail. Web servers are very reliable, and most companies do a good job 24/7/365. But when something goes wrong, will they care about you? Some companies figure, "Why sweat $90 a year?" Make sure you have a host that you can call any time of the day or night, as a trouble ticket waiting for 12 hours when you have a business prospect looking at your site simply will not cut it. The best host in the world is **www.ourgig.com**.

5. What low- or no-cost options would you recommend for selling products on a Web site, such as PayPal integration or other shopping carts? Is all shopping cart software essentially the same? For a Web site with hundreds of products, what shopping cart software would you recommend? What do you recommend for SSL?

If we are talking a beginner and little cost, you are looking at a hosted solution. I would always suggest **http://mals-e.com**, since you can get all the features you will need and installed software as you grow. The cheap SSL certificates that I would suggest are from **www.thawte.com**, if we are not talking little or no money.

6. There are dozens of companies that you can buy domain names from. Is there any company in particular that is better than the others, and why? Is there any advantage to buying several domain name types for my domain, such as .com, .biz, .us, and .net?

Really, Register.com or GoDaddy are perfect registrars. Let us just say for the individual, there is really no substitute, and your key factors are accessible support, protections, and control.

7. When designing a Web site, we want to ensure compatibility with major Web browsers, such as Microsoft Internet Explorer, Mozilla Firefox, Google Chrome, and others. Do you have recommenda-

tions for how to design the site to ensure maximum compatibility and user functionality?

The same standard: less is more, use something like Microsoft Expression Web, and, of course, try out other browsers as you build.

8. *What is a useful CSS technique that you use often? What is the most common font you use when designing Web pages? What advice can you give regarding Web site navigation?*

I think 99 percent of surfers like Verdana. For navigation, keep to six or seven top-level items and not too many sub-levels. Try placing non–revenue generating information in the footer.

9. *A challenge of any new Web site is obtaining search engine rankings. What practical advice can you give to someone with a new Web site to achieve visibility in major search engines?*

Make sure your home page text speaks to what you are doing — top engines check. Have text links available to key pages, and make sure that if you code keywords, they are really in your site content. List your sites in relevant directories and other sites. Where possible, take advantage of several online tools — most are different and help you in various ways. Google search for terms like: "check my Web site," "check my HTML," and "speed-test my Web site." You will learn and grow much more than just installing something.

10. *If you could only give three pieces of advice, what would you tell a business or individual as they attempt to build and/or establish a viable Web presence?*

- Do not overload your site with useless info, images, clip art, and JavaScript effects.
- Only publish what looks good to you and perhaps a close friend. If you cannot make something look right online, it is better to say, "Call us or e-mail for more on…"

- Practice, revise, practice.

*Frank Moten was born in New York City and raised in Englewood, New Jersey. Frank's closest neighbor was the great jazz man Dizzy Gillespie, and over the next decade and with Dizzy's support and guidance, Frank pursued his music career, appearing at venues like Carnegie Hall, the Apollo, and the Beacon Theater. Frank decided to combine his love for music and business with his technical expertise. Frank saw the kind of impact the Internet was having on the entertainment industry and realized that it could be a beneficial tool for emerging entertainers as well. Frustrated by the badly designed, overpriced Web sites that existed for independents at the time, Frank founded **www.OurGig. com**. Combining his professional experience with his vast knowledge of the entertainment industry, Frank is now able to provide new artists and entertainers with a highly visible, professional Web presence. You may contact Frank at services@ourgig.net or on the Web at **www.ourgig.com**.*

Interview with Navin Ganeshan

1. How does someone begin the process of determining what they should put on their Web site, what design elements it should have, how navigation should function, and what the overall appearance should be? When starting with a blank HTML document, what steps or techniques would you recommend to get to a finished product?

You can create an attractive and valuable Web site in 10 easy steps:

1. **Start with your audience:** You know your business inside and out; your audience does not. Make sure that your Web site clearly communicates what your business is and what you offer.

2. **Plan your online image:** Definitely think about the image you want your Web site to portray. The look and feel should match your offline business and its mission.

3. **Make your color scheme pleasing and appropriate**: Using too many different colors can distract from your design. Choose up to four main colors in your color palette and stick with them consistently throughout your site. Make sure your colors match or complement your logo and are appropriate for your business. For example, red might be an unappealing color for a financial business.

4. **Do not switch fonts**: Maintain consistency with one or two fonts. Think about the Web sites you visit. Different fonts, sizes, styles, and spacing distract your audience from what you are trying to say. Hint: Do not use all capitals and italics or switch font colors. Pick one font/style/color for your headlines and one for your text, and use it on all pages.

5. **Think readability**: Reading text on a computer screen is different from reading text on paper. Avoid long paragraphs or blocks of text. Keep your writing concise and on message.

6. **Post contact information on every page**: Customer service is the leading reason for customer loyalty. Make sure your audience knows how to contact you wherever they are on your site.

7. **Plan your navigation**: Make the structure of your Web site logical and easy to navigate. Do not lose credibility with broken links or too many pop-up screens. You should provide a link to your home page from every sub-page to keep customers from getting lost. A search feature can help customers get the information they need quickly and easily.

8. **Fast-loading sites convert the most sales**: Limit the number and size of graphics. Users will not wait forever for a graphic to load and will abandon your site. Consider people visiting from a dial-up connection or from a mobile device and ensure that pages load quickly.

9. **Help customers find your Web site**: Determine and use appropriate keywords and meta tags to make sure your Web site comes up on popular search engines. Think about words your audience will type into a search. Make a list and use these frequently.

10. **Keep your content fresh**: Many businesses set up a great Web site, but then forget about it for months on end. If content is not updated regularly, search engines (and customers) will assume your site is dead. Also, maintaining a blog page on your site can be a great way to express yourself and also attract attention to your business.

2. There are many Web design products available, such as Microsoft FrontPage, Microsoft Expression Web, and Adobe Creative Suite. For a beginner who wants to have a professional Web site, yet use a fairly simple-to-use Web design product, what would you recommend and why?

If you do not have the time, Network Solutions has a team of graphic designers who are educated in Web 2.0 design standards, understand the basic design rules for successful Web sites, and know how to add the creative punch to make your Web site stand out from the crowd.

3. What type of image format do you recommend using on Web sites? There are several different formats, such as GIF, JPEG, and PNG — is there a difference? Is one better than the other?

Different standards allow for different levels of quality and features in an image. But for basic images and graphics, any of these formats will work just fine.

4. How much should someone spend on Web site hosting? Is there a Web hosting platform or other features we should specifically be looking for? If you were to recommend a Web hosting provider, who would it be?

You should not spend more than $30 per month on Web hosting. For Web hosting, I would recommend Network Solutions. At 99.99 percent, our Unix uptime rating is the best it gets. And our secure servers are continuously monitored for potential hacker activity as well as performance, so you can feel confident that your Web sites are always up and running.

5. *What low- or no-cost options would you recommend for selling products on a Web site, such as PayPal integration or other shopping carts? Is all shopping cart software essentially the same? For a Web site with hundreds of products, what shopping cart software would you recommend? What do you recommend for SSL?*

Shopping carts are definitely not all the same. Some companies like Yahoo! Small Business, eBay ProStores®, and WebStore by Amazon will charge an additional fee for every sale you make, and others only support certain payment methods or gateways.

Network Solutions' e-commerce solution does not charge per transaction, and it works with numerous payment gateways to give you the most flexibility. Secure transactions will bring you peace of mind — Network Solutions is also a leading provider of SSL certificates.

6. *There are dozens of companies that you can buy domain names from. Is there any company in particular that is better than the others, and why? Is there any advantage to buying several domain name types for my domain, such as .com, .biz, .us, and .net?*

Network Solutions is a pioneer of domain name registration. We developed our system in 1993 and currently offer the most wide-ranging list of general extensions (gTLDs) and country-specific extensions (ccTLDs) of any domain name registrar.

7. *When designing a Web site, we want to ensure compatibility with major Web browsers, such as Microsoft Internet Explorer, Mozilla Firefox, Google Chrome, and others. Do you have recommendations*

for how to design the site to ensure maximum compatibility and user functionality?

As far as design, it should be clean and crisp, making sure every page is easy to read, and should follow a logical reading path for both the human eye and the search engine spider.

8. A challenge of any new Web site is obtaining search engine rankings. What practical advice can you give to someone with a new Web site to achieve visibility in major search engines?

Step one in your search engine optimization plan is to identify a target key phrase. This key phrase should have high traffic, low competition, and market viability. The Google Keyword Tool is a great place to find key phrases that meet these criteria. Step two is to build a Web page around that phrase, including it — or a slight variation — in each of the key on-page elements: title tag, meta description, meta keywords, header tags, and body copy.

One of the most common Web site characteristics that can hinder search engine rankings is when the title tag of each page of your site is the same, such as your company name. Each page on your Web site should have a unique title tag that represents the content on the page. For example, instead of a page title like "John Doe Communications, Inc.," create a title that represents exactly what the page is about. Something like, "Discount phone systems — John Doe Communications."

9. If you could only give three pieces of advice, what would you tell a business or individual as they attempt to build and/or establish a viable Web presence?

It is critical to remember that you have a small window of opportunity to make your site compelling enough for a person to stay focused on it. Make it as simple as possible for someone to find and read the messages that you want to communicate. The more a person needs to click on a site to find what they are looking for, the less likely they stay and become a customer.

As the senior director of the Web Presence product line, Navin Ganeshan is responsible for Network Solutions' Web site, hosting, e-commerce, and security products, and for finding new ways to help small businesses get online. Navin's previous roles at Network Solutions include managing the engineering team that developed the company's Web site product and later managing data strategy and business intelligence as the Director of Enterprise Data Services. Prior to Network Solutions, Navin managed the development of online insurance ratings products for Tower Street as a subsidiary of AMS. Throughout his career, Navin has spoken at many industry conferences, participated in standards bodies such as ACORD, and most recently spoke about customer relationship management and campaign modeling at the Dreamforce 2008 conference.

Interview with Tammy Schultz

1. How does someone begin the process of determining what they should put on their Web site, what design elements it should have, how navigation should function, and what the overall appearance should be? When starting with a blank HTML document, what steps or techniques would you recommend to get to a finished product?

Before you start designing a Web site, you must determine the site's function, determine who your target market is, determine the search terms you want the site to appear under, and decide how visitors will navigate the site.

Site function: A Web site basically has three functions: to attract new clients, to support current clients, or for online sales. A site can do all three, but each one requires specific items to be present.

A new client will want to know what you can do for them, where you are located, how to contact you, and what makes your company different. This is a first impression. A current client knows who you are but needs to be reminded of the services or products you offer. He or she also needs to be informed of new services or products and any specials you are running.

For online sales, the site needs to be selling on every page. Similar to a grocery store placing chocolate chip cookies next to the milk cooler, you need to create a "need to have it now" or "impulse" feel to your site.

Target market: You should know who your target market is. If you do not know who is buying your products or services, how can you market to them? You might be able to sell to anyone, but what demographics are most likely to buy from you? You are looking at things like age, gender, income level, location, and type of business. The design of your Web site needs to cater to your target market.

Let us say that you sell video games. Your target market would be males between the ages of 16 and 30. What is it that they want? They will want access to new games, demo games, perhaps secrets to playing games. How about a way for them to connect with other gamers? They want entertainment. However, if you are selling hearing aids, your market is totally different. Now, you are selling to people in their 50s, 60s, and 70s. These people did not grow up with computers; they are not used to them and are not looking to be entertained. They want information and answers to their hearing problems. They want a site that is easy to read and navigate; they are also looking for customer service.

Search terms: You should have an understanding of the search terms people will use when looking for sites similar to yours on search engines. Web site content is the most important element in determining where a site appears on search engines. Without pertinent content, a Web site will not place well.

That content needs to include your search terms. Keep in mind that these search terms should be what potential clients are using, not what you would use. These are often very different. Not sure what they will use? Do some research. Ask current clients what they would search for if they were looking for your company today. Ask your sales team what products or services people are asking them for. If you are a local business, your location should be part of your search terms. Another thing to think about is narrowing your text to more specific things. For example, if you sell cuckoo clocks, you should be using cuckoo clocks and not just clocks.

Navigation: Map out your Web site. Most of us would not take a week-long trip without an idea of where we are going. The same should be true of your Web site. Create an outline of all the pages you want to have on your site. I recommend that you work on this outline for two to three days. Do a little, then come back to it. This list becomes your wishlist if time and money do not matter. After a few days, you can let reality set in and say, "OK, I only have X amount to spend. What can I do for that?" Now, you can select what is most important, and you also have a plan for phase two and phase three.

Once you have determined what will be on the site, think about how people will navigate it. Keep in mind that the site will grow, and you want to ensure your navigation will grow with it. People look for navigation at the top or on the left-hand side. Because your site is a marketing tool and the purpose of it is to sell your products or services, do not make it difficult for people to navigate it. Keep things simple and easy to use — a Web site navigation system is no place to be "cute."

2. ***What type of image format do you recommend using on Web sites? There are several different formats, such as GIF, JPEG, and PNG — is there a difference? Is one better than the other?***

That all depends on what the image is and what it is being used for. Each image type has their benefits and disadvantages. A JPEG is great for photos, as you can get a high-quality image at a reasonably small file size. However, if the image needs to have any transparency, a JPEG will not work, as they do not support transparency. If an image requires transparency, a PNG or GIF would work. A PNG works great for transparency; however, they are typically a larger file size, leading to a longer load time for the page. A GIF works for transparency and has a better load time, but the quality is not nearly as good.

3. How much should someone spend on Web site hosting? Is there a Web hosting platform or other features we should specifically be looking for? If you were to recommend a Web hosting provider, who would it be?

There are tens of thousands of places you can host your Web site. The main thing is to find a hosting company that provides the services you need. Think about what the site will need as it grows. At the beginning, you may not need a shopping cart, but if that is in your plan, then go with a hosting company that has a workable shopping cart that you can grow into. If you are new to Web design, I would suggest going with a local company. It will be easier for you to develop a working relationship with them, and you may find you get better support. If they also provide Web design services, all the better. As your site grows, you may find that you no longer can or want to maintain your site. Price is an option, but so is support and server uptime. Do not be fooled by low monthly prices. Ask questions about their support, their server uptime, how much space you are allowed, and how many e-mail addresses you can have. Ask for references and call them. Ask if they will be renewing their contract.

Keep in mind that a hosting company is not in business to help you design your site — that is what you hire a designer for. Their support will be limited to ensuring your site is up and running, not walking you through the design process while you do it yourself.

Here in the Midwest, the average monthly hosting fee for a static site is about $15 to $20 per month. If you have an online store, the cost is about $45 per month. I recommend Green Bay Net (**www.greenbaynet.com**), located in Green Bay, Wisconsin.

4. What low- or no-cost options would you recommend for selling products on a Web site, such as PayPal integration or other shopping

carts? Is all shopping cart software essentially the same? For a Web site with hundreds of products, what shopping cart software would you recommend? What do you recommend for SSL?

Like hosting companies, there are thousands of shopping cart packages available. Some are easy to use with templates but look just like others created with that same program. Some allow customization, but these will require additional time to learn how to use. The best advice is to ask questions and make sure that the shopping cart not only does what you want it to do today, but what you will need it to do next year or in five years. It might be more expensive upfront, but in the long run, it is better to not have to change shopping carts as you grow. Before you purchase a shopping cart, merchant account provider, or SSL certificate, select your hosting provider. Your provider will very likely have a shopping cart option and may provide an SSL certificate. This will save you money, and you will be able to get support from one place. If you use programs such as Amazon, ProStores, or Yahoo!, keep in mind that these stores will only run on their systems and cannot be moved to another provider. This may become an issue if you outgrow these stores, as it would mean recreating your entire storefront.

You will need to have a way to process credit cards. Again, there are many options: PayPal, Google Checkout, or a merchant account with your bank. Do not commit to any merchant account until you know who will be hosting your Web site and what storefront you will be using, as different companies support different gateways. If you have a merchant account now, be sure you are able to use it for non-swipe transactions.

5. There are dozens of companies that you can buy domain names from. Is there any company in particular that is better than the others, and why? Is there any advantage to buying several domain name types for my domain, such as .com, .biz, .us, and .net?

For a long time, Network Solutions was the only place to purchase domain names, but in 1999 this was opened up to other companies, such as Go-Daddy. Today there are hundreds of places to purchase a domain name, and prices will vary. On average, you will pay about $10 per year for a domain name.

Here are some things to keep in mind when selecting a domain name:

- **Go with the .com**: The .com domain name is a lot like 800 numbers. If you see 800-123-4567, you know it will be toll-free. In a lot of cases, people will say, "Use my 800 number, 877-123-4567." The .com is the first extension someone will try if they do not know your domain name. Never go with the .net or .org if the .com is a competitor of yours. You will just be sending them business.

- **Use your business name**: If you are a new business and the name you wanted to use is already taken, then select a different business name. If you are not able to change your business name, then get creative with your domain name. How about using your tag line or another catchphrase?

- **Do not abbreviate, or use "non-letter" characters in your domain name**: People type so much these days that they do not mind a few extra letters in a domain name. It is more important that the domain name be memorable, easy to speak, and easy to spell. For example, a client of mine had the domain name **www.the-business-news.com**. Looking at it, it does not look that bad, but read it out loud to yourself — "the dash business dash news dot com." That is a mouthful, and people do not get it the first time they hear it. We changed the domain name to **www.thebusinessnewsonline.com**. A little longer, but easier to say, understand, and remember.

- **Use a memorable domain name**: Many domain names are the same as the company name, which is good, but often the company name is hard to spell and does not say what they do. That is where a memorable domain name comes in. This is a domain name that you can use anytime people will hear or see your domain name and need to remember it (radio, billboard, TV, or networking). Your memorable domain name should say what you do, be short and easy to remember, and point to your primary Web site. How important is this to have? If you plan to utilize radio, TV, or billboards to advertise your Web site, then it is important. For example, which is easier to remember: BernatzCosmeticDentistry. com or BeautifulTeeth.com?

Here are some things to help you come up with a memorable domain name:

- What problems do you solve for clients? When people come to you for your products or services, what do you do for them? A massage therapist might use NoMoreStressToday.com, or a brake shop may use WeStopAnything.com.

- What benefits or results do your clients see? How do clients benefit by working with you, or what results will they see? Do you save them time? Will they make more money? Will they have a healthier life? If you are a Web site designer, you might use GetResultsFromYour Website.com. An accountant might use MoreMoneyForYou.com.

- Describe what you do. Do you have a business name that does not say what you do? You can use a memorable domain name to do that for you. For example, the name of your company is Myers International, which does not say what you do. Your main domain might be Myers.com, but your memorable domain could be Elec- tricHoists.com. Now you know that they deal with electric hoists.

To register a domain name, you can go to **www.domainsbyvirtualtech. com**. The above domain names were made up for this article and may or may not be currently available.

6. *When designing a Web site, we want to ensure compatibility with major Web browsers, such as Microsoft Internet Explorer, Mozilla Firefox, Google Chrome, and others. Do you have recommendations*

for how to design the site to ensure maximum compatibility and user functionality?

When you start the project, have all the major browsers open and keep checking each one. You will not be able to get the site to be the same in all major browsers. However, it should be as close and functional as possible. With older browsers, some of the newer bells and whistles might not work the same or might not work at all, but the site still needs to be fully functional. By having all the major browsers open throughout the design process, you will be able to catch issues as they arise and not have to go back and change them later. Having to go back and make changes can lead to other parts of the site not working.

7. What is a useful CSS technique that you use often? What is the most common font you use when designing Web pages? What advice can you give regarding Web site navigation?

Everything designed should be fully CSS-driven, with no in-line styles and no deprecated font tags. If everything is CSS-driven, it will be more compatible with all the newer browsers. This philosophy makes updating and changing the site much easier and faster. I like to put footer information and navigation systems into includes.

The most common font I use when developing is Arial. It is a clean, crisp, easy-to-read font that most people are familiar with. Because it is installed on just about every computer, there is no major issue with availability. If the site is more elegant, I like to use a font such as Georgia. Georgia is also fairly clean and easy to read, but still has the elegance of a serif font. Other fonts that are good choices include Verdana, Trebuchet, and Comic Sans®.

Navigation of your site should be easy to use and easy to find for both site visitors and search engines. Keeping in mind that your Web site is a marketing tool and it is meant to sell your product or service, you want people to be able to look around. Do not be cutesy with it. If it is a link to your products, call it "Products." Do not create a navigation that might look cool but forces the site visitors to hunt around for it. People want information now — they do not want to have to work for it. Your navigation should include a link to the home and contact pages. You always want to give people the chance to start over again, and you never want them hunting for your contact information. Even if your phone number is on every page, you still should have a contact page. People are trained to look for "Contact" when they want to contact you. Keep your navigation consistent throughout the site. The easier it is for people to get around, the longer they will stay.

8. A challenge of any new Web site is obtaining search engine rankings. What practical advice can you give to someone with a new Web site to achieve visibility in major search engines?

Search engines can be a challenge, but if you take your time and create a site that is search-engine friendly, you can have great success. One thing to keep in mind is that it takes time to have a site appear in the "natural" or "organic" listings. On average, it will take nine months to have a new site appear on the first page of Google. If you want your site to appear right away, you will need to go with a pay-per-click campaign such as Google AdWords.

Search engines have a hard time indexing a site built totally in Adobe Flash. Flash is a great program for certain elements such as a slideshow, but not for the entire site. Because there is no visible text-based content, the search engine has nothing to index.

Search engines look at a variety of things when determining if and when your site will appear in the natural listings. Here are the main ones to focus on:

Site content: Search engines love content. They want to index a site that has useful information to the site visitors. The content on your Web site needs to be in text format. If you cannot highlight the text, copy, and paste it into another program, then the search engines cannot "read" it; they will not index a "blank" page. Your content should be of use to the site visitors, not just a sales pitch. Of course, you want to sell your product or service, but you also need to provide useful information to the site visitors. Educate them about your industry and what they should look for when making a purchase. Add articles and press releases to build content.

If you have more than four search term phrases that you want to target, then create search–term specific pages. These pages provide information specifically about a certain product or service. Bodacious Basketry (**www.bodaciousbasketry.com**) makes handmade custom baskets. They wanted to get noticed for their dove release baskets, so we created a page dedicated to dove and butterfly release baskets: **www.bodaciousbasketry.com/dove-release-baskets.htm**. The meta tags and page content are all about dove and butterfly release baskets. If you search Google for "dove release baskets" or "release baskets," they are No. 1. And in both cases, you are taken directly to the dove release basket page rather than their home page.

When writing your Web site content, keep in mind that you are writing for search engines, not your ninth-grade English teacher. You want to have good spelling and grammar, but you may also break rules such as using the same word over and over in the one paragraph. Use your search terms as often as you can within the text of your Web site. If you are an accountant, do not say "our services;" instead, say "our accounting services." Just adding a few extra words into the text of your Web site will make a big difference.

Tile Roof Specialists (**www.tileroofspecialists.com**) installs tile roofs. Below are two examples of possible first paragraphs for their Web site.

Example 1

Tile Roof Specialists, LLC is a roofing contractor that installs and repairs roofs. Tile Roof Specialists is accredited for the successful installation of many roofs and has over 129 years of combined installation experience through its five owners and dedicated installers.

Example 2

Tile Roof Specialists, LLC is a Wisconsin-based tile roofing contractor specializing in the installation of clay tile, natural slate, and concrete tile roofs. We install and repair tile and slate roofs throughout Wisconsin (Madison, Milwaukee), Michigan, Minnesota, Iowa, Illinois, Indiana, Ohio, and Missouri. Tile Roof Specialists is accredited for the successful installation of hundreds of tile and slate roofs and has over 129 years of combined installation experience through its five owners and dedicated installers.

Either is correct; however, Example 2 provides more useful information to search engines.

Page naming and internal text links: As you start to create your Web pages, think about what you are naming the pages. Giving Web pages descriptive names not only will help you to manage the site, but will help the search engines to know what is on each page. Arcways (**www.arcways. com**) builds custom spiral and curved stairs. When we created their site, we named the page on curved stairs **curvedstairs.asp**. We could have used **cs.asp** or **curved.asp**, but **curvedstairs.asp** is more descriptive.

"Click Here" and "Learn More" are great action statements to get people to click on a link. However, from a search engine perspective, having your text link include the search term is more effective. In the case of Arcways, rather than having a link read, "Click here for more information" and then linking to curvedstairs.asp, it is more search-engine friendly to have the text read, "Learn more about curved stairs" and link it to curvedstairs.asp.

Link popularity is the number of links to your site. The search engines assume that the more links there are to your site, the better and more informative your site is. However, you want relevant links to your site, not just links. For example, if you are a zoo, having a link from Betty's Salon is not relevant, and too many of these types of links can hurt your site. However, a link from a national zoo site or *National Geographic* would build up your link popularity.

To build your link popularity, you need to ask for links. Ask associations you belong to, vendors, suppliers, and complementary businesses for links to your site. You can also build your link popularity by getting your site listed on search engines and Internet directories, and by submitting press releases, videos, and articles to online sources.

To get an idea of how many sites and what sites are linking to you, go to Google or Yahoo! and in the search box type in "links:www.yourdomainame.com."

A sitemap is an outline of your Web site that links to every page of your site. It gives search engines a fast and easy way to index your entire site, and these can be easily added to any site. Just create a page named "Sitemap" (with the appropriate extension) and create an outline. You can also use an XML sitemap (**www.xml-sitemaps.com**).

Meta tags: There has been a lot of discussion about meta tags and whether you need them or not. I say yes, you still need them, and you need to take time to create them. Meta tags are found in the code of your Web site and could consist of many tags. The ones that I feel you need for search engines are "Title" and "Description."

Title: Your meta title tag should be no more than 10 words and include your most important search terms. You should not use your company name, unless it is one of your top search terms. Try to avoid fluff words such as "and," "if," and "or." If you are limited in your service area, then use the area you do business in as part of your title.

Description: Your description is basically a classified ad for that Web page. Keep it to fewer than 30 words and repeat some of the terms used in your title. Also, put your company name here. Because the description is what appears when someone does a search, make it exciting and give the searcher a reason to click on your Web site link while keeping your search terms.

To see if your current site has meta tags or to see those of your competition, open a browser and go to the Web site you want to review the meta tags for. Click on "View." A drop-down menu will appear; click on "Page" or "Page Source." This will open a new window. The meta tags are found between the **<head></head>** tags.

Here is an example of what the meta tags look like live:

<head>
<title>Sheet Metal Fabrication - Sheet Metal Fabricator - Wisconsin</title>
<meta name="description" content="Muza Sheet Metal of Oshkosh, Wisconsin is a sheet metal fabricator providing Architectural Sheet Metal, Industrial Ventilation, Dust Collection, Composite Panels, or HVAC/Dust Collection Service. "/>
</head>

Meta tags should be customized for every page of your Web site. Ideally, both the title and the description should be unique, or at a minimum, just the title. Customize it to what is included on that page. Think about people searching and how you want them to find that page.

ALT tags are another way to add search terms to your Web site for search engines. ALT tags are attached to images and would appear if someone has images turned off or if the Web site is being read to the visitor. These tags are required by current Web standards and offer an excellent opportunity to increase your search-term density.

Online guerrilla marketing techniques: Guerrilla marketing is a concept you may be familiar with. The term was made popular by the book *Guerrilla Marketing Attack* by Jay Conrad. The book talks about what a small business can do to compete with a large company that has an unlimited marketing budget. Most of the marketing techniques discussed in the book are free or low-cost and simple to do. This article will take the guerrilla marketing concept and apply marketing options found on the Internet.

- **Signature files:** These "files" are found at the bottom of every e-mail message you send out and should include your name, company name, Web address, phone number, and tag line. By using a signature file, you are constantly advertising your business, for free. The tools to set up a signature file can be found in your e-mail program. Try to avoid using fancy fonts or images as part of your signature file. Keep it short and sweet.

- **Uploading videos to YouTube:** It is free to upload videos to YouTube, and they link back to your site, thus building your link popularity. Web surfers are researching products and services via YouTube. You can also track how many times your video is reviewed and if people subscribed to be notified when you post another video.

- **Discussion groups:** Also called "online forums," these are groups of people who "get together" to discuss a common interest. You can use discussion groups to promote your business by finding a group that attracts your target market and then actively participating in the discussion. Your participation must be a benefit to the group and not a sales pitch. Answer questions with free advice and ask questions of your own. These back-and-forth conversations will start to position you as an expert in your field and someone whom people will look to for answers. To find a discussion group, search for "discussion group" on your favorite search engine.

- **Press releases:** I am sure you are currently using press releases to keep the local media informed of activities at your business. Online press release services distribute your press release to online sources including search engines and online publications. You should be using online press releases to announce new products, employees, or awards your company has won. To find places to submit your press release, search for "online press releases" on your favorite search engine.

- **Writing and submitting e-zine articles:** By writing an article for an e-zine (online newsletter), you can quickly position yourself as an expert and receive free exposure for your business. Most e-zine editors are looking for free articles to put in their e-zine. In exchange, they will allow you two or three lines for a bio and contact information. One downside to writing an article is that you need to be able to write a good article. If you are not talented in this area, you may need to hire an editor to review. A good place to start is to search for "submitting e-zine articles" on your favorite search engine.

- **Creating an e-zine:** Having a company e-zine is a great way to stay in touch with your clients and potential clients. E-zines are a free way to keep clients up-to-date with new products and services, and helps to educate them on changes within your industry. However, you need to be able to write and come up with articles on a regular basis. There are a number of people looking for outlets for their articles.

9. If you could only give three pieces of advice, what would you tell a business or individual as they attempt to build and/or establish a viable Web presence?

Take your time and do some research. Creating a Web site is no different than opening a store on Main Street, U.S.A. You need to have a plan as to the content of your Web site, what it will look like, and where it will be hosted.

If you are designing the site yourself, spend some time looking at portfolios of professional Web designers. What are the elements that make a good design? Use those. Your Web site will become an important part of your business and marketing, and you need to have one rather quickly.

If doing it yourself will delay the launch of the site by more than a month, then hire someone to do it for you. It will cost you more, but it will be working for you faster; plus, you will have time to focus on other parts of the business.

Tammy Schultz is president and co-owner of Virtualtech Web Site Design and Promotion, Inc. Tammy started Virtualtech in 1997 when she saw that small businesses needed help taking advantage of marketing on the Web. Today, Virtualtech has more than 300 clients in 26 states and focuses on Web site design, Web site maintenance, and Internet marketing. Because of the commitment to its clients, Virtualtech still has its very first client. Tammy may be contacted at tammy@virtualtech.com.

Interview with Dale DeHart

1. How does someone begin the process of determining what they should put on their Web site, what design elements it should have, how navigation should function, and what the overall appearance should be? When starting with a blank HTML document, what steps or techniques would you recommend to get to a finished product?

We always recommend starting with the viewpoint and preferences of your target audience. What is the message that you are trying to convey (benefits of your product or service, positive outcomes associated with the content of your site)? How would this message be best portrayed to your specific demographic?

Once you have the message written down, always try to tell the story with positive benefit-oriented imagery. iStockphoto is a great — and inexpensive — place to get images that will match your message.

Navigation? Keep it simple. Always try to keep your audience no more than one click away from your most-desired outcome.

2. There are many Web design products available, such as Microsoft FrontPage, Microsoft Expression Web, and Adobe Creative Suite. For a beginner who wants to have a professional Web site, yet use a fairly simple-to-use Web design product, what would you recommend and why?

None of the above; we would start with a template based on an open-source content management system — our favorite is Joomla! These templates are inexpensive, sometimes free, and offer great design flexibility to anyone willing to put in a little time experimenting. In addition, it immediately puts you into a database-driven solution that is easy to maintain (no HTML required). Anyone who knows MS Word can maintain a Joomla! Web site.

3. *What type of image format do you recommend using on Web sites? There are several different formats, such as GIF, JPEG, and PNG — is there a difference? Is one better than the other?*

Each of these formats has strengths and weaknesses; the GIF format, for instance, supports animation and the others do not. The JPEG supports many more color variations, making it better for photos and images where color rendering is critical. The PNG format was intended to have the strengths of the GIF (other than animation) with better color density and fewer patent restrictions. So yes, read up and choose the format based on the application.

4. *How much should someone spend on Web site hosting? Is there a Web hosting platform or other features we should specifically be looking for? If you were to recommend a Web hosting provider, who would it be?*

We think $15 to $20 per month is a reasonable hosting fee that allows enough margin to the provider that they can deliver great service in real time. We recommend CartikaHosting — for companies that do not host with us, that is. There are dirt-cheap hosting companies out there that throw you into a server farm and provide very little support when you need it.

5. *What low- or no-cost options would you recommend for selling products on a Web site, such as PayPal integration or other shopping*

carts? Is all shopping cart software essentially the same? For a Web site with hundreds of products, what shopping cart software would you recommend? What do you recommend for SSL?

Once again, Joomla! has an extension called VirtueMart that simply plugs into the site and has all the features of a world-class shopping cart program — and it is open-source, in case customization is required. We encourage people, though, to list their requirements when it comes to shopping carts. If someone has some very specific things they want to do with their cart, there is a chance that any given solution will not support that particular feature. For SSL, we use Comodo® — it never lets us down and is reasonably priced.

6. There are dozens of companies that you can buy domain names from. Is there any company in particular that is better than the others, and why? Is there any advantage to buying several domain name types for my domain, such as .com, .biz, .us, and .net?

We always recommended Network Solutions until they started reserving domains on their own and reselling them back to customers at a higher cost. We will not even do a search on NS anymore for fear they will gather the information and reserve the domain before we do. Now we use NameCheap™ — hate the name, love the company — for reasonable prices and great service.

7. When designing a Web site, we want to ensure compatibility with major Web browsers, such as Microsoft Internet Explorer, Mozilla Firefox, Google Chrome, and others. Do you have recommendations for how to design the site to ensure maximum compatibility and user functionality?

For the beginning designer, we would start with a template that has already been validated and 100-percent table-less CSS, if at all possible. That way, you have a head start and are less likely to fall into a browser-trap.

8. What is a useful CSS technique that you use often? What is the most common font you use when designing Web pages? What advice can you give regarding Web site navigation?

We use a CSS technique that moves the main content of the page as close as possible to the top — search engines like not having to wade through lots of code to get to the meat of a message.

On fonts, almost always a sans-serif, like Verdana, Arial, or Trebuchet.

9. A challenge of any new Web site is obtaining search engine rankings. What practical advice can you give to someone with a new Web site to achieve visibility in major search engines?

Before you start writing the content for your site (and yes, content is the key to high rankings), think about the keywords that users are likely to search to find the information you are providing. Then use those keywords a few times in the content to assure that the search engines will know that your site is about those topics.

Keep your theme focused as tightly as possible; remember, you are trying to convince Google that you are the absolute expert on your particulate topic, and it is hard to do that if you stray too far afield.

And finally, do not waste your title meta tag — it is really important to get your keywords in there.

10. If you could only give three pieces of advice, what would you tell a business or individual as they attempt to build and/or establish a viable Web presence?

- Do competitive research and understand carefully whether you can effectively differentiate yourself from others on the Net that are in the same market.

- Stay away from Flash if you want to attract search traffic — I cannot tell you how many people we have had to rescue from a Flash Web site.
- Call 1-866-644-SOHO.

*Dale DeHart is the President and founder of SOHO Prospecting, a professional marketing services company in Camarillo, California, that provides marketing services and strategies for small and medium-sized independent businesses. Dale's technical and business background led him to excel in senior management positions with several leading high-tech corporations, including Hewlett Packard, TRW, and Motorola. In 1997, Dale established his own management consultant company, DeHart Consulting, LLC, providing companies   including California Amplifier, Harmonic, Fujitsu, and Xilinx — with business strategy and development support. Dale launched SOHO Prospecting as a division of DeHart Consulting, LLC in 2001 to provide comprehensive marketing solutions to companies across the business spectrum. You can contact Dale at 1-866-644-SOHO or **www.sohoprospecting.com**.*

Interview with Stephanie Fredrickson

1. How does someone begin the process of determining what they should put on their Web site, what design elements it should have, how navigation should function, and what the overall appearance should be? When starting with a blank HTML document, what steps or techniques would you recommend to get to a finished product?

The process of determining what should be put on a Web site is based on the type of Web site you have. If you are selling a product, you want to feature that product. You also want to tailor the site elements and graphics to the audience you are trying to reach. For instance, if you are selling baby items, you would want your site to look like a boutique or have a baby theme. You need to have a basic understanding of color and design theory to determine which type of graphics or design elements to put on your site. Colors convey different feelings.

The steps I would recommend when starting with a blank HTML document to get to a finished product is to study how a basic style sheet (CSS) is put together and create your graphics with a graphics editor (Adobe Photoshop or Illustrator). If you cannot do that, then you should start with a Web site template that has pre-made graphics in it.

2. *There are many Web design products available, such as Microsoft FrontPage, Microsoft Expression Web, and Adobe Creative Suite. For a beginner who wants to have a professional Web site, yet use a fairly simple-to-use Web design product, what would you recommend and why?*

I would recommend Dreamweaver, only because it is simple to use, and if you have to build your Web site yourself, it has all the tools to do it properly. If you are a beginner and do not want to spend the money — Dreamweaver is higher on the price scale — there are quite a few WYSIWYG editors like Dreamweaver that are much more inexpensive. You can do a Google search to find one that fits your needs, and you also have to consider if it is for a PC or a Macintosh.

3. *What type of image format do you recommend using on Web sites? There are several different formats, such as GIF, JPEG, and PNG — is there a difference? Is one better than the other?*

It depends on what type of graphic you are going to be adding to your site. If you are using a photograph, it needs to be optimized and saved as a JPEG. Any other type of graphic can either be GIF or PNG. The only time to really use a PNG on a Web site is when you have an image with a transparent background.

4. *How much should someone spend on Web site hosting? Is there a Web hosting platform or other features we should specifically be looking for? If you were to recommend a Web hosting provider, who would it be?*

I recommend using LAMP servers (Linux, Apache, MySQL, Perl) only because I am partial to PHP coding, and most of the CMS and shopping carts I use only work on LAMP servers. Most developers like me use MySQL for database creation and PHP to pull from those databases. Basically, it is all choice and what type of site you want to develop. Some people swear by Windows hosting and servers because they have never used LAMP servers and use FrontPage to design. Others cannot live without Linux hosting like me, and use Dreamweaver, MySQL, and PHP to develop sites.

Cost depends on what you are looking for hosting. For example, if you want a hosting provider that includes a special shopping cart or CMS already in their database, then you might pay more. If you are planning on putting videos on your Web site, then you might have to pay more for a higher bandwidth plan to accommodate that. A basic Web site should be pretty inexpensive for a yearly plan and accommodate most Web sites that even sell hundreds of products. I personally use and recommend HostGator.

5. What low- or no-cost options would you recommend for selling products on a Web site, such as PayPal integration or other shopping carts? Is all shopping cart software essentially the same? For a Web site with hundreds of products, what shopping cart software would you recommend? What do you recommend for SSL?

I would recommend two different ways of going about this. The first would be to use WordPress and install a free shopping cart plug-in from **www.wordpress.org**. There are many shopping cart plug-ins for WordPress that integrate with PayPal, and the only fees you have are those associated with PayPal.

The second low-cost way to easily sell products on a Web site is OptionCart. It is a MySQL database-driven catalog system that works in conjunction with the Mals-E shopping cart system to sell and display products with unlimited pages, categories, and other features like a guestbook and wholesale option.

The best place to get an SSL certificate is either directly through your hosting company, if they offer it, or GoDaddy. You should hire a professional to set it up for you, unless you truly know what you are doing.

6. There are dozens of companies that you can buy domain names from. Is there any company in particular that is better than the others, and why? Is there any advantage to buying several domain name types for my domain, such as .com, .biz, .us, and .net?

I personally do not know if one place is better than another. GoDaddy is where I have always purchased my domain names from. I think there can be an advantage to purchasing the .biz or .net of your particular domain name to protect it. Then someone cannot use that particular domain to start up a business with the same name as yours. Doing this can help stop name squatters from stealing business or traffic from your Web site.

7. When designing a Web site, we want to ensure compatibility with major Web browsers, such as Microsoft Internet Explorer, Mozilla Firefox, Google Chrome, and others. Do you have recommendations for how to design the site to ensure maximum compatibility and user functionality?

Design and code your site with the newest CSS standards; do not use tables, and your site will look the same in all major browsers.

8. What is a useful CSS technique that you use often? What is the most common font you use when designing Web pages? What advice can you give regarding Web site navigation?

All CSS techniques are invaluable when designing a site. The CSS technique I use the most and is consistent throughout my coding is my reset style sheet, which sets my margins and padding for columns.

The most common font I use when designing sites are sans-serif fonts (Arial, Veranda, and Helvetica), which are fonts that do not have the small features called "serifs" at the end of strokes. Sans-serif fonts are much easier to read onscreen than serif fonts (such as Times New Roman and Georgia).

The best advice I can give on Web site navigation is to clearly know what pages you want your audience to visit. This will help you determine whether to use a vertical or horizontal navigation, tabs, or sliced images. Personal preference will dictate the best type of navigation for a given site.

9. A challenge of any new Web site is obtaining search engine rankings. What practical advice can you give to someone with a new Web site to achieve visibility in major search engines?

Do keyword research for your site using **www.google.com/sktool/#**. This will help you determine the best keywords to use in meta tags and meta descriptions. Also, if you are selling products, use keywords in the title of each product and write original product descriptions. Never steal content from other sites. That could get you penalized by search engines. Google has a section where they give tons of advice on SEO that is the standard for all sites: **www.google.com/support/Webmasters**.

10. If you could only give three pieces of advice, what would you tell a business or individual as they attempt to build and/or establish a viable Web presence?

1. Knowledge is power in the world of Web design. Web standards and CSS styles are always changing, and you need to keep up with new techniques.

2. Just because you have a Web site does not mean you are going to have a million visitors to your site. Make sure you have a well–thought out business plan and a budget for marketing your Web site. For individual or personal sites, this is not such an issue because you do not necessarily have to promote a personal blog the way you promote an online retail business.

3. Hire a professional Web designer that is trained to develop professional and personal Web sites and graphics if you encounter technical challenges beyond your realm of expertise.

*Sweet Boutique Design, LLC has been providing boutique and blog owners with trendy designs since 2007. SBD is a small design studio located in Michigan with clients from all over the United States, Canada, and Europe. Stephanie is an experienced Web and graphics designer who is a member of the AIGA (American Institute of Graphic Arts). Even though Stephanie has a flair for fun and whimsical boutique illustrations and Web sites, she also caters to other types of clients, such as schools and small business owners. Services offered include e-commerce, informational Web site design and development, custom WordPress theme designs, one of a kind graphics, and whimsical illustrations. You can contact her by phone at 1-810-599-3542, on the Web at **www.sweet boutiquedesign.com**, or by e-mail at admin@sweeetboutiquedesign.com.*

Interview with Howard Sherman

1. How does someone begin the process of determining what they should put on their Web site, what design elements it should have, how navigation should function, and what the overall appearance should be? When starting with a blank HTML document, what steps or techniques would you recommend to get to a finished product?

Conceptually, a Web site should be a natural, seamless extension of your business. Your Web site is your storefront on the Internet, and that is how the Web site should be designed from page one.

Navigational considerations are mainly a matter of personal choice — navigation buttons on top? On the left side? Should the buttons not be buttons at all but text links to other pages? These details are not so important; making the Web site easy for your Web site visitors to navigate is really all that matters.

When starting from scratch, have a rough idea of how many Web pages you plan to have ("About Us," "Online Store," and "FAQ," for example) and first design the skeleton of that Web site by creating the navigational links or buttons that work between and among all the pages. With that done, put the meat on the skeleton by writing in the content for each page.

2. There are many Web design products available, such as Microsoft FrontPage, Microsoft Expression Web, and Adobe Creative Suite. For a beginner who wants to have a professional Web site, yet use a fairly simple-to-use Web design product, what would you recommend and why?

Microsoft Expression Web is an excellent product for a beginner to start with because it is not much different than using Microsoft Word. There is very little in the way of a learning curve if you are looking to produce a basic, presentable Web site. Because most of the inhabitants of planet Earth know how to use Word, those same people can sit down and get right to work with Expression Web.

3. What type of image format do you recommend using on Web sites? There are several different formats, such as GIF, JPEG, and PNG — is there a difference? Is one better than the other?

GIFs are excellent because they are very small and therefore load very quickly. JPEGs have a great range of depth in terms of picture quality overall, and also tend to be smaller than TIFFs or PNG files. Web site visitors are very impatient. Conventional wisdom says you have 10 to 15 seconds of a visitor's undivided attention as they determine if your Web site is where they want to be or not. Do not kill that valuable time with slow-loading images. There are dozens of graphic file formats out there, but GIF and JPEG should be used whenever possible. There is seldom a reason to use any other.

4. How much should someone spend on Web site hosting? Is there a Web hosting platform or other features we should specifically be

looking for? If you were to recommend a Web hosting provider, who would it be?

A good hosting plan runs about $10 per month and will have sufficient storage and bandwidth for startup Web sites. If your Web site is heavy on files — movie clips, multimedia presentations, or large amounts of content in general — or draws lots of Web site traffic, upgrading to a $25 monthly plan should do the trick.

Choosing Linux or Windows depends largely on what you plan to do with your Web site. Some shopping carts like VP-ASP will only run under Windows, while others like Zen Cart will run other either platform. Generally, Linux is held as being more reliable and more secure. I have found the latest Windows Web servers to be just as good.

I can confidently recommend two Web site hosting companies I personally deal with. I have found them very responsive in handling personal support requests, and they are very new-user friendly. For Windows hosting, I strongly suggest Eric Lammer's Krack Media in Maine, and for Linux Web hosting, Darrel Carpenter's Las Vegas Web Hosting is the way to go. My own Web sites are on Darrel's servers, yet many of my clients requiring Windows servers are hosting their Web sites with Eric.

5. *What low- or no-cost options would you recommend for selling products on a Web site, such as PayPal integration or other shopping carts? Is all shopping cart software essentially the same? For a Web site with hundreds of products, what shopping cart software would you recommend? What do you recommend for SSL?*

I always recommend PayPal for three very important reasons: Setting up PayPal for payments is very simple, straightforward, and — even more importantly — PayPal is very neutral in consumer-vendor disputes. Where a conventional credit card company will pull the funds out of your account at the mere whisper of a customer complaint or chargeback, PayPal has a methodical case method where a final decision about a purchase dispute is not made until both sides have been heard out and all evidence and documentation presented. PayPal may have slightly higher fees, which I feel are more than balanced out by the ease of use and the very fair way PayPal handles disputes. And here are the best part — after 60 days, a dispute will not be considered as valid. Credit card banks can "whack" your account several months after a sales transaction; PayPal holds the deadline for disputes at just two months.

As far as shopping carts go, I have worked with VP-ASP for a number of clients and find it to be by far the most flexible and powerful while being rather simple to manage with any number of projects once it is up and running.

6. *There are dozens of companies that you can buy domain names from. Is there any company in particular that is better than the others, and why? Is there any advantage to buying several domain name types for my domain, such as .com, .biz, .us, and .net?*

Your Web hosting company is the best place to buy domain names, as they will effortlessly integrate the domain name registration into the setup of your Web site hosting. It is a needless hassle to buy a domain name from one place, then set up hosting somewhere else. Web site owners should buy as many derivatives of their name as possible. You do not want someone purchasing MyWebsitename.net, or MyWebsitename.biz when you own MyWebsitename.com because that can be a competitor looking to tap into your Web site brand and cause brand confusion that may lead people to their Web site instead of yours.

7. *When designing a Web site, we want to ensure compatibility with major Web browsers, such as Microsoft Internet Explorer, Mozilla Firefox, Google Chrome, and others. Do you have recommendations for how to design the site to ensure maximum compatibility and user functionality?*

I am a purist, so I tell everyone to write their Web site in plain HTML. HTML will load perfectly in any Web browser out there, and the search engines eat HTML Web pages like candy. A pure HTML Web site will rank much higher on search engine listings than any other type of Web site, with all other things being equal.

8. *What is a useful CSS technique that you use often? What is the most common font you use when designing Web pages? What advice can you give regarding Web site navigation?*

I do not dabble with CSS, but some of the Web site designers that work for me do. CSS can be nice with adding some flair, but my advice is not to overdo it.

9. *A challenge of any new Web site is obtaining search engine rankings. What practical advice can you give to someone with a new Web site to achieve visibility in major search engines?*

Link marketing. Link marketing is the "secret sauce" to getting picked up and placed high on the search engines. Google's own algorithms for factoring a Web site's placement in search results weighs the number of links a Web site has pointing to it very heavily.

SEO is certainly critical, but link marketing is the missing link. Think of SEO as the engine that will get you located on the search engines, then consider link marketing as the fuel for that engine.

10. *If you could only give three pieces of advice, what would you tell a business or individual as they attempt to build and/or establish a viable Web presence?*

Add fresh content all the time. Visitors are put off by stale Web sites that are infrequently updated because the perception is that your Web site is not serious about what it is offering. The search engines also love content, as more and more content on your Web site pertaining to your Web site's subject matter increases the gravitational pull of potential visitors, leading to higher search engine rankings.

If you are selling products, you must offer the most liberal refund policy possible. If you take my advice and use PayPal, you can refund a customer's money within 60 days and have your PayPal processing fees refunded to you as well. A 60-day money-back guarantee tells customers you believe in the products you are selling and also gives the customer peace of mind that they cannot make a mistake in making a bad purchase decision because they have the comfort of knowing they can always return it in a fairly long amount of time. Paradoxically, the longer your return policy, the lower your return rate. People procrastinate, like we all did with term papers. For days and then weeks, the thought persists that they have plenty of time. Then the deadline comes, and it is too late.

Get good at copywriting. Copywriting is the way to sell online. Buy books on the subject and follow all the examples. Join a good blog like John Carlton's blog for lots of copywriting insights or, even better, purchase one of his training courses. Ditto for Dan Kennedy's material. You can have the best products at the lowest prices with a lifetime return policy, but if your Web site's copy is weak, then your sales will suffer.

*Royal Geeks Founder Howard Sherman leads a team of top-notch professionals in every sphere of technology — Linux gurus, Apple Macintosh mavens, Web site designers, customer service specialists, and IT consulting pros — to deliver world-class service and support to consumers and businesses worldwide, encompassing all sectors of the technology universe. He also publishes interactive fiction through the parent company, Malinche Entertainment, at **www. malinche.net**. Howard can be contacted by e-mail at howard@royalgeeks.com or on the Web at **www.royalgeeks.com**.*

Interview with Michael Dubendris

1. How does someone begin the process of determining what they should put on their Web site, what design elements it should have, how navigation should function, and what the overall appearance should be? When starting with a blank HTML document, what steps or techniques would you recommend to get to a finished product?

The answer to this question depends on a lot of factors. First off, referring to a "blank HTML" document is misleading, as the times when HTML in and of itself was a mainstay of Web design and development are long gone. More than ever, developing a Web site involves an immense amount of behind-the-scenes programming, and the line between simple Web site creation and full-fledged application development have become blurred. If you are in need of a large-scale LAMP (Linux, Apache, MySQL, PHP) deployment, creating your own Web site may not be the best path. This is unless you are utilizing a bundled preconfigured software package, such as a CMS. That is a popular choice that is also more likely if you are trying to construct your own Web site with little to no money.

It is best to have an idea of what you are going to want to put on your Web site beforehand — what kind of information you want to convey and in what manner — when deciding on a format. For example, blogs are a very popular Web site format these days; they have even gained credibility as a legitimate news source. If you have many frequent updates, this may be a good format to choose. However, if your content changes less frequently, or your Web site is more business-oriented, a blog format may not be the best choice.

If you are looking for more of a "business card" type format for your Web presence, Flash may be a good choice. Flash Web sites tend to have less changing content and are generally visually appealing. Of course, Flash sites in general are much more resource intensive, and while most people these days have access to broadband connections, it is important to keep in mind that this is not always the case.

For Web site navigation, the biggest key is to make sure your navigation structure remains the same throughout your Web site. The home page should serve as a template for the rest of the Web site, because your users will be expecting this. Navigation should be grouped together to make things easy on the user, and as a general rule, you should consider avoiding placing important links at the top of the page. This is because as we browse the Internet, we in general train ourselves to avoid things we do not recognize or think of as advertisement — which is often located at the top of the page. In a large Web site with plenty of content and pages, a search feature is almost always necessary. The most important thing to consider when planning your sitemap is that the user is comfortable with the format. Other rules are just guidelines, but above all you want to test the site and get feedback. If the user does not enjoy the experience, it does not matter what rules you have followed.

Sometimes it is best even to sketch out your layout on a piece of paper. My process generally involves writing an actual outline with bullet points defining the different pieces of the Web site, followed by a few sentences or a paragraph briefly describing what kind of content will go on those sections. Once this is done, it is pretty easy to map out the site and realize what kind of navigation structure you are going to want to use. From there, I would actually sketch out on paper a drawing of what I would like the layout to look like to give me an idea of where on each page I want each element. This gives you a pretty decent idea of how the site is going to flow, and I find that it works very well.

2. There are many Web design products available, such as Microsoft FrontPage, Microsoft Expression Web, and Adobe Creative Suite. For a beginner who wants to have a professional Web site, yet use a fairly simple-to-use Web design product, what would you recommend and why?

I suppose it is all a matter of personal preference and what you have available to you at the time. For the most part, they achieve similar things for inexperienced users. It is important not to get too caught up in the drag-and-drop, point-and-click nature of these applications, though. It is very important in creating a successful Web site that you understand the source code that drives your creation. These WYSIWYG software applications do help in the beginning, but becoming reliant on them hinders serious development. The greatest feature of these applications is the ability to do a split screen source code and Web site preview, which allows you to see your modifications in real time.

3. What type of image format do you recommend using on Web sites? There are several different formats, such as GIF, JPEG, and PNG — is there a difference? Is one better than the other?

Each image format has a specific use. GIF and PNG files both allow for transparency. GIF also allows for animations but generally has lower quality then PNG or JPEG. JPEG is best for large image files that do not contain transparency such as photos. So to answer the question — yes, there are differences, but no, one is not better than the other.

4. How much should someone spend on Web site hosting? Is there a Web hosting platform or other features we should specifically be looking for? If you were to recommend a Web hosting provider, who would it be?

As far as hosting goes, you tend to get what you pay for. There are several sources of free Web hosting out there, but many of them are plagued with forced advertisements and other limitations. Web hosting on a whole is fairly affordable at under $5 per month for most of the lowest-tiered packages. There are limitations on these and any Web hosting packages though, ranging from insufficient bandwidth to limitations on what kinds of scripts you are allowed to run. Almost any hosting package should be sufficient for a very basic HTML page to be hosted without much concern for bandwidth utilization. The other benefit of paying for Web hosting is that almost any hosting plan will provide you with your very own IP address, which is essential if you plan on purchasing your own domain name and have it pointed at the correct server.

Most modern Web sites can live happily on a system consisting of a software bundle known as LAMP. LAMP stands for "Linux, Apache, MySQL, and PHP." When searching for a Web host, I would look for these things specifically. Linux is the underlying operating system, but any Windows-based platform is an easy substitute for most sites; it mostly depends on personal preference. Though I do prefer working with Linux-based systems, I did not invent the acronym. Apache is the name of the Web server software. The majority of the Internet is powered by Apache Web servers, and to host any kind of content on a Web site, you need a Web server to serve that content. The last two are the most important, though. MySQL is an SQL database that many large Web sites and Web applications depend on to store and retrieve data in tables. Lastly, PHP is a scripting language that is immensely popular. There are several others you are likely to come across. For the majority of people, unless you know specifically what resources and languages you are going to need (for example, you know you plan on going into Ruby on Rails® development), looking for a Web host providing this LAMP functionality is a good starting point.

If you are tech-savvy, the Web host I recommend is Linode (**www. linode.com**). Though not technically a Web host, Linode is a Virtual Private Server, which gives you complete access to an entire system which you can configure exactly to your liking. It is affordable (relatively), with plans starting at $20 per month, and whatever requirements you have, you can add to the system yourself. An environment like this is almost a must-have for any serious development, though for more casual Web sites, this may be overkill. It depends on how much control you like to have.

5. *What low- or no-cost options would you recommend for selling products on a Web site, such as PayPal integration or other shopping carts? Is all shopping cart software essentially the same? For a Web site with hundreds of products, what shopping cart software would you recommend? What do you recommend for SSL?*

PayPal itself provides fairly effective methods of integration, and for low or no cost, it is hard to beat. The SSL is taken care of, and customers are presented with the trusted name of the PayPal company.

6. There are dozens of companies that you can buy domain names from. Is there any company in particular that is better than the others, and why? Is there any advantage to buying several domain name types for my domain, such as .com, .biz, .us, and .net?

The most important domain type is .com, without question. Obviously, if you are an organization, you may want a .org domain, but the term "dot-com" is defining of the Internet era. If a potential customer or viewer of your Web site knows the name of your Web site but not the address, chances are the first thing they will do is type in www.yourcompany.com. Absolutely, .com is better than any other, but the appeal to owning several different domain types is still there. This prevents other unrelated entities from starting similar Web sites or unrelated Web sites with a similar address.

7. A challenge of any new Web site is obtaining search engine rankings. What practical advice can you give to someone with a new Web site to achieve visibility in major search engines?

Use meta tags. SEO is still very important, but as search engines like Google become more advanced, it is easier and easier to find yourself in the search listings. Posting your URL in blogs and other relevant mediums (not spam) helps with rankings.

8. If you could only give three pieces of advice, what would you tell a business or individual as they attempt to build and/or establish a viable Web presence?

Get a good domain name, one that is easy to remember and will not get confused with something else. The domain name is as important as your brand name; it is how people will know you and how you will gain exposure.

Establish a good layout. This means use appropriate fonts, use effective navigation and search features, and in general, just make the Web site a pleasure to use — or at least not a chore.

Establish cross-browser compatibility. There is nothing worse than having a developer forget to test on a platform and alienating that entire audience.

Michael Dubendris is the founder of Rummex, LLC. In addition to managing a team of talented developers and designers, he is also employed as a test engineer by Cisco Systems. He can be contacted at mdubendris@rummex.com.

Interview with Greg Richards

1. How does someone begin the process of determining what they should put on their Web site, what design elements it should have, how navigation should function, and what the overall appearance should be? When starting with a blank HTML document, what steps or techniques would you recommend to get to a finished product?

Putting the structure of the Web site on paper is the first step. A nice-looking design is nothing without properly structured content, because after all, users visit your site to take in information.

Before even designing the look, decide what content is going to go into the site. Once you get the content inventory done, then you can wireframe it, determine the user flow, and then the design elements will fall into place. Remember, you might be iterating through these steps more than once before you have the final design you will be happy with.

2. There are many Web design products available, such as Microsoft FrontPage, Microsoft Expression Web, and Adobe Creative Suite. For a beginner who wants to have a professional Web site, yet use a fairly simple-to-use Web design product, what would you recommend and why?

For **www.MatrixWebs.com**, the Adobe products — especially Photoshop, Illustrator, and Dreamweaver — are the way to go. They are the top graphic design tools any designer should become familiar with, and many jobs will require that you know them. With the proliferation of blogs, you should be able to easily find tutorials to help you with everything from beginning to expert techniques for these excellent programs.

3. What type of image format do you recommend using on Web sites? There are several different formats, such as GIF, JPEG, and PNG — is there a difference? Is one better than the other?

It all depends. But our general rule of thumb is: Pictures or images with gradients — JPEG; any other images with solid colors — GIF; and for elements with alpha transparent shadow effects — PNG.

4. How much should someone spend on Web site hosting? Is there a Web hosting platform or other features we should specifically be looking for? If you were to recommend a Web hosting provider, who would it be?

Nowadays, Web site hosting is such a small overhead cost. When it comes to platform, it is really on your choice of coding environment. The open-source Linux platform generally runs cheaper than Windows-based servers. Always search for reviews on different Web hosts, and take time to shop around. If a price seems too good to be true, then it probably is. Remember: You get what you pay for.

5. What low- or no-cost options would you recommend for selling products on a Web site, such as PayPal integration or other shopping carts? Is all shopping cart software essentially the same? For a Web site with hundreds of products, what shopping cart software would you recommend? What do you recommend for SSL?

The three biggest cart systems that I hear of are Magento™ Commerce, Joomla!, and Zen Cart. All are open-source, based on PHP, and require the Linux platform.

If you would rather not plug in those cart systems, you can easily hook up a payment system via PayPal. PayPal will take care of the difficult options for you for a small fee.

6. There are dozens of companies that you can buy domain names from. Is there any company in particular that is better than the others, and why? Is there any advantage to buying several domain name types for my domain, such as .com, .biz, .us, and .net?

We have purchased from different companies, and my personal experience was good with each. GoDaddy, Aplus.net, and Network Solutions are all good options, with my preference being Network Solutions. Purchasing different extensions should be used more to protect your domain name rather than creating multiple pointers to a given site. You do have to draw the line somewhere, though; the **.com** and **.net** extensions are the important ones.

7. When designing a Web site, we want to ensure compatibility with major Web browsers, such as Microsoft Internet Explorer, Mozilla Firefox, Google Chrome, and others. Do you have recommendations for how to design the site to ensure maximum compatibility and user functionality?

Develop in compliance with the W3C standards. Make your site accessible for users with disabilities; make sure it degrades nicely for older and mobile browsers; and test, test, test. Simply install all of the major browsers out there and open your site in them. In one browser, it may look rock-solid and pixel-perfect, but in another it may look completely broken. Unfortunately, compatibility is one of the hardest aspects of Web development that takes experience.

For those of you who say, "Microsoft does not allow me to install more than one version of Internet Explorer, so I never test older versions," do not let that be an excuse. Simply download the free Microsoft Virtual PC and get the free VPC images that Microsoft provides for IE7, IE8, and more.

8. What is a useful CSS technique that you use often? What is the most common font you use when designing Web pages? What advice can you give regarding Web site navigation?

We love using image sprites. It speeds up load times of common image elements used throughout the site. Our list of favorite techniques can go on and on. Let us just say that CSS in general is a must-learn for Web designers and developers. The most common fonts we use in our designs are Arial and Verdana; sans-serif fonts are just more readable in nature.

When it comes to Web site navigation, I usually try to limit clients' main menu options to six items, maybe eight max. After that, in my opinion, the options start to look overwhelming — unless, of course, you are designing an e-commerce Web site with the main product categories as the main menu, then you have an exception.

One other thing to remember is that users usually have a short attention span. Given the way we work now, with multiple tabs opened with multiple sites and numerous other programs running in the background, it is always important to have identifying elements on a page that will help the user to get their footing when they are browsing. For example, for sites that have deep linking structures, offer breadcrumbs so they know where they came from and what they are drilling down to.

9. A challenge of any new Web site is obtaining search engine rankings. What practical advice can you give to someone with a new Web site to achieve visibility in major search engines?

Achieving visibility in search engines is not easy and does not come fast. Unless you put a good amount of money into a major marketing campaign and/or publicity stunt to get your name out there, it does take time. We would say the top things to do are to start a blog discussing topics relevant to your business, making your company active in social networking sites, and sending out useful and informative e-mail marketing campaigns.

10. If you could only give three pieces of advice, what you would tell a business or individual as they attempt to build and/or establish a viable Web presence?

Plan ahead, think of what makes you different from everyone else, and keep your customers happy, as word-of-mouth is the strongest form of referral.

*Greg Richards is the owner and president of **www.matrixWebs.com**. With 13 years of experience in the IT industry, Greg established MatrixWebs in 1999. Greg's primary roles are in technical sales, software design, and project management. He can be contacted by e-mail at grichards@matrixWebs.com.*

Interview With Scott Buresh

1. How does someone begin the process of determining what they should put on their Web site, what design elements it should have, how navigation should function, and what the overall appearance should be? When starting with a blank HTML document, what steps or techniques would you recommend to get to a finished product?

The process of determining what appears on your site is purely specific to your business, objectives, and goals. Many times, new site owners will want to replicate or mimic other sites in their industry without truly positioning their own site to meet business goals. Foremost, you should address what your site purpose is. Is it to sell products? Provide information? Advertise?

Once you have that information, the process of site design and development truly has guidance. You want to perform competitive analysis, dissecting what the competition is doing wrong and doing right. Often, you will find site survey data on publications like *Internet Retailer* that provide the top sites in a particular industry. This information is extremely useful to drive your design and development process, as it provides you with real data on how visitors rate top Web sites. These sites are rated on design, ease of use, navigation, and other important site evaluation elements.

In any event, your site needs to prominently and effectively position the most important site elements. If you are driving registrations for a seminar, that call to action needs to appear prominently on the page, above the page fold, and easily allow visitors to give information. The key is to remove as many road blocks as possible to achieve a site action. If there are pieces of the process that do not make sense, get rid of them. Focus on the end result — what you truly need, and what the visitor truly wants to see.

One of the first things I do is conceptualize what I will be producing: the final product. And then I begin coding rough "editions" — that is to say, I start with very basic geometric shapes and then refine the Web site down into greater and greater detail; you could liken this process to how an artist creates an art piece. They start with basic shapes and refine down until they get their final product. Also, I usually always try to stick with using **<div>** elements, as they are much more flexible than **<table>** tags, because if I need to move things around, **<div>** elements are infinitely easier to adjust.

Another technique that I use is to break down the Web page into parts; some examples of basic parts include the header, the content area, a navigational area, and a footer. These sections are all independent of each other, unless one needs to be located inside another.

2. There are many Web design products available, such as Microsoft FrontPage, Microsoft Expression Web, and Adobe Creative Suite. For a beginner who wants to have a professional Web site, yet use a fairly simple-to-use Web design product, what would you recommend and why?

The Adobe suite is by far the most robust, as it includes Dreamweaver and Photoshop, plus many other tools: InDesign®, Bridge, Version Cue®, and

Illustrator. The only downside is the upfront cost of the entire suite; there are, however, plenty of free alternatives. GIMP is a free and open-source Photoshop alternative, and back when I began learning about Web pages and HTML, I was coding with Notepad.

I like to use Dreamweaver only for its HTML highlighting. I rarely, if ever, use the WYSIWYG editor of Dreamweaver, just because it almost always produces un-maintainable code. Also, if I create a Web site mockup using Photoshop, I will only slice out important pieces of the mockup and never the whole thing, as Photoshop also produces un-maintainable code when using its slice export command.

3. What type of image format do you recommend using on Web sites? There are several different formats, such as GIF, JPEG, and PNG — is there a difference? Is one better than the other?

There is a place for different image formats. I use GIFs for any design or layout images such as background images and borders because of their generally smaller size. I use JPEGs for other images, such as a person's picture or an illustration — think of the pictures in a wedding album on a Web site. JPEGs, in my opinion, are usually bigger in size than GIFs, but that is because they can be of better quality. However, the newest format on the block, so to speak, is the PNG format. PNGs are different in that they can have real transparent backgrounds; the other two formats have to fake it — JPEGs much more than GIFs. More often you will find PNGs as floating image overlays to make something "pop."

4. How much should someone spend on Web site hosting? Is there a Web hosting platform or other features we should specifically be looking for? If you were to recommend a Web hosting provider, who would it be?

There are generally two different flavors of hosting: shared and dedicated. Shared hosting is usually very cheap (a few dollars a month); the only downside is that you are sharing a single server with a number of other

Web sites, which means you could take a performance hit, should another site on that server see a spike in traffic. Dedicated hosting is where you pay for the privilege of having your Web site run on its own server — or servers, if you need more than one. The plus side is that you have the full server's power to yourself — should you have a lot of traffic, this is a good thing — but the only downside is that it is quite a bit more than standard shared hosting.

Usually your hosting platform (or operating system) is generally determined by what kind of backend code, if any, your Web site could be running (PHP, ASP/ASP.NET, Perl, or Ruby on Rails). Generally speaking, I prefer the Linux environment; I have found it to be easier to work with. Though Windows does have a nice user interface, I have found that Linux offers the server administrator a lot more power in how his or her server works.

I generally do not recommend Web hosting providers, just because there are so many. One of the big things to ask any hosting provider, especially for shared hosting, before signing on to a service is how much control you get through the hosting provider's control panel. You do not want to get stuck with very little control over your Web site.

5. *What low- or no-cost options would you recommend for selling products on a Web site, such as PayPal integration or other shopping carts? Is all shopping cart software essentially the same? For a Web site with hundreds of products, what shopping cart software would you recommend? What do you recommend for SSL?*

There are literally hundreds of free and open-source e-commerce software packages, and there are just as many that you will have to shell out money for. More often than not, when you are paying for shopping cart software, you are going to have to host with the shopping cart's owner, and when that is the case, you will not be allowed to change the underlying code should you want to modify it to work differently. Usually, this is to maintain certification like PCI compliance, which is a very hard certification to get, and one that is equally hard to maintain.

It has been my opinion that all shopping cart software is the same. They all do the same exact thing, as they display products and allow customers to buy them. The big differences in shopping carts come when you have to administer them through the backend or administration area. Some are super simple, and others are robust. Quick Google searches can net reviews of the many different shopping cart vendors. From there, you can usually visit the Web sites of top-rated vendors and find demonstration versions of their software. I would highly suggest that anyone looking for a shopping cart vendor take the time to carefully comb over an administration section to ensure it meets all of the criteria you have hopefully already set before setting out on your search for a vendor. The last thing you want to do is pay out any kind of money (if you take that route), and find out that you are majorly limited in what you can accomplish.

Whether you have 10 or 10,000 products, all of the most popular software will scale very well and will not even sweat under the potential increased load. As for any particular brand of software, I have never found one that I am 100-percent pleased with; I generally look for one based on the client's criteria.

As for SSL, generally the more well-known a CA (Certificate Authority) is, the more you are going to pay. Admittedly, I will usually only buy from Web sites that display SSL certificates from the most popular CAs — VeriSign, for instance. But, in actuality, all SSL certificates are the same, and all do the exact same thing: ensure the Web site you are visiting is actually the Web site you are visiting, as well as encrypting traffic to and from the verified Web site.

6. There are dozens of companies from which you can buy domain names. Is there any company in particular which is better than the others and why? Is there any advantage to buying several domains name types for a domain, such as .com, .biz, .us, and .net?

From a strict SEO perspective, the only domains we have seen that appear to get preferential treatment are .edu domains, and this is primarily because not just anyone can have them.

From a branding standpoint, however, we still recommend a .com domain. If you are considering a .net or a .biz simply because some other company already has that name, you are already setting yourself up for brand confusion. A .net is a distant second in terms of a visitor's perspective.

Having said that, we own most domain extensions of our company and 301-redirect them back to our dot-com domain. This is primarily a means to prevent other people trying to capitalize on our brand, however; it is more of a defense mechanism than a marketing tactic.

7. When designing a Web site, we want to ensure compatibility with major Web browsers, such as Microsoft Internet Explorer, Mozilla Firefox, Google Chrome, and others. Do you have recommendations on how to design the site to ensure maximum compatibility and user functionality?

As I noted above, I generally build a Web site through a revision process. At the end of each revision, I check the Web page's compatibility with all of the browsers and then fix issues as they arise. As far as maximum compatibility goes, I always try to go for the "lean" side — that is, I like to keep things simple. "Simple" means less HTML code, and in my opinion, the less HTML code, the less chance you will run across elements misaligned or out of proportion.

8. What is a useful CSS technique that you use often? What is the most common font you use when designing Web pages? What advice can you give regarding Web site navigation?

One of the first techniques I always suggest is to use a CSS reset, which are simple CSS declarations that help to reduce browser discrepancies by "normalizing" things like line heights, margins, paddings, font sizes, and so on. Additionally, I do not like to have thousands of different declarations for elements that all basically do the same thing — and I have seen this before; again, the mantra "simple is usually better" always sings out in my head. While sometimes mandatory, I do not like using a lot of CSS hacks to get things to work in the varying number of browsers; I always find myself coding for ease of cross-browsers usage. Of course, this usually makes maintaining these Web sites pretty simple. The most common font is typically Arial or Times New Roman in 10- to 12-point font. Site navigation should be cleanly organized, aligned well with business objectives, and as streamlined as possible.

9. A challenge of any new Web site is obtaining search engine rankings. What practical advice can you give to someone with a new Web site to achieve visibility in major search engines?

It is an unfortunate fact — brand new Web sites have a more difficult time achieving search engine success for competitive phrases than their older counterparts, particularly on Google. However, the worst thing that a new site owner can possibly do is presume that they are "too late to the game" and decide not to pursue this marketing channel at all. A good search engine optimization company should be able to effectively work with a new Web site, setting the foundation for a remarkable success story while still achieving steadily increasing short-term benefits.

The issues

There are many reasons why new Web sites — and a search engine optimization company that frequently works with them — face an uphill battle. What follows is only a few of the major stumbling blocks.

The Google sandbox

There is much debate as to what exactly the Google sandbox is, and even debate as to whether it actually exists. More than one search engine optimization company has noted that there seems to be a "penalty" assessed to new Web sites, especially those that seem to gain too many inbound links too fast. This is all conjecture, but this would make sense. Inbound links factor largely in Google rankings, and therefore many sites that were already popular in Google began selling links from their sites based upon that popularity — a practice that goes against Google's terms of service. However, text link buying is very hard to police. The sandbox makes sense in this scenario, because Google seems to be saying, "We may not be able to stop people from buying text links, but they are going to pay a pretty penny for them before we will give them any ranking boost because of them." This is more conjecture, of course, but it is a popular theory in the numerous search engine optimization forums.

Lack of links

Unfortunately, here a new Web site is faced with the opposite problem. Links to new Web sites are called into question, but without incoming links, a new Web site has a slim chance of performing well on Google. This catch-22 is obviously a sore spot for many owners of new Web sites.

Trustworthiness

For many years, a common search engine optimization strategy was to set up numerous new Web sites all for one company, each geared toward targeting a different search term. This was largely due to the fact that search engines used to place a much higher importance on the home page of a Web site, rather than interior pages. Over time, search engines caught on to this trick, and as a result, new domains are now looked at more skeptically. The prevailing wisdom seems to be that while it is relatively easy and inexpensive to set up a new Web site that targets a certain term, a Web site that has been around for much longer and has a breadth of content has much more to lose and is less likely to attempt to "game the system."

The solutions

Does this mean that you should not hire a search engine optimization company to work on your new Web site? Not at all. In fact, it is in the very beginning of your Web site planning that a long-term strategy should be put into motion, a strategy that still offers positive results in the short term.

Before you build

It is important to get your search engine optimization company involved as early as possible before you build your new Web site. Not only are there many technical issues that you should be aware of before you begin design (such as linking architecture, types of text to use, and balancing your SEO efforts with your brand), but there are also strategies that can be set in motion at the outset that will counteract some of the stumbling blocks listed above. If you involve your search engine optimization company after you have built your new Web site, much of the work you have done will likely need to be redone with a long-term strategy in mind.

Targeting appropriate phrases

A good search engine optimization company will tell you that targeting a highly competitive phrase with a brand-new Web site can be an exercise in futility. However, this does not mean that you cannot achieve initial success on search engines. The trick is to target less competitive phrases at the outset and to begin tackling the more competitive phrases later. For instance, let us assume that your company makes custom widgets and that "custom widgets" is a very competitive search phrase. A search engine optimization company working on your new site might recommend that you instead target less competitive variations of the term, such as "custom-made widgets" or "custom widget manufacturing." Because these terms are less competitive, you will be more likely to obtain high rankings for them with your new Web site. You can thus enjoy highly targeted traffic in the beginning of your campaign and eventually target more competitive and popular phrases as your site gains traction, quality inbound links, and a reputation for usefulness.

Make your site a resource

A quality search engine optimization company will encourage you to turn your new site into an industry resource. You can do this by providing educational content about your industry in the form of articles, white papers, and other forms of non-biased content. There are many benefits to this approach, one of the primary being that such content attracts inbound links without any effort on your behalf. In addition, such a resource area builds your credibility in the eyes of your potential customers and serves to educate them in all stages of the buying cycle, so that when they are ready to make a purchase, you will likely be first in mind.

Build links

While making your new site a useful resource is a great way to attract inbound links, this does not mean that you should not also be seeking them out. Your search engine optimization company should get your site included in many general directories (such as the Yahoo! directory and Business.com), but even more importantly, in directories that are specific to your industry. Not only do these links help to boost your search engine rankings over time, but they are also a quality source of targeted traffic.

Keep your content fresh

A search engine spider will revisit your site frequently if your content continues to increase and evolve frequently. A site that has been optimized for three years with no changes to its content will usually not fare as well as a site that has content that is consistently updated. It is as if the search engine is saying, "Well, this old stuff still looks good, but it certainly is not the newest stuff out there about this topic." This so-called "freshness factor" can have a large impact on rankings, particularly with new Web sites.

Although it may seem that achieving search engine success with a brand-new Web site can be a daunting prospect, it need not be, if done properly. Hiring a skilled search engine optimization company is a good first step. There is little use in lamenting the difficulty before you or feeling that you have already fallen too far behind to begin. As an old Chinese proverb reminds us, "The best time to plant a tree was 20 years ago. The second-best time is today."

10. If you could only give three pieces of advice, what would you tell a business or individual as they attempt to build and/or establish a viable Web presence?

1. **Have a business plan.** Yes, the Web does indeed change the way that many of us go about doing business, but the Web is not a substitute for a viable idea and a well-thought strategy. Too often, I see people who take the "ready, fire, aim" approach — they figure that they will build the Web site and then sort out how they will go about doing business later. I cannot think of any of these examples that succeeded in the long run.

2. **Be aware that your site is a reflection on your business, and act accordingly.** No amount of traffic is going to make a huge impact on a Web site that was built by your 10-year-old nephew. I am not saying that you should go out and spend $50,000 on a Web site, but find a designer whom you are comfortable with and make sure you can walk away if you do not like the prototypes. This is un-biased advice — my company does not offer Web site design. We often turn down search engine marketing business from companies that have Web sites that are overtly amateurish and that have ter-rible conversion rates, unless the company is willing to bring in an outside designer.

3. **Offer something of value to your visitors.** The Internet is full of brochure-ware Web sites that serve the sole function of extolling the virtues of the business. Yet studies show that when people come online, they are primarily searching for information. By provid-ing helpful, nonbiased information on your Web site — informa-tion that helps people to address a certain issue or solve a certain problem — you can reach visitors much earlier in the buying cycle (when they are still in research mode). It is a longer-term approach, but if you only focus on the low-hanging fruit, there is a good chance that your product or service will be commoditized in the mind of the buyer, as they already know exactly what they want and are now comparing several vendors. Offer valuable informa-tion at all stages of the buying cycle, and you will be rewarded by winning a one-horse race in the end.

Scott Buresh is an internationally recognized SEO expert. He has been featured in respected publications such as Entrepreneur, Success, DMNews, Business to Business, *and the* Atlanta Business Chronicle *for his exceptional online marketing talents and managerial style. His articles on the search enging marketing (SEM) industry have been translated into eight languages and have appeared in numerous influential industry publications. Scott was also a contributor to both* The Complete Guide to Google Advertising *(Atlantic, 2008) and* Building Your Business with Google for Dummies *(Wiley, 2004), and he has been cited in several national publications as a leading expert in his field. In 2001, Scott utilized his experience as an SEO expert to co-found the Search Engine Consortium of Atlanta (SECA), a leading organization of SEM specialists dedicated to promoting the discipline of search engine marketing in the city of Atlanta and beyond. You can contact Scott at sburesh@mediumblue.com.*

Interview with Stefan Mischook

1. How does someone begin the process of determining what they should put on their Web site, what design elements it should have, how navigation should function, and what the overall appearance should be? When starting with a blank HTML document, what steps or techniques would you recommend to get to a finished product?

The process should start on paper with a list of things you want to promote, or a list of things you feel are important for your site visitors to see — these items will be your main menu items. Once you have refined that down to, say, the top 5-10 items, you can start sketching out your basic page structure. This is where leaning on Web templates can come in handy; prefabricated template collections can allow you to quickly scroll through a bunch of design possibilities much more quickly than you could if you were designing from scratch. Once you have the basic style/look you want, you can look at purchasing the template that closely resembles what you want, and then modify it. Or, you can start putting your first page in HTML together from scratch, based on the template you picked.

2. There are many Web design products available, such as Microsoft FrontPage, Microsoft Expression Web, and Adobe Creative Suite. For a beginner who wants to have a professional Web site, yet use a fairly simple-to-use Web design product, what would you recommend and why?

I would not use FrontPage because it generates really bad code that may cause you problems with modern Web browsers. Besides, FrontPage was replaced with Expression Web a few years ago. Beyond that, your choice of Web design software is your choice. They all have pros and cons, and much of the time, it comes down to taste. That said, you do not have to use a Web design package at all. Many Web designers actually prefer to design Web pages by hand using a simple text editor. In that case though, you will need to learn HTML and CSS.

3. What type of image format do you recommend using on Web sites? There are several different formats, such as GIF, JPEG, and PNG — is there a difference? Is one better than the other?

JPEG is used for photographs because it can produce the best results with the smallest file size. The smaller the file size, the better when it comes to the Web. GIF and PNG are better for images like your typical logo where the colors are solid and you have sharp lines. Think of logos like Microsoft's or Adobe's, and you should get the idea. Between PNG and GIF, PNG is the better choice because it has a lot of capability — most notably, PNG can have a fading (graduated) transparency that allows you to create cool affects with overlaid images in your Web pages. GIF does allow for transparent backgrounds, but it is a simple off/on transparency, so you cannot create a lot of cool-looking effects that you can with PNG.

4. How much should someone spend on Web site hosting? Is there a Web hosting platform or other features we should specifically be looking for? If you were to recommend a Web hosting provider, who would it be?

For basic sites (most sites), your run-of-the-mill PHP-based hosting package should run you say $3-$4 per month. I recommend you get PHP hosting because many popular Web tools are written in PHP, like blogs, CMS, and forums.

5. **What low- or no-cost options would you recommend for selling products on a Web site, such as PayPal integration or other shopping carts? Is all shopping cart software essentially the same? For a Web site with hundreds of products, what shopping cart software would you recommend? What do you recommend for SSL?**

Not all carts are the same. Some are very simple and easy to deploy, while others are a lot more flexible in terms of how much you can configure them, but that comes at a cost of complexity. I would recommend for most new sites that you just use PayPal to process your credit cards, and then if the volume really increases, you may later on consider another provider. PayPal is safe and well-known; they process credit cards and e-checks, along with PayPal accounts, of course. If you use PayPal, you will not need to get an SSL certificate because PayPal will take care of that for you. We have our own cart software that integrates with PayPal: **www.killerphp.com/tutorials/shopping-cart-tutorial**. It comes with a series of video tutorials and is a fully functional and easy to configure shopping cart. Yes, a shameless plug; it is the cart we use on our own pages.

6. **There are dozens of companies from which you can buy domain names. Is there any company in particular which is better than the others and why? Is there any advantage to buying several domains name types for a domain, such as .com, .biz, .us, and .net?**

Domain name registration is a commodity now — no major difference between the companies for the most part. Just be sure the domain name is in your name and not the registrar's. The distinction between .com, .net, and other domain types is not nearly as important as it was. I would still go with .com personally, if I can, but I am kind of old-school that way.

7. *When designing a Web site, we want to ensure compatibility with major Web browsers, such as Microsoft Internet Explorer, Mozilla Firefox, Google Chrome, and others. Do you have recommendations on how to design the site to ensure maximum compatibility and user functionality?*

Just stick to Web standards code. A good Web design software will take care of that for you.

8. *What is a useful CSS technique that you use often? What is the most common font you use when designing Web pages? What advice can you give regarding Web site navigation?*

The most useful CSS technique: IE Conditional Comments. This allows you to take care of the common problem of making your pages work on both IE and other browsers.

IE does not play by the rules sometimes. I created a free video showing you how to use Conditional Comments: **http://www.killersites.com/ blog/2006/ie-conditional-comments-video.** Common font: depends on the type of site you have and the subject matter. If, for example, your site was on classical pianos, then I would lean toward a script font for the headers. If, on the other hand, you were building a site about clowns, then I would have a more fun font for the headers. Never use flowery, hard-to-read fonts for your paragraphs.

Use simple fonts like Arial, Helvetica, etc. Navigation: Keep it simple and in the same spot on every page.

9. *A challenge of any new Web site is obtaining search engine rankings. What practical advice can you give to someone with a new Web site to achieve visibility in major search engines?*

Content is king. Build a good site and the engines will come.

10. If you could only give three pieces of advice, what would you tell a business or individual as they attempt to build and/or establish a viable Web presence?

Start simple and higher a good designer to establish a solid foundation. Once you have that in place, it is easier to build up from there. Remember that a good-looking site creates a good first impression. A crappy-looking amateur site does not. Would you go to your first meeting with a client wearing old shorts with paint blotches all over it?

Stefan Mischook started designing Web sites in 1994 and has written Web-based software using 8-9 programming languages. He now runs a group of popular educational Web sites, including **www.killersites.com**, **www.killerphp.com**, **www.csstutorial.net**, *and several others. You can find his articles and tutorials on a monthly basis, published in magazines that appear around the world. You may contact Stefan at stefan@killerphp.com.*

Interview with Brian Combs

1. How does someone begin the process of determining what they should put on their Web site, what design elements it should have, how navigation should function, and what the overall appearance should be? When starting with a blank HTML document, what steps or techniques would you recommend to get to a finished product?

Prior to even considering design elements, you need to decide what you want the Web site to accomplish, and define your metrics for success or failure. This paints the picture of the finished product, so that you have a reasonable chance of getting there.

Next, the interactive elements of the site need to be defined. This is basically anything other than plain text or graphics, which are supported by the default HTML pages. These other elements may require technical programming/integration to make them work with your site. You need to determine what you can implement yourself and what you cannot.

Then it is a matter of deciding what technical platform to use. I really like WordPress, which is most known as a blog platform. It can also be customized to be used as a regular Web site (either with or without a blog integrated). This then gives you access to custom themes (the look and feel of a WordPress site) as well as the hundreds of WordPress plug-ins, which allow you to expand the functionality of the site.

2. There are many Web design products available, such as Microsoft FrontPage, Microsoft Expression Web, and Adobe Creative Suite. For a beginner who wants to have a professional Web site, yet use a fairly simple-to-use Web design product, what would you recommend and why?

I do not love any of the beginner applications, as they tend to create horrible code and unprofessional-looking sites. If you have a little bit of background in design, take the time to learn Dreamweaver, which is incredibly powerful.

And do not be afraid to start from a template and then customize it yourself. If you know a bit of HTML and have a decent eye for design, but do not have the ability to create high-quality design yourself, a template can be a great shortcut.

There are a number of WordPress themes available, both for free and for nominal fees ($25-$50). These can then be customized to your needs.

And even if you cannot do the customization yourself, finding someone to customize an existing WordPress theme is generally less expensive than creating a design from scratch.

3. What type of image format do you recommend using on Web sites? There are several different formats, such as GIF, JPEG, and PNG — is there a difference? Is one better than the other?

I do not really use anything other than GIF and JPEG. GIF is best for line art such as logos. JPEG is best for photos and images with the complexity of photos, as the color palette is larger than GIF.

4. How much should someone spend on Web site hosting? Is there a Web hosting platform or other features we should specifically be looking for? If you were to recommend a Web hosting provider, who would it be?

I have a bias for open-source solutions, and prefer a Linux (or similar) machine with PHP. I believe it provides a wider range of tools than a server on the Microsoft platform does. Most any hosting provider should be able to give you this.

Be sure to do some research on the hosting provider before you sign up with them. You do not always get what you pay for. Reviews for any established hosting provider should be easy to find.

I like to work with local companies when I can. You may pay a bit more, but being able to actually reach someone, and have them actually care when you have a problem, is worth quite a bit. Here in Austin, Texas, I like Midas Networks quite a bit, but every good-sized city will have a large selection of quality hosting providers.

To a certain extent, the amount you pay depends upon your traffic and computing needs. It is not unreasonable to expect to pay $20 a month or so to start. You can find cheaper, but you may get what you pay for.

5. What low- or no-cost options would you recommend for selling products on a Web site, such as PayPal integration or other shopping carts? Is all shopping cart software essentially the same? For a Web site with hundreds of products, what shopping cart software would you recommend? What do you recommend for SSL?

For simple and cheap payment systems, PayPal and/or Google Checkout are the way to go. You may still want these integrated with your site. Depending upon the technology you are using, this can be easy or hard.

Both charge transaction fees (as do all payment solutions), so these need to be built into your cost of goods.

All shopping card software is not the same. The quality of your checkout process can make a huge difference in your shopping cart abandonment rate, and thus your profitability.

If you are just starting out and you need to watch your pennies, you might want to look at one of the turnkey shopping cart services, such as Shopify. Then, when the company is rolling, look at one of the more powerful solutions such as Volusion.

In any case, before making a decision, look at the checkout process of some of the sites listed as examples and see if you like them. Some systems allow only one checkout process, while others allow considerable customization.

6. *There are dozens of companies from which you can buy domain names. Is there any company in particular which is better than the others and why? Is there any advantage to buying several domains name types for a domain, such as .com, .biz, .us, and .net?*

I do not think the domain name company you use makes all that much of a difference, as long as you are hosting with someone reputable and reliable. I like GoDaddy because they are cheap, although their checkout process is quite irritating.

It is not that important to get the various TLD versions of your domain, in my opinion. You want to choose one version and make it authoritative in any case.

On the other hand, they do not cost much, and grabbing them will minimize the potential for confusion in the future.

7. **When designing a Web site, we want to ensure compatibility with major Web browsers, such as Microsoft Internet Explorer, Mozilla Firefox, Google Chrome, and others. Do you have recommendations on how to design the site to ensure maximum compatibility and user functionality?**

The most important thing to do is stay away from Microsoft's hosting platform. Its wiz-bang functionality seems to have more problems with cross-compatibility than anything else.

Next, the more your HTML and CSS conform to industry standards, the less likely you are to have problems. But, in any case, always test it out on a large number of browsers. I like to set up the site in a staging area and ask my friends and business associates to take a look — call it a sneak preview. That will usually get you a wide sample set of computers, operating systems, and browsers, and you will certainly hear about any problems.

8. **What is a useful CSS technique that you use often? What is the most common font you use when designing Web pages? What advice can you give regarding Web site navigation?**

I use Arial for a lot of my sites. I tend to prefer sans-serif fonts for body text.

The most important thing with Web site navigation is to keep it simple and intuitive. Try to keep the most important data within a couple of clicks of the home page.

On any particular page, too many choices are generally worse than not enough choices.

9. A challenge of any new Web site is obtaining search engine rankings. What practical advice can you give to someone with a new Web site to achieve visibility in major search engines?

Do not set your expectations too high. The search engines have a definite bias against new sites, and you are not likely to rank for any competitive keywords for quite some time.

If you are targeting users from a particular geography however, the "local listings" for Google, Yahoo, and Bing may be the way to go. The anti-new bias is not nearly as strong there.

The best way I have seen to accelerate the process in Google is through PR. I had a client with a new site that rolled out to considerable press from trusted sites such as the *Wall Street Journal*. They even gave him links. This allowed him to rank for moderately competitive terms in just a few weeks. These sorts of links are not available to most of us, however.

Another thing to do is to set up a placeholder page. Once you know your domain, even before you build the site, put up a "Coming Soon" page on that domain. Make it the default page for the site. Then place a link to the domain from somewhere else on the Web (any page that is indexed by the search engines will do). This link will direct the search engines to the page, and once they find it, the site starts "aging" in the search engines' calculations right away, rather than when you put the completed site up.

10. If you could only give three pieces of advice, what would you tell a business or individual as they attempt to build and/or establish a viable Web presence?

1. **Define your goals beforehand.** You cannot know how well you are doing unless you have metrics of success. And install an analyt-

ics system to let you know what is happening on your site. Even if it is just Google Analytics, having access to data and information is critical.

2. **Do not be afraid to launch before everything is perfect.** While you do not want the site to come across as unprofessional in any way, you also do not want a BMW sitting in your garage with no wheels. Get it on the road and fix things there. You will be amazed at how inspired you are to improve the site once it is public.

3. **Consider using WordPress (or something like it) to implement your site.** This not only provides access to a wealth of existing design and technical solutions, but also will make it much easier for you and your staff to manage the site over time.

As an online marketing expert and Internet pioneer, Brian Combs specializes in bringing measurability to marketing. In May 2009, Brian founded Ionadas Local to help geographically focused companies be found on the Internet.

Before this, he was founder, senior vice president, and chief futurist at Apogee Search, the largest search engine marketing firm in the Southwest, where he was tasked with charting the firms path through the choppy and constantly changing waters of the online marketing sea. Prior to founding Apogee Search, Brian was director of marketing and business development for Journyx, the leading provider of Web-based time and expense management solutions. At Journyx, he oversaw all marketing and strategic partnership activities. Prior to this, he was the senior market analyst in the strategic planning group of Globeset, an Austin software developer backed by Citibank, American Express, Chase Manhattan, and Compaq Computer. At Globeset, Brian was responsible for detecting trends and predicting changes within the financial services industry.

His opinions on the future of the Web and Internet marketing have been included in The Wall Street Journal, The Houston Chronicle, *and* The SEO

Bible *by Jerri Ledford. He is a regular speaker at industry conferences and events. Brian may be contacted at combs@ionadas.com.*

Interview with Johnny Truant

1. How does someone begin the process of determining what they should put on their Web site, what design elements it should have, how navigation should function, and what the overall appearance should be? When starting with a blank HTML document, what steps or techniques would you recommend to get to a finished product?

I actually do very little design from scratch anymore. I work mainly in WordPress blog software (as I operate mainly in the blog space), and there are tons of free WordPress themes out there. Tons. Even premium themes like Thesis and Woothemes cost far, far less than anything custom, and some of these are customizable in themselves (Thesis, particularly). As such, because most of my customers are on a shoestring, I find it is easier to either find and use a free or cheap existing WordPress theme, or to customize an existing theme, than to start from scratch. Why reinvent the wheel unless your needs truly call for something with fully custom branding?

2. There are many Web design products available, such as Microsoft FrontPage, Microsoft Expression Web, and Adobe Creative Suite. For a beginner who wants to have a professional Web site, yet use a fairly simple-to-use Web design product, what would you recommend and why?

I have only ever used Macromedia (now Adobe) Dreamweaver. I used to use FrontPage and now cannot find enough bad things to say about it. Dreamweaver is standards-compliant and will not rewrite your code like some other programs that think they are smarter than you.

However, when working with CSS, I tend to code by hand. This is not easy and not intuitive for beginners, so I would stick with HTML. And yes, I would still suggest Dreamweaver. It makes sense and will not make a mockery of your code.

3. What type of image format do you recommend using on Web sites? There are several different formats, such as GIF, JPEG, and PNG — is there a difference? Is one better than the other?

I use JPEGs for pretty much anything. I give lip service to the idea that I should use JPEGs for continuous tone images (like photos) and GIFs for graphics with few colors, but I am not strict about it and honestly feel it does not much matter if you just kind of always use JPEGs. I do not use PNGs. They tend to be space hogs, unnecessarily huge. And never use GIFs for continuous tone images (like photos) unless you need a transparent background (for which GIFs are required). They cannot reproduce a continuous tone image well enough using only the 256 colors allowed to GIFs.

I would say using all JPEGs is probably a good default position for 99 percent of all people.

4. How much should someone spend on Web site hosting? Is there a Web hosting platform or other features we should specifically be looking for? If you were to recommend a Web hosting provider, who would it be?

I overspent for hosting for years and have decided since that the vast majority of Web users (and especially beginners) should never pay more than $10 per month for hosting. There simply is no reason. There are no features beyond the two plans I use for everything (including my own sites and my own clients) that anyone but super-specialists would ever need.

I recommend a HostGator plan called "Baby" and a GoDaddy plan called "Deluxe." Both are under $10/month, and both allow for unlimited Web sites to be placed on them and have absolutely no limits on how much a user can upload. There are also no limits on bandwidth. Why buy something more expensive?

5. What low- or no-cost options would you recommend for selling products on a Web site, such as PayPal integration or other shopping carts? Is all shopping cart software essentially the same? For a Web site with hundreds of products, what shopping cart software would you recommend? What do you recommend for SSL?

I think most beginning sellers can get by just fine using **www.e-junkie.com** as their product management software, integrated with PayPal, Google Checkout, or both. That setup covers most people.

If you want advanced affiliate management and product-specific affiliate marketing materials — or want to be able to upsell buyers of a specific product with custom, product-specific auto responders — then get a full-blown cart. I would not move to a cart until one of those things is true; the expense outweighs the benefit for most people. Of these, I like **www.1shoppingcart.com.**

If you have many products in specific categories with many different colors, sizes, varieties, or whatever, you should use store software, not cart software. I have always used **www.shopsite.com**, which handles the store creation for you.

6. There are dozens of companies from which you can buy domain names. Is there any company in particular which is better than the others and why? Is there any advantage to buying several domains name types for a domain, such as .com, .biz, .us, and .net?

I like GoDaddy because it is easy to use and cheap, but in general I feel that a registrar is a registrar. I would not be picky. As to multiple domains, the only real reason I see is to get more search engine juice for a given term (the term in the URL) or if you think people will not be smart enough to figure out to add ".com."

7. *When designing a Web site, we want to ensure compatibility with major Web browsers, such as Microsoft Internet Explorer, Mozilla Firefox, Google Chrome, and others. Do you have recommendations on how to design the site to ensure maximum compatibility and user functionality?*

CSS seems to have finally solved many of the browser compatibility issues, but really the only way to find out is to test throughout the process. I have found Firefox to be the best judge overall, especially if you design on a Mac and do not have easy access to Explorer.

8. *What is a useful CSS technique that you use often? What is the most common font you use when designing Web pages? What advice can you give regarding Web site navigation?*

I use CSS mainly to style text and to position page elements. I am old-school and still (probably ill-advisedly) do most of my design using tables. I use divs to position "odd elements" or when I worry that a table will behave differently in different browsers. Divs are also great when you want an absolute position.

For fonts, I stick with the common families because everyone has them. I like Arial for most text and Verdana a lot of times for blogs. I am not a fan of serif fonts like Times for body text, but it all depends on preference. Serif works better in print than on screen, for some reason.

Navigation: Keep it obvious, and I do mean stupidly obvious. Then read Steve Krug's usability manual *Don't Make Me Think!* and pay close attention to all of it.

9. A challenge of any new Web site is obtaining search engine rankings. What practical advice can you give to someone with a new Web site to achieve visibility in major search engines?

1. Do not be cute. Be obvious. People hate to think online and will leave your site a long time before they figure out that "Fine purchasings" is the location of your store.

2. Your site does matter. As hard as this is to describe, the look of your site must match the personality of your brand and your industry.

3. Be cost-conscious, but not cheap. This is a major business asset, so treat it like one. Do not pinch every single penny.

Johnny B. Truant has carved out a niche as "the guy who makes technology stupidly simple." Johnny began building Web sites professionally, as well as writing for print magazines, in the late 1990s. It took him another decade to launch his Internet career, and did so in 2008 as a humor blogger. Johnny began writing a weekly column about his attempts to build a business online. It all came together when Johnny wrote his first report, a free e-book called How to Launch a Blog in Under an Hour for Super Cheap, Even if You are a Total Idiot. *Johnny realized he had a hit on his hands when, within a few days, the free e-book had been downloaded more than 400 times. Since that time, John has written guest posts for mega-blogs Problogger and Copyblogger, as well as continued his weekly IttyBiz column and appeared on many other popular blogs. He lives with his sons and two children and continues to write his own blogs at* **www.LearnToBeYourOwnVA.com** *and* **www.TheEconomyIsntHappening.com**. *Johnny can be contacted at Johnny@theeconomyisnthappening.com.*

Chapter 18

WEB DESIGN
SUCCESS STORIES

CASE STUDY: STEPHEN ANTISDEL

Stephen Antisdel
WorkingPerson.com
FurnitureFind.com

The story behind the success of **www.WorkingPerson.com** could rc ally be traced back to an earlier successful online business: **www.FurnitureFind.com**. After 20 years in the brick-and-mortar home furnishing business, we launched this early online furniture site in 1996. We designed and built it internally, learning as we went along, and experienced strong organic growth over the next several years. A key point is that we developed proprietary best practices for SEO and site design that contributed to very high search engine placement and better-than-average conversion in a very tough category.

Based on our success at bringing targeted traffic to our site and then converting the visitors to customers, we survived the dot-com crash in 2000-'01 and emerged as a leader in the space by 2002. We sold the company in 2003 and started doing e-commerce consulting work. Although we signed a multi-year non-compete to stay out of the online furniture business, we kept our proprietary IP and methods.

In 2005, we met up with WorkingPerson.com — as consultants, initially — and were very impressed; we saw great potential in the business model. The CEO, Eric Deniger, had built a true destination retail store in a tiny town (pop. 400). He had a deep understanding of the space and was focused on serving the work apparel and footwear customer better than anyone else, with more breadth and depth of product, a strong service ethos, and value pricing. He had his Web site up, but was paying multiple outside consultants to try to build and market the site, with mixed results.

Seeing the potential, we joined forces with Eric in 2005 and went inside to rebuild the Web site and manage the online marketing. Using 2004 online sales as a baseline, by the end of 2005, we would have outgrown the e-commerce business by about three times. In 2006, the online revenues were up nearly four times over 2005. Between 2007 and 2008, online sales more than doubled again. Key design features incorporated as we improved the WorkingPerson.com site: detailed, custom-created product descriptions; multiple, high-quality product images on thousands of products; customer reviews; customer ratings; customer comments throughout the site; improved multi-path navigation; improved site search; new, faster, easier cart design (only one page to have to enter purchase info); chat; ticket system; easier returns systems; upgraded site serving capabilities to handle millions of page views per month; and a thousand other improvements along the way — you are never done.

Then came the marketing: SEO using our proprietary methods (the WorkingPerson.com site is on page one of Google on thousands of terms); SEM testing 50,000 keywords and key phrases; data feed optimization; and e-mail campaign management.

By late 2005, word started getting out on the success we were having building WorkingPerson.com, and we started getting calls to help other businesses with their Web design and marketing efforts. That interest led to the decision to launch AVID Commerce as a separate services division of the same holding company that owns WorkingPerson.com — now, we are "brother-sister" companies.

Other AVID Commerce clients now include companies as diverse as Veada.com (OEM boat seating manufacturers); **ArtPassion.com** (custom framed art); **GreenfishSports.com** (high-quality bicycles and gear); **BathtubStore.com** (direct sourcing of vintage bathtubs and more); and **JLPowellUSA.com** (unique, high-quality men's sporting apparel), among others.

WorkingPerson.com has been on the *Internet Retailer* Top 500 (largest e-retailers) list for 2007, 2008, and 2009. The parent company, Working Person's Store, won a spot on the *Inc.* 500 in 2008 (fastest-growing private companies in America) and numerous other awards.

In 1996, I led the build-out of what was probably the world's first online furniture store: **www.furniturefind.com**. This was a DIY project: We taught ourselves HTML, tested and refined various design and navigation elements to optimize conversion, reverse-engineered the early search engines (essentially inventing SEO best practices), and generally learned as we went. What we learned worked very well: The site was consistently at the top of the search engines.

With strong organic search visibility — and good conversion metrics — we were able to compete successfully with the many VC-funded competitors (many of which had tens of millions in startup funding) that sprung up during the late '90s dot-com boom. Then, when the dot-com meltdown hit, as our competitors imploded, we emerged from the rubble as the leading Web site. (We were one of the Top 100 highest-traffic Web sites in the world, and by 2001, we were No. 1).

Post script: We sold FurnitureFind.com to a venture capital group in 2003 (but kept our SEO and conversion-design IP) and launched what is today AVID Commerce to help other companies do high-performance Web site design, SEO technologies, and strategy. I also started teaching as an adjunct professor, teaching a number of business classes at Indiana Tech; no surprise that e-commerce is my favorite subject.

Stephen Antisdel is e-Business Analyst and Chief Executive Officer of AVID Commerce. Stephen is an Adjunct Professor at Indiana Institute of Technology's College of Professional Studies. He was a co-founder and former CEO of FurnitureFIND Corporation. Following the sale of the company to a venture capital group, he became a co-founder and Chief Executive Officer of AVID Commerce. His e-business innovations have been covered by Business Week, The Wall Street Journal, Investors' Business Daily, Business 2.0, Newsweek, Furniture World, Furniture Today, *and National Public Radio. He has shared his business perspectives as a presenter for Hewlett Packard; the International Conference of Better Business Bureaus; the Consumer Electronics Manufacturers Association; and business conferences in London, Atlanta, Las Vegas, the University of Michigan, Indiana University, and the Internet Retailer Conference in San Jose. Stephen can be contacted at stephen@ avidcommerce.com and* **www.avidcommerce.com**.

CASE STUDY: NANCY STRONG

Nancy Strong
LightenYourWorkLoad.com

Building my own Web site was a challenge I was not sure I wanted to undertake. However, the alternative was something I could not afford at the time. I was taking a class called Expert VA Training offered by Kathy Goughenour (**www.expertvatraining.com**). My main goal for this course was to get my new real estate virtual assistant business started, which included setting up a Web site.

DISCOVERING A GOOD DOMAIN NAME

My first challenge was to come up with a good domain name. Not only would this be my domain name, but also my company name. It had to reflect what I wanted to provide to the real estate community. After much research and input from family, friends, and colleagues, I chose Lighten Your WorkLoad (**www.lightenyourworkload.com**).

ANALYZING KEYWORDS

Finding the right keywords for my Web site was the next step. This involved thinking of the things I would be doing in my new business and discovering the keywords and keyword phrases I would need to use in my content and titles. This may seem like a daunting task to many people who have never thought about putting a Web site on the World Wide Web, but it is an extremely important step. This is called SEO and may not seem relevant to the average person; however, if you want your Web site to come up in the first few pages of a Web search, this is extremely important. Most people do not go beyond the first few pages when they search for something; I know I do not. If I cannot find what I am searching for in the first few pages, I will try different words for my search.

After a while, exploring keywords became a game, almost an addiction. There were times I would sit for hours looking for keywords and phrases that would be a possible fit. What could I say or write, or how would a phrase fit into my writing? I produced an Excel spreadsheet with all of the keywords I had looked up and made several worksheets for each category I was thinking of including on my Web site.

WRITING CONTENT

Next came the fun part: learning how to write content for my Web site and where to put these keywords I had discovered. Keywords must be placed strategically within the Web site's content. This enables the search engines to scan the content to find the keywords that are related to the Web site. I learned where the ideal placement of the keywords and keyword phrases were to go to enable the search engines to recognize the Web site.

The key to writing text is not to make sure keywords are placed correctly, which is very important, but to make sure the content is "talking" to the person reading the Web site. Direct the content to them. Use the word "you." Speak their language.

I have always found it an excellent idea to have someone, or several people, read what I have written and make comments. Not only did I query my family, but Kathy Goughenour, my coach and mentor, was such a wonderful help to me. She had written so many Web pages for real estate agents when she was a virtual assistant that she knew how to write for the Internet and made suggestions to get me headed in the right direction.

The amazing thing about the Internet and learning something new like designing your Web site is how much information is out there for your use. People are always willing to help you figure out a problem. Most of this information can be found free of charge.

ADDING PHOTOGRAPHS

Once the content was written, I had to start thinking of photographs to include on the Web site. People love pictures, and a Web site needs as many as you deem necessary, but not too many. There were numerous places to find photographs. I could use my own, which I did for many. Other avenues were **www.istockphoto.com** and **www.flickr.com**. There are many other Web sites where photographs can be obtained, but make sure they are obtained legally.

ESTABLISHING PAGES

There were many other things I needed to learn for SEO, writing, and constructing my Web pages. I feel as though I learn something new if not daily, then weekly. There were several pages needed for my Web site: the home page, of course, which is the introduction to my business; FAQ is self-explanatory. I want people to know what I provide and how much I charge, so there is my "Services and Rates" page. There must be a "Contact" page for anyone interested in contacting you, and I have included a "Portfolio" page as well. A Web site needs to be continually updated and revised, or your Web site will not be attractive to the search engines. A terrific section to include in your Web site is a blog. But be warned, you need to consistently update your blog for it to be effective (**http://featherinyourhat.com**).

BUILDING YOUR WEB SITE

So the next question for me was how to go about getting my Web site designed and on the World Wide Web. Funds are tight, and the best solution for someone to design my Web site for me was through a Web designer Kathy Goughenour recommended. They were very good, and the price was reasonable. But it was not really something I could afford. They wanted $599 for the Web site design using one of their pre-existing templates, plus $30 a month for hosting. For a year, that came to $960. I did not really have $960. The alternative was to design my own Web site, but I was not sure what to use.

My search started out with two alternatives to designing my own Web site: either iWeb® — an Apple application — or WordPress.org. I investigated both and decided to go with iWeb due to the fact I am very familiar with Apple software. I have been a Mac user since 1989 and I have never regretted that choice. Then I had to consider hosting. I knew GoDaddy had a hosting service and started investigating. The first thing that came up on GoDaddy when I logged in was their Website Tonight Web design. This intrigued me. I could do everything under one roof, so to speak. They had video and testimonials from people who had used Website Tonight. These people had never built a Web site themselves and raved about the ease. Website Tonight had a large assortment of templates, and everyone said computer software knowledge was not a necessity. The best part was the affordability. For Website Tonight and a year of hosting, the cost would be $170.

GoDaddy was not as easy as people had said on the videos and testimonials. There are two ways you can use Website Tonight for inputting your content. One is what they call Design, which is basically word processing. Of course, this was my choice. The other choice is HTML, if you know how to write HTML. I had no idea how HTML was written and did not want to learn. GoDaddy allows you to type in the content, and they format the HTML automatically. This was great if no mistakes are made or something a little different is needed from what they have to offer. I realized I needed a little HTML knowledge to make the Web site work the way I wanted. But all in all, GoDaddy was basically very straightforward. Their support is quite helpful, which in my case was key. If I could not find the answer in their help area, I could submit a ticket with my questions, and they usually responded within 24 hours. There were times I had to call them and speak with a support tech. They were always friendly and eager to help with questions and problems.

GoDaddy is a bit cumbersome to work with, especially because I work on a Mac. I did get one tech who also uses Mac, and he informed me that GoDaddy works well with the Sunrise browser. So I downloaded Sunrise and had a little better luck getting my Web pages written and designed.

There were many times when I would need to edit a page and the design would go gray; I could do absolutely nothing. So I would have to close the window and launch my design again. This was a problem if I had done a lot of work on that particular page without saving it first. I learned if I was going to edit a photograph or do something with a link, I needed to save my work first and then go back into the page and do my edits. It makes the process go a bit slower and therefore is a drawback, but not a show-stopper.

I was also receiving daily SEO tips from Search Engine Workshop (**www.searchengineworkshops.com**). This is one of those amazing free services you will find on the Internet. I have found these daily SEO tips very helpful. One thing they highly recommend is to have a sitemap on your Web site and have every single page link to that sitemap. The reason for this is the search engine robots can then go to any page within your Web site and not get lost or stuck. Robots like to freely roam Web sites. So this was another page I needed to add to my Web site. I went to Search Engine Workshop to see what their sitemap looked like and what they did and basically formatted my sitemap after theirs. It seemed logical to me — look at what the pros do and follow their instruction.

BLOGGING

I also wanted a blog, as my mentor had said that keeping a blog updated is good exposure and helps with the search robots. My first thought for a blog was WordPress because my daughter had a WordPress blog. But I found that to have a WordPress blog connected to my GoDaddy Web site, I would need to host the blog as well. Even though WordPress was free, the hosting was not. The difference in cost between hosting a

WordPress blog and GoDaddy's Quick Blogcast was nominal. If I went with GoDaddy's Quick Blogcast, everything would be under one roof, so to speak. The added cost was a total of $56 for an entire year. So my out-of-pocket expenses for designing a Web site with one year of hosting and a blog was less than $230.

Designing my Web site on GoDaddy with Website Tonight and adding a blog took approximately one month. I did not think that was too bad. I was just starting to get a few virtual assistant clients, so my time was available.

LAUNCHING LIGHTENYOURWORKLOAD.COM

March 13, 2009 was the Web site publish date. I was so excited. Something that I had been working on since December 2008 was coming to fruition. When I hit the "Publish" button, the elation I felt was unbelievable. I had learned so much in such a very short time, and something I had never thought I would ever do in my life was now becoming a reality.

Once published, which took approximately 24 hours after hitting the "Publish" button, I knew there would be changes and revisions needed. I informed my family, friends, and colleagues and asked them all to review my Web site and let me know what errors they found. There were a few. The biggest were discovered on the Internet Explorer browser. Figures, as I work on a Mac. This is when I needed to learn HTML.

LEARNING HTML

During the whole process of writing my Web site on GoDaddy, I had never gone to the HTML side of the pages. This was about to change. There were wonky fonts discovered and mistakes that needed HTML changes. I figured by this time, what the heck, I have actually published a Web site, so how difficult can HTML be? Much to my surprise, it is not as difficult as I had imagined. I did write software for Martin Marietta back in the 1970s, so I was not as intimidated as I thought I would be.

This has produced another challenge I am embracing with my whole heart. As if I do not have enough on my plate, I have started reading *HTML, XHTML and CSS for Dummies* by Andy Harris. There have been numerous times in my business and Web site design where I have looked for HTML code needed to accomplish something that I wanted a certain way. Again, with all of the information on the Internet, free most of the time, it is fairly easy to find the answers. But I figure with some of the issues I have been confronted with, the best choice is to learn HTML.

This will help in my business, and I may find another avenue in which I can make money.

ANALYZING THE WEB SITE'S SUCCESS

My Web site has been published for almost three months. I cannot say I have had success in acquiring clients from this Web site as of this date. However, I have had people visit the Web site and go through my pages. A service GoDaddy provides is Visitor Statistics. These statistics enable me to see what is happening when people search for a keyword or phrase I am using and what they do when they go on my Web site. Since my Web site was published, there have been more than 4,500 successful server requests, and this is increasing. According to the statistics from GoDaddy, there have been almost 1,500 successful requests in the past seven days. I average approximately 50 blog visits a day. This is not resounding success, but for three months, it is a good start.

HELPING OTHERS WITH THEIR WEB SITES

My daughter had been laid off in January of this year. She was having no success in finding a job in her field of archaeology, nor in the workplace as a whole. She found an interesting video on Internet marketing and did a lot of research. She wanted to start her own Web site.

At first she attempted to use WordPress.org for a Web site, but the restrictions she was encountering made her decide to use GoDaddy, as I did. I have helped her with some of the aspects of her Web site. In the meantime, she had a job offer to work at the North Rim of the Grand Canyon to do archaeological survey work for the National Forest Service. She did get her Web site published before she left, but there are many pages she has not been able to complete and keep up-to-date, as Internet service is very limited where she is. I did get her sitemap, or "Coordinates" page, as she calls it, written and published this past weekend. I am hoping there will be a chapter in this book with her experiences as well.

This experience has helped me in my business endeavors. I am currently working with a group of virtual assistants for a real estate agent. We each have our expertise and are assisting her in updating her Web site, contact management system, and adding video. Because of some of the challenges I encountered with GoDaddy and learning some HTML, I have been able to incorporate her contact management system with her Web site.

I am also in discussions with a family member to develop a Web site for him in a new enterprise he is pursuing. There are going to be challenges, as everyone needs and wants different things on their Web sites. But with my experiences in developing my Web site, I feel I am up to the task.

*Nancy Strong has been small business owner with her husband, Dan, since 1989. Starting a small business opened their eyes to the many aspects that are needed in succeeding as small business owners. Nancy has been on the inside of their businesses, doing what is needed to assist in the development of sales, from creating strong relationships with customers to preparing quotes, forecasts, payroll, and quarterly and year-end accounting. Because of Nancy's attention to detail, their businesses have been a success. Nancy started using computers in the 1970s while working at Martin Marietta as a computer programmer. She is experienced on both Macs and PCs. Nancy helps build businesses at **www.lightenyourworkload.com**. You can contact Nancy at Nancy@Lighten YourWorkLoad.com.*

CASE STUDY: SUSAN MARX

Susan Marx
SusanMarxDesign.com

I figured out what information I wanted on my site and how I wanted it structured. Then I created a layout in Adobe Illustrator. I used Dreamweaver to help code the Web site.

I use Dreamweaver (and HTML) to design sites for my clients as well. As an art director/graphic designer, it is important to have a Web site, primarily to show my work to potential clients. And because Web site design happens to be one of the services I provide (along with print and display design), I want mine to look visually interesting and provide useful content.

Several years ago when I would set up meetings, I would have to carry along a large portfolio containing hard copies of all my projects. Now I rarely carry one — I simply direct people to my Web site. So before

I even have an initial meeting with a client, they have usually had a chance to review my work. I put out an e-newsletter once a month, and people can sign up to be on the mailing list on my Web site, too. Also, I occasionally speak at universities and chambers of commerce on design and marketing. People can sign up on my site to get information about that as well.

Susan Marx Design helps small- to mid-size companies strengthen their visual presence. Whether you are a corporation that wants to share your products and services, a non-profit in search of donors, or an entrepreneur with an exciting venture, they can help create cohesive presentations in print and on the Web. Susan can be contacted at susan@susan marxdesign.com or **www.susanmarxdesign.com***.*

CASE STUDY: PABLO SOLOMON

Pablo Solomon
PabloSolomon.com

As an artist, several things are necessary for success. Of course, there is the obvious: creative talent. However, equally important is name recognition and the ability to stay in contact with collectors, galleries, and art critics. In the old days, this was very difficult. In addition, the galleries had a virtual plantation system in which you either played servant to them or had little or no chance for success. The Internet allowed artists to "leave the plantation" and to contact collectors directly to show their work to a worldwide audience. Of course, we must still maintain a business relationship with galleries and gain the favor of critics and museums. Today, one can now function as an equal, and not as a slave to the system.

I may have been one of the first visual artists to recognize the freedom and empowerment that the Internet had the potential of providing for artists. Luckily, my wife also recognized the value of the Internet early. She actually developed a concept for the Texas Parks and Wildlife system in connection with Texas Highways in which tourists could go to the computer and find out what wildflowers were blooming along which highways: **www.Bluebon.net** was a big hit. In fact, she received a citation from the

State of Texas for her work and was featured in the state magazine *Fiscal Notes*. Not bad for a woman who spent most of her career as a model and then account executive for some of the major fashion designers. In fact, she has brought a lot of her sales and promotion experience to my art career. So we began experimenting with an art Web site as early as we could get an Internet connection out here on the ranch, around the year 2000.

At first it was excruciating. We tried using Dreamweaver, and it drove us nuts. Then a fortuitous chain of events occurred: First, our original Internet provider went out of business and was bought out by Earthlink. At the time, we did not realize what a good thing that would turn out to be because Earthlink provided free Web space and provided a template called Trellix to make your own Web site. They have upgraded this template several times to the point that now you have lots of options, and it very simple to use.

My Web site has exposed my work to collectors and art writers around the world. It has led to our meeting other artists. In fact, we have been the guests of artists in France and the Netherlands due to our meeting them on the Internet. When we put out a call to photographers suggesting a joint project in which they photographed models with my work, we had no idea how successful it would be. We had world-class photographers coming to our ranch. We even had one short film done on my work with model Niecy Moss over a period of years that aired on HBO. Several of the photographers won awards for the work they did; one even got a write-up in the *New York Times* art section, and the photos ended up in the most prestigious gallery in the world. This also led to shows for me and many magazine write-ups.

So building our own Web site has turned me from just another artist to one of the most recognized names in the art world today. Amazing, considering it basically only cost us some time and $21 a month.

*Pablo Solomon is an internationally recognized artist known primarily for drawings and sculptures of dancers. He has been featured in books, magazines, newspapers, radio, TV, and film. Currently, he lives and works with his wife Beverly on their historic 1856 ranch north of Austin, Texas. You can see his work at **www.pablosolomon.com**.*

CASE STUDY: KOINONIA BUSINESS WOMEN'S ORGANIZATION

Koinonia Business Women's organization
KBwomen.com

The Koinonia Business Women's organization started out as a simple idea that continues to grow and develop even now. Because this business/ministry/organization was starting locally but was meant to expand in stages, we needed a Web site that would do exactly the same thing. We needed to establish one central online hub where Christian women in business could find out more about who we are. Our site had its "small beginnings" launch out of necessity, although we had a vision for its functionality, look, and content far beyond what it started out as. That is all right. At first just getting something up "live" felt good, although also frustrating because it was not perfect. Then again, waiting until everything is perfect is dangerous for most businesses or projects. Sometimes, something evolving is better than nothing.

Since I already had experience with HTML and Web design, we decided to do the site ourselves. We still do, but will most likely give the task over to someone else eventually for updating. In the first six months of existence, the Web site underwent major transformation twice. Having full control of the site ourselves has given us great flexibility in making changes and additions. As services and product offerings have been added, so have pages to the site. Certain pages need changes often (like the "Events" page), yet some have content that remains constant (such as the "About Us" page). We have received nice feedback on the site. Even when we were relatively unknown, people who found the site would tell us it made us look like a big organization. That was exciting.

Today, all of our online efforts direct potentially interested people to our site. We like to incorporate features like Twitter feeds, audio messages, and other interactive and free services to make our site more interesting for visitors. Our site helps us collect e-mail addresses for our free e-zine automatically, which is great. People also use the site to RSVP for our networking meetings, to register and pay for workshops and teleseminars, or to find out about our other upcoming events.

We would recommend to every small business owner that they learn enough about Web sites and Web design that they could update their own sites, even if someone else does the initial design. There is still much to be learned and implemented. KBWomen.com has been a work of love.

The Koinonia Business Women's organization offers teleseminars on business, goals, and life-purpose topics, as well as having local networking groups, mastermind groups, the KBWomen Radio show, *BLING* e-zine for Christian women in business, conferences, video skits for churches and ministries, The Wall of Prayer, and speaking.

*For more information, visit **www.kbwomen.com** or e-mail questions@kbwomen.com. Also, you can visit The Wall of Prayer at **www.thewallofprayer.com**.*

CASE STUDY: KELLY CANULL

Kelly Canull
KellyCanull.com

In 1996, at the age of 22, I decided to start my own soul reading and life coaching business called Coaching From Within. At that time, I had no idea what a Web site was or how beneficial having one would become in my life. I would see clients in person, and I built my business locally, based on word-of-mouth for many years. Every time I moved, I would have to start by business from the ground-up, networking like crazy to meet clients in my new towns. In 2005, after moving to Colorado, I set up my business in a small office area and used my usual marketing tactics to build my clientele base. It was slowgoing, and I knew there had to be a better way. The next day I was daydreaming about reaching more people worldwide with my work, and that is when it dawned on me: Why do not I use the World Wide Web?

At this point, the Internet had proved itself to be a valuable place for others I knew to put their work on display to the world, so I thought perhaps it may just work for my business as well. In one day, I made three appointments with three different Web designers. Two were to be over the phone and one was in-person. That day, the man I was to meet in-person was a no-show, and neither of the designers I was to meet with over the phone called me.

As an intuitive, I believe there are no accidents, so I realized it was a sign that I was to develop my Web site on my own. But I had no idea where to turn or what to do to start on the path of creating my own Web site. The next day, I started to research Web companies that would allow me to create my own site with ease and at an affordable rate. I found a few, but after going through their tutorials, I felt bad that there was no way I could do this without a company with a format that was easy for someone like myself to follow.

The next morning, I received a random e-mail. I quickly checked out the Web site and scrolled down to the bottom to see that it was powered by a company called **www.citymax.com**. I could not believe what I was seeing — a company that allows you to try it out for two weeks free of charge and, if you decide to use them, only costs $20 a month. I could not resist, and I signed up right away, saving even more money (now only $16 a month) by purchasing a six-month package.

I spent the next week creating my own Web site. I felt empowered in ways that I had not felt before. My inner critic was now silent, and I had regained my confidence that this new portal was going to open new avenues for me in ways I was not even clear about in the beginning. Two of the most important things that I wanted to have before I learned about building my own Web site was access to be able to change the content whenever I wanted, and a newsletter where I could build up my business. This company had handed me a golden key. It was so simple that I could edit my site a hundred times a day if I wanted (and I came close when I first created it), as well as easily add new components to the site as I went along.

In January 2007, I launched my Web site to all my family, friends, and past clients. I started by creating a weekly newsletter in which I sent them inspirational stories that I would write in alignment with the work I was doing. I used the newsletter as a way of reaching out to let others know that they were loved, as well as build my client base. This tool alone brought my newsletter distribution list from 200 to 2,000 in just a year. The second factor — being able to change the content in a minute's time — was also significant in helping me build my business. Initially, the only portion of my business that I had on my site was my

An Inward Journey: A Guide to Living Your Best Life, and started a program called "Break Free from The Money Game" that needed to be highlighted on my site as well. Having access to my Web site where I could play around with the content and change it on a dime was important to me and to those whom received what I had to share. Not only did I have the freedom to change the content, but I would also change out pictures and even the entire template in an instant whenever I felt it needed updating.

In 2007, I did not know what my goals were beyond putting my work out into the world on the Internet. I knew in order to do that, I would need a creative Web site that drew people in and did not take a lot out of me, both mentally and financially. Finding **www.citymax.com** was a gift. It allowed me the space to be creative and develop a Web site that looked and felt professional, while costing me only $16 a month.

Here are a few other ways that having a Web site has changed the dynamic of my business:

1. I used to accept checks and had to wait to receive the payment before I would schedule a client. Having them pay online gave me the freedom to book my clients sooner as well as more often.

2. I used to have an office where I would see my clients in person. Having this Web site allowed me to switch to working remotely with clients over the phone from all over the world.

3. After my book was published, my Web site was an important portal that initially drew people to my book, yet once there, they were able to see all the other services I provided as well.

4. Being able to change the layout, content, pictures, and overall theme of my site in only seconds is one of the greatest perks to building my own site.

Today, I am continuing to use my Web site as a portal to bring people to my business and gifts I have to offer the world. I have recommended **www.citymax.com** to others I have seen who really want to create a Web site for their business, yet do not know where to get started. My business continues to grow every day because I have the freedom to promote what I am doing to a large audience that has selected to receive my newsletters as well as all of the people who find my site through the Web.

Building a Web site for my professional business is the best thing I have ever done to accomplish my goals of reaching a worldwide audience. It was simple, affordable, and empowering all in one. I invite you to walk down this path of self-empowerment and create your own Web site this week — it may just change your life forever, like it did mine.

Kelly Canull has shown individuals for more than 20 years how to remove the limitations, restrictions, fears, doubts, and obstacles that no longer serve them, while simultaneously showing them how to tap into their inner guidance. She guides individuals back inward where they access the voice, feelings, and wisdom of their souls so they can live their phenomenal life. To learn more about her work, visit **www.kellycanull. com,** *or e-mail her at aninwardjourney@gmail.com.*

CASE STUDY: EFREM R. JASSO

Efrem R. Jasso
INeedAWife.com

Back in 1998, I was mentoring two recent college graduates on Internet development and marketing. These two young men were ten years my junior and had invited me out to a local bar for drinks one weekend. Chris inquired into a couple of dates that I had gone on the previous weekend. I told him that the women were nice but the chemistry was not quite right. He made a sad face and jokingly said, "Aw, what's next for the old man now?" I was 30 years old at the time, mind you. I sort of mock-slapped at him and said, "You know what, I am going to set up a Web site. This is what I do for a living — I am going to market myself on the Internet." My friend Jason laughed and said, "Yeah, what are you going to call it, I-Need-A-Wife-dot-com?" We all laughed and continued drinking.

30 days later and well after sobering up from that night, I received a letter from the InterNIC, the governing authority on domain name registration. It was a bill for a domain name that I (apparently) had registered that night after I got home: Ineedawife.com.

My immediate thought was, "What am I going to do with this? I cannot believe I actually registered this!" I sat on the letter for a day or so, and after some thought I decided that it would be a riot to go ahead and pay for the name and to build a site for it, just to see what kind of response it would get. I had absolutely no real intent of looking for a wife; I just wanted to see what would happen.

Coming from a background in art history and fine arts, and having worked in the Internet development arena for four years at that time, I pooled together my resources and designed a simple site. The home page was artfully done with rich golds and browns and had these little buttons that looked like milk chocolate bars that you could pluck right off of the page and eat. I scanned a copy of Raphael's famous painting of two angels gazing up toward the heavens, and I Photoshopped myself between them, smiling and looking down at them — I thought it was cute at the time.

In the site, I added a "Bio" page that listed some of my musical, artistic, historical, and gastronomical likes and passions. I also included a simple contact form so people could easily contact me. I coded the form so that the subject line of each e-mail that came from it would be fixed and easily recognizable. This also helped me filter those e-mails directly into an inbox created just for that stream of contact (that I was not really sure was going to happen).

To button things up and make sure that readers of the site would know exactly what this was all about, I transcribed the story I started with above in this document — how the concept was "born." To this I added the fact that I was not really looking for a wife, but would just sort of let things happen as they may. I was also the first one to poke fun at myself by saying that "I can hear it now: People will say, 'Why did not you register I Need A Life.com?'"

On the back end of the site I had done some keyword tagging and coding so that the site would show up high in the search engines when people typed in keywords or phrases such as "dating" or "relationships." Little did I know how effective this would turn out to be.

I launched the site on January 1, 1999, and pretty much left it to its own devices out on World Wide Web. I had almost forgotten about it for a couple of weeks until I came home one night after work and opened up my e-mail software. It was January 27, a Wednesday. I had just sat down to have dinner and see what was going on in the news. In the background, my hard drive was happily chugging away as the e-mail continued to download, and download, and download.

I looked up to notice that the unread messages were starting to run in the 3,000 range and almost fell out of my chair. I immediately started scanning them to see what happened to cause such an immediate and unexpected flood. I got about half way through the 3,000-plus e-mails and came across a letter from a woman that read, "Congrats on your mention in *USA Today*! I hope you find the woman of your dreams."

I grabbed my car keys and ran out of the door to go to the local book seller and pick up a copy of *USA Today*. I raced back home and spread the paper out on my dining room table to look for this "mention" of my site but was disappointed not to see anything on it at all. Then it occurred to me to look online at **www.usatoday.com**.

There I was, on the front page of **USAtoday.com**: "Hot Site of the Day / Hot Site of the Week: Help Efrem Find the Woman of His Dreams." After the initial shock and joy of seeing my mug on a national news source, I called my Web hosting provider and asked to speak to a friend whom I knew there named Rob. I let him know what just happened as a sort of heads-up to watch for an increase in traffic on the local shared hosting server that I was on.

Over the next three months, I would receive more than 44,000 more e-mails from all around the globe. I kept a running tally daily as new mail poured into the **Ineedawife.com** inbox I had created. I had a woman from Tanzania write to say that the tribal elders wanted to discuss the matter of dowry and that I should come straight away to Tanzania. I received an e-mail from a man in Paris offering to pamper me and give me a life of luxury. One woman wrote, "I am too old for you, honey, but I will help you find the woman of your dreams!" The outpouring of support and offers was overwhelming. Some women (and men) sent pictures of themselves — clothed or otherwise.

While all of this was happening, I started receiving phone calls from local and national media sources, all wanting to do interviews with me on why I created the site and what I was really looking for. FOX television sent a camera crew to my house for a taped interview that would run on their news broadcast. The Associated Press called for a phone interview. UPI also interviewed me, as did no fewer than 14 "morning drive show" radio programs, including the Howard Stern Show.

From a media coverage perspective, I had hit the motherload. You cannot get that kind of coverage unless you are a hit or a crook these days.

The site was getting millions of visits weekly, and the traffic was leaping off the charts.

In the meantime, while all of this press attention was taking place, a woman named Jennifer Smith in Madison, Wisconsin, was screening online singles ads for her boss. He did not know much about how the whole Internet singles ads thing worked, so she volunteered to help him out and save him from some of the crazier postings.

In her searches, she was mildly complaining to herself that every time she put in a keyword for relationships or dating, my site would pop up in the top of her search list. She finally decided to have a look and see what the site was all about. Her immediate thought upon loading the site was, "What kind of a sad sack would set up a Web site like this?"

Being a techy and also an editor, she read through the site and made some mental notes to the effect of, "Well, at least he writes well and there are not any typos." I had an AOL Instant Messenger plugin on the Web site and invited anybody looking at the site to contact me via the messenger. With all of the press coverage, I was getting dozens of requests to chat every night that I logged into the site.

On June 29, 1999, Jennifer was one of the people who took me up on the invitation and contacted me through the instant messenger. When she did, she came at me like a first-rate reporter with a slew of questions that left me, well, type-less. "Hiya, name's Jennifer. Just came from your Web site. Clever little domain hook you got goin' there. What's the real story? You really looking for a wife? I see you work as a Web developer. You make good money doing that? I do the same thing. Just wondering how the pay compares."

She came right out and told me, "I am not looking for a relationship, I just got out of a bad one and my boss was asking me about online singles ads, so I started to screen some for him. Did you know your site comes up at the top of the search list on that stuff?" My response: "Uh... hi." Pretty lame response by any measure. Needless to say, we chatted for a while, and I was able to answer all of her questions, one after the other, but it was pretty slowgoing for the first few days.

Those initial disjointed, shaky chats turned into some pretty deep conversations about art, technology, life, travel, and a wealth of other topics. Naturally, the chats turned to flirting, and I asked if she would send me a picture of herself because she had the opportunity to see mine on the site. She sent a picture via e-mail, and I was gaga over her eyes. The online chats turned into phone calls a couple of nights a week, and then a couple hours per night several nights per week.

At some point, I offered to fly her out to Michigan (where I was living at the time) for a weekend. She agreed, and I booked a ticket for her two months out. She had a friend at the time who was doing some digital work for a certain agency with a three-lettered acronym. This friend offered to have me "checked out" by one of his contacts at the agency. She said, "OK, but I only want to know if anything bad comes up — no other personal stuff." On my end, I had my mother's boyfriend (a law enforcement officer) do some digging around just to be safe. We both notified friends and family of what was going on and who we would be meeting. As we continued to talk (every night at this point), it started to feel like waiting for two months for her to come out was too long, so I booked a flight to Madison from Detroit that weekend.

The walk to the plane terminal gave me a firsthand feel for what it must be like to be a rock star. As I rounded the corner to the jetway, a small gaggle of teenage girls were standing around talking when one of them looked toward me and said (loudly), "That's him! That's the I Need A Wife guy! I will bet he's going to see her!" They half-approached me and asked if I was going to see the "girl" in Wisconsin. I just smiled and said, "Yes, I am." They sent me off with a hearty round of "Good luck!" followed by a bunch of giggling and "Oh my god!"s.

When I got to the airport in Madison, it was hot and sunny. I was wearing sunglasses and was having a hard time adjusting to the light inside of the airport, so I walked off the jetway and into the terminal, looking for Jennifer. You know that feeling you get when somebody is staring at you, the one where the hair on the back of your neck stands up? I got that and immediately focused in on where she was — standing behind a large, concrete support pillar with just her head poking out as if making ready to hide if she did not like what she saw. I spotted her, smiled, and walked up to her and said, "Hi, Jennifer." She stepped out from behind the pillar and we hugged for a long time. We spent a wonderful weekend together in and around Madison, and at the end of the weekend, we both knew that we wanted to spend more time together.

The next year was filled with flights back and forth between Michigan and Wisconsin, and we decided to move in together. Jennifer came to Michigan to live with me, and by spring of 2000, we were engaged to be married. We got married on May 13, 2001 and just celebrated our eighth anniversary. We have a beautiful, bright 6-year-old son named Deacon and live in Madison, Wisconsin — all thanks to the Web site I created, **www.Ineedawife.com**.

*Efrem R. Jasso got his start in technology in 1994 at an engineering firm in Dearborn, Michigan, just outside his birth city of Detroit. Building off his academic background in fine arts, he started off doing graphic design and Web development, and after a few years he moved into IT project management for one of the nation's largest telecommunications companies. Efrem is available for freelance IT work and consulting and is looking to sell the domain name **www.Ineedawife.com**. He can be contacted at efremj@purgatorio.com.*

CASE STUDY: TEENA ROSE

Teena Rose
ResumeToReferral.com

Since 1999, the layout, content, and overall design of my Web site have been my undertaking. In the beginning, I took on Web development myself, primarily based on cost. Good copy writers and Web site designers do not come cheap. A high cost could not be afforded, especially for a low-revenue startup business like mine.

Over the years, my knowledge surrounding Web site design increased, so my continued involvement with developing my company Web site contributed to my passion for it and was no longer based on cost. I absorbed the design and content ideas from others and continued to present my own unique versions over the many Web site designs I have created over the last 10 years. Overall, my site has gone through probably a dozen major changes.

Unlike previous Web site versions, I conducted a slew of research and gave the layout, content, and amenities plenty of thought before starting this time around. The research phase pained me because my last design was an utter flop (I was losing money while I spent hours toil through expert advice, books, and online articles) for a variety of reasons: The layout was too spacious, visitors did not have easy access to the navigation bar, and the content was not as keyword-heavy as it should have been. Live and learn, right?

The latest redesign has been the most time-consuming. I started by first identifying the various essentials that affect the everyday visitor to my Web site, as well as the eye-catching sales elements that are effective in turning prospects into clients. Here are the seven steps I followed, from pre-planning to going "live:"

- First, I read several books from well-known authorities on branding, e-commerce, customer relationship management, and the online customer experience. It is easy for someone to say, "Write from the viewpoint of prospects and clients," but sometimes it is easier said than done. So I took the liberty of learning from the experts to find out what I did wrong with my last design — and all those before it, for that matter.

- Second, I researched CSS code and how it could effectively replace lengthy HTML code. The new Web site does take advantage of CSS code, and an external style sheet, but the coding has a long way to go before it is optimal, I feel. A complete CSS conversion is a work in progress.

- Third, I focused on writing content that would appeal and reach out to both existing customers and visiting prospects. The overall idea was to develop a distinct Web site that stood out from the thousands of others (in and outside of my industry), and I feel I accomplished that by using a conversational style to my writing.

- Fourth, I utilized an F formula for the layout, placing important information in the header, left column, and within the top half of each page. Researchers have learned Web site visitors' eyes tend to travel within an F pattern when scanning Web sites. For leads and sales, the transformation has worked well.

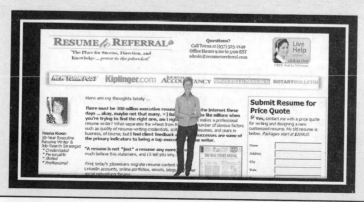

- Fifth, I wrote keyword-dominant taglines and rewrote content to shift from a company focus to a "me" focus. After all, I am the face of the company — adding personality to the business would have been impossible if I stayed with the stuffy company persona I used previously.

- Sixth, I incorporated live help along with easy access to phone and e-mail, making contact exceptionally easy for Web site visitors. Prospective buyers are a hot commodity; therefore, the thought of each spending even seconds trying to find contact information was just out of the question.

- Lastly, I added a personal host to greet visitors. Surprisingly cost-effective, adding a personal greeter was a smart move as well. Factoring my target audience, I selected a slightly older woman who was conservatively dressed. She complements me and my business, rather than outshining it.

During the initial stages, I thought the process would never end. It is amazing how much help and guidance is out there. It is rather overwhelming, actually. But the pain and suffering of the latest redesign was definitely worth the effort — and I probably saved a few thousand just by doing the work myself.

How do I know the new site design is a success?

- First, I am receiving a two-fold increase in leads.

- Second, I have received great comments from those who call.

- Third, I am seeing an attractive increase in revenues.

Teena Rose is a professional speaker, career coach, book author, former columnist, and top-endorsed resume writer and job strategist. She leverages job-search collateral (résumé, cover letters, and executive bios), applying social networking, personal branding, online portfolios, and new technologies and tools to further benefit the careers of her top-echelon clientele. She is also author of Start Your Résumé-Writing Business: The Ultimate Resource for Building a $100,000 Résumé-Writing Business, *which you can download at* **www.resumebiz.com**. *Teena can be contacted at admin@resumetoreferral.com.*

CASE STUDY: MARY MCMANUS

Mary McManus
NewWorldGreetings.com

In April 2007, when I decided to launch New World Greeting Cards, customized poetry for all occasions. I knew that a Web site was critical to the success of my business. Fortunately, my husband, Tom, is — among his other technical talents — a Web site designer. He chose to build my Web site using Linux/Open Source. He chose a hosting service that supports Linux. Using a standard template from Drupal for content management, we made small modifications to begin building the Web site. Since its inception, we have added features such as audio and video. We also added a GUI editor. I am able to manage most of the content myself, though, for adding audio, video, and photos, I rely on Tom's expertise. Our hosting for the Web site and e-mail is only $6.99 per month, and paying 12 months in advance, we receive a discount. Tom provides consultation to other businesses through **www.bostonlinux.net** to help them build low-cost, highly successful Web sites.

My business, **www.newworldgreetings.com**, began with one or two orders and now, including book sales, we do more than $1,000 per month in business. I have more than 500 unique visitors each month, and visit time ranges from two minutes to 30 minutes. But my Web site is more than a site to promote business; it is a site where I share my journey of inspiration, courage, faith, and determination from post-polio survivor to Boston Marathon finisher; from taking a leap of faith and leaving the security of a full-time, award-winning career as a VA social worker, to becoming an entrepreneur in order to heal my life, mind, body, and spirit. It has also been used to help with our fund raising efforts when I ran the 2009 Boston Marathon to raise money for Spaulding Rehab Hospital. We raised $10,535 for Spaulding Rehab Hospital.

Mary McManus is an award-winning social worker, a post-polio survivor, and a Boston Marathon finisher. Mary always had a passion for writing and loved creating customized poetry for all occasions. Her friends and family would often comment that she should work for a major greeting card company. In December, 2006, Mary was diagnosed with post-polio syndrome (PPS) at Spaulding Rehab Hospital. Mary left her work at the VA in May 2007 and created New World Greeting Cards, customized poetry for all occasions. She received a publishing contract from Publish America, and New World Greetings: Inspirational Poetry and Musings for a New World was released in December 2007. She donates 20 percent of the proceeds of the sale of the book to Spaulding's Polio Fund. You can go to her Web site at www.newworldgreetings.com to see samples of her work, read reviews, and listen to interviews.

CASE STUDY: KATE ROTHACKER

Kate Rothacker
LocalMemories.com

I primarily design scrapbook pages, not Web pages. Being married and a mom to four teen-to-adult children, joining the Internet revolution was not a motivating desire for me when I began my scrapbooking business in 2001. But having a business in this century, with any sort of market awareness, depended on it. So, with no budget for hiring a Web designer, I learned basic HTML from books and an online course to put together a very simple Web site about the scrapbook services I offer.

Beginning with a horse-and-buggy shaped cutout for sale to the scrapbooking tourists that visit Lancaster County, Pennsylvania, I created designs specific to my home area and wanted to make them available online for travelers to be able to add to their memory books when they got home. Thus the Web site **www.localmemories.com** was born.

The Web site includes information on my collection of elements designed around local attractions, as well as scrapbook-for-hire services, album imprinting, and hosted weekend scrapbooking events (called "crops"). The site is not flashy and does not use forms or even have a shopping cart. Yet people have been contacting me in growing numbers for my scrapbooking services. Web traffic has come from each of the service varieties offered, but by far the most traffic has been for the weekend crops. Eventually, Local Memories opened a dedicated location for these retreats; a private home equipped with tables, lighting, and tools, specifically for small groups of scrapbookers — and enough beds for them to spend the weekend. Named the "Cozy Crop House," this business clearly needed a Web address of its own.

One tip put to use early on was to register a variety of domain names, but use a redirect to the main site rather than having several different domains hosted. So, besides **www.imprintedalbums.com** and **www.scrapperforhire.com**, we also registered **www.cozycrophouse.com**.

Business has continued to grow, and I am looking at additional expansion, including franchising the Cozy Crop House. I recently arranged a barter for a professional redesign of my site to improve the graphics and add some functionality. But it was my low-cost, home-spun version of a Web site that grew the business to the point that the barter was attractive to the Web designer.

Especially with the Cozy Crop House, I knew I had something great to offer to other people like me. The Web site allowed me to post details and photos online for my potential guests so that they could find out how to experience it firsthand and get the word out to others. I cannot imagine it growing the way it has without being online.

Kate Rothacker is the founder of Cozy Crop House, a scrapbook retreat house company. She resides in Lancaster County, Pennsylvania, and can be reached at cozycrophouse@gmail.com.

CASE STUDY: MATT MCCORMICK

Matt McCormick
JetCityDevices.com

About three years ago, I quit a job at Microsoft and started my own company helping small business build their own Web sites. Since then, I have transitioned to running my own online business. Through those experiences, I have learned a lot about building and marketing a Web site. Unfortunately, I cannot give great advice on cheap tools for building a site since I am a developer and write all of my own code. However, here are a few lessons I have learned:

- Start with the smallest set of features you absolutely need, nail them, and then build from there. Too many people try to build everything into the initial version of a site when what they really need is just to get something up that brings in customers.

- Write good and concise copy for your Web site. If you cannot do it, find someone who can — save money with a friend who will often do it for dinner or a beer.

- "Hire" professionals to do the design. "Hire" may be as simple as using something like **www.templatemonster.com** to get a great-looking design for under $100.

- Make calls to action on your site easy to find and easy to use. It is crazy how many sites make this hard to do.

- Use Google. This includes: Google Webmaster Tools to get your site listed with them, Google AdWords to turn on traffic immediately, and Google Local Business (if you are local) to get some easy and great-quality organic rankings.

- Put a short, descriptive title on each page of the Web site. This is one of the easiest ways to get good organic search results.

- Do A/B testing. Again, Google makes this easy with its AdWords system.

*Matt McCormick spent three years with Microsoft working on Windows Media® Center and then about two years working on the MSN Messenger product. In 2007, he decided to start his own company building Web sites for small companies. In January 2009, he put his Web site consulting and development business on hold and focused solely on his new company, which offers online cell phone repairs and accessories. Matt can be reached at **www.jetcitydevices.com**.*

CASE STUDY: BRAINSPARK MEDIA

BrainSpark Media
BrainSparkMedia.com

Problem: In today's Internet-savvy world, a visitor spends just eight seconds scanning a Web site for interest. With this realization, Brain-Spark Media recognized that their Web site did not significantly prove the company's full capabilities in that one shot, eight-second chance.

As a full-service interactive agency in Denver, Colorado, BrainSpark Media helps its clients optimize their online presence for tangible results, but finding their own tangible results became the driving force in an overall rebranding effort, which culminated with the new **www.brainsparkmedia.com**. With top-tier, successful clients, including McKesson, 21c Museum Hotel, PENTAX Imaging, TopSchool, and GeoEye, BrainSpark realized that they needed to become their own No. 1 client.

Solution: In order to obtain the desired outcome, the BrainSpark team decided to not only update the brand and Web site, but to take the time to evaluate how each piece would fit into new marketing goals using a minimal amount of cost. As the new colors and logo took shape, the company's top designers and developers discussed priorities for the Web site. The main goal, as decided, was to create a Web site that featured the company's portfolio and development capabilities in a clear, attractive, and professional way. The use of BrainSpark's internal resources to complete the site and also the simplification of the site to emphasize the portfolio kept down complex development costs.

Goals for the solution immediately dropped into place:

- Become its own client to showcase features and capabilities on the Web site.

- Rely on their strong branding and emphasize its new look with a subtle color scheme to highlight the "spark" in BrainSpark.

- Capture the visitor immediately with simple, easily navigated elements on the Web site home page.

- Use Flash features to captivate the visitor and introduce brightly colored images and portfolio pieces.

- Guide the visitor to news and information using the latest Internet trends and communication tools.

- Retain the visitor's interest with a wide depth of Web site content.

Result: The clarity and proficiency of BrainSpark's redesigned Web site produced immediate success for both the company and their clients in lead generation, positive client feedback, and two interactive/digital advertising awards.

The following information details BrainSpark's success after relaunching their Web site in January 2008:

- 2008 Silver Summit Creative Award by the Summit International Awards

- 2008 Gold Davey Award by the International Academy of the Visual Arts

- 20 percent average increase in Web traffic

- Considerable positive feedback from current and former clients

- Lead generation from prospects and former clients

- Reinforced company's capabilities and quality overall

*BrainSpark Media is a Denver-based, award-winning interactive agency dedicated to helping clients optimize their online presence for tangible results. They blend project experience, keen analysis, and a versatile process to formulate the right strategy for each project. This intelligence drives tactical yet practical design fused with technical know-how to create user experiences that build brands and boost business performance. They can be contacted at **www.brainsparkmedia.com**.*

CASE STUDY: JENNIFER SMITH

Jennifer Smith
ThriveHere.org

Our Web site — like our mission — is unique in the world of economic development and serves to set us apart nationally and internationally.

The name of our organization, Thrive, was chosen specifically because it is an end benefit (you, your family, and your business all thrive here), and because it is a highly adaptable marketing and co-branding tool. This end benefit, then, became the Web site name, as we found in our research that "destination" or "verb-based" domain names were eliciting positive response rates (for other examples of co-branding, see **www.thrivehere.org/promote**).

As a startup organization (2007), our Web site was the first external marketing and communications effort we undertook, and currently remains the main international gateway to the Madison, Wisconson region. To date, the majority of our communications focus has been regional outreach targeting information to our target sectors, our regional partners. Therefore, we have relied on our Web site to be the cornerstone of our presence to national and international audiences. As we move farther into the social media sphere, we continue to bring those tools into the Web site — for example, a Twitter feed.

We have heard that the unique design and content of our site has attracted attention to the region and to our organization both nationally and internationally from a range of end users — site selectors, those looking to move here, and those looking to expand business here.

Site selectors comment on the color scheme and "softer" feel of the site and how that reinforces our strategic goals and our region's quality of life offerings — a big draw for regions (and people) these days. This unique design also means our site is often more memorable, which is another comment we hear often.

Those looking to relocate here (personally or professionally) have also commented on the breadth of content and visual appeal, unusual in many ways, and the creative nature of some of the elements on the site (like our customized postcards, for example: **www.thrivehere.org/ postcard**), which reinforces the creative flavor and opportunities in the area.

We measure the effectiveness of our site with standard metrics — traffic patterns, downloads, and time on site. From this data, we can see that we have steady traffic, high stickiness rate, and traffic and use patterns that seem to be consistent with what we planned for. We also gauge the effectiveness from word-of-mouth and other intangibles that we know are critical — and hard to measure.

For example, employers in the region have the option of using our site in unique ways to promote their businesses and for recruiting workforce. One of the area's largest recruitment agencies, The QTI Group, uses customized pages on the Thrive Web site for high-level positions for which they recruit both in and out of state. These pages function as the first doorway a candidate sees to the region.

Peter Gray, Manager of Professional Recruitment for QTI, said that, "As executive recruiters at The QTI Group, our job is often to persuade people to consider moving to the Madison region for a job opportunity. The team at Thrive has been very helpful in customizing pages into announcement pages for our job opportunities. We have gotten great, positive feedback from our candidates about the Thrive Web site. It is the first impression of the Madison region for many people we speak with around the country, and it is a great marketing tool for the region.

"For example, I was just speaking with executives in Kansas City, Seattle, and New York who are candidates for positions in the Madison region. None of them has ever been to Wisconsin, and all of them were very impressed with the Madison region from the Thrive Web site." Happy ending — the candidate from Kansas relocated.

We use a proprietary backend CMS developed by a local business, Acumium. With Acumium, we planned the navigation and layout of our site, wrote the content, populated the site, and directed the look/feel/usability standards. Another local design firm helped with the wireframe design, based on our logo and branding standards. This design scheme (playing off the word "thrive") allows our staff to make regular updates, which keeps the Web site fresh and up-to-date. It is very low-cost for us, yet reinforces the brand and end message.

While it was a little nerve-wracking to launch a site so radically different from standard economic development Web sites, it reinforced both our organizational vision (economic development and quality of life together) and our regional brand or flavor (intellectual curiosity and innovative, creative energy) — and it has worked.

Some features of our Web site:

- Navigation tailored to a broad spectrum of users, including: site selectors and entrepreneurs; those looking to move or expand a business; those seeking to move to the area; those in the area seeking events, new opportunities, arts and culture info; and "trailing spouses" moving to the area seeking info on jobs, schools, health care, recreation, and assets of the region (**www.thrivehere.org/livehere**).

- Integration with LOIS (Location One Information System), a searchable site selection and research tool (**www.thrivehere. org/communities**).

- Intensive data and startup resources (**www.thrivehere.org/ business**).

- Tagged article system so articles are sorted and fed simultaneously into relevant areas of the Web site in a streaming format and into an opt-in RSS feed.

- Twitter feed brought into page (see for an example: **www. thrivehere.org/biotechnology** — check the "related Thrive info" box).

- Digital assets like postcards (**www.thrivehere.org/postcard**), media library, and a research/white papers area.

- Examples of customized recruitment pages: **www.thrivehere.org/portage** (careers at Divine Savior hospital in Portage) and **www.thrivehere.org/gentel** (careers at Gentel Biosciences).

*Jennifer Smith is the Director of Communications for Thrive. Thrive is the regional economic development enterprise for the eight-county Madison, Wisconsin region, growing the region's economy in ways that preserve and enhance quality of life. They may be found online at **www.thrivehere.org** and may be contacted at 1-608-443-1960 or info@thrivehere.org.*

CASE STUDY: TINA HILL

Tina Hill
KidzSack.com

Quite often I have heard that ignorance is bliss, and I have to say that in my case, it was true. I started my business on a shoestring budget, just $200, and that included my Web site as well. I got the idea for my product, Kidzsack, and could not start it fast enough. I do not have a business background, so the idea for a business plan never even entered my mind. I knew these few truths: I had an idea that I needed to develop and get into production, and I needed to have my product seen. Therefore, a Web site was essential.

Lucky for me, I had read the book *Mommy Millionaire*, in which the author highlights a few Web site-making companies that are on the cheap. The book mentions **www.godaddy.com** and **www.homestead.com**. I ended up going with Homestead because I liked their selection of stock Web sites better. They offer about 2,000 stock Web sites to choose from with all different themes, colors, and categories. Some of their many selections include Web sites geared toward catering, landscaping, interior design, and general business service, which was the direction I went in. What struck me about the stock Web site that I chose were the colors. I wanted green and purple to begin with, and when I came across a stock Web site on Homestead that offered that, I knew it was a good fit.

Homestead offers a cheap package with an easy SiteBuilder feature for uploading your images and text. I believe my monthly payments are $8.99 a month for hosting the five-page package. I am just a startup, but as my company grows, I can go to the platinum package, which will give me an option for more pages and e-commerce. For now, I am good. I am very comfortable with taking baby steps and letting my business grow slowly. My husband and I are not high-tech people, and this Web site has made it very easy to navigate and is extremely user-friendly.

I believe that every business needs to have a face, and if you are not a brick-and-mortar store, what better way to provide that than with a Web site? Now more than ever, people are very conscious of their purchases and spending, and because of the Internet, they are able to research products and companies. Being able to demonstrate your product is a huge selling bonus. I cannot imagine why anyone would miss out on an opportunity like that. Also, with a Web site, you have a real chance to connect with people and let them see the story behind the product. On my Web site, **www.kidzsack.com**, I show the product, demonstrate it with a video, and give the story behind the product. The last page of my Web site lists all my online catalog and retail locations.

For a company still in startup mode, I consider myself a huge success. In my first year of business, I broke even and hope to make a profit in my second year. Because of the constant marketing that I do, pitching my story to newspapers, magazines, TV shows, blogs, and news channels — all done online — I have gained publicity, which leads more people and search engines to my Web site.

*Tina Hill is the owner of **www.kidzsack.com**. Kidzsack was founded in fall 2007 with the goal of creating an environmentally conscious and creative product. Kidzsack products are designed to inspire creative play with the highest level of quality and safety. Kidzsack is located in West Newbury, Massachusetts. Tina can be contacted at tina@kidzsack.com.*

CASE STUDY: TAM HANNA

Tam Hanna
tamspalm.tamoggemon.com

My entry into the handheld computing sector in general, and the Web publishing business in specific, should probably be considered one of the least-planned success stories in the Western world: I bought a cheap, used Palm IIIc™ to be more productive in my day job in the family's business.

The quality of Web content available about these devices left me frustrated. I thus set out to run a little blog about the Palm OS® in my spare time. I initially chose Google's Blogger service (**www.blogger.**

com). Though in itself it is pretty good, it was a decision that came to haunt me later.

TamsPalm (**http://tamspalm.tamoggemon.com**) started off with me posting a long post every few days. As readership grew, I eventually recruited some readers as authors, who created more content. All of that eventually required categories to keep the stuff accessible for readers and Google alike.

Keep in mind that this all took place in 2004; back then, the only way to get categories was to host a blog on your own. We chose WordPress and began the painful operation of switching our blog over manually. Today, all of this would be handled by a script.

This brings us to lesson one: Start your blog on your own domain — even if it costs more. Never ever go with a hosted blog service; it will cost you a lot in the long run.

We were busy getting out of the Google sandbox when hosting once again became an issue. We were featured on a Web site called Slash-Dot, which drove thousands of visitors to our site within minutes. Unfortunately, our host turned out to be completely unable to handle the traffic, which led to us loosing potential readers who simply could not reach our site.

Moving away from them involved the use of an attorney and a bit of data loss. However, I owned the domain myself, which means that readers and Google noticed nothing but a short downtime.

Lesson two: Cheap Web hosts are bad news. Content-wise, Tamoggemon managed to carve out a style of its own (last but not least thanks to renowned Austrian publicist Dr. D. M. Kohrs, who has had an integral part in shaping the company). We do not run every story, but instead focus on the important ones. Updates are scheduled across the day so that something on the site always keeps changing — this attracts further readers.

Wikimedia® Commons (**http://commons.wikimedia.org**) has enabled us to embed pictures next to articles — use the HTML code **<img src="URL" style="float: left; margin:5px;">** at the top of the post. This has turned out to be extremely popular with our readers.

Dr. Kohrs extended our WordPress platform with a few useful plug-ins. Our related posts tool can no longer be downloaded, but it has served us greatly by offering more content to visitors. The send-post-via-e-mail tool unfortunately was not as successful — it was rarely used.

Eventually, our news sites grew so big that we decided to sell ad space to third parties. This generated publishing-derived revenue, which allowed me to pursue a press ID from the Vienna Journalists Club (**www.wjc.at**).

After having talked about all these tricks, it is time to look at the business side of things. Leaving revenue from ad sales aside, Tamoggemon has benefited from its news services in two ways. First of all, added visibility meant less advertising costs to sell our software; nobody can charge you for a banner on your own Web site.

The second — and just as valuable — benefit was access to information. Manufacturers were much more attentive to support requests and provided samples of upcoming devices for review. This allowed us to gain a significant edge on the competition. Finally, it is an ego thing. Believe me that you will never forget the day when the first fan approaches you on the road.

Tam Hanna is the CEO and founder of Tamoggemon Limited, an Austrian company that specializes in mobile computing software and publishing.

Chapter 19

SUMMARY

There is nothing more gratifying than creating your own Web site from the beginning stages to watching others visit your site, interact with you, buy products, and exchange information. The Internet is amazing, and establishing your own Web presence in the form of a Web site, blog, or social networking site is an accomplishment you can be proud of. Your Web site, blog, or social networking site is accessible around the world by nearly anyone. For little or no money, you can establish a permanent Web presence that will serve you for many years. There is no other form of marketing or advertising that lets you instantly advertise to the world, and the return on investment for your Web site can be mind-boggling. You can instantly sell products around the world, reach new customers, expand your business lines, and reach friends and family across continents.

This book has not only armed you with the knowledge to create your own Web site for little or no money, but it has also taught you how to optimize it for search engines, establish a blog, use PPC advertising, and establish an affiliate marketing campaign. The goal of this book was to provide you with practical advice, knowledge, and understanding of the tools, skills, and applications to help you build a Web site for little or no money. There are plenty of guides that can help you take your Web site and your design skill level to the next level. If you design your Web site with sound SEO fundamentals, using the practical knowledge and advice from proven industry Web design experts and the success stories included here, you are well on the way to achieving tremendous success on the Web.

It is gratifying achieving success based on your own efforts. I am 100 percent confident that anyone can create an attractive, productive, and profitable Web site or blog for little or no money, and without advanced training or skills. I wish you the absolute best success with your Web design adventures and look forward to hearing your stories. If you wish to share your experiences and success stories with me, feel free to e-mail me at bruce@ brucecbrown.com, and I will gladly share them with my readers and post them on my blog. You can also find me on Facebook.

Best of luck from sunny Florida,
Bruce C. Brown

Chapter 20

RECOMMENDED REFERENCE LIBRARY

It is highly recommended that you build a quality reference library to assist you with your overall Web design, online marketing, SEO, and overall business planning. While there are plenty of excellent books on the market, I definitely recommend you add the following to your library. All are available through Atlantic Publishing Group, Inc. (**www.atlantic-pub. com**). Once you decide on which Web design application to use — such as Dreamweaver, Expression Web, or WebPlusX2 — you may want to invest in books dedicated to honing your skills in these applications.

How to Use the Internet to Advertise, Promote and Market Your Business or Web Site With Little or No Money

Interested in promoting your business and/or Web site, but don't have the big budget for traditional advertising? This new book will show you how to build, promote, and make money off your Web site or brick-and-mortar store using the Internet with minimal costs.

This new book presents a comprehensive, hands-on, step-by-step guide for increasing Web site traffic and traditional store traffic by using hundreds of proven tips, tools, and techniques. Learn how to target more customers to your business and optimize your Web site from a marketing perspective. You will learn to target your campaign, use keywords, generate free advertising, apply search engine strategies, and learn the inside secrets of e-mail marketing.

The Complete Guide to All Aspects of Google Advertising — Including Tips, Tricks, & Strategies to Create a Winning Advertising Plan

Are you one of the many who think Google is simply a search engine? Yes, it is true that Google is the most popular search engine on the Web today. More than 275 million times a day, people use Google and its related partner sites to find information on just about any subject. Many of those people are looking for your products and services. Consider this even if you don't have a Web site or product. There are tremendous opportunities on the Internet and money to be made using Google.

Google has created numerous marketing and advertising products that are fast and easy to implement in your business today, including AdSense, AdWords, and the Google APIs. This new book takes the confusion and mystery out of working with Google and its various advertising and marketing programs. You will learn the secrets of working with Google —without making costly mistakes. This book is an absolute must-have for anyone who wants to succeed with advertising on Google. This book teaches you the ins and outs using all of Google's advertising and marketing tools. You will instantly start producing results — and profit.

The Ultimate Guide to Search Engine Marketing: Pay Per Click Advertising Secrets Revealed

Is your ultimate goal to have more customers come to your Web site? You can increase your Web site traffic by more than 1,000 percent through the expert execution of pay-per-click advertising. With PPC advertising, you are only drawing highly qualified visitors to your Web site. PPC brings you fast results, and you can reach your target audience with the most cost-effective method on the Internet today.

Master the art and science behind PPC advertising in a matter of hours. By investing a few dollars, you can easily increase the number of visitors to your Web site and significantly increase sales. If you are looking to drive high-quality, targeted traffic to your site, there is no better way than to use PPC advertising.

The Complete Guide to E-mail Marketing: How to Create Successful, Spam-Free Campaigns to Reach Your Target Audience and Increase Sales

Researchers estimate that by 2008, e-mail marketing revenues will surpass $1.8 billion dollars annually. Are you getting your share? According to Jupiter Research, 93 percent of U.S. Internet users consider e-mail their top online activity. E-mail is a fast, inexpensive, and highly effective way to target and address your audience. Companies like Microsoft, Amazon, Yahoo!, and most Fortune 1000 firms are using responsible e-mail marketing for one simple reason: It works. It generates profits immediately and consistently.

In this book, you will learn how to create top-notch e-mail marketing campaigns, how to build stronger customer relationships, generate new qualified leads and sales, learn insider secrets to build your e-mail list quickly, deal with spam filters, and learn the optimum days and times to send your e-mails.

How to Open and Operate a Financially Successful Web-Based Business (With Companion CD-ROM)

With e-commerce expected to reach $40 billion and online businesses anticipated to increase by 500 percent through the year 2010, you need to be a part of this exploding area of Internet sales. If you want to learn about starting a Web business, how to transform your brick-and-mortar business to a Web business, or even if you're simply interested in making money online, this is the book for you.

You can operate your Web-based business from home and with very little start-up money. The earning potential is limitless. This new book will teach you all you need to know about getting started in your own Web-based business in the minimum amount of time. This book is a comprehensive, detailed study of the business side of Internet retailing.

The Secret Power of Blogging: How to Promote and Market Your Business, Organization, or Cause with Free Blogs

If you have a product, service, brand, or cause that you want to market online inexpensively, then you need to look into starting a blog. Blogs are ideal marketing vehicles. You can use them to share your expertise, grow market share, spread your message, and establish yourself as an expert in your field for virtually no cost.

In this book, you will learn how to create top-notch blog marketing campaigns, how to build stronger customer relationships, generate new qualified leads and sales, and learn insider secrets to build your readership list quickly.

Word Of Mouth Advertising Online & Off: How to Spark Buzz, Excitement, and Free Publicity for Your Business or Organization With Little or No Money

Word-of-mouth marketing (WOMM) is the least expensive form of advertising, and often the most effective. People believe what their friends, neighbors, and online contacts say about you, your products, and services — and they remember it for a long, long time. Word-of-mouth promotion is highly valued. There is no more powerful form of marketing than an endorsement from one of your current customers. A satisfied customer's recommendation has much greater value than traditional advertising because it is coming from someone who is familiar with the quality of your work.

The best part is that initiating this form of advertising costs little or no money. For WOMM to increase your business, you need an active plan in place to create buzz. If your business is on the Web, there is a myriad of possibilities for starting a highly successful viral marketing campaign using the Internet, software, blogs, online activists, press releases, discussion forums and boards, affiliate marketing, and product sampling. Technology has dramatically changed traditional marketing programs. This up-to-date book covers it all.

How to Open & Operate a Financially Successful Web Site Design Business (With Companion CD-ROM)

According to a 2007 survey by Netcraft, there are more than 108 million Web sites worldwide. Every Web site needs to be designed. *The Pricing & Ethical Guidelines Handbook* published by the Graphic Arts Guild reports that the average cost of designing a Web site for a small corporation can range from $7,750 to $15,000. It is incredibly easy to see the enormous profit potential.

Here is the manual you need to cash in on this highly profitable segment of the industry. This book is a comprehensive and detailed study of the business side of Web site design. This superb manual should be studied by anyone investigating the opportunities of opening a Web design business and will arm you with everything you need, including sample business forms, contracts, worksheets and checklists, and dozens of other valuable, time-saving tools that no entrepreneur should be without.

The Complete Guide to Writing Web-Based Advertising Copy to Get the Sale: What You Need to Know Explained Simply

Since the advent of the Internet, and since more and more people are making purchases online, writers have had to adapt to composing copy for the Web. Contrary to what many people think, writing for the Web and writing for print are not the same and involve very different skill sets. Instead of struggling to find the right words, copywriters should read this book from cover to cover to discover how to write sales-generating copy.

This book will teach you how to make your copy readable and compelling, how to reach your target audience, how to structure the copy, how to visually format the copy, how to pull in visitors, how to convert prospects to paying customers, how to compose eye-catching headlines, and much more.

Internet Marketing Revealed: The Complete Guide to Becoming an Internet Marketing Expert

This is a carefully tested, well-crafted, and complete tutorial on a subject vital to Web developers and marketers. This book teaches the fundamentals of online marketing implementation, including Internet strategy planning, the secrets of search engine optimization, successful techniques to be first in Google and Yahoo!, vertical portals, effective online advertisement, and innovative e-commerce development. This book will help you understand the e-business revolution as it provides strong evidence and practical direction in a friendly and easy-to-use self-study guide.

You will find a variety of teaching techniques to enhance your learning, such as notes, illustrations, conceptual guidance, checklists of learned topics, diagrams, advanced tips, and real-world examples to organize and prioritize related concepts. This book is appropriate for marketing professionals as well as Web developers and programmers who have the desire to better understand the principles of this fresh and extraordinary activity that represents the foundation of modern e-commerce.

Online Marketing Success Stories: Insider Secrets from the Experts Who Are Making Millions on the Internet Today

Standing out in the turmoil of today's Internet marketplace is a major challenge. There are many books and courses on Internet marketing; this is the only book that will provide you with insider secrets. We asked the marketing experts who make their living on the Internet every day — and they talked. This book will give you real-life examples of how successful businesses market their products online. The information is so useful that you can read a page and put the idea into action right away.

With e-commerce expected to reach $40 billion and online businesses anticipated to increase by 500 percent through 2010, your business needs guidance from today's successful Internet marketing veterans. Learn the most efficient ways to bring consumers to your site, get visitors to purchase, how to up-sell, how to avoid oversights, and how to steer clear of years of disappointment.

Amazon Income: How Anyone of Any Age, Location, and/or Background Can Build a Highly Profitable Online Business with Amazon

The Internet affiliate program industry is one of the largest and fastest growing digital revenue generators in the world, with more than $65 billion in total income brought in during the 2006 fiscal year, and this is because of programs like Amazon's Associate program, which has been around for more than a decade and allows casual, everyday users of the Internet to install widgets and links on their Web sites that link back to Amazon products.

Users like you can earn commissions of up to 15 percent on products that your Web site visitors purchase when they visit Amazon. With the world's largest online retailer as a potential source of income, you can generate endless streams of income as a result.

No matter where you are from, how old you are, and what your background is, you can build and run a highly profitable business with Amazon. This comprehensive book is written to show you exactly how to do so. You will learn every detail necessary to complete the transformation from casual Internet user to Amazon guru in just a matter of weeks, making unfathomable amounts of money by selling Amazon products, your own products, starting a store, promoting outside projects, and making referrals.

The Small Business Owner's Handbook to Search Engine Optimization: Increase Your Google Rankings, Double Your Site Traffic... In Just 15 Steps — Guaranteed

This book is ideal for small business owners who want to learn an efficient and effective process for dramatically improving their Web site's search engine rankings and doubling their site's monthly unique visitors.

A business owner does not need to know technical skills like Web programming to be successful at search engine optimization. Instead, business owners will rely on marketing skills and the ability to think like their customers and prospects versus an ability to write HTML or other form of Web programming. Business owners will learn how to select keywords that are proven performers, blend the keywords into site content, boost site popularity, and more. This practical and tactical guide includes a free SEO toolkit and other valuable resources that will help business owners increase the return on investment generated by their Web sites. Business owners will also receive a detailed blueprint with specific checklists to follow throughout the 15-step process.

Google Income: How Anyone of Any Age, Location, and/or Background Can Build a Highly Profitable Online Business with Google

Google is the largest Internet company in the world. In the 2006 fiscal year, the company generated more than $6 billion in profit, and more than 90 percent of that income is generated through the use of their advertising program AdWords, a program that paid out more than $3 billion in the same year to advertising partners. The opportunity to make money with Google is so great that entire companies have been built around working with the search and advertising giant, and if you are properly situated, you can tap into that market and start generating your own massive profits.

There are dozens of ways to start making money with Google, and because of its digital nature, anyone can do it from anywhere in the world. This book leaves absolutely no stone unturned in cataloging for you every possible method through which you can generate and maintain steady income streams through the world's largest search engine.

GLOSSARY

Ad: For Web advertising, an ad is almost always a banner, a graphic image, or a set of animated images (in a file called an animated GIF) of a designated pixel size and byte size limit. An ad or set of ads for a campaign is often referred to as "the creative." Banners and other special advertising that include an interactive or visual element beyond the usual are known as rich media.

Ad impression: An ad impression, or ad view, occurs when a user pulls up a Web page through a browser and sees an ad that is served on that page. Many Web sites sell advertising space by ad impressions.

Ad rotation: Ads are often rotated into ad spaces from a list. This is usually done automatically by software on the Web site, or at a central site administered by an ad broker or server facility for a network of Web sites.

Ad space: An ad space is an area on a Web page that is reserved for ads. An ad space group is a group of spaces within a Web site that share the same characteristics so that an ad purchase can be made for the group of spaces.

Ad stream: The series of advertisements viewed by the user during a single visit to a site.

Ad view: A single ad that appears on a Web page when the page arrives at the viewer's display. Ad views are what most Web sites sell or prefer to sell. A Web page may offer space for a number of ad views. In general, the term "impression" is more commonly used.

Affiliate: The publisher/ salesperson in an affiliate marketing relationship.

Affiliate directory: A categorized listing of affiliate programs.

Affiliate forum: An online community where visitors may read and post topics related to affiliate marketing.

Affiliate fraud: Bogus activity generated by an affiliate in an attempt to generate illegitimate, unearned revenue.

Affiliate marketing: Revenue-sharing between online advertisers/ merchants and online publishers/ salespeople whereby compensation is based on performance measures, typically in the form of sales, clicks, registrations, or a hybrid model. Affiliate marketing is the use by a Web site that sells products of other Web sites, called affiliates, to help market the products. Amazon.com created the first large-scale affiliate program, and hundreds of other companies have followed since.

Affiliate merchant: The advertiser in an affiliate marketing relationship.

Affiliate network: A value-added intermediary providing services such as aggregation for affiliate merchants and affiliates.

Affiliate software: Software that, at a minimum, provides tracking and reporting of commission-triggering actions (sales, registrations, or clicks) from affiliate links.

Accessibility: The degree that a Web site can be accessed by people with disabilities.

Animated GIF: A GIF file that is animated or has motion.

Apache: A popular Web server.

Bandwidth: A measure of how fast data can be transferred between two computers.

Banner: A form of a graphic image that typically runs across a Web page or is positioned in a margin or other space reserved for ads. Banner ads are usually GIF images. In addition to adhering to size, many Web sites limit the size of the file to a certain number of bytes so that the file will display quickly. Most ads are animated GIFs, as animation has been shown to attract a larger percentage of user clicks. The most common larger banner ad is 468 pixels wide by 60 pixels high. Smaller sizes include 125 x 125 and 120 x 90.

Beyond the banner: This is the idea that, in addition to banner ads, there are other ways to use the Internet to communicate a marketing message. These include sponsoring a Web site or a particular feature on it; advertising in e-mail newsletters; co-branding with another company and its Web site; contest promotion; and, in general, finding new ways to engage and interact with the desired audience.

Behaviorally targeted advertising: A method of compiling data on Web visitors, such as surfing history, gender, age, and personal preferences, to later target them with tailored ads.

Black lists: Blocks mail from known spam sources.

Blog: A blog is a type of Web site that uses a dated log format for building its content.

Booked space: The number of ad views for an ad space that are currently sold out.

Brand, brand name, and branding: A brand is a product, service, or concept that is publicly distinguished from other products, services, or concepts so that it can be easily communicated and usually marketed. A brand name is the name of the distinctive product, service, or concept. Branding is the process of creating and disseminating the brand name.

Browser: Software that is used to view and locate Web sites on the World Wide Web.

Caching: In Internet advertising, the caching of pages in a cache server or the user's computer means that some ad views will not be known by the ad counting programs and is a source of concern. There are several techniques for telling the browser not to cache particular pages. On the other hand, specifying no caching for all pages may mean that users will find your site to be slower than you would like.

Campaign: A campaign consists of one or more ad groups. The ads in a given campaign share the same daily budget, language and location targeting, end dates, and distribution options.

Cascading style sheet (CSS): A technology used to control the presentation and layout of a Web page.

Client side: Applications or software downloaded and run by the user's Web browser, rather than on the Web server.

Click: A click occurs when a visitor interacts with an advertisement.

Click-through: A click-through is what is counted by the sponsoring site as a result of an ad click. In practice, click and click-through tend to be used interchangeably. A click-through, however, seems to imply that the user actually received the page. A few advertisers are willing to pay only for click-throughs rather than for ad impressions.

Click rate: The click rate is the percentage of ad views that resulted in click-throughs.

Common gateway interface (CGI): Technology that lets a Web browser communicate with a program on the Web server.

Content management system (CMS): A collection of tools designed to allow the creation, modification, organization, and removal of information from a Web site.

Cookies: A small text file downloaded to a user's computer that can be used to track user activity on a Web site or store user information about a visitor.

Domain name: A unique name that identifies one or more IP addresses.

Download: The transfer of files from a remote machine, or Web server, to a user's machine.

Dreamweaver: Web page authoring application from Adobe.

E-commerce: The process of buying, selling, and transferring money through the Internet.

Expression Web: A Web–page authoring application from Microsoft.

File size: The amount of space that a file takes up when stored on a disk; measured in bytes, kilobytes (K), megabytes (MB), or gigabytes (GB).

File transfer protocol (FTP): The most common way of transferring the files from one computer to another across a network.

Firewall: Software to protect networks from unauthorized access.

Flash: A vector-based, multimedia technology that can be embedded in HTML pages, typically in the form of animations. Entire Web sites may be developed in Flash.

Fold: "Above the fold," a term borrowed from print media, refers to an ad that is viewable as soon as the Web page arrives. You do not have to scroll down or sideways to see it. Because screen resolution can affect what is immediately viewable, it is good to know whether the Web site's audience tends to set their resolution at 640 x 480 pixels or at 800 x 600 — or higher.

FrontPage: A Web page authoring application from Microsoft.

GNU image manipulation program (GIMP): An open-source graphics creation and manipulation application.

Graphic interchange format (GIF): A popular image file format.

Hit: The sending of a single file, whether an HTML file, an image, an audio file, or other file type.

Home page: The first page a user sees when visiting a Web site.

Hypertext markup language (HTML): The language of the Web. Web pages are written in HTML.

Hypertext Transfer Protocol (HTTP): The protocol used to transfer Web pages on the Internet.

Impression: An impression occurs every time an ad is loaded onto a user's screen. Impressions are how most Web advertising is sold, and the cost is quoted in terms of the cost per thousand impressions (CPM).

Insertion order: An insertion order is a formal, printed order to run an ad campaign. Typically, the insertion order identifies the campaign name, the Web site receiving the order, the planner or buyer giving the order, the individual ads to be run and who will provide them, the ad sizes, the campaign beginning and end dates, the CPM, the total cost, discounts to be applied, reporting requirements, and possible penalties or stipulations relative to the failure to deliver the impressions.

Internet: A worldwide collection of computers all connected together to form a huge network.

Internet information services (IIS): A Web server created by Microsoft.

Internet protocol address (IP address): A unique number assigned to each machine connected to the Internet to identify it uniquely.

Internet service provider (ISP): The entity that provides users with connectivity to the Internet.

JavaScript: JavaScript is a client-side scripting language used to create dynamic Web pages. JavaScript should not be confused with Java, the full-featured programming language.

Joint photographic experts group (JPG or JPEG): A popular image file format.

Keyword: A word or phrase that a user types into a search engine when looking for specific information.

Keyword searches: Searches for specific text within a document or Web page that contains matching one or more words specified by the user.

Link: An object on a Web page that connects the user to another section of the page, the Web site, or the Internet. Links are normally a different color to stand out from the rest of the text on a page.

Linux: An open-source operating system.

Macintosh (Mac): An Apple Macintosh computer.

Markup: The process in which text and other data is converted into Web pages by using HTML tags.

Meta tags: Hidden HTML directions for Web browsers or search engines. They include important information such as the title of each page, relevant keywords describing site content, and the description of the site that shows up when a search engine returns a search.

MP3: The file extension for MPEG. They can be embedded into Web sites to provide audio.

Newsgroups: Topic-specific discussion and information exchange forums open to interested parties.

Non-permission marketing: An e-mail message that is or appears to be sent to multiple recipients who did not request it, even though they may be in the right target market.

Open-source: Programs that permit the source code to be distributed, thereby allowing programmers to alter and change the original software.

Paint Shop Pro Photo X2: A powerful graphics application.

Photoshop: The industry standard graphics application.

PHP hypertext preprocessor (PHP): A server-side programming language designed for Web programming.

PNG: Portable Networks Graphics; a loss-less, compressible file format for images on the Web.

Pixel: The smallest point of light that a monitor can produce.

Practical extraction and reporting language (Perl): A server-side, interpreted programming language commonly used with CGI.

Relational database management system (RDBMS): A database management system that allows data arranged in a tabular form to be related to data in other tables via common fields.

Screen reader: Software that reads the content of the screen aloud to a user.

Search engine marketing (SEM): Promoting a Web site through a search engine. This most often refers to targeting prospective customers by buying relevant keywords or phrases.

Search engine: A special site that provides an index of other Web site addresses listed according to keywords and descriptions in the original page.

Search engine optimization (SEO): Making a Web site more friendly to search engines, resulting in a higher page rank.

Secure shell (SSH): A secure way of transferring information between computers on a network.

Server-side: Programs that reside on the server and that a user can interact with through the CGI, or more directly, through the Web server.

Spam: An unwanted e-mail message sent in bulk to thousands of addresses to try to advertise something.

Spam posts: Messages posted to an e-mail discussion group, chat rooms or bulletin boards that are off-topic or distinctly promotional.

Splash page: A splash page (also known as an interstitial) is a preliminary page that precedes the regular home page of a Web site and usually promotes a particular site feature or provides advertising.

Sponsor: Depending on the context, a sponsor simply means an advertiser who has sponsored an ad and, by doing so, has also helped sponsor or sustain the Web site itself.

Universal resource locator and uniform resource identifier (URL and URI): A string of characters used to identify a resource on the Internet. Commonly called the domain name.

Unix: An operating system commonly used for Web servers.

Unique visitor: A unique visitor is someone with a unique address who is entering a Web site for the first time that day or some other specified period. Thus, a visitor who returns within the same day is not counted twice. A unique visitor count tells you how many different people there are in your audience during the time period, but not how much they used the site during the period.

Upload: The process of moving files from a local computer to a remote computer.

User session: A user session occurs when someone with a unique address enters or reenters a Web site each day or some other specified period.

View: A view refers to either an ad view or a page view. There can be multiple ad views per page views. View counting for ads should consider that a small percentage of users choose to turn the graphics off and do not display the images in their browser.

Visit: A visit refers to a Web user with a unique address entering a Web site at some page for the first time that day, or for the first time in a lesser time period. The number of visits is roughly equivalent to the number of different people who visit a site. This term is ambiguous unless the user defines it, as it could mean a user session, or it could mean a unique visitor that day.

Web accessibility initiative (WAI): A W3C initiative aimed at improving the accessibility of the Web.

Web content accessibility guidelines (WCAG): A set of guidelines to make a Web site accessible.

Web designer: A person who designs Web pages.

Web developer: A person who performs programming for a Web site.

WebPlus X2 Website Maker: A Web page authoring application from Serif.

Web server: The computer (and software) that hosts a Web site.

Web site: A collection of Web pages available on the World Wide Web through a Web server.

World Wide Web Consortium (W3C): Developer of specifications and guidelines for the Web.

eXtensible hypertext markup language (XHTML): This next-generation language uses the same expressions and basic code as HTML but also complies with the XML standard. It helps to create Web sites that contain more features, functionality, and flexibility than ones created using HTML.

BIBLIOGRAPHY

Crowder, David A. *Building a Website for Dummies*. Indianapolis: Wiley Publishing, Inc., 2007. Print.

MacDonald, Matthew. *Creating Web Sites: The Missing Manual*. Sebastopol, California: O'Reilly Media, Inc., 2006. Print.

Author Biography

Bruce C. Brown is an award-winning author of nine books as well as an active duty Coast Guard officer, where he has served in a variety of assignments for nearly 25 years. Bruce is married to Vonda and has three sons: Dalton, Jordan, and Colton. His previous works include *How to Use the Internet to Advertise, Promote and Market Your Business or Web Site with Little or No Money*, winner of a 2007 Independent Publisher Award, as well as *The Ultimate Guide to Search Engine Marketing: Pay Per Click Advertising Secrets Revealed*, winner in the USA Best Books 2007 Award program. He also wrote *The Complete Guide to E-mail Marketing: How to Create Successful, Spam-free Campaigns to Reach Your Target Audience and Increase Sales; The Complete Guide to Google Advertising: Including Tips, Tricks, & Strategies to Create a Winning Advertising Plan; The Secret Power of Blogging: How to Promote and Market Your Business, Organization, or Cause With Free Blogs; Returning From the War on Terrorism: What Every Veteran Needs to Know to Receive Your Maxi-*

mum Benefits; The Complete Guide to Affiliate Marketing on the Web: How to Use and Profit from Affiliate Marketing Programs; and *Google Income: How ANYONE of Any Age, Location, and/or Background Can Build a Highly Profitable Online Business with Google.* He holds degrees from Charter Oak State College and the University of Phoenix. He currently splits his time between Land O' Lakes, Florida and Miami, Florida.

His books have been consistent best-sellers and have been recipients of prestigious awards such as the "Best Book – USABookNews.com," "Winner – Independent Book Publisher (Silver/Gold)," "INDIE Excellence Awards," and "Book of the Year – Foreword."

Index